THE LAMB'S BOOK OF LIFE

Will your name be found written therein

by

Carl Brice

authorHOUSE®

AuthorHouse™
1663 Liberty Drive, Suite 200
Bloomington, IN 47403
www.authorhouse.com
Phone: 1-800-839-8640

© 2008 Carl Brice. All rights reserved.

No part of this book may be reproduced, stored in a retrieval system, or transmitted by any means without the written permission of the author.

First published by AuthorHouse 9/10/2008

ISBN: 978-1-4343-7497-4 (sc)
ISBN: 978-1-4343-7498-1 (hc)

Library of Congress Control Number: 2008902238

Printed in the United States of America
Bloomington, Indiana

This book is printed on acid-free paper.

TABLE OF CONTENTS

PREFACE xi
INTRODUCTION xiii
ACKNOWLEDGMENT xv
MISSION STATEMENT xvii

DAY ONE 1
   PRAY FOR THE NATION OF ISRAEL 1
   THE BOOK 7
   DO YOU KNOW IF YOU ARE LOST? 9
   GET COVERED WITH THE BLOOD
   OF THE LAMB 13
   CAN A MAN LOSE HIS SALVATION? 17
   Four Things That May Make You
   Question Your Salvation 19
   ARE THERE MANY WAYS TO INTERPRET
   THE BIBLE? 25
   SOVEREIGNTY OF GOD 27
   REVELATION OF GOD'S CHARACTER 28
   GOD'S TWO PRIORITIES FOR MANKIND 32
   The Number One Priority 32
   The Number Two Priority 33

DAY TWO   34
   YOUNG PEOPLE LEARNING THE TRUTH   34
   Believing the True God 34
   TRAIN YOUR KIDS FOR RELEASE 37
   ONE BLOOD FOR ALL NATIONS 39
   DIFFERENT FLESH FOR DIFFERENT SPECIES 40
   SIN INTRODUCED INTO THE WORLD 40
   Our Ancestors Disobeyed God 40

DAY THREE 47
DID YOU KNOW! 47
One-hundred Biblical Points of
Informational Knowledge 47
Paradise and Hell or Hades 88
Hell, Hades or Sheol 90
Lake of Fire 91
A Few Examples of Ungodly Prayers 113
Life 114
Power 114
Voice 116
God Gave Them Up to Three Kinds of Rejected
Lifestyles 150
CURSED 175
BLESSED 175
PREDESTINATION 206
ADOPTION 207
FORGIVENESS OF SINS 207
THE LESSON 221

DAY FOUR 233
THE TEN COMMANDMENTS 233
Two Tables of Stone 233
WHAT IS FORNICATION 235
CLEAN AND UNCLEAN ANIMALS 239
Food Consumption Authorized by God 239
BLESSINGS OF OBEDIENCE
(Deuteronomy 28:1-14) 243
CONSEQUENCES OF DISOBEDIENCE
(Deuteronomy 28:15-68) 244
WHO WROTE THE SIXTY-SIX BOOKS OF
THE BIBLE? 250
FIVEFOLD MINISTRY 253
SPIRITUAL GIFTS 254

QUALIFICATIONS OF BISHOP, ELDER
AND DEACON 257
  Qualification of Bishop..257
  Duty to Elders 258
  Qualification of Deacon 258
  Pastoral Office Responsibilities 258

DAY FIVE..260
  LOVE AND CHARITY..260
  The Way of Love—Book of 1 Corinthians 260
  THE BEATITUDES OF JESUS CHRIST 263
  The Eight Character Blessings Taught by Jesus...............263
  GRACE AND MERCY...266
  Grace...267
  Mercy 270
  WISDOM 271
  FAITH VS FEAR 272
  Faith Pleases God..273
  Faith Healing..277
  Fear is from Satan 279
  Your Worse Fear Will Come upon You 282
  POWER OF PRAYER 283
  Pray in Faith 284
  Prayer in Worship 285
  Prayer in Confession 285
  Pray in Adoration 286
  Pray in Praise 286
  Pray in Thanksgiving 287
  Pray in Intercession...287
  Hindrance to Prayer..288
  Answer to Prayer...291
  FIVE SENSES OF MANKIND 293
  1) SIGHT..294
  2) HEARING 294
  3) TOUCH 294

4) SMELL 294
5) TASTE 294
THE TRYING OF YOUR FAITH 296
Wrestle with God..296
Your Test of Faith by Fire 297
JUDGMENT / CONDEMNATION 303
DEATH AND LIFE IS IN YOUR TONGUE 305
PROPHECY VS SPEAKING IN TONGUES 308
THE LAST DAYS...312
OLD TESTAMENT—JUDGMENT OF GOD 313
NEW TESTAMENT—JUDGMENT OF GOD 315
  1) The Cross Judgment 315
  2) The Believers' Self-Judgment Seat of Christ 315
  3) The Chastisement by the Father 316
  4) The Bema (Judgment Seat) of Christ 317
  5) The Tribulation 318
  6) The Judgment of Gentile Nations 320
  7) The Great White Throne Judgment 321
  8) The Judgment of Angels 322
WHAT IS THE WRATH OF GOD? 324
FINAL WRATH 325
THE JUDGMENT 326
THE GREAT DAY OF GOD'S WRATH 327
THE SEVEN SEALS 327
The 144,000 Sealed 329
The Numberless Multitude 331
THE SEVEN TRUMPETS...332
The Angel and the Little Book 334
THE VIALS OF WRATH 335
DESCRIPTION OF SATAN..337
ARE YOU STILL IN CAPTIVITY?..............................341
THE WILL OF SATAN...342
SPIRIT OF THE ANTICHRIST 345
POWER OF DEMONS 347

Demons Recognize God and Know His Laws 349
DAY SIX 352
   IS JESUS CHRIST THE ONLY WAY? 352
   Jesus was Prophesied in the Old Testament 356
   JESUS, THE HOLY SEED 358
   THE MANY MIRACLES OF JESUS 360
   The Spirit of the Lord was upon Jesus 362
   REPENT FOR EVERLASTING LIFE 363
   THE GIFT OF SALVATION! 364
   REMEMBER THE SABBATH DAY 366
   Consequences of Failing to Honor the Sabbath 369
   THE ARMOR OF GOD 371
   Description and Purpose of this Armor 371
   The Armor of God in Detail 372
   The Armor of God Consist of Six Pieces 372
   HOW TO WALK UPRIGHT BEFORE THE LORD 373
   Walking in the spirit 377
   Signs Shall Follow Them Who Believe 382
   WE MUST FOLLOW JESUS 384
   Power Received for the Task 385
   THE CHURCH 388
   CHRIST'S RETURN FOR HIS CHURCH 391
   THE FIVE CROWNS OF GLORY 391
   1) INCORRUPTIBLE CROWN—Victor's Crown 393
   2) CROWN OF LIFE—Martyr's Crown 393
   3) CROWN OF RIGHTEOUSNESS—
   For Those Who Love His Appearance 394
   4) CROWN OF GLORY—Elder's Crown 394
   5) CROWN OF REJOICING 395
   DESCRIPTION OF THE KINGDOM OF HEAVEN 396
   WHO IS THE HOLY SPIRIT? 399
   The HOLY SPIRIT is All We Need 402
   BLASPHEMY AGAINST THE HOLY GHOST 404
   The Unforgivable Sin 404

DAY SEVEN 406
  THE BOOK OF LIFE 406
  SIX QUESTIONS ASKED IN DAY ONE 407
  1) What is the Book of Life? 407
  2) Whose Book Is It? 407
  3) Why is there a Need for Such a Book? 408
  4) What Happens If My Name Is Not Found In The Book Of Life? 409
  5) How Do I Get My Name in the Lamb's Book of Life? 409
  6) How Do I Keep My Name Written Therein? 410
  HEAVEN OR HELL 412
  Where Will You Spend Eternity? 412
  THE LAKE OF FIRE 413
  THE END OF SATAN—THE BEAST AND THE FALSE PROPHET 416
  THE NEW HEAVEN AND THE NEW EARTH 417
  The Holy City / The New Jerusalem 417
GLOSSARY 423

PREFACE

The information gathered in this book is designed to take you on a spiritual journey concerning the will of God. The Holy Bible is a book of God's prophecies, principles, and commandments designed to be a beacon of light unto his human creation. God knew beforehand we were going to have a rough journey through this wicked and dangerous world. In the beginning, Adam and Eve had it made in the garden—living a life free of sin. Once their act of disobedience caused sin to enter into this world, the spirit of death and hell received their assignment. The God of love, mercy, and forgiveness sent his only begotten Son named Jesus from glory down to earth to save the souls of mankind. Some may ask the question, what are we saved from. The correct answer is that we are saved from God's wrath that will be poured out onto the earth without mixture in the last days. This wrath is a form of God's judgment that will be executed upon this sinful world. This sounds like doom, and it is to all who reject God and his precious gift he has provided for his creation. This gift is the good news of the gospel of Jesus Christ, who is the Messiah—the only one worthy to die on the cross for the sins of the entire world. This same God-sent Messiah is also the only one found worthy to open the Lamb's book of life. At the completion of this book, you will come to know many glorious things about your Creator. You will understand how each and every one of us is fearfully and wonderfully made by God. Also, you will be convinced that your way is the wrong way if it is not in line with the precious Holy Bible. We must remember that God knows best when it comes to what he has created.

INTRODUCTION

The knowledge contained in this book is designed to give the reader a new outlook on life concerning the will of God. Whosoever reads this book will be convinced in their heart that it is time to make that ultimate decision. The ultimate decision of whose side you are on. All who are on the Lord's side, let them come to Jesus right now. The information contained in this book will share valuable researched biblical knowledge with the reader. Hopefully, it will also clear up any false knowledge one may have pertaining to God's holy word. This factual information is formulated to cause a hunger for wisdom and knowledge that can only be satisfied by the word of God. While we attempt to gain biblical knowledge for ourselves, we cannot forget about our youth of today. They are a major concern for the development and growth of our nation's future. They are being taught not to serve God. This wicked world's system has taught our youth against acknowledging and worshiping a God they cannot see. Therefore, if our young people are not trained and taught about the Lord in their homes and churches, they will grow up lost forever in a world saturated with sin. Satan will have won their hearts over, and they won't even know what hit them. The cares and concerns of this world have totally consumed the majority of our young people. Everything we see with our eyes causes us to desire such things as wealth, riches, lust and beauty. We are taught to lust after the things that we feel will satisfy the desires of our flesh. The Bible teaches us to be concerned with each other and love one another. That's not what the world system teaches. The world system trains us to step on one another, lie, cheat, steal, and do whatever it takes to get to the top. The question is—the top of what? In addition to this way of life, we are taught to appear to be righteous, even when we are not. The world system also teaches us that the one who dies with the most toys win. The writer of this slogan forgot to tell you what it is exactly that you win. Whoever wrote that slogan had no clue about the judgment of God. Mankind is so bogged down with daily tasks and responsibilities, that there is little or no time left to spend with the God of all creation. There is no time left at the end of our day to even notice all God's heavenly glory set before us. The world's system also controls what the world media releases to the public.

Today, that includes everything we see and hear. The media is not always positive when reporting news concerning Christianity. They often treat this topic as if it is a storybook, myth or fable. Society attempts to make the world feel simple-minded if they even think about believing in a Holy God they cannot see with their natural sight. In other words, they try to make every thing concerning God not politically correct. We as Christians know better. That's part of God's mystery revealed to those who love him. Those who have not learned to love God cannot experience a personal relationship with him. Jesus said it best when he stated that the world cannot know him. Our mission as a believer in Christ is to teach everyone about his beautiful gospel message. We must make sure that everyone knows he is the only begotten Son of the true and living God. Jesus is the only one who can save us from his final judgment to come upon this world. This wrath is one of the final prophecies to be fulfilled in the coming days ahead. The Bible has not failed yet, when it comes to fulfilling all the prophecies written therein. Don't you think its time to pay attention to what has already been revealed so far?

ACKNOWLEDGMENT

I would like to dedicate this book of biblical knowledge to the glory of our Lord and Savior, Jesus the Christ. I feel blessed and privileged to be inspired to share the knowledge of God with all who have an ear to hear. I thank God for blessing me with wonderful parents who raised four boys to adulthood according to the word of God. I give honor to my earthly father Charles Perry Brice and my earthly mother Linda Mae Brice who have both gone on to be with the Lord. They taught each one of their sons to love God and always care for one another. I am very grateful for the structured discipline they imparted unto each of us. They truly loved us enough to correct all of our wrongful behavior growing up. Mom and Pop Brice could swing a mean belt. Unlike the world today, it caused us to grow up with love and respect for ourselves and others. Thank God for the tough love they imparted into each one of us. All parents deserve to be honored by their children because God commanded it to be so. I would also like to thank my Pastor, Superintendant Elmer R. Hess Sr. and First Lady Missionary Luella Hess, also my Assistant Pastor, Elder Elmer R. Hess Jr. and Missionary Anita R. Hess of First Pentecostal Church of God in Christ. I am truly grateful for all their prayers, instruction and guidance in the word of God. They have truly been an inspiration in my spiritual walk with the Lord.

However, most of all, I give special thanks to my precious Aunt Willa Mae Bell who recognized the anointing of the Lord on my life through a godly conversation we were having one day. It was she who suggested that I share our wonderful conversation we were having with those who normally would not hear such truth. My sweet auntie's main heart felt concern was for our precious youth of today, and how they so desperately needed to hear a word from the Lord. She saw and felt the desperate need for our young people to be reintroduced to the true and living God. She realized like most Christians that the wicked world system appears to be gaining ground when it comes to our young people. She felt this book would be an excellent tool to enlighten all souls to seek more of the true and living God. She is and always will be an inspiration in my life. I truly thank the Lord for my Aunt Willa

Mae and the influence the Matthews family had on our generation. Even though my family and nearest kinsmen at one time walked in darkness, it was the Matthews family who worshiped the Lord before us. Some laughed and some listened, however, in the end, we all had to choose to serve the Lord if we wanted to be saved. The fact is my Auntie Mae and her family had found what we all needed to find if we wanted to spend eternal life in the kingdom of God! I truly thank God for this blessed woman of God. God Bless you Auntie Mae, I love you!

I would like to give special thanks to the staff at Author House Publishing for their expertise in editing, designing and formatting this book. It was an extreme pleasure to work with the publishing house staff during the development of this project. Thank you for all the professional team members who were assigned to help and guide me through this process. Thank you Author House Publishing, God bless you!

MISSION STATEMENT

Our mission is to use anointed words of wisdom in book form in order to reach lost souls for the kingdom of God. These words are designed to educate and stimulate the mind of every human being. The Holy Bible says God's people are destroyed for lack of knowledge. Our mission is to provide the necessary knowledge which will prevent the destruction of mankind. Once this literature is fully absorbed, the words written in these books will feed your spirit and cause a spiritual hunger to rise up within you. We at Carl Brice Book Ministries acknowledge Jesus Christ as the Holy Redeemer who voluntarily laid down his life for the sins of the entire world. Therefore, let your spirit be fulfilled as you receive biblical knowledge intended to maximize your spiritual growth.

Carl Brice Book Ministries
P.O. Box 120
Battle Creek, Michigan 49016-0120

Contact us on the Web

Web Site
  Visit our web site at:
  www.EdifyYourSpirit.com

E-mail Address
  E-mail us at:
  CarlBrice@edifyyourspirit.com

HOLY SCRIPTURE REFERENCE

All biblical scripture references made in this book were inspired and taken from the King James Version of the Holy Bible.

DAY ONE

PRAY FOR THE NATION OF ISRAEL

We must pray for the peace of Jerusalem if we want the United States to continue to be a blessed nation. The two flags which appear on the front cover of this book signify the correlation and peace between the Nation of Israel and the United States of America. The flag displayed on the back cover showing both the United States and the Nation of Israel combined is not meant to dishonor its meaning by any means. This flag display is to imply togetherness and the importance thereof. To some individuals, these images will probably mean absolutely nothing. However, to the Christian born-again believers and the chosen covenant people of God, it means we are on the Lord's side. Whether this world believes it or not, there are only two sides to life. There is a side which leads to eternal life in Christ Jesus, and then there is a side which leads to eternal separation from God. This means that God has his side and the devil has the other. The question is which side are you on? All nations, tribes and kindreds throughout the entire world are welcome into the family of God. Therefore, there is no excuse for anyone to feel left out. The Bible tells us that Jesus died for the sins of the entire world and not just for a few individuals. The only requirement is that you must believe it in order to receive it.

Scripture

"For God so loved the <u>WORLD</u>, that he gave his only begotten Son, that <u>whosoever believeth</u> in him should not perish, but have everlasting life" (John 3:16).

The Lord is not willing that any souls should perish, but that all should come to repentance. There is truly a blessing for the souls who enter into the family of God. Did you know that whosoever blesses the seed of Abraham will be blessed by God? Likewise, whosoever curses the seed of Abraham will be cursed by God. This is a biblical fact whether you believe it or not!

Now the question remains, who is Abraham's seed? The seed of Abraham consist of the twelve tribes of Israel who are God's chosen covenant people. Therefore, the Nation of Israel and the land God gave Abraham and his seed are both blessed and protected by God. The Lord also made Abraham the father of many nations, which means his covenant family has been extended. Jesus Christ came, died, and rose from the dead so that all souls by FAITH would have right to the Tree of Life. Without faith it is impossible to please God. This is why it requires faith in the risen Savior in order to be saved in this sinful world. Once saved by faith and the blood of Jesus Christ, these redeemed souls are adopted into the family of God. This now qualifies the redeemed of the Lord to be sons of God and seed of Abraham. This means they too are now considered covenant people of God who have been cleansed by the blood of the Lamb. There are born-again Christians and Christian Jews spread throughout all the United States praying and interceding for this great nation. I know the unsaved souls would like to think that the size of their military forces is what decides the outcome of a war. If this was true, the Nation of Israel would have been destroyed a long time ago! If this was true, the Lord's servant and deliverer named Gideon would have never defeated the 135,000 army of Medianites soilders with only the 300 men of Israel whom God set apart. God's protective hand was and still is upon the Nation of Israel and whosoever supports them. The Nation of Israel is God's chosen covenant people. No one can destroy them. It is the Lord who fights their battles supernatural, the same way he fights for the born-again believers of today. If you do not believe it, ask all of the nations who have attempted to destroy Israel over the centuries with greater armies. Maybe at some point man will stop scratching his head and realize that God is still very much in control of his world. There is coming a day when God will destroy all nations who wage war against the Nation of Israel.

Scripture

"In that day will I make the governors of Judah like a <u>hearth</u> of fire among the wood, and like a torch of fire in a sheaf; and they shall devour all the people round about, on the right hand and on the left: and Jerusalem shall be inhabited again in her own place, even in Jerusalem" (Zechariah 12:6).

> *"In that day shall the Lord <u>**DEFEND**</u> the inhabitants of Jerusalem; and he that is feeble among them at that day shall be as David; and the house of David shall be as God, as the Angel of the Lord before them. And it shall come to pass in that day, that I WILL SEEK TO DESTROY ALL THE NATIONS THAT COME AGAINST JERUSALEM"* (Zechariah 12:8, 9).

I'm sure there are individuals in this country who feel that the United States is a blessed nation based on their works. I'm here to tell you that the United States is blessed and will continue to be blessed as long as we support the Nation of Israel. We as a country must continue to pray for the peace of Jerusalem. The chosen people of God known as the Jewish nation have always been welcome in this great USA. Whether you believe this or not, this is the only reason the United States has prospered all these years. If this country received rightfully what it deserved, it would be doomed, just like other areas of the world where Christ is not proclaimed. However, the same way God shows grace and mercy toward his followers, he has also shown grace and mercy toward their land.

Scripture

> *"If my people, which are called by my name, shall humble themselves, and pray, and seek my face, and turn from their wicked ways; then will I hear from heaven, and will forgive their sin, and will HEAL THEIR LAND"* (2 Chronicles 7:14).

There is a blessing to those who pray and embrace the people of God. Whosoever blesses the children of Israel; God himself will bless and prosper that nation.

Scripture

> *"Pray for the peace of Jerusalem: they shall prosper that love thee. Peace be within thy walls, and prosperity within thy palaces. For my brethren and companions' sake, I will now say, Peace be within thee. Because of the house of the Lord our God I will seek thy good"* (Psalms 122:6-9).

The peace that God extends in these verses provides completeness, health, justice, prosperity, and protection to anyone who embraces his chosen people. We must fully understand that Jerusalem is the capital Holy City of this world. This sacred land is indeed the gateway to the heavens. The Bible tells us that Jesus will sit on the throne of King David in the holy city when he returns to rein over this world. Therefore, let us stay connected to the covenant people of God and honor the Promised Land he has given them. God smiles on the USA and blesses this nation with his mighty hand. We must be very careful not to think too highly of ourselves nor allow our worldly knowledge to out smart us. There are several brilliant minds according to the world's standard that hold very important positions of authority throughout the land. These so called brilliant minds actually feel as if they are contributing to the outcome of this world. The truth is the ending has already been determined by God. It is spelled out in detail in the Holy Bible. This is why not many wise, mighty, or noble men after the flesh are called of God. They are too smart for their own good. These souls are too busy trying to gain the whole world, and in the process will end up loosing their very soul.

Scripture

"For ye see your calling, brethren, how that not many WISE MEN after the flesh, not many MIGHTY, not many NOBLE, are called: but <u>God hath chosen the foolish things of the world to confound the wise</u>; and God hath chosen the weak things of the world to confound the things which are mighty; and base things of the world, and things which are despised, hath God chosen, yea, and things which are not, to bring to nought things that are: that NO FLESH should glory in his presence. But of him are ye in Christ Jesus, who of God is made unto us WISDOM, and RIGHTEOUSNESS, and SANCTIFICATION, and REDEMPTION: that, according as it is written, <u>He that glorieth</u>, let him <u>glory in the Lord</u>" (1 Corinthian 1:26-31).

"For what shall it profit a man, if he shall gain the whole world, and lose his own soul? Or what shall a man give in exchange for his soul? Whosoever therefore shall be ashamed of me and of my words in this adulterous and sinful generation; of him also shall the Son of man be ashamed, when he cometh in the glory of his Father with the holy angels" (Mark 8:36-38).

The grace of the Lord is upon all who humble themselves. However, God will resist the proud at heart. They are given over to their vain imagination. It is hard for these souls to receive the Lord into their heart because they feel they have a better method. This type of person thinks that only weak minded individual reach out to God. This may be describing you! These individuals give glory to themselves over the things God has truly blessed them with. The saints of God know that all glory belongs to the Lord. The Bible teaches us that God is a jealous God who does not share his glory with anyone. He is the creator of everything and everyone. Therefore, we must understand when you are the original owner; this is the only time jealousy is justified.

Scripture

"He hath shewed strength with his arm; he hath scattered the proud in the imagination of their hearts" (Luke 1:51).

"But he giveth more grace. Wherefore he saith, God resisteth the proud, but giveth grace unto the humble" (James 4:6).

"Thus saith the Lord, Let not the WISE MAN glory in his wisdom, neither let the MIGHTY MAN glory in his might, let not the RICH MAN glory in his riches: But let him that glorieth glory in this, that he understandeth and knoweth ME, that I AM the Lord which exercise lovingkindness, judgment, and righteousness, in the earth: for in these things I delight, saith the Lord" (Jeremiah 9:23, 24).

The question to ask yourself is this, are you smarter than the God who created you? If your answer is yes, continue to sleep on. If your answer is no, keep reading this blessed book and be edified. God is very much in control of his world. The Bible tells us that the heart of the king is in his hand.

Scripture

"The king's heart is in the hand of the Lord, as the rivers of water: he turneth it whithersoever he will" (Proverbs 21:1).

This verse of scripture shows that God has the heart and mind of the rulers in authority in his hand. The Lord is very much in control of his world. We as spirit beings in earthen vessels are also used by God to fulfill his agenda in the earth. The unfortunate thing is Satan has an agenda also. He is the tempter and accuser of this world. When a man refuses to follow the Lord, he automatically helps fulfill the devil's purpose, which is to ultimately defy God. For this reason, we as American's must be very careful when it comes to our moral value. Remember, God is still watching while his holy angels record every word uttered and every deed performed by man. Nothing is hid from the eyes of the Lord.

Scripture

"And I saw the dead, small and great, stand before God; and the books were opened: and another book was opened, which is the Book of Life: and the dead were judged out of those things which were written in the books, according to their works" (Revelation 20:12).

This verse of scripture was witnessed and scribed by John the apostle when he was called up to witness the Revelation of Jesus Christ. These books and their purpose were mentioned by the angel who spoke with John while he was being revealed the end time prophecy. The book of the Revelation of Jesus Christ completes the last book to seal the canonization of the Holy Bible. All souls not covered with the blood of the Lamb will be judged by God out of these sacred books at the Great White Throne Judgment. Remember, this is the judgment of the spiritually dead souls who rejected the grace of God. This is the judgment where you do not want to be present. One good reason why you should not want to be there is because Satan, the false prophet, the beast and the entire demonic host will be there. Unless you like hanging out with the devil, this is not the place for you!

THE BOOK

What is the book of life?
Whose book is it?
Why is there a need for such a book?
What happens if my name is not found written in this book?
How do I get my name to appear in the Lamb's book of life?
How do I keep my name written therein?

The Lamb's book of life is that sacred book God has in heaven which contains all the names of men and women who have been saved by the blood and sanctified by the Spirit of God. Those who have been saved by the blood have been washed in the blood of the Lamb. Their sins have been forgiven and covered by faith in the risen Savior who is Jesus Christ our Lord. The word sanctified means set apart for God. Therefore, everyone who has freely accepted Jesus Christ as Savior and Lord will find their name written in the Lamb's book of life. The reason why this book is called the Lamb's book of life is because God the Father, God the Son, and God the Holy Spirit are one. Furthermore, Jesus was the only one worthy to open this sacred book. The Bible also tells us that God foreordained before the foundation of the world the souls who would answer the call of God. This tells us that some men and women are predestined to reject the salvation of the Lord. We must never forget that Jesus Christ willingly laid his life down to redeem our souls from the hand of the enemy. This same God sent Messiah known as Jesus the Christ came down from glory and offered himself as a living sacrifice so that we all could inherit eternal life in the kingdom of God. Therefore, to the ones who reject the risen Savior of this world, there is no redemption for their souls. Salvation is a free gift from the true and living God to all who have a mind to receive. Only God knows who will freely accept his only begotten Son Jesus, and who will not.

Scripture

"According as he hath chosen us in him before the foundation of the world, that we should be holy and without blame before him in love: Having predestinated us unto the adoption of children by Jesus Christ to himself,

according to the good pleasure of his will, To the praise of the glory of his grace, wherein he hath made us accepted in the beloved" (Ephesians 1:4-6).

Those who receive Jesus as Lord have been saved from the wrath of God which will appear very soon. Those who reject the risen Savior are condemned already and the wrath of God abides on them. This topic will be discussed in more detail later in this book. The opening six questions regarding the book will also be addressed and explained later in this text. The question everyone needs to know is this. Where does a man go when he wants to hear directly from God? We go to the one and only place where we can be certain that we are hearing exactly what God has to say. That one important place is called the Holy Bible—the anointed word of God. There is no other such book in the world that has been canonized specifically for this purpose. However, there are a large number of religious books written over the years that men worship out of. Many of these same books were developed primarily because man disagreed with what he found in the word of God. This type of rebellion is what motivates an individual or group to develop a religion or denomination that only accepts part of the Bible. When we reject the holy word of God in any or all parts, we are headed for trouble. This is referred to as the buffet style religion. This type of religion allows you to scroll through the entire Holy Bible and just pick out what you want to eat. In others words, you just pick out the parts you agree with, as if God almighty made a big mistake and needed your help. I can assure you the word of God was inspired by God for his divine purpose and not ours.

Scripture

"All scripture is given by inspiration of God, and is profitable for doctrine, for reproof, for correction, for instruction in righteousness: That the man of God may be perfect, thoroughly furnished unto all good works" (2 Timothy 3:16, 17).

The Holy Bible has the POWER to cause men to walk perfect while guiding them to their assigned good works. The Holy Bible was not given to man for the purpose of just gaining knowledge or winning arguments.

The Christian born-again believer studies the Bible in order to learn how to perform the works of Christ while they remain in the earth. This knowledge and wisdom found in the word of God is designed to strengthen our faith as it leads us to perform these good works. When a man takes it upon himself to change or ignore the word of God, he has openly rejected the word of life. This man has allowed his imagination to convince him that he can do it or say it better than God. This is a dangerous state of mind to adopt simply because there will be other souls who will also be led away from God watching you. This is a form of rebellion that a man enters into when he disagrees with the almighty God who is HOLY. We as Christians, seek to develop a relationship with the Savior Jesus Christ. He is the Savior of the entire world and not just a select group of people. The Lord Jesus is God's plan and free gift for the salvation of all nations, tribes and kindreds. This is the relationship we ought to be seeking; not some other doctrine which is geared to exalt men to receive the glory that only God is worthy of receiving. When this type of religion is practiced, more emphasis is placed on rituals and traditions than on a willingness and obedience to serve and obey the will God. Religions that seek to do things according to their own philosophy are clearly rejecting the perfect will of the Lord. Anyone who rejects God and his only begotten Son, Jesus, will spend eternity in the lake of fire.

Scripture

"And whosoever was not found written in the book of life was cast into the lake of fire" (Revelation 20:15).

Now you have learned that it is very crucial that your name be found among other names which God has chosen to appear in his precious book called the Lamb's book of life. Continue to read this vital information and learn more of the true and living God who created all things for mankind to care for and enjoy.

DO YOU KNOW IF YOU ARE LOST?

This particular question is one which most people cast out of their mind. Not only do they not think about it, some do not realize they are lost. There are souls who do not know Jesus Christ in the pardoning of their sins. This is because they are not convinced they are in need of a Savior. They have convinced themselves that everything is just fine in their lives. This could even be describing you. Until we realize that we are as filthy rags before the eyes of God, we will not recognize that we are lost and on our way to a devil's hell. We must avoid the lake of fire and brimstone at all cost. This final judgment comes immediately after the Great White Throne Judgment of God. This may sound harsh, but it is so very true. We are all in desperate need of the cleansing blood of Jesus—the only innocent blood capable of washing our sins away. We have to first believe that God is real. Then we also have to believe that the devil is real. This will keep us from being deceived by his many wicked devices. Everyone who believes that they can make it into the kingdom of God based on their good works is already deceived. Since the wages of sin is death, this proves that no one can escape the judgment of God. No man or woman can enter into the kingdom of God without the Lord's provision for sin. This clearly teaches us that no one can save themselves. We all need the blood of Jesus to cover and pardon our sinful nature in order to avoid the death penalty God placed on sin. The good news is God's provision for sin is free. Therefore, there is no excuse for the soul that chooses to perish without the grace of God. The word of God tells us that we are all as filthy rags in the eyes of God.

Scripture

"But we are all as an unclean thing, and all our righteousness's are as FILTHY RAGS; and we all do fade as a leaf; and <u>our iniquities</u>, like the wind, have taken us away" (Isaiah 64:6).

This is why our loving God sent us his only begotten Son to save us from two areas of concern. The first area of concern is the wrath of God which will be poured out without mixture on a dreadful world contaminated with sin. This world is so engulfed in sin that it must be destroyed or regenerated by fervent heat. The second area of concern is to avoid the second death, which is the final judgment in the lake of fire. The saints of God are not appointed to either one of these judgments of God. They have been spared. This is the good news of the gospel of Jesus Christ. Jesus accomplished this salvation when he willingly went to the cross and laid down his life to be atonement for all who will receive his free gift of salvation. Without this free gift, mankind's very soul is condemned forever. When God formed man out of the dust from the ground and breathed life into his nostrils, man became a living soul. What some men fail to realize is that same soul God gave to mankind will live forever somewhere. Where you end up is your choice and your choice alone. God has given every person the right to choose. This is not make-believe folks. This is your eternal life we are talking about. Please, let not the enemy (Satan) deceive you any longer into thinking everything is okay. This form of deception creeps in when we overload our lives with the cares and concerns of this world. Satan tries to convince mankind that there is no God. Unfortunately, there are those men and women who buy into this deception as they mock God's very existence. When you hear people make fun of God, this is very sad for the Christian believer, for they know that the one who uses the Lord's name in vain will not go unpunished. This type of bad behavior is detrimental to their very souls. The Holy Bible lets us know that nonbelievers cannot know or even comprehend the word of God. This is because they have blinders on their eyes which were placed there by God's enemy known as Satan. The Bible describes the unbeliever as a NATURAL MAN. The natural man has no spiritual discernment at all. He has been totally conformed to this wicked world system which is under the influence of Satan himself. Everything concerning the word of God is foolish in the eyes of the natural man. What they don't realize is God said, "The fool has said there is no God." Therefore, let us not be offended any longer when men do not receive the word of the Lord. The word of God is like a seed of life. Once the seed is planted in their mind, someone else will come along and water that same seed. They plant more scriptures on top of scriptures. The best part of all is God will give the final increase in his perfect timing. This means that God will cause that soul to receive his wake-up call, just like he has done for us. Then they too will step over from darkness into the marvelous light. We must continue to plant those precious seeds of scripture and leave it up to the Lord to wake them out of their dark sleep.

Scripture

"But the natural man receiveth not the things of the Spirit of God: for they are foolishness unto him: neither can he know them, because they are spiritually discerned" (1 Corinthians 2:14).

This describes everyone who feels like they are in no need of a Savior. They will continue to walk in darkness without the revelation of God. Hopefully, those who are spiritually dead will one day awaken to the knowledge of the Savior Jesus Christ. We all have sinned in our lives and come short of the glory of God. When we are blinded by Satan, the only sin we see are the sins of others. This trick of the enemy is a dead give-away of that particular soul walking in darkness. Satan knows that the unbeliever thinks he or she is better off than the born-again Christian believer. This same enemy also knows that all unbelievers view the Christian population as nothing more than HYPOCRITES! If this is you, then you have just been deceived because you still possess what is known as a stoney heart. Now you are classified as a finger pointer. That is a person who loves to point the finger and judge others, even when God commanded us not to. Remember, Satan too is known as the accuser of the brethren. Therefore, when we judge others, whose character are we really imitating? The Bible tells us that whosoever judges another, condemns his own self. When this behavior is practiced, it is a true sign of an unbeliever, or a spiritually immature Christian. This person's spiritual vision is so limited; they can only see the sins of others. God so loved the world that he gave his only begotten Son as a living sacrifice for all sin. Every sin committed by man carries the death penalty whether large or small. Therefore, we must realize that no one will escape the judgment of God. Only God can make the necessary provision for man to be pardoned from his righteous judgment. There is only one way to the kingdom of God regardlous of what most people think. Jesus said it best in this next verse of scripture.

Scripture

"Jesus saith unto him, I AM the Way, the Truth, and the Life: NO MAN cometh unto the Father, but by me" (John 14:6).

All souls must eventually accept the risen Savior if they want to be saved from the wrath of God. This is the plan of God regarding the salvation of all mankind. Therefore, accept Jesus as Lord and Savior and get covered with the precious blood of the Lamb.

GET COVERED WITH THE BLOOD OF THE LAMB

Scripture

"For God so loved the world that he gave his only begotten Son, that whosoever believeth in him should not perish, but have everlasting life. For God sent not his Son into the world to condemn the world; but that the world through him might be SAVED" (John 3:16, 17).

"Neither is there SALVATION IN ANY OTHER: for there is none other name under heaven given among men, whereby we must be SAVED" (Acts 4:12).

Remember, Jesus had no sin; however, he loved us enough to die in our place on that rugged cross because of our sins. The innocent blood of the Lamb of God was shed for the remission of sin. The Bible teaches us that without the shedding of blood, there cannot be remission of sin (Hebrews 9:22). For this reason, we all need to be covered with the blood by faith in Christ Jesus who is the Savior of the world. To those who are ready to accept Jesus Christ as Lord and Savior, pray this prayer with me. If you are reading this passage, then it is not too late.

LORD JESUS,

NOTHING IS HID FROM YOUR EYES.
I AM A SINNER.
I CONFESS TO YOU ALL OF MY SINS.
COVER ME WITH YOUR PRECIOUS BLOOD.
WASH ME WHITER THAT SNOW.

THANK YOU FOR CASTING MY SINS IN THE SEA OF FORGETFULNESS NEVER TO BE REMEMBERED AGAIN.
I BELIEVE THAT YOU ARE THE RISEN SAVIOR SENT BY GOD ALMIGHTY WHO DEFEATED DEATH, HELL AND THE GRAVE TO ALL THAT BELIEVE.
THANK YOU FOR TAKING MY PLACE ON THAT RUGGED CROSS FOR THE SINS I HAVE COMMITTED AGAINST YOU.
THE LIVING SACRIFICE YOU MADE FOR US ALL ALLOWS US TO SPEND ETERNAL LIFE WITH YOU IN YOUR NEW KINGDOM.
TODAY, I BELIEVE IN MY HEART AND CONFESS WITH MY MOUTH THAT YOU ARE MY LORD, AND THE SAVIOR OF MY SOUL.
I NO LONGER WANT TO LIVE MY LIFE MY WAY.
I TOTALLY SURRENDER MY ALL TO YOU.
THANK YOU FOR YOUR GRACE AND MERCY THAT YOU HAVE GIVEN ME.
MAKE ME A VESSEL OF HONOR TO SERVE YOU IN THE EARTH.
I WILL BOLDLY CONFESS YOUR HOLY NAME BEFORE ALL MEN.
THANK YOU FOR SAVING MY SOUL FROM YOUR RIGHTEOUS JUDGMENT.
THANK YOU FOR ALLOWING MY NAME TO BE WRITTEN IN THE LAMB'S BOOK OF LIFE.
I LOVE YOU LORD JESUS!
AMEN.

Scripture

"That if thou shalt confess with thy mouth the Lord Jesus, and shalt believe in thine heart that God hath raised him from the dead, thou shalt be SAVED. For with the heart man believeth unto righteousness; and with the mouth confession is made unto SALVATION. For the scriptures saith, Whosoever believeth on him shall not be ashamed" (Romans 10:9-11).

THE LAMB'S BOOK OF LIFE:

Welcome to the family of God which is the body of Christ. You have just allowed Jesus Christ to save your soul from his great wrath and perfect judgment to come. Your life has also been spared from the second death which is the lake of fire. Your spirit and soul has now been redeemed by God. Now you have to tell someone. By telling at least one soul seals your confession onto salvation. If you were able to pray the prayer of salvation and believe what you prayed, something supernatural just happened to you on the inside. A new man was just birthed in your spirit. Now the Spirit of God called the Holy Spirit has connected with the spirit of man. This is called being born again of the Spirit of God. Now you have two natures so to speak. The old man which is your sinful nature has been dominated and surpressed. Your new nature which is your spiritual nature is what God has extended his grace and mercy toward. This nature is where the Holy Spirit of God dwells. It is now known as the temple of God. Now you have to decide which one of your natures you will feed and develop. If you feed you old nature with lustful desires, you will continue to sin and grieve the Holy Spirit. You will find yourself repenting for sin on a regular basis suffering the consequences thereof. If you feed your new nature with the word of God, old things will indeed pass away, all things will become new. Then your total mind will be renewed to conform to the perfect will of God. Remember, Jesus said in his word, "Man does not live by bread alone, but by every word that proceeds out of the mouth of God." This means, we must feed our spirit man everyday with a daily dose of God's holy word. We must learn to love the word of God whether we like it or not. Remember, God knows best for what he has created. When we starve our spirit man by refusing to spend time in the word of God, that old natured flesh man will rise up again. You want to avoid this from occurring at all cost. Everyone who prayed the prayer of salvation must know and understand that not just anybody can speak the words of redemption. The Bible teaches us that the Holy Spirit has to influence the proclamation of Jesus Christ as Lord. Without the Holy Spirit's involvement, it cannot be done. Therefore, if you still are hesitant to receive the free gift of salvation that God offers, now you know why. The Holy Spirit has to be present.

Scripture

> "*Wherefore I give you to understand, that <u>NO MAN</u> speaking by the Spirit of God calleth Jesus <u>accursed</u>: and that <u>NO MAN</u> can say that <u>Jesus is the Lord</u>, but by the Holy Ghost*" (1 Corinthians 12:3).

Those who love the Lord will never speak ill nor curse Christ with their mouth. The Bible tells us that it cannot be done. On the other hand, those who despise the Lord and choose not to believe in him will never proclaim Jesus as Lord and Savior as long as they are in that state of mind. This is why the wicked world system of unbeliever's hates the name of Jesus. Have you ever noticed that you never hear unbelievers speak the name Jesus from their lips? They may talk about the god in their imagination. They may even use the Lord's name in vain. Some may even talk about other false gods. This is when individuals make up in their own mind what and who they think God should be. Of course this is not accurate. Only the Holy Bible can give us the true character and nature of the ture and living God. The bottom line is this, if you do not know Jesus the Son, you definitely do not know God the Father.

Scripture

> "*Who is a liar but he that denieth that Jesus is the Christ? He is antichrist that denieth the Father and the Son. <u>Whosoever denieth the Son</u>, the same <u>hath not the Father</u>: but he that acknowledgeth the Son hath the Father also*" (1 John 2:22, 23).

When we accept Jesus Christ as our Lord and personal Savior, this causes our names to remain written in the Lamb's book of life. Now let's move on and learn more about this loving God who gave us all a second chance at eternal life. This second chance was given when Jesus Christ redeemed us back from the enemy into the hands of our loving God. This free gift of salvation is what qualifies us to become the sons and daughters of God.

Scriptures

"For ye are all the children of God by faith in Christ Jesus" (Galatians 3:26).

"But as many as received him, to them gave he power to become the sons of God, even to them that <u>believe on his NAME</u>: Which were born, not of blood, nor of the will of the flesh, nor of the will of man, but of God" (John 1:12,13).

We are now in the family of God. All born-again Christian believers have been legally adopted into God's righteous family. When we became born-again Christians, our adoption was made final in the family of God. This is one family you cannot just enter into; you have to be born in by the Spirit of God. There is no cost or entry fee to obtain membership in God's family. All he requires is our faith, belief and confession in his only begotten Son named Jesus and then we will be saved.

CAN A MAN LOSE HIS SALVATION?

Once saved, are you always saved? This is a question that baffles all types of belief systems and religious organizations across the globe. The best way to answer this question correctly is to search out the Holy Bible. We as born-again Christian believers know what the requirements are to obtain salvation. The question is how do we maintain it? Can salvation be lost? We as saints of God know that we have to first of all accept Jesus Christ as our Lord and Savior. This involves us believing in our heart that Jesus is the risen Savior of the world. Once we believe, then all we have to do is confess the Lord with our mouth. After our confession goes forth out of our mouth, this is when our salvation is activated. Then the Holy Spirit which is the Comforter comes and dwells on the inside of us to help us and guide us to all truth. Jesus clearly tells us that we should be careful not to lose our crown which is our heavenly reward.

Scripture

"Behold, I come quickly: hold that fast which thou hast, that no man take thy crown. Him that over cometh will I make a pillar in the temple of my God, and he shall go no more out: and I will write upon him the name of my God, and the name of the city of my God, which is New Jerusalem, which cometh down out of heaven from my God: and I will write upon him my new name. He that hath an ear, let him hear what the SPIRIT saith unto the churches" (Revelation 3:11-13).

Jesus tells us that he is coming back quickly and for us to protect our crown. Christians know that rewards will be given out at the Judgment Seat of Christ. This is the Judgment that you want to be a part of. The Great White Throne Judgment is where you do not want to appear. Let us discuss the many issues that may hinder one's salvation. Those who confess Jesus as Lord must stay on course and keep their focus on Christ. When a believer loses focus on Christ, can this cause that soul to turn back from the faith? This is a question we will have to search out. Jesus taught his disciples the importance of ministering the kingdom of God to the lost souls of this world. Jesus called many disciples during the course of his ministry, however, some turned back. The question is will the souls who turned back make it into the kingdom of God? This is what Jesus had to say concerning two people he chose to follow him.

Scripture

"And he said unto another, FOLLOW ME. But he said, Lord, suffer me first to go and bury my father. Jesus said unto him, Let the dead bury the dead: but go thou and preach the kingdom of God. And another also said, Lord, I will follow thee; but let me first go bid them farewell, which are at home at my house.

And Jesus said unto him, NO MAN, HAVING PUT HIS HAND TO THE PLOUGH, AND LOOKING BACK, IS FIT FOR THE KINGDOM OF GOD" (Luke 9:59-62).

Jesus lets us know here that anyone who comes into the knowledge of his salvation and turns back or even looks back is not fit for the kingdom of

God. This tells us how valuable the salvation of the Lord is viewed by God. We should highly value it as well. There are several things that can cause you to come up short. Whether or not it will cause you to be cast into the lake of fire is something God will have to decide. Many have their own view on this theory. Let's talk about the things that we know of.

Four Things That May Make Your Question Your Salvation

1) Turning back from the faith.

This is a topic that we just examined. Believe it or not, there are those in this world who have reversed their belief system. For example, there have been cases where souls have reverted from Christianity back to Judaism. The question is, "Was that soul ever really saved in the first place?" Judaism is the Jewish religion that ushered in Christianity. They practice monotheism based on the teachings of the Holy Scriptures and the Talmud. The Talmud is a collection of books and commentary complied by Jewish rabbis from A.D. 250 to 500. There were more than 2,000 scholars or rabbis who worked over a period of 250 years to try to understand the meaning of God's word for their set purpose. Out of these efforts they produced the Talmud. We, as Christians, must remember that Jesus encountered the same attitudes among the Pharisees even before the Talmud existed. Jesus confronted the Pharisees in that day that also had similar type attitudes.

Scripture

"But he answered and said unto them, Why do ye also transgress the commandment of God by your traditions" (Matthew 15:3)?

Jesus explained to the stiffed neck Pharisees that they paid more attention to their man-made traditions as opposed to what the word of God actually said. They plotted to kill Jesus who was actually God manifested in the flesh, yet they called themselves Jewish temple leaders. So there are souls out there who will and have turned back from the faith. Jesus tells us that all whom God gives him, not one will HE cast out.

Scripture

> *"All that the Father giveth me shall come to me; and him that cometh to me I will in no wise cast out. <u>For I came down from heaven</u>, not to do mine own will, but the will of him that sent me"* (John 6:37, 38).

The Bible tells us that God foreordained all souls who will be saved before the foundation of the world. Notice that Jesus tells us that all souls given to him by God, HE will not cast out. Notice that Jesus did not say that they could not leave the faith on their own. Remember, man has freewill to make his own decision—whether or not he wants to continue to follow the Savior is totally left up to him. This is why the Lord encourages the Christian to finish his race, not allowing his faith to fail him. We as Christians must continue to work out our salvation with fear and trembling.

2) Failure to repent for sin.

The Bible tells us that once we receive the salvation of the Lord by repentance, belief, faith, and confession, we must not let future sins ever go without repentance. This is what the beloved disciple named John had to say about covering our sin.

Scripture

> *"If we say that we have no sin, we deceive ourselves, and the truth is not in us. If we CONFESS our sins, he is faithful and just to forgive us our sins, and to cleanse us from all unrighteousness. If we say that we have not sinned, we make him a liar, and his word is not in us"* (1 John 1:8-10).

> *"My little children, these things write I unto you, that ye sin not. <u>And if any man sin</u>, we have an advocate with the Father, Jesus Christ the righteous: And he is the propitiation for our sins: and not for ours only, but also for the sins of the whole world"* (1 John 2:1, 2).

This is part of the wonderful gift—that Jesus died on the cross to give to all who will accept him as Lord. It is called the grace of God. The precious blood of Jesus the Messiah covers and cleanses all of our sins—past, present and future. This is not a license to sin with malice, God forbid we even consider such a thing. This is why it is very important to recognize that we do not need to feel guilty once we have confessed our sins to God. Let us not assume that we have freedom to sin whenever we please. When we confess our sins, God is faithful to forgive and cleanse us at the same time. God forbid if we ever feel like we can take advantage of God's perfect grace. Jesus being our propitiation means he defends us to God the Father if we sin as a believer. Jesus reminds God that he has already paid the price for our sins. His precious blood, which came from God almighty, covers the sin stains of mankind. As a believer, if we commit a sin and fail to repent, that sin remains uncovered. When we repent, we agree with God that what we did is an offense to him. We then ask for his forgiveness and turn from that sin. If we fail to ask God for his forgiveness, this is the same as condoning the sinful behavior. Paul the apostle said it best. He explains that he had a constant battle in his flesh against sin, just like all born-again believers.

Scripture

> *Apostle Paul said, "For I know that in me (that is, in my flesh,) dwelleth no good thing: for to will is present with me; but how to perform that which is good I find not. For the good that I would I do not: but the evil which I would not, that I do. Now if I do that I would not, it is no more I that do it, but sin that dwelleth in me"* (Romans 7:18-20).

> *"For I delight in the law of God after the inward man: But I see another law in my members, warring against the law of my mind, and bringing me into captivity to the law of sin which is in my members. O wretched man that I am! Who shall deliver me from the body of this death? I thank God through Jesus Christ our Lord. So then with the mind I myself serve the law of God; but with the flesh the law of sin"* (Romans 7:22-25).

Paul the apostle clearly lets us know that our flesh will war against our spirit all of our days. When a man has been born of the Spirit of God, his spirit connects with God's Spirit. This is when the Comforter, also known as the Holy Spirit shows up to aid the new born Christian. With the help of the Holy Spirit, that born-again believer can keep the old flesh man under subjection. The new man who was born of God cannot sin. However, the old man has not totally disappeared. He's still there. As long as we walk in the Spirit of God which unvolves the will of God, we will overcome our flesh. The minute we look back and begin to walk in the flesh, the old flesh man will show up everytime. This is why we must stay in the word of God daily. We must also learn to meditate on the word of God day and night. We must keep the faith and remain quick to repent in case we stumble. The apostle told us that the law of sin warred against his mind. This is a result of the sin nature inherited from our great ancestor Adam. The constant thoughts and deeds of sin will ultimately produce at the end the death in our flesh. Never allow yourself to become complacent toward sin—knowing that the wages of sin is still spiritual death when we fail to repent to God. Repentance is a privilege only given to the righteous saints of God for their belief in the risen Savoir. Let us not abuse this privilege. God knows the intent of each one of our hearts. The only way we can walk free of sin is through the word of God and the presence of the Holy Spirit. This is where the true power comes from which allows the born-again believer to walk upright before the Lord. The flesh of mankind will be in a constant battle with sin the remainder of its days in the earth. However, never forget, we have the victory in Christ Jesus through the blood of the Lamb and the grace of God.

Scripture

"This I say then, walk in the Spirit, and ye shall not fulfill the lust of the flesh" (Galatians 5:16).

Therefore, with the war that is before us, let us always repent from the heart for anything that is not like God. Let us never forget that we have an advocate, and his name is Jesus.

3) Lack of forgiveness.

When we refuse to forgive one another, God refuses to forgive us. How then can our sins be washed away and covered if we do not have God's forgiveness? This is a very serious issue that many take for granted. The one who ignores this command to forgive others often feels justified in their actions. They fail to understand that the principle of forgiveness works both ways. Anyone who fails to follow this commandment of God causes their very soul to be endangered of the judgment. The Bible is very clear concerning the stipulation of forgiveness.

Scripture

Jesus said, *"For if ye forgive men their trespasses, your heavenly Father will also forgive you: But if ye forgive not men their trespasses, neither will your Father forgive your trespasses"* (Matthew 6:14, 15).

This is the stipulation in the prayer that Jesus taught his disciples to pray. This is not an option. It is a command directly from God. We are the ones who have no choice in the matter. Lack of forgiveness puts us in a state of being not forgiven by God. This is definitely not a good place to be. Once we come into the knowledge of Jesus Christ, this is the time to surrender all and start doing his will instead of our own.

4) Hatred for the brethren.

This is a very important issue that has many brothers and sisters still in bondage, even today. This area covers anyone who has hatred in their heart. Many Christians claim to confess Jesus as Lord, yet they still struggle with hatred, racism, and lack of love toward one another. This is what the beloved disciple John wrote about in the book of 1John. The apostle explained how important it is to love and not hate one another.

Scripture

"He that saith he is in the light, and hateth his brother, is in darkness even until now. He that loveth his brother abideth in the light, and there is none occasion of stumbling in him. But he that hateth his brother is in darkness, and walketh in darkness, and knoweth not whither he goeth, because that darkness hath blinded his eyes" (1 John 2:9-11).

Since Jesus is the LIGHT that shines on the world, darkness is a result of remaining in sin. We must learn to love all nations in order to come into the knowledge of Christ Jesus as Lord. There is no room for hatred in our hearts, nor will there be in the kingdom of God. God made all nations of mankind with one blood from one flesh of men. What right does anyone have to take it upon themselves and choose to hate their brother? God created mankind in his own image and likeness. This means when mankind chooses to hate one another, they forget about the God who created them. When a man hates his brother, it is impossible for that man to love God. This covers all racist human beings. As long as individuals struggle with racism toward their brothers and sisters, they cannot share a relationship with God. Remember this biblical fact for as long as breath remains in your body.

Scripture

> *"God that made the world and all things therein, seeing that he is Lord of heaven and earth, dwelleth not in temples made with hands; Neither is worshiped with men's hands, as though he needed anything, seeing he giveth to all life, and breath, and all things; And hath made of <u>one blood all nations of men</u> for to dwell on all the face of the earth, and hath determined the times before appointed, and the bounds of their habitation; That they should seek the Lord; if haply they might feel after him, and find him, though he be not far from every one of us"* (Acts 17:24-27).

Unless you are willing to continue to walk in sin and darkness, understand that when we choose to hate, we violate the commandments of Jesus to have love, one to another. We do not have the right to rebel against God, especially after what he has done for us on the cross at Calvary. Let us remember Jesus is still making intercession for us as our advocate every time Satan accuses us. Therefore, choose to no longer walk in darkness, but enter into the marvelous LIGHT of the Lord. The question still remains, "Can you lose your salvation when you choose to rebel against God? What do you think? Remember this, Jesus tells us in his word that whosoever endures to the END shall be saved.

Scripture

> Jesus said, *"And many false prophets shall rise, and shall deceive many. And because iniquity shall abound, the love of many shall wax cold. But he that shall endure unto the end, the same shall be saved"* (Matthew 24:11-13).

Since this statement is true, our job is to endure to the end, staying rooted and grounded in the word of God. Let us not be the one who the scriptures refer to as turning back or being deceived. Endure yourself until the very end and be among those who enter into God's glorious kingdom.

ARE THERE MANY WAYS TO INTERPRET THE BIBLE?

This is a common statement that is often made by individuals who have not come to the knowledge of God. Unbelievers will often say that the Bible can be interpreted in any way you choose to believe. This is a very untrue statement. The Lord thy God only intended his holy word to be interpreted the way he intended it to be understood. When skeptics and unbelievers read the word of God, their motives are not honorable. Their intentions are not in order. Skeptics will often read the Bible for the purpose of attempting to prove others wrong. Their intention is not to gain a closer walk with God, but to fine fault in the word itself. They have within them what is called a rebellious spirit. The fact is, they will never understand nor come to love the word of God with that type of attitude. Before you can understand the word of God, you must believe in God and have faith that his word is true. Then the Bible will not seem confusing at all. The Lord himself will give you a personal revelation of his holy word. In addition, God rewards those who seek him with a pure and diligently heart.

Scripture

"But without faith it is impossible to please him: for he that cometh to God must believe that he is, and that he is a rewarder of them that diligently seek him" (Hebrews 11:6).

This should explain why the skeptic believer finds it quite confusing and feels like the Bible can be interpreted in many ways. To a person who truly disbelieves the Bible in his heart, there is no revelation from God for that person. Unbelievers are the way they are primarily due to their unwillingness to change the way they live. They have not come to the point where they are willing to totally surrender to the will of God. They have refused to discipline their lives in order to conform to the commandments God has given. There are many consequences listed in the Bible for obedience and disobedience. We, as men and women in the earth must make the decision to either obey the CREATOR, or continue to submit our lives to the creature. Your decision will decide your destiny. That is why when it comes to teaching or trying to explain the content of the Holy Bible, you need a revelation from God. When men and women lack the revelation of God concerning his holy word, this is when interpretation errors can and will arise. The Holy Bible has marvelous power contained in its content. False teachers have often taken its content and used it for personal, wicked, and even financial gain. Those who use the Bible in this fashion will truly have their day of judgment.

Scripture

"But there were false prophets also among the people, even as there shall be false teachers among you, who privily shall bring in damnable heresies, even denying the Lord that bought them, and bring upon themselves swift destruction. And many shall follow their pernicious ways; by reason of whom the way of truth shall be evil spoken of" (2 Peter 2:1, 2).

False teachers and false prophets will never fully understand the word of God. They use God's word for immoral purposes. The true essence of the Holy Bible is to be a guiding light to all who believe in the true Creator of the universe. This guiding light leads the way to the precious kingdom of God. When you read and believe the Lord's love letter he gave to the children of men, then it will be a lamp unto your feet, and a light unto your pathway.

Therefore, understand this, God wants us to understand his holy word. We must come correctly when it comes to seeking the Lord. This is the only fullproof way to be certain that we understand the true revelation that the Holy Spirit gives. We must seek God with a pure heart, and then we will learn to rightly divide the word of truth. Jesus told us in the Holy Scriptures how to make this possible.

Scripture

"Jesus answered and said unto him, If a man love me, he will keep my words: and my Father will love him, AND WE WILL COME UNTO HIM, and make our ABODE with him" (John 14:23).

Jesus promised that he and God will take up residency inside those who love him. This is a true blessing to have the Spirit of God living on the inside of all born-again believers. Thank God that we have the Lord with us where ever we go. This means, we are never alone. Therefore, let your little light shine before men so that they will be compelled to glorify God in heaven.

SOVEREIGNTY OF GOD

We as Christians have a responsibility to explain to others how the almighty God is sovereign. This means that God is the Creator of all things and above all things. There is no one, nor anything greater than he. God is above and superior to all others. He is the supreme authority over the universe. Nothing is far greater.

Sovereignty of God—the theological term which refers to the unlimited power and authority of God, who has sovereign control over the affairs of history, nature, and the universe.

Scripture

"Hast thou not known? Hast thou not heard that the everlasting God, the Lord, the Creator of the ends of the earth, fainteth not, neither is weary? There is no searching of his understanding" (Isaiah 40:28).

The Lord God was referred to by many names based on his character and functions he performed toward his chosen people. Each one of these specific names carried its own meaning which helped explain his sovereign rule. Here is a list of just a few to remind us of who God is and the many functions he performs for us on a regular basis.

Elohim – The Creator, the one who speaks things into existence.
El-Shaddad – God all mighty.
Adonai – He is my Lord, he controls everything, our owner.
El El Yun – He is the Most High God who ruleth.
Elrauh – He is the God who seeth thee, when no one else can.
Jehovah – The God who keeps his covenant with his people.

Jehovah-Jireh – He is the God who provides all of our needs.
Jehovah-Nissi – He is the God who gives us the victory.
Jehovah-Rophe – He is the God who gives us health and healing.
Jehovah-Shalom – He is the God of peace.
Jehovah-Shannah – He is the God near to us, he is always there.
Jehovah-M'Kaddesh – He is the God who sanctifies.
Jehovah-Sabiyose – He is the Lord of Host, he is our protection.

These are just a few names and functions that the God of Abraham, Isaac and Jacob is known by. These names help draw a big picture of the true essence of the almighty God. Even though every name has a different character and function assigned to it, there is still only one God. He is known by many names to those who love, honor and worship him with a pure heart.

REVELATION OF GOD'S CHARACTER

God is the one who created and sustains the universe. God provided mankind with the revelation of himself, through the natural world and through his Son, Jesus Christ. This great revelation of God can only be found in the Holy Bible. This holy book lets us know that God is the same yesterday, today, and forevermore. The Bible further helps us to understand both the existence and true nature of the almighty God.

> God is holy.
> God is love.
> God is righteous.
> God is wisdom.
> God is truth.
> God is eternal.
> God is all powerful.
> God is all knowing.
> God is a spirit.
> God is everywhere.
> God is matchless.
> God is hope.

Hope is what I would like to address concerning our young people of today. The word of God has been taken away from our young people. This precious word of God is very rarely discussed, even in our homes. Today's youth are making major decisions for themselves which do not include God. This behavior is being allowed by parents improperly training and teaching their children the ways of the Lord. Some parents of today are overworked—having little time if any to spend with God. This makes it nearly impossible for our children to learn the valuable principles that the word of God teaches. We as parents have a responsibility to teach and pass down the knowledge of God to our younger generation. By doing so, we keep the love of God alive and present among us. The Bible tells us that God's people will be destroyed for their lack of knowledge in his holy word. Today's modern child psychiatrist, psychologist and counselors have adopted a new approach to raising children. The problem is most of society has bought into their ideas and views. God has given us instruction in his word on everything concerning the affairs of mankind. The Bible contains all knowledge pertaining to how mankind is to walk in the earth. We as human beings have a responsibility to read and search out the Creator, who is our heavenly Father. The only way this can be accomplished is if we study the Holy Bible. The Holy Bible is the only real truth that remains in the earth. What makes this wonderful book so special? Its entirety was inspired by God himself!

Scripture

"All scripture is given by inspiration of God, and is profitable for doctrine, for reproof, for correction, for instruction in righteousness" (2 Timothy 3:16).

Many men have taken the word of God and manipulated its meaning. Wicked men influenced by the enemy—Satan—have been guilty of distorting God's word for selfish reasons to accomplish their evil deeds. Wicked men use this as an excuse to cause division among one another. This is exactly what the evil one (Satan) wants to see happen among men. One thing is for sure…God's word has stood the test of time. When we seek the Lord with a pure heart, the revelation of the Lord will come upon us. This keeps us from reading the word of God and not understanding what we read. God wants to see a sincere interest in our hearts toward him. He does not want us reading his word for the wrong purpose. Unfortunately, some read the Bible for the purpose of tripping up the saints of God. They do not believe the Bible themselves, so they read to gain knowledge to use it against the Christian born-again believer. These souls are worse off than God's enemies. The enemies of God, known as Satan and his demonic forces at least believe God. Remember, they were once a part of God's kingdom. They believe the word. They know the word. They just choose not to obey the word of God. They just rebel against everything that has anything to do with God. This is the will of Satan. Skeptic men in the earth, who do not believe, lack faith in the one true reality of this world, the word of God. They are full of doubt and disbelief. They actually do not know what the real truth is. That's why they are deceived by the enemy. Remember, God wants us to know his plan for our salvation. This way, we can share knowledge and information with other souls concerning the blessings of God. We also have a responsibility to share the knowledge concerning eternal life in the kingdom God he has prepared for each of us.

Scripture

The Bible tells us, *"For the preaching of the cross is <u>to them that perish foolishness; but unto us which are saved it is the power of God</u>"* (1 Corinthians 1:18).

When the preaching of the cross goes forth out of the mouth of the righteous souls, all those who disbelieve have called it foolish teachings. While the unbelieving souls mock God, the righteous souls receive power from on high. By faith in the only begotten Son of God, we are saved and given eternal life in the kingdom of God.

Scripture

The Bible also states, *"But the natural man receiveth not the things of the Spirit of God: for they are <u>foolishness</u> unto him: neither can he know them, because they are spiritually discerned"* (1 Corinthians 2:14).

Hopefully this knowledge will keep us from getting discouraged when ministering to unbelievers. This knowledge of scripture can also be shown to the unbelievers to help them understand why nothing makes sense to them. They can read it for themselves and see it with their own eyes right in the word of God. Then they will understand that the word of God was not meant for them to know based on their disbelief. God's mighty word will forever be a mystery to the unbelieving souls of this world. Therefore, to the one who has faith to believe, be encouraged when seeking the Lord? All his wisdom and knowledge will surely bless your life.

Scripture

"But without faith it is impossible to please him: for he that cometh to God must believe that he is, and that he is a rewarder of them that diligently seek him" (Hebrews 11:6).

That's right—it's profitable to seek our Lord and study his word. God is very much aware that his word contains POWER. Any time we read from the Holy Bible, we hear directly from the voice of God. That's why when we quote God's word pertaining to our situation or need, God delivers us. The main key to life is to trust in God. God has set principles in the universe that if followed, we will receive the benefits they produce—principles like sowing and reaping, giving and it shall be given unto you, and showing pity for the poor, etc. God blesses all these things and much more according to his holy word.

Scripture

"He that hath pity on the poor lendeth unto the Lord; and that which he hath given will he pay him again" (Proverbs 19:17).

The Bible further tells us that blessed is he who considers the poor, the Lord will deliver him in his time of trouble. Therefore, when we take care of each other as God intended, God takes care of us in our time of need—no matter what or how large the need is. Remember, we are our brother's keeper! God honors his word, and he is not a man who would ever lie or fail!

GOD'S TWO PRIORITIES FOR MANKIND

The God of this universe is the great <u>I AM</u>. God has only asked mankind to seek two things in life. This means, there are only two priorities that God has instructed for us to do. If we will do these two things, God will provide the remainder of our needs. This may sound very far fetched, especially when we live in a world that teaches us to go after our needs. The problem with this method is we are doing it backwards. The laws, rules and principles of God's kingdom are totally opposite according to the world's point of view. The next few scriptures will explain how the Lord takes care of us when we focus and trust only in him.

Scripture

> *"Therefore take no thought, saying, What shall we eat? or, What shall we drink? or, Wherewithal shall we be clothed? (For after all these things do the Gentiles seek:) for your heavenly Father knoweth that ye have need of all these things. <u>But seek ye first the kingdom of God</u>, and <u>his righteousness</u>; and all these things shall be added unto you. Take therefore no thought for the morrow: for the morrow shall take thought for the things of itself. Sufficient unto the day is the evil thereof"* (Matthew 6:31-34).

The Number One Priority

The number one priority according to the word of God is for mankind to <u>SEEK FIRST THE KINGDOM OF GOD</u>. All we are required to do in this earth is to seek the kingdom of God with our whole heart. This is our first priority in life as we know it. When we seek other things, we are outside the will of God. That's when confusion, strife and struggles in life appear. Many brothers and sisters live their entire lifetime before they realize the Lord's two priorities for mankind. This will often happen when we choose not to read the word of God for ourselves. Another explanation could possibly be when we choose to continue to seek after selfish desires which please our flesh. Either way, we miss out on an opportunity for the Lord to shower us with all of our needs. This keeps us from wasting time hunting down everything we need and desire for ourselves. God is willing and able to provide for our every need without effort. All we have to do is follow his direction. We must be willing to do it God's way, which is the only way. Then we will enter into his rest.

The Number Two Priority

The number two priority according to the word of God is for mankind to <u>SEEK THE RIGHTEOUSNESS OF GOD</u>. By seeking the Lord's righteousness, we fulfill our obligation set by him. God said in his word, if we seek his kingdom and his righteousness, he will provide everything else in life that we would ever need. This principle is so simple that many Christians pass right over it. Our part involves these two commands. The key is that you have to believe and trust that God is who he says he is, and then you will understand this passage of scripture. The believer who has accepted Jesus as Lord must continue seeking God's kingdom and righteousness all the days of his life. When the believer seeks God's kingdom and righteousness, then all these things (material things) <u>SHALL</u> be added unto him. When our priority is spiritual, God will take care of the natural or material things. We must remember, "When God guides, he will provide." When we seek the kingdom, we seek and search out the word of God. When we seek God's righteousness, we seek, accept and follow the Savior Jesus Christ the righteous. Then our priorities have been fulfilled. The ending of the above verse tells us that we should not worry about tomorrow. The Bible teaches us that sufficient unto the day is the evil thereof. This means that each day has its own amount of trouble assigned to it. These troubles are considered to be serious challenges that all have to be responsibly handled. The Bible further explains to us that we should never worry about hypothetical situations and problems that may arise tomorrow. This is a total waste of time and thought process when we allow ourselves to worry about things before they happen. The truth is most things we choose to worry about never occur. Therefore, always remember God's two priorities that he requires of us, and then we can completely trust God as he supplies our every need.

DAY TWO

YOUNG PEOPLE LEARNING THE TRUTH

Believing the True God

Young people, did you know that God created man in his own image and likeness, and that means you? Many of our young people today have chosen not to seek God for themselves. When this occurs, they have bought into the many deceptions and distractions of this world. Our young people have gotten caught up in the world's system and found themselves believing that life as they know it is perfectly normal. They take on the attitude that everything is just fine with them living the way they have chosen to live. The world system has been designed and influenced by God's enemy known as Satan. Mankind has been spiritually blinded by the enemy and does not even know it. The biggest mistake young people make today is refusing to seek the Lord. The cause of this major setback occurred when they were not taught by their parents to love and worship God as a young child. We have to train our children in the admonition of the Lord, whether they like it or not. This is part of their training process. Have you noticed that most children if given half the chance would never make sound decision for themselves? If we allow our children to raise themselves, they would definitely come to ruins because they know no better. Young people…don't wait until you are too old and burnt out to acknowledge the true and living God. The truth is some young people don't make it. The ones who do make it to adulthood without serving God find themselves wasting valuable time in life. Learn about the Lord and receive his blessings while you are young enough to enjoy them. Whatever a man sows in his life, he will also reap in abundance one day. This principle applies whether we sow into good or bad ground. Both good and bad ground is a representation of the many different kinds of things we do and say while we are in the earth. Everything will produce a harvest according to whatsoever seed was sown. Therefore, learn to sow into good ground so that you can reap the benefits of your chosen crop. Always remember this, Jesus loved us enough to die in our place so that we could live now and well into eternity with God. We owe the Lord Jesus our very life he saved when he died on the cross for us. Therefore, let us be about our Fathers business and remain connected to each other in the earth. We must never forget who we are in Christ Jesus. Every man and woman has the opportunity to be considered a son of God. Remember, Adam was the first man created in the image and likeness of God. All of mankind are created equal and are the true descendants of Adam and Eve. When we understand this truth, we as a nation will no longer struggle with separation issues.

Many ethnic groups—due to lack of knowledge still struggle with this ignorance because they have rejected the word of God. Many men who call themselves men of God still struggle with issues of bigotry. There are actual ministers in this world today who teach that God created all races of people <u>separately</u>. This is not true according to the holy word of God. When dealing with the human race. The best example that can be viewed is to think of you as having many offspring. Several centuries later, your same offspring start to complain about their distant relatives. The same truth applies today. Regardless of how we choose to look at it, Adam and Eve are still the great ancestors of us all. Men have rejected the word of God for centuries. The question is, "Whose report will you believe?" There are men who want separatism in this world to satisfy their own discomfort and prejudice, just like there are men willing to disobey the word of God. Since God has said in his word he has no respect of persons. This means to have respect of persons is of the devil. Remember one thing. When someone willingly disobeys the word of the Lord, they have just taken on the will of God's enemy. Satan also has a will that he is trying to get accomplished in the earth. The question remains, whose agenda will find their way into your soul? Man has always tried to rationalize the many mysteries of God. God tells us in his word not to lean on our own understanding. He instructs us to trust him with all of our heart, even when we do not fully understand our situation. This is why we walk by faith, and not by our natural sight! The wickedness of wanting to be separate will always cause men to grow distant from one another. The devil knows that when mankind fails to come together, this weakens their ranks. In other words, when mankind is divided, they fall further into sin, which causes the devils wicked kingdom to enlarge. Always remember that a braided rope of many strands will always be stronger than a single strand of rope. When humans are separated, this makes it very easy for the enemy to infiltrate their mind. The Bible teaches us about the flood in Noah's day when God saved only eight souls. These were the souls of Noah and his immediate family only. After the flood, the Bible tells us that Noah's three sons repopulated the entire earth. This factual information clearly destroys any foundation attempting to support that all ethnic groups were created separately in the beginning. God destroyed all human life form except Noah, his wife, and their three sons and their wives. All mankind and animals left upon the earth were destroyed by the flood. We must keep in mind that God only made reference to sparing eight souls. The only way this theory concerning God creating other ethinic groups before he created Adam could stand, would be if none of the other ethinic groups had souls. Then it would stand to reason that some human beings are running around with out a soul. Regardless of how much some people have the need to feel special; this theory does not line up with the Holy Bible concerning the creation of mankind. Meanwhile, when the Bible said Noah gathered creatures of all kind, this particular term creature did not include other human beings. The unfortunate thing is that there are certain individuals today who preach this theory. We as born-again Christian believers trust in the Holy Bible which tells us this.

Scripture

"And the sons of Noah that went forth of the ark were Shem, and Ham, and Japheth: and Ham is the father of Canaan. These are the three sons of Noah: and of them was the whole earth overspread" (Genesis 9:18, 19).

Since the whole earth was overspread by Noah's sons, this means all nations of men are related to one another just like in the beginning with Adam. Every human being since the flood, and those who are alive today, are descendants of Noah and his three sons, by way of the first man Adam. Therefore, let us stop separating ourselves and realize we are all related, whether we like it or not! We must learn to show love and respect for all nations, kindreds and tongues. Remember, God loves everything and everybody he fashioned. Has it ever occurred to you that God placed all the different types of pigment into the human DNA upon creation? I'm sure if God wanted every human being to look exactly the same, he would have made us that way. You do remember that he is God Almighty? Therefore, why are we trying to figure out how God created us as opposed to just obeying his commands? The problem with human nature is we put more effort on questioning what we don't understand, instead of receiving what we do. One day when you meet God face to face, feel free to ask him why the skin of some human beings he created are shaded and others are not? I'm sure God would love to answer that question for you! On top of being all related to one another, we must never forget that we all bear the image and likeness of God.

TRAIN YOUR KIDS FOR RELEASE

To the parents raising young children…teach your children to value life. Show them how to look forward to establishing responsibility in their future. Slowly add responsibility to their lives as they begin to grow. As they grow older, increase their responsibility so that their life develops purpose. This will prepare them for this cruel and wicked world which they are about to enter into. The better you prepare your children as young adults, the better they will be prepared for life's many challenges. If you fail to prepare your children for life, both you and they will be sorry. When we fail to teach our children to clean, they become slobs. When we fail to teach our children how to cook, they will be forced to depend on others. When we fail to teach our children how to take care of business, they will lack responsibility. The number one thing we must never fail to teach our children is how to obey the Lord. This one major principle will save their lives. Without this valuable knowledge, our children will indeed perish. The Bible tells us that God's people are destroyed for lack of his knowledge. The example of the eagle is one that should be looked at very carefully. The mother eagle builds a sufficient and comfortable nest for her young. Before she conceives, she finds an adequate mate. This mate is tested several times having to retrieve little twigs dropped by the female eagle from different heights. This test is to prepare the male for the time when her young are ready to be winged. Before the female eagle selects a mate, he has to convince her that he will be skillful in retrieving her young. As the baby eagles begin to grow, the mother starts to remove the nest bed little by little. What the young eagles do not realize is their mother placed thorns in the bottle of their nest. These sharp thorns are to encourage the young eagles at the right time to fly the coop. The same principles should apply to our young adults if we properly prepare them for the world—both spiritual and mentally. They will be glad to leave the nest and experience their new life in this great big old world. On the other hand, if we fail to prepare them properly, they will want to remain home forever. The reason they refuse to leave their nest is because we as parents have made it too comfortable for them at home. They lack the necessary skills to be self-sufficient. Take the rich and wealthy for example. Those who properly prepare their children, regardless of their wealth, their children turn out fine. Those who give their children everything without effort or labor, especially when it's not deserved will raise unmotivated, ungrateful heathens. Their children grow up and sit down waiting for their parents to die. In some cases, they even assist their parents in leaving this life. Then they will abuse everything that their parents worked hard to achieve. This is very cruel, but very true in many cases. The Lord gives us instruction on how we should train up our children. Those who follow God's instructions, their offspring will be fruitful. Those who do not follow the word of the Lord will suffer the consequences.

Scripture

"Chasten thy son while there is hope, and let not thy soul spare for his crying" (Proverbs 19:18).

"The desire of the slothful killeth him; for his hands refuse to labor" (Proverbs 21:25).

"Train up a child in the way he should go: and when he is old, he will not depart from it" (Proverbs 22:6).

Training our children involves discipline, correction, training and loving. We have to discipline them so that they have respect for themselves and others. We have to correct them when they are wrong so that they understand that consequences are inevitable. We have to train them in the way they should go so they will be sensitive to the voice of God. We have to love them so that they will not lack self-esteem. However, the most important one is to train them and teach them according to the will of God. This training is priceless. The word of God teaches us that once trained, they will not depart from their original training when they become old. They will always come back to God and his righteous behavior if the proper foundation was laid. Likewise, if all they have is the wicked world's instruction, rest assure, they will ultimately rely solely on what they have learned.

ONE BLOOD FOR ALL NATIONS

Adam was the first man created by God. We are all descendants of Adam by way of Noah and his three sons. Noah's sons, Shem, Ham and Japheth, repopulated the entire world after the flood. This clearly tells us that not only was Adam the first man, it also lets us know we all have both the blood of Adam down to Noah running warm in all of our veins.

Scripture

"And hath made of <u>one blood all nations of men</u> for to dwell on all the face of the earth, and hath determined the times before appointed, and the bounds of their habitation; That they should seek the Lord, if haply they might feel after him, and find him, though he be not far from every one of us" (Acts 17:26,27).

The Bible says all men are of one blood. There may be different medical blood types according to the various DNA findings, however, God said, one blood for all nations. We are fully convinced that having different blood types does not prevent one from being related. Since the blood type comes primarily from the male line, then in most cases if not all, the child's blood type will always be different from the mother. Therefore, this is not a good example to argue whether or not blood type matters. God said one blood for all nations. The question is whose report will you believe?

DIFFERENT FLESH FOR DIFFERENT SPECIES

There are different types of flesh according to the word of God and it is not between men. Let us see what the God who created all flesh has to say about his different types of flesh.

Scripture

"All flesh is not the same flesh: but there is one kind of flesh of men, another flesh of beasts, another of fishes, and another of birds. There are also celestial bodies and bodies terrestrial: but the glory of the celestial is one, and the glory of the terrestrial is another" (1 Corinthians 15:39, 40).

God distinguishes the flesh between mankind, animals, fish and birds. God also makes the distinction between angels and inhabitants of the earth. Hopefully this will clear up any questions that anyone may have had concerning this issue. When you have questions about life in the future, they all can be answered from the word of God. The Holy Bible has addressed every issue that man can ever imagine.

SIN INTRODUCED INTO THE WORLD

Our Ancestors Disobeyed God

Adam and Eve were the first human beings created by God in this earth. They are our true original ancestors. Unfortunately, they disobeyed God. This act alone introduced sin into the world. God the Father is a Holy God that cannot look upon sin. Satan, that old serpent, deceived Eve in the Garden of Eden. Eve ate of the forbidden fruit from the tree of the knowledge of good and evil. After Eve ate, she gave also to Adam with her; and he did eat. This information is found in Genesis 3:6. We were lost in this world without God. We were in desperate need of a Savior. God saw to it that he provided us with one since mankind was incapable of saving himself. If we had to depend on mankind, we would be headed for eternal damnation in the lake of fire. This may sound harsh to some; however, there are those who still depend on mankind.

Scripture

The good news is, *"For God so loved the world that he gave his only begotten Son, that whosoever believeth in him should not perish, but have everlasting life. For God sent not his son into the world to condemn the world; but that the world through him might be saved"* (John 3:16, 17).

God loves us unconditionally. He created us in his own image and likeness for a reason. This love caused him to send his only begotten Son into a dying world. Jesus, the Son of the living God came into this world to pay the ultimate price for sin once and for all. This is the Godhead, being God the Father, God the Son and God the Holy Spirit, and these three are one God! I've explained it to you this way so that the next scriptures found in the book of John, chapter 1, verses 1-3 and 10-14 will reveal who Jesus truly is and was, as he walked the face of this earth. The scriptures reveal the true identity of Jesus our Lord and Savior. The book of John, the beloved disciple, the same apostle having privilege to look into the kingdom of God, was instructed to write the book of the revelation of Jesus Christ. John the apostle wrote these words to the body of Christ.

Scripture

"IN THE BEGINNING WAS THE WORD, AND THE WORD WAS WITH GOD, <u>AND THE WORD WAS GOD.</u> ALL THINGS WERE MADE BY HIM; AND WITHOUT HIM WAS NOT ANY THING MADE THAT WAS MADE" (John 1:1-3).

Verses 10-14 read,

V: 10 HE WAS IN THE WORLD, AND THE WORLD KNEW HIM NOT.

V: 11 HE CAME UNTO HIS OWN, AND HIS OWN RECEIVED HIM NOT.

V: 12 BUT AS MANY AS RECEIVED HIM, TO THEM GAVE HE POWER TO BECOME THE SONS OF GOD, EVEN TO THEM THAT BELIEVE ON HIS NAME:

V: 13 WHICH WERE BORN, NOT OF BLOOD, NOR OF THE WILL OF THE FLESH, NOR OF THE WILL OF MAN, BUT OF GOD.

V: 14 AND THE WORD WAS MADE FLESH, AND DWELT AMONG US, (AND WE BEHELD HIS GLORY, THE GLORY AS OF THE ONLY BEGOTTEN OF THE FATHER,) FULL OF GRACE AND TRUTH.

In essence, the WORD which is God left all his glory in heaven, wrapped his own self in a flesh suit and entered into the earth realm through the womb of the Virgin Mary. This miraculous act was necessary so that God could be on man's level when it was time to pay the ultimate sacrifice for the sins of this world. He came in the form of the Godhead as the only begotten Son of God the Father. This may still be a mystery to most, but the word of God is all-knowing and all true. John the apostle referred to Jesus as the <u>WORD</u> which is <u>GOD</u>. The Lord Jesus made this statement himself.

Scripture

Jesus said, *"I and my Father are one"* (John 10:30).

"Jesus said unto them, Verily, verily, I say unto you, Before Abraham was, I AM" (John 8:58).

This second verse mentioned is a very important statement made by Jesus Christ himself. In the book of Exodus, Moses told God that the children of Israel would want to know the name of who sent him. God told Moses to tell the children of Israel that <u>I AM</u> sent you. This is the same name Jesus told the Jews when they questioned him about being greater than Abraham. Jesus was letting the Jews know that he and God are one in the same. Jesus was the manifestation of God in the flesh that the Old Testament Holy Scriptures prophesied about. The Old Testament Scriptures called him IMMANUEL, which means, God with us! This is why he came with power and dominion over the entire universe. The laws of nature did not apply to Jesus the Christ. The Bible tells us that he (the Lord) came into this world and they (the Jews) rejected him. They knew him not. The Jews were the ones who should have been anxiously awaiting the Messiah's coming since they had privilege to the Holy Scriptures.

Scripture

"And Moses said unto God, Behold, when I come unto the children of Israel, and shall say unto them, The God of your fathers hath sent me unto you; and they shall say to me, what is his name? What shall I say unto them? And God said unto Moses, I AM that I AM: and he said, Thus shalt thou say unto the children of Israel, I AM hath sent me unto you. And God said moreover unto Moses, Thus shalt thou say unto the children of Israel, The Lord God of your fathers, the God of Abraham, the God of Isaac, and the God of Jacob, hath sent me unto you: this is my name for ever, and this is my memorial unto all generations" (Exodus 3:13-15).

Jesus Christ was born of the Virgin Mary without a flesh Father in order to dwell among us and die for all of our sins. Jesus had the blood of God in his veins as he walked the face of the earth. This had to be done in order to create a way back home to be in the presence of the Lord. Jesus rectified the disobedience of Adam in the garden, bridging the gap back to the kingdom of heaven. We must remember, since Jesus died willingly on the cross at Calvary and rose again on the third day, we have been given a direct line to God in the name of our Lord and Savior Jesus Christ. The Bible explains that the <u>WORD</u> was <u>GOD</u> in the beginning. Then the WORD (Jesus) was made flesh and came to this earth. Jesus came in the form of the Godhead as the only begotten Son of God to dwell among men. God's purpose was to sacrifice his one and only Son for the sins of all mankind once and for all. What wicked men fail to understand is this very important principle of God—the principle of sin being committed in the flesh, therefore the same sin had to be likewise dealt with in the flesh. God said the wages of sin is death. This promise will not change because God has spoken the words. Therefore, even God is not willing to violate his own spoken written word. The only way God could redeem us was to cover our sin with the innocent blood of Jesus. No more sacrificing innocent animals is required. The blood of animals was only a temporary covering for sin until the Lamb of God could be manifested. This Lamb of God named Jesus paid the ultimate price for us all. We have been bought and paid for; therefore, we should be grateful and appreciative for what God has done for us. Let us also be willing to serve the Lord with our whole heart. Have you ever wondered why this world has a problem when the name of Jesus is spoken out loud? I want you to really understand why this world truly has a problem with this name. There is unexplainable power in the name of Jesus. The name of Jesus the Christ is above every other name that has ever, or will ever be spoken with the angelic or human tongue.

Scripture

"Wherefore God also hath highly exalted him, and given him a name which is <u>ABOVE EVERY NAME</u>" (Philippians 2:9).

"Neither is there salvation in any other: for there is none other name under heaven given among men, whereby we must be <u>SAVED</u>" (Acts 4:12).

This verse of scripture clearly cancels out all other belief systems in this world. No other religion or belief system can or will save the souls of mankind. This means that if you serve someone or something other than Jesus the Christ, you are wasting your time, and your sins are weighed heavily upon you. This is not a very good state to be in, knowing that your very soul is lost and on its way to hell. The good news is no one has to remain in that state once they have learned the truth about God's saving grace. This is not a time to be prideful. Remember, pride is what was found in Lucifer (the devil) before he was cast out of the kingdom of God. We must try and understand that the true and living God loves us unconditionally. His love was so great for his creation that he sacrificed his only begotten Son for us. Let me ask you a question! Would you give the life of your only child, or even one of your children for that matter to save this sinful world? That question may sound a little soft. Let's take it to another level. Would you give the life of your child to save the life of everyone in the world housed on deathrow? While you struggle with your answer, the God we serve gave his only begotten Son so that sinners like you and me could have eternal life in God's kingdom. Not only some souls, but all souls can come to the foot of the cross and cast their sins upon the Lord. No matter what sin anyone has committed in this world, God is willing to forgive that soul. This is the kind of God we serve. You can be sure that no other form of religion known to man has it where their <u>god</u> sacrificed his or her life for his or her followers. Jesus took it a step further. He not only endured pain, suffering and a severe beating leading up to the cross, he died, rose again on the third day and promised to resurrect all believers unto eternal life in his kingdom. You will never find this kind of unconditional love anywhere else in this world God created. This is the true test of who really cares for the souls of this world. The shepherd gave his life for his sheep. Jesus said it like this in the word of God.

Scripture

"I AM the good shepherd: the good shepherd giveth his life for the sheep" (John 10:11).

Realize that this is a spiritual world we live in. The unbeliever cannot begin to imagine everything that goes on around him. He is too full of the cares and concerns of this world to even attempt to see clearly. The born again believer realizes and fully understands that the name of Jesus is the only name by which men can be saved. This is the will of God the Father, not some religion made up by the wicked minds of men condoning their ungodly lifestyles. The blessing concerning the salvation of the Lord is this. What God has offered to this world is a <u>FREE GIFT</u> that requires both the belief and confession of mankind. In order to believe and confess this truth, one must have faith. Without this kind of faith, it is impossible to please God. We as souls in the earth must stop trying to fit God into our sinful little lives. We must come to the knowledge of his word and conform to his will. This is where salvation lies. It is available to everyone. No one has been excluded. There is no salvation in stubbornness and hardness of heart. This is why anyone that goes into hell, and then on to the lake of fire, only has themselves to blame.

Scripture

"For by grace are ye saved through faith; and that not of yourselves: it is the gift of God" (Ephesians 2:8).

This world of nonbelievers may not be ready to accept the word of God. They cannot bring themselves to believe that Jesus was manifested in the flesh and dwelled among men in the earth. This is and was God's own plan to save our souls from the lake of fire. Sin has a death penalty assigned to it. We had to be washed in the blood of Jesus in order to be spared this great condemnation. Once God speaks a law into existence, it cannot be changed. He is the King of the universe. Those who understand how a kingdom operates when a king speaks, also understands that his words become law. This is why it is so important that we accept Jesus as Lord. God has spoken it into his word. There is no other way to his heavenly kingdom. This is God's plan for us; not a plan that man has devised. Remember, receiving the free gift of salvation is for the purpose of saving your SOUL. You can either take it or leave it. The choice is up to you. Just don't say you were never told!

DAY THREE

DID YOU KNOW!

One-hundred Biblical Points of Informational Knowledge

This section is designed to educate the unbeliever as well as further enhance those who believe. The day-to-day grind can overload our lives to the point that we leave ourselves with very little time to spend with God. The information found in this section will bring your focus back on track. This section is designed to inform you of significant factual events found in the word of God. Some of this information may seem elementary to the biblical intellectual. However, to the one who has not taken the time to explore all the wonderful things concerning the Creator, this information will greatly enlighten your spirit. Hopefully, this powerful word will turn on your holy light and cause a spiritual hunger for more of the true and living God. Remember, this information is geared to jump-start your desire and quest for more biblical wisdom and knowledge. Then you will understand that there is only one place in this world where you can receive this kind of truth. That one place is the written word of God, commonly referred to as the Holy Bible.

1) Did you know that in the beginning God created the heavens and the earth? This statement will sound very simple to some, and to others, it will establish their biblical foundation. Remember, there are some souls who still believe in evolution and the Darwinian Theory. You may be one of them! Therefore, we must understand that God spoke this world into existence and it manifested itself. God created all things in the earth in six days and he rested on the seventh (Sabbath day). Whether the six days are measure in time or out of time is not for us to know at this time. The Bible teaches us that God created all that he created in six days, and then he rested. Instinctively, animals do exactly what God created them to do. They operate out of instinct. This also applies to other living things such as plants, flowers, trees, and grass, etc. They, too, carry out their assigned function in the earth. Man is the only creature who struggles with obedience issues and the true purpose for which he was created. This is due to the great fall and disobedience of the first man Adam. As a result of sin, the world has been affected greatly. Even though the world has been affected by the sin of man, God is still very much in control. We all have a purpose in life whether we believe it or not. Blessed are those who find it.

Scripture

"Thou art worthy, O Lord, to receive glory and honor and power: for thou hast created all things, and for thy pleasure they are and were created" (Revelation 5:11).

Man insists on walking this earth in an attempt to find his own way. This is why we must seek the Lord and his direction at all times, even when we feel like we are in charge. Mankind will often think that he knows where he is going most of the time. However, the precious word of God lets us know that mankind doesn't have a clue.

Scripture

The Bible tells us, *"O Lord, I know that the way of man is not in himself: it is not in man that walketh to direct his steps"* (Jeremiah 10:23).

Since the Bible teaches us that we do not know our way in life, let us not continue to waste time seeking our own direction. Let us totally depend on the Lord to direct our steps. When we attempt to walk without God, we wander in the wilderness like lost sheep. God gave us all freewill and the right to choose. The choices we make will provide the appropriate consequences we will face. Likewise our words we choose to speak from our lips will help pattern and design our future destiny.

2) Did you know that Cain and Abel were not born in the likeness of their father, Adam? Cain and Abel were the first souls born of a man and woman in the history of this world. Adam was created by God who formed him out of the dust of the ground. Eve was formed by God who used one of Adam's ribs in order to fashion her. In essence, Eve was taken from within the man. The Bible teaches us that God created both male and female when he made man. Therefore, all he had to do when it was time to create woman was to separate her from within the man. This way, man and woman will always be connected to one another. They are made for each other. Adam said it best when he spoke of what Eve meant to him.

Scripture

"And Adam said, this is now bone of my bone, and flesh of my flesh: she shall be called Woman, because she was taken out of Man" (Genesis 2:23).

"And the Lord God caused a deep sleep to fall upon Adam, and he slept: and he took one of his ribs, and closed up the flesh instead thereof; and the rib, which the Lord God had taken from man, made he a woman, and brought her unto the man" (Genesis 2:21, 22).

God performed the first surgery where the patient was put to sleep during the operation. I bet you thought the doctors thought that up? The Holy Bible holds the answers to all things done under the sun. When God finished separating both male and female, Eve was presented to Adam by God. She showed up on the scene as both a wife and a help-mate. This union was formed as soon as the couple came together as man and wife. God ordained their covenant of marriage which was honorable before his eyes. For this reason, be careful who you link yourself too sexually. The consummation establishes a one flesh union between a man and a woman. Adam and Eve's covenant was ordained by God who created them for this union.

Scripture

"Adam knew Eve his wife; and she conceived, and bare Cain and said, I have gotten a man from the Lord. And she again bare his brother Abel" (Genesis 4:1-2a).

The two young boys grew up and the elder brother Cain ended up slaying his younger brother Abel. Cain became wroth with Abel over his offering to God. God was pleased with Abel's offering, but displeased with Cain's offering. The Bible tells us that the second son, Abel, presented a more excellent offering to the Lord than his elder brother, Cain. Abel's offering was blessed and accepted by God, whereas Cain's offering was not. The two sons born to Adam and Eve started the precedence of the second son being the blessed of God. Throughout the Bible, the second son received the covenant blessing of God instead of the firstborn on many occasions. Despite how tradition would have it, the first born son has always been rightfully entitled to the birthright according to the worlds system. Since God is the Creator of all things, this means he can do whosoever he pleases when it comes to his rules.

Scripture

"And in process of time it came to pass, that Cain brought of the fruit of the ground an offering unto the Lord. And Abel, he also brought of the firstlings of his flock and of the fat thereof. And the Lord had respect unto Abel and his offering: But unto Cain and his offering he had not respect. And Cain was very wroth, and his countenance fell" (Genesis 4:3-5).

The birth of Adam and Eve's two sons came after they had sinned against God and was dispelled from the Garden of Eden. The two young men grew as their father Adam toiled in the wilderness. One day, Cain became so angry that he murdered his own brother—the first murder committed in the history of this world. This murder served as a reminder to Adam and Eve that the wages of sin is death. Sin has a way of causing uncontrollable situations and consequences to occur throughout an entire lifetime.

Scripture

"And Cain talked with Abel his brother: and it came to pass when they were in the field, that Cain rose up against Abel his brother, and slew him. And the Lord said unto Cain, Where is Abel thy brother? And he said, I know not: Am I my brother's keeper? And he said, What hast thou done? The voice of thy brother's blood crieth unto me from the ground. And now

art thou cursed from the earth, which hath opened her mouth to receive thy brother's blood from thy hands; When thou tillest the ground, it shall not hence forth yield unto thee her strength; a fugitive and a vagabond shalt thou be in the earth" (Genesis 4:8-12).

Exactly how Cain slew his brother is not clear. The Bible described it as Cain rose up against his brother and slew him. Whether he was struck in the head, pushed off a mountain, choked, or strangled, we do not exactly know. After the murder, we are not sure whether or not Cain buried Abel's body in an attempt to hide it from the Lord. What we do know is that God told Cain that Abel's blood cried out to him from the ground. This caused the ground to be cursed for Cain. From that day forward, nothing would yield to him because he took an innocent life and caused innocent blood to be shed. We must remember that all souls were created in the image and likeness of God. For this reason, we are all precious and valuable in the sight of the Lord.

Scripture

"And Adam knew his wife again; and she bare a son, and called his name Seth: For God, said she, hath appointed me another seed instead of Abel, whom Cain slew" (Genesis 4:25).

The Bible tells us that when Seth was born, he resembled his father, Adam. According to the Bible, this was the beginning or the first evidence where sons and daughters started to resemble their parents.

Scripture

"And Adam lived a hundred and thirty years, and begat a son in his own likeness, after his image; and called his name Seth" (Genesis 5:3).

Based on this information, it is apparent that Cain and Abel did not resemble their father Adam. This makes you wonder where Adam's blood came from since he was the first man. Just remember this, God fashioned man out of the dust of the ground and breathed his Spirit into him. Man became a living soul and a speaking spirit. When man received the spirit of God, he was given the ability to also create things by speaking them into exsistence.

The Bible refers to Adam the first man as a living soul, then makes reference to Jesus Christ as the last Man Adam referring to him as a quickening spirit.

Scripture

"And so it is written, The first man Adam was made a living soul; the last Adam (Jesus) was made a quickening spirit" (1 Corinthians 15:45).

3) Did you know in the book of Genesis there lived a man named Enoch who did not experience death in the earth? The word of God tells us that Enoch was so righteous that God took him off the face of the earth.

Scripture

"And Enoch walked with God: and he was not; for God took him" (Genesis 5:24).

"By faith Enoch was translated that he should not see death; and was not found, because God had translated him: for before his translation he had this testimony, that he pleased God" (Hebrews 11:5).

God took Enoch off the face of the earth without him seeing or experiencing death. Enoch was the father of the oldest man who ever lived named Methuselah. Methuselah lived to be 969 years old. He was the grandfather of God's faithful servant; the patriarch named Noah, builder of the Ark. Enoch was not the only man who did not experience death in the earth.

There also lived a man named Elijah. This prophet of God was the second man God chose not to experience death in the earth. Elijah was caught up in a whirlwind witnessed by his servant and helper, the prophet Elisha.

Scripture

"And it came to pass, as they still went on, and talked, that, behold, there appeared a chariot of fire, and horses of fire, and parted them both asunder, and Elijah went up by a whirlwind into heaven" (2 Kings :11).

God is a God of order. Everything God does, he does for a reason. Some scholars feel that the two witnesses God makes mention of in the end times are Enoch and Elijah. This is because they are the only two souls who have not experienced death in the flesh throughout the history of this world. The purpose of God sparing these two trusted servants is to fulfill the end time prophecy to take place during the great tribulation period. This involves the two witnesses sent by God into the earth to be a final witness to the souls that were left behind when the trumpet of God sounds. Since these two great patriarchs are the only men who have not seen death in the flesh, it is pretty obvious that they will see their death later as the scriptures unfold. God is the alpha and the omega, the beginning and the end, the first and the last. He knows all things and has made provision for all things. In the event God had chosen someone else, they would have had to die twice.

Scripture

"And I will give power unto my two witnesses, and they shall prophesy a thousand two hundred and threescore days, clothed in sackcloth. These are the two olive trees and the two candlesticks standing before the God of the earth" (Revelation 11: 3, 4).

"And when they shall have finished their testimony, the beast that ascended out of the bottomless pit shall make war against them, and shall overcome them, and kill them" (Revelation 11:7).

"And they heard a great voice from heaven saying unto them, Come up hither. And they ascended up to heaven in a cloud; and their enemies beheld them" (Revelation 11:12).

The Bible tells us that this event will probably occur during the last half of the tribulation period. The witnesses will proclaim a message of judgment and the need for repentance during the tribulation period. They will be slain by the beast. Their bodies will lie in the streets and be on display for the whole world to see. Three days later, they will be resurrected from the dead before the eyes of those who inhabit the earth during that time. Their resurrection from the dead will be the same as what Jesus Christ and all who chose to follow him experienced. Their bodies will then ascend into the heavens to fulfill the prophecy of God. This timeframe of three days is similar to the timeframe Jesus was raised from the dead. Jesus opened the portal and paved the way for us all to be resurrected in the last days. Salvation is assured to all who call upon the name of the Lord. Unfortunately, if you are not born again and did not enter in through the straight-gate, you will miss the opportunity to dwell in the house of the Lord forever. If you miss this opportunity, you automatically will find yourself dwelling among the enemies of God in a place of outer darkness for all eternity. This place is well known as the lake of fire. Then you will have no one to blame but yourself because you chose to be set apart from the almighty God.

4) Did you know that fallen angels took for themselves wives of the daughters of men? The Bible tells us that the offspring of these unions produced giants in the earth.

Scripture

"And it came to pass, when men began to multiply on the face of the earth, and daughters were born unto them, that the sons of God saw the daughters of men that they were fair; and they took them wives of all which they chose" (Genesis 6:1-2).

There are two basic possibilities in the mind of some scholars. Some feel that this verse refers to (angelic) non-human beings such as those mentioned in the book of Job chapter 1: verse 6 and chapter 2: verse 1. Some scholars feel that this verse refers to a godly line of Seth, Adam's third son mentioned. The daughters of men were explained by some scholars as being the daughters of Cain—the cursed son of Adam who murdered his brother, Abel. Some scholars refer to this as the godly and ungodly offspring of man. The problem here is that when Adam disobeyed God, sin was introduced into the world. Therefore, all of Adam's offspring would have been sinners by nature. The fact that we are all descendants of Adam indicates that we all came from the same stock. The question came up whether or not angels enter into marriage? The Lord Jesus told us when asked by his disciples about the wife of the seven brothers that died without producing seed to their brother spouse, whose wife would the women belong to in the resurrection (Matthew 22:25-30 and Mark 12:20-25)? Jesus answered them by saying, "Angels do not enter into marriage." But remember this, these are rebellious/fallen angels who live and take pleasure in disobeying God. Therefore, the Lord Jesus said angels do not marry, however, fallen angels neither obey God nor dwell among God's holy angels anylonger. For this reason, the scripture in the book of Genesis, chapter six is clearly referring to fallen angels and not sons of men. After the angelic beings took wives of the daughters of men, the daughters conceived and produced supernatural mighty men. In the Old Testament, when referring to the sons of God, the Bible is referring to the angels whether they are heaven's host or the fallen angels cast down with Satan. In the New Testament, when the term, sons of God is used, it is referring to the born-again Christian men and women of God. This is based on how Jesus Christ redeemed man and died on the cross at Calvary for us all. We have been adopted into the holy family of God. Therefore, we became the sons of God which is his righteousness. We were lost and separated from our heavenly Father in desperate need of a Savior. Then the Savior appeared in the form of the only begotten Son of God named Jesus. This Savior is the same one prophesied as the coming Messiah who possessed the blood of God which ran warm in his veins. Jesus paid the ultimate price for the sins of this world when he shed his precious blood on the cross for mankind.

Scripture

"And the Lord said, my spirit shall not always strive with man, for that he also is flesh: yet his days shall be an <u>hundred and twenty years</u>. There were GIANTS in the earth in those days; and also after that, when the sons of God came in unto the daughters of men, and they bare children to them, the same became mighty men which were of old, men of renown. And God saw that the wickedness of man was great in the earth, and that every imagination, of the thoughts of his heart was only evil continually. And it REPENTED the Lord that he had made man on the earth, and it grieved him at his heart. And the Lord said, I will destroy man whom I have created from the face of the earth; both man, and beast, and the creeping thing, and the fowls of the air; for it repenteth me that I have made them" (Genesis 6:3-7).

These scriptures teach us that the sons of God (fallen angels) took them wives of the daughters of men and impregnated them. These angels were spirit beings that were able to interact with human beings for the purpose of engaging in sexual intercourse with the daughters of men in the earth. This perverted act was not in the will of God. The offspring of this union produced half-spirit and half-human beings. These were supernatural beings that were very large in stature.

Scripture

"But Noah found grace in the eyes of the Lord" (Genesis 6:8).

Noah was a just man and the Bible describes him as perfect in his generation. The Bible goes on to say that Noah walked with God. God flooded the earth shortly after that which took care of all living beings in the earth except Noah and his immediate family. The way this was written in the Bible can lead us to believe that the sons of God referred to the rebellious/fallen angels that were a part of Satan camp. Some scholars agree with this explanation. Since all souls came from Adam and his offspring, this would qualify the bloodline of Adam to be called the sons or daughters of men. The next question is what happened to the fallen angels—the spirit beings?

Scripture

"And the angels which kept not their first estate, but left their own habitation, he hath reserved in everlasting chains under darkness unto the judgment of the Great Day" (Jude 1:6).

This Holy Scripture describes the whereabouts of the fallen angels who were cast out of heaven along with Lucifer (the devil) when they rebelled against God. First of all we know that the word of God teaches us that they were cast down to the earth initially before man was created.

Scripture

"And his tail drew the third part of the stars of heaven, and did cast them to the earth" (Revelation 12:4a):

This verse of scripture is referring to Lucifer, also known as Satan when he was cast down from heaven. This enemy of God influenced one third of the heavenly host to follow him. The Holy Scriptures refers to them as the stars of heaven. Therefore, when Lucifer was kicked out of heaven, he became known as the devil and Satan. God was not willing to allow this enemy to rule this earth. God fashioned a man and attached him to the earth he formed. This God created man was given a flesh suit and made lord over what God had created. This is when Satan found a way to tempt Eve and cause Adam to disobey God in the Garden of Eden. That was the beginning of all of our trouble. The Bible taught us that God now has reserved the fallen angels in everlasting chains under darkness until that great day of the Lord. These angelic beings have been since locked down and held in chains in darkness. There can no longer be anymore intermixing sexually between angelic and human beings. However, the spirit of Satan still roams the earth like a lion seeking whom he may devour and whose mind he may invade. Therefore, study and learn the word of God and live free of the devils demonic influence.

5) Did you know that the Bible tells us that Noah was a just man and perfect in his generation? Noah walked with God and served him as a just man. God saved eight souls—Noah and his wife, his three sons, Ham, Shem and Japheth and their wives. No other human beings survived the flood according to the word of God. Noah lived in a time that mankind had become so wicked in the earth that God repented that he had made man. God spoke to Noah and gave him instruction on the dimensions of an ark he was to build. The large boat type vessel was set to be three hundred cubits (450 feet) in length. The breadth was to be fifty cubits (75 feet) wide. The height of the vessel was to measure out at thirty cubits (45 feet) high. Cubits were measured at approximately eighteen inches long. This general distance was determined by measuring the distance between a man's elbow and the tip of his finger. Noah was instructed to take a pair of every animal on their journey in order to prevent total extinction. God specifically instructed Noah to take every clean beast by sevens, and every unclean beast by two.

Scripture

> *"Of every clean beast thou shalt take to thee <u>by sevens</u>, the male and his female: and of beasts that are not clean <u>by two</u>, the male and his female. Of fowls also of the air by sevens, the male and the female; to keep seed alive upon the face of all the earth"* (Genesis 7:2-3).

The building of the ark took approximately one hundred and twenty years (120yrs) to complete. During this time, Noah preached the entire time warning the people about the coming flood. With all the preaching and warning, Noah received not one convert among them. What would we honestly say about a preacher in this day and age who preached for decades with only an eight-member congregation? You would probably question and criticize whether or not he was truly an anointed man of God. This goes to show you, it's not in the numbers; it's in the message from the word of God. Noah found grace in the eyes of the Lord and was privileged by God to regenerate the human race through his three sons and their wives. His obedience to the voice of God allowed him and his family to be saved when everyone else perished off the face of the earth. The fact that it had never rained before, the people were reluctant to believe it was going to rain in a dry desert. The word of God is still warning the world today in the same manner. God is pleading with us in his holy word to get covered with the blood of his only begotten Son Jesus, but only a few souls are willing to take heed. When Christ returns for his Church body of born-again believers, those who disbelieve, just like in the days of Noah, will not be saved nor protected from the wrath of God's final judgment. Just like in the days of Noah's flood, so will it be again in the days of the coming of the Lord. The lost souls will be forced to go through the tribulation period in the earth. This period will begin immediately follow the Lord's return for his church body of believers. The Bible warns us that this day will be like the day God sealed Noah's family in the ark. Noah had faith to believe God's warning and obeyed his instructions to build an ark made of gopher wood. We have the same option today to believe and be saved by the risen Savior who is Jesus the Christ. Noah was six hundred years old at the completion of the ark when the rains came upon the whole world. The flood was so great that it covered the highest mountain upward of fifteen cubits which is actually about twenty-two feet. Nothing on land or in the air could survive.

Scripture

"And the waters prevailed exceedingly upon the earth; and all the high hills that were under the whole heaven, were covered. Fifteen cubits upward did the waters prevail; and the mountains were covered. And all flesh died that moved upon the earth, both of fowl, and of cattle, and of beast, and of every creeping thing that creepeth upon the earth, and every man: All in whose nostrils was the breath of life, of all that was in the dry land died" (Genesis 7:19-22).

God destroyed all creation except Noah and his family and everything that was in the waters. The waters were not tampered with according to the Holy Bible. All living things that God created in the bodies of water still exist today. One of the most significant eye-opening events pertaining to Noah and the ark was the covenant God made with Noah and all his creation. The Lord God placed a sign in the heavens to be looked upon until the end of time. This sign is to be a constant reminder of God's mercy and compassion he shows toward man and all his creation.

Scripture

And the Lord said, "And I will establish my covenant with you; neither shall all flesh be cut off any more by the waters of a flood; neither shall there anymore be a flood to destroy the earth. And God said, This is the token of the covenant which I make between me and you and every living creature that is with you, for perpetual generations: I do set <u>MY BOW</u> in the cloud, and it shall be for a <u>token of a covenant</u> between me and the earth. And it shall come to pass, when I bring a cloud over the earth, that the bow shall be seen in the cloud: And I will remember my covenant, which is between me and you and every living creature of all flesh; and the waters shall no more become a flood to destroy all flesh. And the <u>BOW</u> shall be in the cloud; and

I will look upon it, that I may remember the everlasting covenant between God and every living creature of all flesh that is upon the earth. And God said unto Noah, This is the token of the covenant, which I have established between me and all flesh that is upon the earth" (Genesis 9:11-17).

God has explained in his word that he would never destroy the earth or mankind again by means of a flood. That beautiful rainbow that we have seen in the sky all of our lives is a mighty sign and token of the almighty God's promise. This beautiful token is a reminder of the covenant God made with mankind and all creatures of the earth. We as believers and inhabitants of God's earth are supposed to acknowledge, remember, and teach to our generations about our covenant with God. This covenant belongs to all who will believe in the word of God. Unfortunately, there are still souls in the earth who believe God's beautiful rainbow seen in the sky after a rain is significant with a four leaf clover and a Leprechaun's pot of gold. How ridicules was this wise tale to have ever been told. This is actually being taught to little children. This wise tail is just as far fetch as the lie parents tell their children on December 25th that Santa is coming. Christmas is the celebration of the birth of the Savior Jesus Christ for those of you who still believe in Santa Claus. The 25th day just happens to be the day that Christians celebrate the best gift the world could have ever received, which is Jesus Christ, the Savior of the world. The world system has made this jolly mystical character called Santa appear to be all knowing and all seeing. Does this remind you of anyone particular? Only God is all knowing and all seeing and all mighty. Parents should never lie to their children for any reason. Eventually, they are going to discover the truth. Then the trust factor will be broken between the children and their parents for the first time. They will begin to be loyal to whoever reveals the truth to them. This is normally their fellow class mates, or perhaps even their friends or enemies. Then parents have the nerve to wonder why their teenagers rebel and turn their loyalty to their friends. Even though, no one loves children more than their own parents. They still go through a stage where they stop trusting their parents and tend to place their trust in the wrong crowd. Lying will cause children to doubt and question everything their parents tell them from then on. Always remember, Christmas is the celebration of the birth of Jesus Christ, that's it! Giving gifts is a wonderful thing because God truly gave us the best gift. Let us not forget that fact during the Christmas season.

Teach your children to be givers, for it is better to give than to receive. Think on this, the name Sa<u>nta</u> switched slightly around also spells Sa<u>tan</u>. The word of God teaches us that this dreadful enemy of God called Satan is the father of lies. Not saying that there is a connection, but we as parents should not be entertaining lies when it comes to our children under any circumstance. Besides, the last time I checked, lying is still a sin and an abomination unto the Lord. We as parents must start to take the word of God serious. When we fail to teach our youth the truth about God, foolish things from the world will be taught to them in its place. This is what causes spiritual blindness. The lies told by this world system will attempt to try and block the true knowledge of God. Only the truth will make you free. Just like in the days of Noah, they laughed in disbelief until it was too late. They failed to believe the preacher when he warned them of the coming event. They chose to believe each other because like minds tend to gravitate toward one another. They were in disbelief and wanted someone to agree with them. Therefore, the next time you see that beautiful rainbow sign in the heavens, instead of thinking of fairytales and four leaf clovers, think of the God who formed man from the dust of the ground. Think of the Lord who sits on high and looks down low as he shows mercy and compassion toward us all. That beautiful seven-colored rainbow we grew up viewing is a glorious sign placed in the heavens from our glorious Creator from on high. The number seven is God's number of completion. The colors God chose to use for his beautiful perfect rainbow are RED, ORANGE, YELLOW, GREEN, BLUE, INDIGO and VIOLET. Pay very close attention to all the glorious things that God has made. They are all around us if we just open our spiritual eyes and take a close look. There are many wonderful breath taking manifestations present all around us. Some can be seen in the heavens, others are attached to the earth. The day we wake up and really pay close attention to nature, is the day we will spiritually come alive. These are the true signs of evidence that God truly exists when it comes to the sun, the moon, the stars, the universe, the galaxies and the numerous planets. These are just a few of many things in the heavens that man cannot take credit for. Think of how the clouds form in the sky which is full of rain. However, if you were to fly in an airplane through the clouds on a dry day, it is like passing through a region of dry smoke. What a miracle this displays at the hands of God. Then there are the miraculous things found here in the earth like the various forms of creation and its many wonders that man cannot claim credit for. Hopefully, you will wake up and realize this beautiful spiritual world you live in and give God all the praise, glory, and honor that only he rightfully deserves to receive. The evidence of all things created is found in the word of God. If you have not read it, you should read it real soon!

6) Did you know that the great patriarch Abraham was one hundred years old when his second son Isaac was born? His wife Sarah was ninety years old when she gave birth to Isaac, their one and only son. Abraham's first born son, Ishmael, was born to Hagar, Abraham's wife Sarah's Egyptian handmaiden. God made his servant Abraham the father of many nations. Abraham is also known as the father of faith. God took Abraham from within the human race and lead him to a far away land to establish his faith family of followers. God knew that when he was to make his appearance into the earth as the Son of God, it was going to require faith in order to believe in him. For this reason, anyone who believes in the risen Savior named Jesus the Christ, the same is the seed of Abraham.

Scripture

The Bible says, *"For ye are all the children of God by faith in Christ Jesus. For as many of you as have been baptized into Christ have put on Christ. There is neither Jew nor Greek, there is neither bond nor free, there is neither male nor female: for ye are all one in Christ Jesus. And if ye be Christ's, then are ye <u>Abraham's seed</u> and heirs according to the promise"* (Galatians 3:26-29).

"Know ye therefore that they which are of faith, the same are the children of Abraham" (Galatians 3:7).

God chose the patriarch Abraham because of his great faith and trust in him. God chose Abraham to be the father of <u>MANY NATIONS</u> because he knew Abraham would teach his generation to obey the laws of God. Abraham taught the love and faith in God to his seed, which passed it on to their generation. We must continue to teach our children the will of God in our homes. When we fail to do so, we cause our children to become caught up and attached to the wicked world system. Unfortunately, the world's system is influenced by the prince of this world, known as Satan. God gave us the command to be fruitful, multiply, and replenish the earth. Part of this command applies to good stewardship. Man should prosper at everything he does in the earth. God will bless everything man puts his hands to when he is obedient unto the Lord. The other part of man's fruitfulness involves training up godly seed to give back to the Lord. When we fail to teach our children the word of God, we raise up ungodly seed to be used at will by the enemies of God. The world has gotten a tight hold on our youth of today. Once this occurs, it's not impossible, but very difficult to get them back! Parents of today do not help the matter much. They allow their children to take part in what the world has to offer. They fail to realize the dangers involved with associating in the wrong environment. By the time they do realize it, it's much too late. These are the parents that have no spiritual discernment concerning the will of God. This is why we have to pass down the knowledge of God to our children. If we are not teaching our children, it's a strong possibility that our parents did not teach us. This goes to show you how fast the love of God can wax cold and get away from us—one generation at a time.

7) Did you know that the great Italian explorer Christopher Columbus believed in the written word of God? There has been great controversy over the years concerning who discovered the America's first. One thing is for sure, based on Christopher Columbus's boldness to launch out into the deep, both North and South America received world recognition, and the Christian faith. Even though the Holy Scriptures were misunderstood in the beginning by men who chose to remain in darkness concerning the true will of God. Eventually, the light of Christ started to illuminate the hearts of men causing them to grasp the proper interpretation of his holy word. Once love was allowed to penetrate the heart of man, this is when they discovered that the word of God applied to all nations, tribes and kindreds. When it came to the courage of Christopher Columbus, he ventured out and set to conquer a land that was new to him. The term conquer should have been use instead of the term discover. Some think it is impossible to discover a place already inhabited by others. The proper Christian way to teach this event in history should be to tell the world that Christianity was brought to a new land. Since the land was already occupied by fellow human beings, the strangers that invaded the region should have been faithful to share God's green earth

with those who already inhabited the land. The Bible teaches us that God placed man over all that he created. This is why God chose to create Adam last among all that he spoke into existence. Nowhere in the Holy Scriptures does it give us permission to cast down a brother who was likewise created in the same image and likeness of God. Since the enemy of God known as Satan roams about seeking whom he may devour, we can always expect evil deeds to be carried out by ungodly men in the earth. The region that Columbus located on his way to India was not uninhabited. Nevertheless, America was eventually placed on the map. Today it is a free country where you can worship according to your own belief. Having the freedom to choose is good, however what we choose will determine our outcome. The beautiful thing about the Italian explorer is that he was a man who believed in the word of God. This was during a time in history when most individuals —including the great scientific minds of that day—believed that the world was flat. Columbus was privileged to the knowledge of the word of God by faith. This does not mean that others were not privileged to the same knowledge in the Holy Bible. What it does mean is that others did not have the revelation or the faith that Christopher Columbus had to believe concerning the word of God. The Lord gives each and everyone of us desires and passions to accomplish in the earth. All we have to do is act upon them. Christopher Columbus had a burning desire to venture out—the Italian explorer knew about this next verse which is found written in the word of God.

Scripture

*"Have ye not known? Have ye not heard? Hath it not been told you from the beginning? Have ye not understood from the foundations of the earth? It is he that sitteth upon the <u>**CIRCLE OF THE EARTH**</u>, and the inhabitants thereof are as grasshoppers; that stretcheth out the heavens as a curtain, and spreadeth them out as a tent to dwell in"* (Isaiah 40:22):

God himself tells us that his wonderful creation called earth is a CIRCLE or ROUND in circumference. We must read, study, and learn what the word of God says. It is a lamp unto our feet, and a light unto our pathway. Christopher Columbus chose to believe the Lord when others did not. The word of God is indeed our manuscript for life. When we fail to adhere to the commandments of God, we waste time wandering through the wilderness being unfruitful in our journey through life.

8) Did you know that the Bible tells us that as long as the earth remains, seedtime and harvest, cold and heat, summer and winter, and even day and night SHALL not cease? This is a direct promise from God himself. God promised us that we can depend on his heavenly signs and wonders he has placed in the heavenly sky. This includes the function of the sun, moon and the stars. Seedtime and harvest means there is a time to plant and a time to harvest; a time to sow and a time to reap. These principles and laws set forth in the earth apply not only to the farmer, but also to every avenue known to man. Everything produces after its own kind. Whatever you sow in the earth, you will also reap a harvest of the same. You will not only reap what you sow, but where you've sown.

Scripture

The Bible tells us, "Where a man's treasure is, there will your heart be also" (Matthew 6:21).

Where ever you put your treasure, there you will find your heart also. This applies to all areas of life. When you find yourself losing ground, pay close attention to your area of interest. The areas that are precious to you, such as praise and worship, marriage, raising children, careers, and friendship will continue to flourish as long as your treasure is there. Whatever loses your heart filled passion and your personal attention in life will start to sink like the titanic. Likewise, whatever area receives your passion and personal attention, the same will give you a harvest—whether it is good or bad. The principles of God work both ways. Therefore, be very careful of the choices you make when it comes to where you sow your seed.

Scripture

"For he that soweth to his flesh shall of the flesh reap corruption; but he that soweth to the Spirit shall of the Spirit reap life everlasting" (Galatians 6:8).

Make sure you always sow into good ground and unto good things. Then your harvest will be without question, a true blessing to your life.

9) Did you know that the Bible tells us we are not to make cuttings in our flesh for the dead, nor print any marks upon our bodies? In this day and age, tattoos and piercings are very popular. Mankind is not to mark, print tattoos, carve, or cut markings in his flesh.

Scripture

"Ye shall not make any cuttings in your flesh for the dead, nor print any marks upon you: I AM the Lord" (Leviticus 19:28).

The Bible tells us that our bodies are the temple of God. They do not belong to us. Therefore, we do not have the right to damage and deface them. If this is a command from God, to act contrary to this law means it becomes the will of God's enemy. When you read the Holy Scriptures, you learn that demons love to harm the body of souls they possess. This is common behavior among demonic influences. Demons love to cut, tear, rip and even burn their victims in an attempt to harm the flesh they possess. Therefore, take heed when you get a strong desire to desecrate your body. This verse of scripture will describe how an unclean spirit behaves inside a human vessel, and how Jesus dealt with him.

Scripture

*"And when he (****Jesus****) was come out of the ship, immediately there met him out of the tombs a man with an <u>unclean spirit</u>"* (Mark 5:2).

"And always, night and day, he was in the mountains, and in the tombs, crying, and <u>cutting himself</u> with stones. But when he saw Jesus afar of, <u>he ran and worshiped him</u>, And cried with a loud voice, and said, What have I to do with thee, Jesus, thou Son of the most High God? I adjure thee by God, that thou torment me not. For he said unto him, COME OUT OF THE MAN, THOU UNCLEAN SPIRIT" (Mark 5:5-8).

Jesus obviously casted out the unclean spirit and sent him into a herd of nearby swine. This particular demon spirit called himself legion and told Jesus that they were many. This means that unclean spirits occasionally will run in droves. You may want to closely examine what frame of mind you are in when making a decision to act contrary to the word of God by marking or piercing your flesh. It just might be the evil spirit within you. Most individuals when ask why they tattooed or pierces their bodies respond with an excuse by saying something like, I went through a divorce, I got fired from my job, I broke up with my boyfriend or girlfriend, I turned over a new leaf, I wanted to be noticed, etc. All these excuses and many more are indications that something got a hold of these individuals. The next time you see someone with a tattoo or a piercing, ask them what was going on in their life when they got their tattoo and or piercing? You will be surprise what their response will be. You will find that something happened to them that wounded their spirit. Evil influences will always attempt to take over the mind of men. We are souls that have a spirit and the Lord provided us with our bodies. Our bodies are earthen vessels which contain our soul and spirit while we remain alive in the earthly realm. Once our flesh dies in the earth, our bodies return to the ground, and our spirit returns to God.

Scripture

"Then shall the dust return to the earth as it was: and the spirit shall return unto God who gave it" (Ecclesiastes 12:7).

"Know ye not that ye are the temple of God, and that the Spirit of God dwelleth in you" (1 Corinthians 3:16).

"What? Know ye not that your body is the temple of the Holy Ghost which is in you, which ye have of God, and ye are not your own? For ye are bought with a price: therefore glorify God in your body, and in your spirit, which are God's" (1 Corinthians 6:19- 20).

Therefore, anything we do against our body, whether it is internal or external, we must do it without authorization from God. Remember, he is our true owner. The Bible tells us the truth—if any man defiles the temple of God which is our body, that man will God destroy.

Scripture

> *"If any man defile the temple of God, him shall God destroy; for the temple of God is holy, which temple ye are"* (1 Corinthians 3:17)?

Thank God for the blood of Jesus and his redeeming power, or we would all be destroyed. The blood of Jesus washes away all of our sin and mistakes we have made in life. Thank God for the atoning blood of the Lamb which taketh away the sins of the world?

10) Did you know that the true and living God of the universe requires our exclusive worship? The first commandment of God commands us to have no other gods before him. This lets us know, despite how we were raised or trained by various traditions; we must serve the true and living God. Every man will worship something in his lifetime. Some people were raised not to serve anything or anybody. Those individuals will end up serving and worshiping either themselves or some other form of abusive sin this world will offer them. We must serve the one true CREATOR of the heavens and the earth—the same CREATOR that spoke this world into existence—the God of Abraham, Isaac and Jacob. He is the God who delivered Moses and the children of Israel out of bondage and captivity in Egypt. He is the same God who delivered Daniel from the lion's den. He is the same God who delivered Shadrach, Meshach and Abednego from the fiery furnace. He is referred to as Jehovah God, the one who sustains this world.

Scripture

> *"Thou shalt have no other gods before me. Thou shalt not make unto thee any graven images, or any likeness of anything that is in heaven above, or that is in the earth beneath, or that is in the water under the earth"* (Exodus 20:3,4).

These two verses of scripture found in the Ten Commandments warn us about serving false idol gods. This same first commandment teaches us that no deity, real or imaginable, is to rival against the true and living God. It's obvious that some are not concerned with this warning. Whether they are concerned or not, the Bible assures us that every knee SHALL bow to the Lord Jesus, and every tongue shall confess to God that Jesus is Lord. Jesus Christ is and will be the one and only judge of this world.

Scripture

> Jesus tells us, *"For it is written, as I live, saith the Lord, every knee SHALL bow to me, and every tongue SHALL confess to God. So then every one of us shall give account of himself to God"* (Romans 14:11-12).

The above verse of scripture is not referring to idol gods thought up and invented or fashioned by the hands of men. This is the one and true God of the universe which is God the Father Jehovah and God the Son Jesus. For centuries, men have looked to other forms of worship to prevent themselves from bowing down to the one true God of all creation. What makes a man want to develop or invent his own god over himself? When a man fashions a statue to worship, that same man feels superior to his self-made image he has made. No one in this earth will ever purposely set a self made image over themselves and truly honor it. That way, a man that creates and fashions his own idol god will only offer false worship toward his self made image. This means he can continue to live a sinful life because he made up the false god he pretends to serve. Therefore, in his mind, there can never be any true judgment or chastisement. Now he is only accountable to what he made up in his own mind. The true God of all creation is far more superior and sovereign than mankind could ever imagine. When a man makes an idol god with his hands, what he is truly saying is that he disagrees and rejects the God who created him. For we know, if a man makes his own god to worship, it still does not answer his question of how he came into existence. Therefore, his worship of his self made image remains in vain. This is called fake worship. This is also a direct rejection of our heavenly Father that sits on high and looks down low everyday at the good and evil deeds of mankind.

Scripture

"But this shall be the covenant that I will make with the house of Israel; After those days, saith the Lord, <u>I will put my LAWS in their inward parts, and write it in their hearts</u>; and will be their God and they shall be my people. And they shall teach NO MORE every man his neighbor, and every man his brother, saying, <u>Know the Lord</u>: for they SHALL ALL KNOW ME, from the least of them unto the greatest of them, saith the Lord: for I will forgive their iniquity, and I will remember their sin no more" (Jeremiah 31:33, 34).

God made a promise and established a covenant with all of his chosen people. The Lord said he will put his laws inside of man, and write them in their hearts. Then there will be no more need to say, know the Lord. This means even when men and women claim to be atheist or agnostic, they will still know of the Lord and his righteousness. The righteousness in this case is the good, just and obedience that God stands for and requires. Atheists choose to believe in themselves instead of bowing down and surrendering to the God who has sovereign rule over this world. The atheist must first know of God in order to choose not to believe in God. Whether they believe in the Savior or not, God still has their breath in his hand. They haven't figured this one out yet. One day they are going to die, then comes the judgment. What will they say then? When a person makes a conscience decision to do evil in his heart, he knows it's wrong. That same person has to override his conscience in order to accomplish whatever evil task he sets out to fulfill. This is how the will of Satan is fulfilled and accomplished in the earth. When we come into the knowledge of the almighty God, we learn to surrender all to him. We make the choice to no longer do things our way. We choose to honor and follow the Lord with the freewill he has given us. Then we are embraced by God into his loving family.

11) Did you know that God laughs?

Scripture

"The wicked plotteth against the just, and gnasheth upon him with his teeth. The Lord shall LAUGH at him: for he seeth that his day is coming" (Psalm 37:12, 13).

The wicked will plot evil toward the just and believe in their heart that they are in the clear. Those who are wicked-minded cannot see their future. If they only could, they would rush to change their ways. The Lord laughs at the wicked because of their deeds, knowing very well that they will pay real soon for their wicked behavior. The last thing you want is to have God almighty laughing at you. God, along with his true followers knows that the day of the wicked approaches rapidly. The Bible tells us that vengeance is mind saith the Lord. The Lord further tells us that it is his job to repay the wicked, not ours. This is why we pray for the souls who persecute and despitefully use us. This is what the Lord Jesus Christ has commanded us to do. True Christian believers understand this passage of scripture which deals with the wicked plotting against the just. This separates the believer from the nonbeliever.

Scripture

"Bless them which persecute you: bless, and not curse" (Romans 12:14).

"Therefore if thine enemy hunger, feed him; if he thirst, give him drink: for in so doing thou shalt heap coals of fire on his head. Be not overcome of evil, but overcome evil with good" (Romans 12:20, 21).

Therefore, let us do well to others despite how others may treat us. When we do well toward our neighbor, this will cause a harvest of greatness to come back to us. The same sowing and reaping principle applies even in this situation. When our brother offends us and does harm to us, it is our personal re-action and response toward that brother which will dictate what type of consequence we reap in return. This method sound foolish to unbelieving souls. However, the Lord gave us this spiritual key found in the word of God which allows us to be incharged of our own destiny. What ever we project outward is what we will receive in return. In other words, no one can ruin our day unless we let them. Therefore, the next time anyone offends you, remember, do not show evil for evil.

Scripture

"See that none render evil for evil unto any man; but ever follow that which is good, both among yourselves, and to all men" (1 Thessalonians 5:15).

Always show love, even in the midst of an offense, then you will have just taken control of your situation. Now since you have projected love toward the offender, that's exactly what you will receive in return. This is why God has told us that he laughs at the wicked because of their expected end. Let us not be the one who God is laughing at, but rather let us be the one who showed compassion. Then we will know that we are worthy to be called the children of God.

12) Did you know that the Bible warns us that we should not associate with the ungodly or anyone who perform evil deeds? This is a command of God that is violated on a regular basis among the born-again Christian community. Most Christians have ungodly friends that they regularly associate with. These types of friendships will always challenge your faith. These individuals who reject the Lord will always try and convince you that it doesn't take all that, or you are giving too much of yourself to God. The problem in their mind is they are not willing to give God any part of themselves. These friends do not have an ear to hear the word of God, neither do they want to know right now. They refuse to change how they live because they do not see the importance of trying to lay down sin. One day, they, too, will perhaps answer the call of God and be set free. Meanwhile, those who have already been saved and washed in the blood of the Lamb must be careful not to let someone else steal their crown of life.

Scripture

"Behold, I come quickly: hold that fast which thou hast, that no man take thy crown" (Revelation 3:11).

"Iron sharpeneth iron; so a man sharpeneth the countenance of his friends" (Proverbs 27:17).

"Blessed is the man that walketh not in the counsel of the ungodly, nor standeth in the way of sinners, nor sitteth in the seat of the scornful. But his delight is in the law of the Lord; and in his law doth he <u>meditate day and night</u>" (Psalm 1:1-2).

This man that the scriptures describe shall be blessed! However, the ungodly and those who walk therein have a different ending. They will stumble all of their days. They are the ones who know the Lord, yet disobey him when it comes to association with the ungodly. The sad thing is they will be eventually sucked back into their old ways of living. Have you ever wondered why church goers often disappear after years of attendance? This is the primary reason why. They live and walk to close to the edge of sin and get sucked back into the worlds system. They start to lower their standards, and the next thing you know, sinful behavior becomes bearable once again. This will always occur when mankind starts to listens to man instead of God. Remember, unrighteous men will always tell you, it doesn't take all that! This is why we have to obey the word of the Lord and come out from among them. This does not mean that we are not to show love toward all God's creations. What this does mean is that we must refrain from allowing those who condone sin to further have influence over our lives. Only those who are strong and mature in their faith can return to certain environments where others tend to still struggle. This is why we must study the word of God to show ourselves approved. Then and only then will we be able to rightly divide the word of truth and avoid the harmful effects of the enemy. Our goal is to become a skillful minister in the army of the Lord. That way, the harmful effects of sinful lifestyles will not cause us to fall away when we are there for the purpose of reaching the lost souls.

Scripture

"For the Lord knoweth the way of the righteous: but the way of the ungodly shall perish" (Psalm 1:6).

God established the term, "guilty by association" long before man ever thought of it. Whatever environment you choose for yourself, that same environment will eventually overtake you. This can be a good thing if your environment is good. However, if your environment is bad, this can and will become a nightmare. No one in their right mind intentionly wants to do badly in life. Some are just impatient as to how they choose to obtain success. Then you have those who will lie, cheat, steal, or in other words, commit sin in order to prosper. The Bible teaches us to care and help one another as we go through this life. The ones who disobey this command, God will send swift judgment upon. The right way to approach success is a willingness to labor and follow the principles of God. This way we remain inside God's perfect will. The Lord's perfect will involves each of us always willing to help one another. When we focus on being our brother's keeper, this also strengthens our Christian walk. This is why we must set our mind on doing good works and ultimately select our environment very carefully. By doing so, this will reduce our struggles and the many pitfalls that life can surely bring. We must learn to stop going against the grain, which is against the word of God. Therefore, to the Christian born again believers, choose your friends wisely so that your destiny will be in peace and prosperity. Remember, who you hang around, you will eventually become. The Bible teaches us helpful ways of how to choose and not to choose our friends. This is a very important principle, whether your ungodly friends think so or not.

Scripture

"Make no friendship with an ANGRY MAN; and with a furious man thou shalt not go; Lest thou LEARN HIS WAYS, and get a snare to thy soul" (Proverbs 22:24-25).

This principle of God not only applies to choosing our friends, but it also applies to choosing a spouse. In this world you have good-natured individuals as well as mean-spirited ones. The good-natured person acts this way because it's their nature. The mean-spirited person acts the way they do because it's their nature. The Bible warns us against taking up company with an angry person. This same principle can be applied to any person with naturally flowing issues. This can be applied to a whoremonger, a thief, a habitual liar, a drug addict, or any other person having habitual unresolved issues in life. When you know someone has these problems upfront, it would be wise not to take up company with that individual. The reason being, in most cases, they will not change. Notice I did say, in most cases. Those who accept Jesus Christ as Lord and Savior will become a new creature in Christ Jesus. Therefore, there is an exception to this principle command. God is the only one who has the power to change who we are. However, to them who reject the cleansing blood of Jesus, their lifestyles will remain the same as they continue to influence those who are in close relationship with them. The scriptures tell us that you run the risk of learning their ways and becoming just like them. Remember, the wisest person who ever lived, who happened to be a king, was eventually influenced by his many foreign wives. King Solomon started out as a strong blessed man with the favor of both God and man upon his life. Then the Lord had to warn King Solomon concerning his many foreign women who openly practiced worshiping idol gods. King Solomon failed to take heed to the Lord's constant warning. After many years, his wives wore him down influencing him to turn against God and build idol gods in high places for his many foreign wives.

Scripture

"And he had seven hundred wives, princesses, and three hundred concubines: and his wives turned away his heart" (1 Kings 11:3).

This was an insult, as well as a sin before God. King Solomon soon thereafter came to himself, repented and returned to the will of God. However, his kingdom was never the same. The point here is that this same principle will happen, even to us. King Solomon was the wisest man to ever live. If his envoriment over took him, then our environment will surely over take us. Therefore, we have to be careful who we link ourselves up with. We are not that strong, even though we may think so. The wisest man who ever lived according to God, fell victim to this very principle? The Lord can wipe away the issues of man when he diligently seeks to follow after Jesus. Those who seek the Lord will also be conformed to the ways of the Lord. This same principle is what causes us to be Christ-like. When we hang around the Lord and study his word diligently, we become just like him! This principle is like a two-edged sword—it will forever cut both ways.

13) Did you know the Bible teaches us that the Lord is our Shepherd, and we shall not want? This verse in Psalm 23:1 was written by King David and inspired by God. This scripture lets us know that God is our Shepherd and source. When we believe this with all of our heart, it will come to pass. If God is indeed our Shepherd, we should not have any wants of any kind. So, if we have wants, we must closely examine ourselves. Maybe we need to question who our true overseer really is! Remember, God is our source and our provider. When we choose to trust in him, he will always see us through. If you seek not after God and the things that pertain to him, then you indeed have another form of overseer. When you do not trust in God, you will trust in the world's system. The problem is that the world system is run and influenced by Satan and his demonic forces. The unbeliever will find this hard to believe because he has no spiritual discernment at all. The unbeliever only believes what he can visually see with his natural eyesight. However, any need that surfaces in the life of the born again believer, he looks to the Lord and his needs are met.

Scripture

> King David said, *"The steps of a good man are ordered by the Lord: and he delighteth in his way. Though he fall, he shall not be utterly cast down: for the Lord upholdeth him with his hand. I have been young, and now am old; yet have I not seen the righteous forsaken, nor his seed begging bread. He is ever merciful, and lendeth; and his seed is blessed. Depart from evil, and do good; and dwell for evermore. For the Lord loveth judgment, and forsaketh not his saints; they are preserved for ever: but the seed of the wicked shall be cut off"* (Psalm 37:23-28).

The scriptures tell us that when we strive to be good men and women of God in the earth, our direction comes from him. When we fall or stumble, the Lord does not give up on us. He upholds us. God gives us the same instruction for one another. When we observe our brother or sister fall into sin, <u>we must not utterly condemn them</u>. We must help them up and be ready to assist them in any way possible. This proves that we are the righteousness of

God and that we belong solely to him. After a long time of observation, King David, the same king who killed Goliath the Giant, observed the righteous souls never being forsaken by God. King David also noticed that the children of the righteous never became beggars. God will always provide for those who love him. The Bible verse tells us that <u>God preserves the saints forever</u>. He indeed is the Shepherd of the righteous. When we as Christians help one another, we are blessed by God. The last verse tells us to depart from all manner of evil and enjoy the blessings of the Lord. This information would not be complete without reference to the scriptures mentioned in Psalms 23.

Scripture

V1) The Lord is my SHEPHERD; I shall not want.

V2) He maketh me to lie down in green pastures: he leadeth me besides the still waters.

V3) He restoreth my soul: he leadeth me in the paths of righteousness for his name's sake.

V4) Yea, though I walk through the valley of the shadow of death, I will fear no evil: for thou art with me; thy rod and thy staff they comfort me.

V5) Thou preparest a table before me in the presence of mine enemies: thou anointest my head with oil; my cup runneth over.

V6) Surely goodness and mercy shall follow me all the days of my life: and I will dwell in the house of the Lord forever" (Psalms 23:1-6).

14) Did you know that we came into this world naked and we will leave the same way? Our souls were sent by God through our mother's womb to establish our birth from man and woman. When we leave this earth at God's appointed time—which no man knows—we will leave all of our accomplishments and possessions behind. The only thing that will follow our spirit and soul are the treasures in heaven that Jesus instructed us to build and store up.

Scripture

John the apostle said, *"And I heard a voice from heaven saying unto me, Write, Blessed are the dead which die in the Lord from henceforth: Yea, saith the Spirit, that they may rest from their labors; AND THEIR WORKS DO FOLLOW THEM"* (Revelation 14:13).

"For we brought nothing into this world, and it is certain we can carry nothing out. And having food and raiment let us be therewith content" (1 Timothy 6:7, 8).

"The earth is the Lord's, and the fullness thereof; the world, and they that dwell therein. For he hath founded it upon the seas, and established it upon the floods" (Psalm 24:1, 2).

Since everything belongs to God almighty, we should have no problem releasing God's holy tithe and offering to help establish the kingdom of God. God's church should be the richest organization in the earth. Unfortunately, the ones who choose to disobey the word of God place their money into the hands of the wicked world's system. These are the same souls who complain about giving the church too much. The house of God is the holy place where the Lord is worshiped and praised. We as Christians know that the world's system is influenced by the prince of darkness. This enemy, Satan, will take advantage of every opportunity possible to turn our hearts away from God. The devil has the world mislead to believe that he doesn't exist. Since a large population of souls truly believes that the devil is not real. This enemy of darkness can continue stealing, killing and destroying the lives of mankind without ever being discovered. Therefore, beware and be careful not to surrender your will to this wretched enemy of darkness.

15) Did you know that God made the sun stand still and the moon stay a day in history? This miraculous event was to assist God's servant, Joshua, in leading the children of Israel into war as they avenged themselves against the tribe of the Amorites. This remarkable event in history should never be forgotten as long as we live.

Scripture

The Bible reads, *"And the sun stood still, and the moon stayed, until the people had avenged themselves upon their enemies. Is not this written in the book of Jasher? So the sun stood still in the midst of heaven, and hasted not to go down about a whole day. And there was no day like that before it or after it that the Lord hearkened unto the voice of a man: for the Lord fought for Israel"* (Joshua 10:13-14).

Joshua had made a request to God not to let the sun go down until his enemies were defeated. Joshua was concerned that the darkness could cause his enemies to overrun them during the night. God fought for the children of Israel causing them to have victory over the Amorites. This event is referred to in the Bible as <u>Israel's long day</u>! There is another day that the sun went down and it was darkened over all the land between the hours of 12:00noon and 3:00 p.m. This was that great day they crucified our Lord and Savior Jesus the Christ on that rugged cross at Calvary.

Scripture

The Bible tells us, "And it was the third hour, **(9:00 a.m.)** *and they crucified him"* (Mark 15:25).

"And when the sixth hour **(12:00 NOON)** *was come, there was darkness over the whole land until the ninth hour* **(3:00 p.m.)**. *And the ninth hour Jesus cried with a loud voice, saying Eloi, Eloi, lama sabachthani? Which is, being interpreted, My God, My God, why hast thou forsaken me"* (Mark 15:33-34)?

Some scholars feel that the darkness was evidently supernatural, since an eclipse of the sun at full noon is impossible. However, we as Christians know that with God, all things are possible.

Scripture

Jesus said, *"And they said, the things which are impossible with men are possible with God"* (Luke 18:27).

God's wrath was poured upon his Son during this time of darkness. At the ninth hour (3:00 p.m.) when Jesus cried out My God, my God, why hast thou forsaken me? Here we have the high cost Christ endured as he atoned for our sins. He was accused by God as our sin-bearer and suffered the agony of spiritual death for us all.

Scripture

"For he hath made him to be sin for us, who knew no sin; that we might be made the righteousness of God in him" (2 Corinthians 5:21).

"Christ hath redeemed us from the curse of the law, being made a curse for us: for it is written, CURSED is every one that hangeth on a tree" (Galatians 3:13).

Then Jesus cried with a loud voice, as a shout of triumph saying, "IT IS FINISHED", and yielded up his Spirit. In other words, having endured the wrath of God's great judgment against sin, he knew he had triumphed over Satan and the curse of sin and death. This is truly the best thing that has ever happened for mankind in the earth. Thanks to God for his tremendous sacrifice on the cross for our sin and the sin of this wicked world.

16) Did you know that God instructed Gideon to reduce his army from 32,000 to 300 men to face the Midianite Army of 135,000 men? Your next question is probably, who is Gideon? I'm glad you asked that question for those of you who may not know. The Lord's servant Gideon was a military and spiritual leader who delivered the tribes of Israel from seven years of oppression by the Midianite nation. The angel of the Lord visited Gideon one day calling him a mighty man of valor and giving him an assignment as a deliverer of God's people. Gideon initially had concerns due to the current oppression they faced against their enemies the Midianites. However, after he continued to converse with the angel of the Lord, he was pleased to serve and develop an army dedicated to God. The Lord wanted to show his glory and victory mightily to the nation of Israel (Judges 7: 2-14). God gave Gideon's army victory over the Midianites and their host. This happens to be another one of God's glorious events that mankind should always remember. This lets us know, even when the odds are against us, we should not worry. God will supernaturally fight the battles of those who love and depend on him. Never focus on the situation at hand, always focus on the Lord.

Scripture

"And the Lord said unto Gideon, The people who where with thee are too many for me to give the Midianites into their hands, lest Israel vault themselves against me, saying, Mine own hand hath saved me" (Judges 7:2).

The Lord reduced Gideon's army twice for the purpose of making it small enough so that God could be glorified. The Lord knows the heart of his people. He knew in advance that the nation of Israel would get puffed up if they prevailed against such a large army with their 32,000 soldiers. However, with an army of only 300 soldiers going up against 135,000, God knew that his people would give him a crazy praise of worship and glory for this outstanding victory. This act of power would bring the Israelites even closer to God. The Lord is always looking for those who are willing to give him what already belongs exclusively to him, his praise and glory!

1) The first reduction involved God directing Gideon to let all the fearful and those who were afraid go home. This sent 22,000 men back to their respective camps.

2) The second reduction involved Gideon following God's instruction of taking the remaining army to the water bank. God told Gideon that all who lapped the water with his tongue, as a dog laps, keep those men. Likewise, everyone who bowed down upon his knees to drink, allow them to return home. The theory is that whosoever was willing to loose focus regarding their personal needs were a danger to themselves and others. This was part of God's reduction strategy. This reduction sent 9,700 men back to their camps. The Lord told Gideon that the 300 men that were left he would save them, and would deliver the Midianites into their hands.

Scripture

> *"And his fellow answered and said, This is nothing else save the sword of Gideon the son of Joash, a man of Israel: for into his hand hath God delivered Midian, and all the host"* (Judges 7:14).

The Lord did not want anyone to say that the Israelite army defeated the large army with their own might. With 300 defeating an army of 135,000, it was clearly viewed without question as the Lord's victory. This great day will always remind us of the power of the Lord and how he will defend those who placed their total trust in him. No matter what battle you may be facing in life, God defends and upholds all who love him and are willing to cry out to his holy name.

17) Did you know that Samson, the strong man, was a true figure in the Bible, unlike Hercules, who was a mythical figure? The Bible tells us Samson was born in the land of Zorah to his Father named Manoah and his barren wife whose name is not mentioned. In the Holy Scriptures, the Philistines wanted to know the source of Samson's great strength. This boggled the minds of the Philistines because Samson was their enemy. The question may arise; did Samson have the appearance of a strong man? It would appear that if Samson looked very muscular, the curiosity would not have been so intense. On the other hand, Samson's strength may have been so significant that his appearance really didn't matter. This biblical historical event found in the Bible may make you wonder whether or not Samson looked abnormal. One thing is for sure…we know that Samson had the anointing of the Lord upon him throughout most of his life.

Scripture

> *"The Angel of the Lord appeared to Manoah's wife and said "Behold now, thou art barren, and bearest not: but thou shalt conceive, and bear*

> *a son. Now therefore beware, I prey thee, and drink not wine nor strong drink, and eat not any unclean thing: For, lo, thou shalt conceive, and bear a son; and no razor shall come on his head: for the child shall be a Nazarite unto God from the womb: and he shall begin to deliver Israel out of the hand of the Philistines"* (Judges 13:3-5).

Samson had supernatural strength, power and the anointing of God resting upon him. Samson was an Israelite from the Tribe of Dan which was one of the twelve tribes of Israel. Samson's life was marred by his weakness for pagan women. This was against God's law, which forbade the intermarriage of Israelites among the many pagan heathen nations. They were idol worshipers who God warned his people against polluting themselves with their practices. Samson refused to listen and went as far as to demand that his parents violate the will of God when it came to selecting him a bride.

Scripture

> *"And Samson went down to Timnath, and saw a woman in Timnath of the daughters of the Philistines. And he came up, and told his father and mother, and said, I have seen a woman in Timnath of the daughters of the Philistines: now therefore <u>get her for me to wife</u>. Then his father and his mother said unto him, Is there never a woman among the daughters of thy brethren, or among all my people, that thou goest to take a wife of the uncircumcised Philistines? And Samson said unto his father, <u>Get her for me</u>; for she pleaseth me well. But his father and his mother knew not that it was of the Lord, that he sought an occasion against the Philistines: for at that time the Philistines had dominion over Israel"* (Judges 14:1-4).

The way the verse of scripture is written, it sounds like Samson was demanding or at least insisting that his parents carry out his request to obtain a daughter of the enemy for him to marry. When Samson's parents were unsuccessful in talking him out of his choice for a bride, they ended up going along with him to accomplish this task. What Samson failed to realize is that God had already sanctified him from birth as a Nazarite. He may have thought he was getting married to the daughter of his enemy, but God clearly had another plan for his life. The wife he ended up betrothing against the will of God was given to another man by her father before Samson could consummate his union. This just happened to be one of the many curses of disobedience spoken of in the 28 chapter of the book of Deuteronomy.

Scripture

> *"Thou shalt betroth a wife, and another man shall lie with her: thou shalt build an house, and thou shalt not dwell therein: thou shalt plant a vineyard, and shalt not gather the grapes thereof"* (Deuteronomy 28:30).

The list goes on and on. There are 14 verses of scripture that pertain to the blessings of obedience and 54 versse of scripture which pertain to the curses for disobedience. Samson walked right into that one. When he discovered that his betrothed wife had been given to another, this sent him into rage and a killing spree. In essence, he began destroying his enemies which he was originally ordained for. Samson destroyed the Philistines crop and ended up slaying a thousand men with the jawbone of an ass. You would have thought that Samson learned his lesson from all of this, however he did not. This is a perfect example of how strong the effects of our sin nature can be without the power of the Holy Ghost. Samson was later led by the same unlawful lust into the arms of another Philistine women whose name was Delilah. Samson eventually became involved with Delilah, a woman from the valley of Sorek. The lords of the Philistines bribed Delilah to entice Samson in order to find the source of his strength. She teased him until he finally revealed that the secret was his uncut hair that was allowed to grow long in accordance with the Nazarite Law. Samson was taught by his family about all the Israelite commands of God. Therefore, he knew the law of God. Yet Samson still went out of his way to violate them. Being constantly warned by his parents about the foreign women and their belief systems. Samson even insisted that his parents go against the will of God when it came to selecting him a wife. This disobedience would later catch up with Samson. Remember, Samson was ordained by God and sent into the earth for a specific purpose. He was a special child called a Nazarite from birth. God had to open the womb of his barren mother in order to fulfill God's purpose. His mission was to deliver the children of Israel from their enemies known as the Philistines. The problem occurred when Samson took his life into his own hands, like most of us do, even today. As long as we walk according to our own direction, we will hit similar pitfalls, just like Samson did until we recognize who God truly is. Samson's life was supposed to be sanctified unto God, yet he decided to satisfy the lust of his own flesh. Since the wages of sin always brings on death and destruction. It did not take long for sin to eventually destroy the life of God's prophet know as Samson. However, God's purpose was fulfilled. Samson destroyed the Philistines and also died himself in the process.

Scripture

"And she made Samson sleep upon her knees; and she called for a man, and she caused him to shave off the seven locks of his head; and she began to afflict him, and his strength went from him" (Judges 16:19).

"But the Philistines took him, and put out his eyes, and brought him down to Gaza, and bound him with fetters of brass; and he did grind in the prison house. Howbeit the hair of his head <u>began to grow again</u> after he was shaven" (Judges 16:21-22).

"Then the lords of the Philistines gather them together for to offer a great sacrifice unto Dagon their idol <u>god</u>, and to rejoice: for they said, Our god hath delivered Samson our enemy into our hand. And when the people saw him, they praised their god: for they said, Our god hath delivered into our hands our enemy, and the destroyer of our country, which slew many of us. And it came to pass, when their hearts were merry, that they said, call for Samson, that he may make sport. And they called for Samson out of the prison house; and he made them sport: and they set him between the pillars. And Samson said unto the lad that held him by the hand, Suffer me that I may feel the pillars whereupon the house standeth, that I may lean upon them. Now the house was full of men and women; and all the lords of the Philistines were there; and there were upon the roof about three thousand men and women that beheld while Samson made sport. And Samson called unto the Lord, and said, O Lord God, remember me, I pray thee, and strengthen me, I pray, only this once, O God, that I may be at once avenged of the Philistines for my two eyes" (Judges 16:23-28).

Samson was a Nazarite unto God and considered one of the great deliverers of the children of Israel from their captivity in bondage for over forty years. This is a perfect example of where persistence prevailed in the end. Delilah was persistent in bugging Samson to reveal his source of strength. She wore Samson down seducing him every step of the way. Whatever we are persistent at in life, we will eventually have. When someone persistently bugs another, the one being bugged will eventually get tired, wore down and give in. Remember this if you ever become the victim of a persistent, stubborn individual. Also remember this when you are in need of showing great tenacity toward something you truly desire. Sometimes we need to be persistent in the things we want and need. This principle works both ways. Be not deceived. Satan uses this principle very often. He is constantly attempting to wear down the saints of God. Unfortunately, most of the time, Satan wins! This goes to show you how effective this method can be. The positive side to this principle allows us to persistently go after anything we want to accomplish that is good. The Lord loves to see his people diligent and persistence when it comes to their prayer life. This allows God to know we desire to have a more intimate relationship with him. Therefore, remember your prayer life and keep it sacred. The sad thing is even Christians sometime forget to pray!

18) Did you know that the most beautiful man born in all Israel was the third son of King David whose name was Absalom? This young man was so beautiful that no blemishes could be found anywhere on his body. This was a perfect looking human being according to the word of God.

Scripture

"But in all Israel there was none to be so much praised as Absalom for his beauty: from the sole of his foot even to the crown of his head there was no blemish in him" (2 Samuel 14:25).

King David made the same common mistake with Absalom that most parents make in raising their children today. The king favored and spoiled his son among his many sons. Even when Absalom raised up against his father the king, and wanted to destroy him, King David still wanted Absalom kept alive. King David's servants accused him of loving his enemy (his son), and hating his friends (his soldiers). This enemy being referred to was obviously the king's rebellious son who turned out to be a rebel. Absalom wanted to dethrone his father at all cost, even to the death.

Scripture

> *"And Joab came into the house to the king, and said, Thou hast shamed this day the faces of all thy servants, which this day have saved thy life, and the lives of thy sons and of thy daughters, and the lives of thy wives, and the lives of thy concubines; In that thou lovest thine enemies, and hatest thy friends. For thou hast declared this day, that thou regardest neither princes nor servants: for this day I perceive, that if Absalom had lived, and all we had died this day, then it had pleased thee well"* (2 Samuel 19:5,6).

King David loved his son and wanted to change the laws to show special favor toward him concerning his attempt to overthrow the kingdom. This made the servants who put their lives on the line feel worthless as servants of the king. These loyal servants vowed to protect King David with their very life. They were happy to perform the mission of protecting their king in the event they had to give up their lives. Yet it appeared that King David was willing to sacrifice his loyal servant's lives in order to save an enemy of the kingdom, namely his son. King David expressed little value for the lives of his men and this hurt their spirits deeply. The servants felt as if the king cared more for his rebellious son who sought his very life, than his loyal subjects who willingly would lay down their life for their king. King David should have taken a course in tough love. Let us learn from this very important lesson. Never favor one child over the other, and always chastise promptly so that your child develops direction, discipline and respect. Always remember, anything you love more than God will always be separated from you. God gives us gifts to enjoy, but never to worship.

19) Did you know that place called hell that most people do not like talking about or thinking about has enlarged itself? That's right, HELL has gotten bigger. Those who end up in hell will be there because of their own choice. Therefore, stop blaming God for your own wicked stubbornness.

Scripture

"Therefore hell hath enlarged herself, and opened her mouth without measure: and their glory, and their multitude, and their pomp, and he that rejoiceth, shall descend into it" (Isaiah 5:14).

So, if you are one of those people who do not like thinking about hell, that's fine. All that means is that you will not think about it. It does not make it magically go away. Just remember, whether you like thinking about it, talking about it, or acting like it does not exist, it's still a real place and a very HOT one! The out-of-sight out of-mind theory will not work this time. The fact is, God has given us his holy word. Hell has indeed enlarged herself! The only way to avoid this place is to make sure your soul is covered with the precious blood of the Lamb, which is faith in Jesus Christ the righteous Savior.

The Bible informs us about a place called PARADISE, HELL or HADES. There is another place I want to make sure you know about. That place is called the LAKE OF FIRE. Jesus taught us the true story concerning the rich man and the poor beggar named Lazarus.

Paradise and Hell or Hades
Scripture

"There was a certain rich man, which was clothed in purple and fine linen, and fared sumptuously every day. And there was a certain beggar named Lazarus, which was laid at is gate, full of sores, and desiring to be fed with the crumbs which fell from the rich man's table: moreover the dogs came and licked his sores. And it came to pass, that the beggar died, and was carried by the angels into Abraham's bosom: the rich man also died, and was buried; And in hell he lifted up his eyes, being in torments, and seeth Abraham afar off, and Lazarus in his bosom. And he cried and said, father Abraham, have mercy on me, and send Lazarus, that he may dip the tip of his finger in water, and cool my tongue; for I am tormented in this flame. But Abraham said, son, remember that thou in thy lifetime receivedst thy good things, and likewise Lazarus evil things: but now he is comforted, and thou art tormented. And besides all this, between us and

you there is a great gulf fixed: so that they which would pass from hence to you cannot; neither can they pass to us, that would come from thence, Then he said, I pray thee therefore, father, that thou wouldest send him to my father's house: For I have five brethren; that he may testify unto them, lest they also come into this place of torment. Abraham saith unto him, they have Moses and the Prophets; let them hear them. And he said, Nay, father Abraham: but if one went unto them from the dead, they will REPENT. And he said unto him, If they hear not Moses and the Prophets, neither will they be persuaded, though one <u>rose from the dead</u>" (Luke 16:19 - 31).

Regarding the rich man's brothers being warned of this place of torment, father Abraham responded by saying, if they will not hear Moses and the Prophets, they will not hear someone who came back from the dead. This statement is even true in our present day and age. Take a look at the world today. Even though Jesus died on the cross for our sins, many refuse to believe he is the risen Savior, even though he was <u>raised from the dead</u>. Therefore, father Abraham must have known exactly what he was talking about. Take heed and learn from this very important true story placed in the word of God for our benefit.

Jesus tells the Pharisees of this rich man and the poor beggar named Lazarus. This event confirmed to the Pharisees and the Lord's disciples that we all have a chance to REPENT and do good instead of evil while we still have blood running warm in our veins. Once death of the flesh comes to claim us, it's too late to make changes concerning eternal life. When Jesus was on the cross at Calvary dying for the sins of the entire world, one of the crucified men made a humble request to Jesus acknowledging him as Lord. The other malefactor chose not to believe.

Scripture

"And one of the malefactors which were hanged railed on him, saying, If thou be Christ, save thyself and us. But the other answering rebuked him, saying, Dost not thou fear God, seeing thou art in the same condemnation? And we indeed justly; for we received the due reward of our deeds: but this man hath done nothing amiss. And he said unto Jesus<u>, Lord, remember me when thou comest into thy kingdom</u>. And Jesus said unto him, Verily

I say unto thee, Today shalt thou be with me in Paradise. And it was about the sixth hour, (12:00 NOON) and there was a darkness over all the earth until the ninth hour (3:00 p.m.). The Sun was darkened, and the Veil of the Temple was rent (torn) in the midst" (Luke 23:39 - 45).

The veil inside the temple was torn from the top downward. This act of God signifies that all born-again Christian believers can now come boldly to the throne of grace in the name of our Lord Jesus Christ. From that day forward, now we can get our needs met by our heavenly Father without the aid of the priest, the prophet or the pope. Jesus is our only intercessor and mediator between man and God. He is all we need to usher us into the presence of the Lord. The shepherds or pastors have been given the anointed job of feeding the flock with the word of God until Jesus returns for his Church body. This body of believers is also known as the body of Christ. This is God's way of making sure that his people are not destroyed for their lack of knowledge. Therefore, whatever you need from God, know that you can go to the Lord for yourself. You do not have to wait on others. However, always remember, where two or three are gathered together in the name of Jesus, the word of God teaches us that Christ is in the midst thereof. This is why fellowship among fellow believers is always a blessing.

Hell, Hades or Sheol

Hell, Hades or Sheol is a holding place of torment where the souls of the spiritually dead are kept. This is a den of lost souls. The souls that are locked in this place of torment and pain are awaiting the final judgment from God. The sad thing concerning these souls is that they will be judged by God without protection from sin. Since the wages of sin is death, their sentence is just that, death. All wicked souls that rejected God and refused to repent will be found there. This place is only a temporary holding facility. Once judged without the Lord Jesus and his saving grace, the lake of fire is their final home for all eternity. The souls of the wicked, such as the rich king who refused to care for the poor man, Lazarus, wasted away their entire life rejecting the will of God.

Scripture

Jesus said, *"For what shall it profit a man, if he shall gain the whole world, and lose his own soul"* (Mark 8:36)?

"By which also he (Jesus) went and preached unto the spirits in prison: Which sometime were DISOBEDIENT, when once the longsuffering of God waited in the days of Noah, while the ARK was a preparing, wherein few, that is, eight souls were saved by water" (1 Peter 3:19,20).

This scripture talks about the longsuffering and patience God had while Noah built an ark in the middle of the desert preaching rain which no one had ever seen before or heard of. God only saved the eight souls of Noah's household. All other creation on land and in the air was destroyed. The disobedient living in that day even had an opportunity to hear the gospel of Jesus Christ preached by the Savior himself according to the above scripture. This is when Jesus descended into the deep during his three day death in the earth. The scriptures tell us that Christ ministered to the souls in paradise. Then he led captivity captive. Likewise, all mankind will have an opportunity to hear the gospel of Jesus Christ so that they too will be given an opportunity to follow the Lord.

Lake of Fire

The lake of fire represents the final place of torment prepared for Satan, the beast, the false prophet and the fallen angels that were cast down from heaven with Satan. The lake of fire is also referred to as the second death. Unfortunately, whosoever does not accept Jesus the Christ as Lord and Savior will end up there experiencing the second death right along with the enemies of God?

Scripture

"And the devil that deceived them was cast into the lake of fire and brimstone, where the beast and the false prophet are, and shall be tormented day and night forever and ever" (Revelation 20:10).

"And I saw the dead, small and great, stand before God; and the BOOKS were opened: and another book was open, which is <u>THE BOOK OF LIFE</u>: and the dead were judged out of those things which were written in the books, according to their works. And the sea gave up the dead which were in it; and <u>death and hell</u> delivered up the dead which were in them: and they were judged every man according to their works. And death and hell were cast into the lake of fire, <u>This is the second death</u>. And whosoever was not found written in the book of life was cast into the lake of fire." (Revelation 20:12-15).

The Scriptures make it clear; anyone whose name is not found written in the Lamb's Book of Life will be cast into the lake of fire and brimstone forever and ever. Just because you may have been taught that HELL and the LAKE OF FIRE doesn't exist does not make it go away. All it does is stop you from thinking about until you get there!

Scripture

"He that believeth on the Son hath everlasting life: and he that believeth not the Son shall not see life; but the Wrath of God abideth on him"
(John3:36).

To as many that accept Jesus Christ as their Lord and Savior, to them, their names will be found written in the Lamb's book of life. Will your name be found written there?

Scripture

Jesus said,

"No man can come to me, except the Father which hath sent me draw him: and I will raise him up at the last day" (John 6:44).

This message is for the reader of this book—to the person reading this sentence right now. If you do not feel God tugging at your heart, don't just sit there. Seek the Lord thy God with a perfect heart and trust not your own perception of things. Be diligent in the study of his holy word. Pray that he draw you into his holy kingdom. God wants all his creation saved from his mighty wrath to come. The reality is that some will choose the creature instead of their CREATOR. Let this not be your choice.

Scripture

Jesus said, *"And this is the Father's will which hath sent me, that of all which he hath given me I should lose nothing, but should raise it up again at the last day. And this is the will of him that sent me, that every one which seeth the Son, and believeth on him, may have everlasting life: and <u>I will raise him up at the last day</u>"* (John 6:39, 40).

20) Did you know when a man fails to honor God with his tithe and offering, he is known as a robber who is robbing God? This tithe and offering is known as the first fruit or the tenth of all our increase. When the Bible calls a man or woman a robber of God that means you are a criminal of the kingdom of God. We have heard of earthly criminals. Now we learn that there is such a thing as a spiritual criminal. That's why all born-again Christians tithe because they choose to believe and obey the word of God. This, among other things, keeps us in good standing with the kingdom in which we are citizens of. As Christians, remember, this world is no longer considered our home. We have been granted citizenship in God's heavenly kingdom. All born-again believers have been adopted into the family of God. This is why we are called ambassadors here in the earth.

Scripture

"Will a man rob God? Yet ye have robbed me. But ye say, Wherein have we robbed thee? In tithes and offerings. Ye are <u>cursed</u> with a <u>curse</u>: for ye have robbed me, even this whole nation. Bring ye all the tithes into the storehouse, that there may be meat in mine house, and prove me now herewith, saith the Lord of Hosts, if I will not open you the windows of heaven, and pour you out a blessing, that there shall not be room enough to receive it" (Malachi 3:8-10).

"And I will rebuke the devourer for your sake, and he shall not destroy the fruits of your ground: neither shall your vine cast her fruit before the time in the field, saith the Lord of host. And all nations shall call you blessed: for ye shall be a delightsome land, saith the Lord of host" (Malachi 3:11, 12).

The Bible further tells us that we pay our tithes on earth to men but God receives them and is keeping record on our behalf. Every dime we give and every dime we hold is being recorded.

Scripture

> *"And here men that die receive tithes; but there he receiveth them, of whom it is witnessed that he liveth"* (Hebrews 7:8).

We have a choice, either we honor our Lord's holy tithe and be blessed in abundance, or we dishonor our Lord and accept the curse with a curse upon our lives. The results will be devastating. God addresses what happens to those who fail to honor him with their substance.

Scripture

> *"Then came the word of the Lord by Haggai the prophet, saying, Is it time for you, O ye, to dwell in your ceiled house, and this house lie waste? Now therefore thus saith the Lord of Hosts; Consider your ways. Ye have sown much, and bring in little; ye eat, but ye have not enough; ye drink, but ye are not filled with drink; ye clothe you, but there is none warm; and he that earneth wages earneth wages to <u>put it into a bag with HOLES</u>.*

> *"Thus saith the Lord of Hosts; Consider your ways. Go up to the mountain, and bring wood, and build the House; and I will take pleasure in it, and I will be glorified, saith the Lord. Ye looked for much, and, lo, it came to little; and when ye brought it home, <u>I DID BLOW UPON IT</u>. Why? saith the Lord of hosts. Because of mine house that is waste, and ye run every man unto his own house. Therefore the heaven over you is stayed from dew, and the earth is stayed from her fruit"* (Haggai 1:3-10).

That's right, God will blow on mankind's resources (money) if we are not doing the right thing and failing to take care of the house of God. The tithe is holy unto the Lord. It does not belong to us. The truth is God has given the earth that he spoke into existence to the children of men to have lordship over. This does not mean that we have the right to forget about God.

Scripture

"Ye are blessed of the Lord which made heaven and earth. The heavens, even the heavens, are the Lord's: <u>but the earth hath he given to the children of men</u>" (Psalm 115:15, 16).

Since God gave us this earth to oversee, we are to subdue it, be fruitful, and be willing to release the tenth and an offering to honor the Lord's sovereignty. All he requires is ten percent of our increase and an offering from the heart presented unto him. This establishes our covenant with the Lord. God created it all and owns it all. He just allows us the privilege to be his caretakers over what he has made while we are alive in the earth. The Lord has given the earth to us to be responsible for until we die in the flesh. This is where the term stewardship comes from. God allows us to be stewards over everything he has created. This is why God created mankind last during the six day creation. His intention was for man to have full dominion over everything he had made. God also gives man vision on the things he wants to manifest in the earth. And all this time, you thought your ideas were your own.

Scripture

"The preparations of the heart in man, and the answer of the tongue, is from the Lord" (Proverbs 16:1).

"Commit thy works unto the Lord, and thy thoughts shall be established. The Lord hath made all things for himself: yea even the wicked for the day of evil" (Proverbs 16:3, 4).

The word of God teaches us that we develop the vision from God in our minds. Then we speak the words with our lips. God takes our words and causes them to materialize in the earth's realm. Many men and women have stolen God's glory and claimed that their thoughts and manifestations came from within themselves. They do not understand this godly principle because they know not the word of God, neither are they spiritually discerned. God is involved in the earth more than we realize. This is why more and more occurrences are finally being recognized as a divine revelation or appointment from God. We must learn to consult the Lord concerning all of our earthly affairs. Getting back to the tithes and offerings we are commanded to participate in. Once we fully understand our position, we realize the more tenth (10 percent) we honor God with, the more ninety (90 percent) he allows us to enjoy. Trust God and see for yourself. Remember, the only things which will last are the things we do for Christ, which is the kingdom of God. All other earthly treasures will fade away. Any and everything we do for God will store up treasures in heaven on our behalf. The benefit of this treasure is that it does follow the saints of God when we leave this earth and enter into the presence of the Lord.

Scripture

> *"And I heard a voice from heaven saying unto me, Write, Blessed are the dead which die in the Lord from henceforth: Yea, saith the Spirit, that they may rest from their labours; <u>and their works do follow them</u>"* (Revelation 14:13).

> *"Lay not up for yourselves treasures upon earth, where moth and rust doth corrupt, and where thieves break through and steal: But lay up for yourselves treasures in heaven where neither moth nor rust doth corrupt, and where thieves do not break through nor steal: FOR WHERE YOUR TREASURE IS, THERE WILL YOUR HEART BE ALSO"* (Matthew 6:19-21).

This verse of scripture clearly lets us know that whatever has our treasure has our heart also. When we withhold God's tithe and offering, this clearly says that we love money more than God! Therefore, make no more excuses as to why you cannot give God his holy tenth part of all your increase. Examine your spending, even if you have accumulated unnecessary debt for yourself. I tell you the truth; there is still room for God if we eliminate the selfish and wicked spending habits totally out of our life. When we honor God with what already belongs to him, we become truly blessed. God said he will open the windows of heaven and pour us out a blessing so large; we would not be able to contain it all. Notice that the ones who complain the most about giving tithes and offerings are the same ones who have the most debt and the worst spending habits. They are the ones who have over-extended themselves because they have not been good stewards over God's property. These are the same ones who have over-extended themselves with debt, and also ungodly habits which cause them to be in want. All one has to do is stop spending foolishly. This means to stop charging up credit cards and buying unnecessary things you cannot afford. Stop supporting ungodly habits like the purchase of alcohol, drugs, cigarettes, marijuana, and all forms of pornographic material of any kind. You will be surprised how much money you can save when you lay down sinful pleasures. This is called wasteful living which is indeed sinful living. All these things harm the body which is the temple where God dwells. When you are ready to serve and worship the true and living God, you will have a change of heart, which causes a change of attitude. Then your mind is on the way to being renewed which will ultimately change your life and your spending habits. The next thing you know, you will start to rise up from where you were and come into a new place where the blessings of the Lord will overtake you. Then you will enter into the land of more than enough. You've tried it your way; now try it the right way.

21) Did you know that God can and will add length of days to your life? This section will teach you about how important wisdom is to every man.

Scripture

"My son, forgot not my law; but let thine heart keep my commandment: For length of days, and long life, and peace, shall they add to thee" (Proverbs 3:1,2).

The Bible teaches us that wisdom also provides us with length of days, riches, and honor. Wisdom is the principle thing according to the word of God.

Scripture

"Wisdom is the principle thing; therefore get wisdom: and with all thy getting get understanding" (Proverbs 4:7).

"Happy is the man that findeth wisdom, and the man that getteth understanding. For the merchandise of it is better that the merchandise of silver, and the gain thereof than fine gold. She is more precious than rubies: and all

the things thou canst desire are not to be compared unto her. <u>Length of days</u> is in her right hand; and in her left hand riches and honor" (Proverbs 3:13-16).

Wisdom causes us to make sound decisions which prevent negative consequences. When our harvest is blessed by God, this will eliminate setbacks in our life. Everything we do in life has a greater consequence we can look forward to. This is why we must learn to use sound wisdom in all of our decisions. Therefore, our future choices in life will be in line with the word of God. Then we can enjoy everything we reap, as a product of what we have previously sown.

22) Did you know that mankind only has one enemy in this world? Did you know that, or are you one of the ones who continue to hold an offense toward your brethren? Satan is the only true enemy in this world on top of being the accuser of mankind. Every since Adam lost dominion to this enemy in the Garden of Eden, he has been the one behind the scenes tempting mankind every step of the way. The world system is temporarily influenced by this defeated devil and his demonic forces. Until we learn to do it God's way, Satan will continue to maintain a level of control over us. We must remember that Satan is behind every wicked deed known to man. Just like God has a will we should be trying to follow, Satan too has his own personal agenda. Only his will is very wicked and evil. The only way the devil can get his will accomplished is by having a willing vessel. Men and women must willingly submit to the enemy in order for him to claim influence over their lives. Jesus died on the cross at Calvary which broke the bonds of captivity from the enemies clutches. Not only has mankind been redeemed, but the works of the devil have been destroyed.

Scripture

"He that committeth sin is of the devil; for the devil sinneth from the beginning. <u>For this purpose the Son of God was manifested</u>, that he might destroy the works of the devil" (1 John 3:8).

Now that Jesus has destroyed the works of the enemy, the saints of God must prepare themselves as well. We as born-again Christians must prepare ourselves to be able to take victory over the devil and his devices. Let us no longer be deceived by the enemy as we accuse our own brothers and sisters for their offenses they have commited against us. The question you must ask yourself is, "Who influenced you when you were an offense toward others in times past?" Your offensive behavior was not godly, neither is the behavior of your brethren when they were an offense to you. You must show mercy if you ever expect to receive mercy from God. Prepare to stand against the wiles of the devil. Know the truth and it will always set you free. Then you can love others unconditionally as Jesus commanded, knowing very well that the enemies of God are at work.

Scripture

"Finally, my brethren, be strong in the Lord, and in the power of his might. Put on the whole armor of God that ye may be able to stand against the wiles of the devil. For we wrestle not against flesh and blood, but against principalities, against powers, against the rulers of the darkness of this world, against spiritual wickedness in <u>high places</u>. Wherefore take unto you the whole armor of God that ye may be able to withstand in the evil day, and having done all, to stand. Stand therefore, having your loins girt about with TRUTH, and having on the breastplate of RIGHTEOUSNESS; And your feet shod with the preparation of the GOSPEL of PEACE; Above all, taking the shield of FAITH, wherewith ye shall be able to quench all the fiery darts of the wicked" (Ephesians 6:10-16).

Without the entire armor of God, we are defenseless against the spiritual wickedness of this world. In addition to wearing God's protective armor, we must have love for one another. Jesus made it clear in the Bible when he said, "A new commandment I give unto you, that ye love one another; as I have loved you, that you also love one another."

Scripture

"By this shall all men know that ye are my disciples, if ye have love one to another" (John 13:34, 35).

We must remember that Satan influences the mind of the brethren. Jesus had to rebuke his disciple Peter once for allowing Satan to enter into his mind. Jesus also stated during the last supper, that Satan entered into Judas to fulfill the betrayal that was prophesied. The important lesson here is that Satan can and will influence the mind of men and women. Jesus wants us to show mercy and forgiveness toward our brethren at all times. Therefore, when our brother commits an offense toward us, understand that Satan has entered into that brother. Never lose your love for one another over an offense. Always remember to pray for those who persecute and despitefully use you. Knowing that anytime we have committed an offense contrary to the word of God, we too fell under the influence of the enemy at that particular moment. Jesus teaches us that love has to be at the center of all things. Without love, nothing else matters. Now that we know who the true enemy is, let us no longer be deceived. Always remember the characteristics of the devil. The Bible teaches us that the enemy, Satan, came to steal, kill and destroy mankind, especially the saints of God.

Scripture

"Then said Jesus unto them again, Verily, verily, I say unto you, I am the Door of the sheep. All that ever came before me are thieves and robbers: but the sheep did not hear them. I am the Door: by me if any man enter in, he shall be SAVED, and shall go in and out, and find pasture. The thief, (Satan) cometh not, but for to STEAL, and to KILL, and to DESTROY: I AM come that they might have LIFE, and that they might have it more ABUNDANTLY" (John 10:7-10).

Never blame God for Satan's handiwork and wicked deception. This is the will of the enemy. His will is to commit all forms of atrocity in the earth and have mankind blame and accuse God falsely. For this reason, we pray that God would remove the blinders from the eyes of the lost souls. Then they will see clearly to serve and worship the one true and living God of this world.

23) Did you know that the Bible teaches us how to enjoy good health?

Scripture

"Trust in the Lord with all thine heart; and lean not unto thine own understanding. In all thy ways acknowledge him, and he shall direct thy path.

Be not wise in thine own eyes: fear the Lord, and depart from evil. It shall be <u>HEALTH to thy NAVAL</u> and <u>MARROW to thy BONES</u>" (Proverbs 3:5-8).

These scriptures teach us that we are to trust God and not our feelings and emotions. When we acknowledge God for who he is, we realize his sovereignty. Then hopefully we will stop thinking we are smarter or equal to our Creator. God then will guide our steps and lead our pathway with his mighty right hand. All we have to do is obey him and depart from an evil lifestyle. This will provide us with <u>GOOD HEALTH</u> all of our days. It's that simple.

24) Did you know that the Bible tells us about seven deadly sins which God hates?

Scripture

"These six things doth the Lord hate; yea, seven are an abomination unto him:

1) A proud look,

2) A lying tongue,

3) Hands that shed innocent blood,

4) A heart that deviseth wicked imaginations,

5) Feet that be swift in running to mischief,

6) A false witness that speaketh lies,

7) And he that soweth discord among brethren" (Proverbs 6:16-19).

These are the behaviors God will reject from fellowship unless we REPENT and put away these evil things. This behavior should not be found among the Christian born-again believers. When Jesus our Lord died on the cross for the sins of the world, he gave power to all who would believe in him.   Now we can say NO to sin, whereas before we could not. By the power of the Holy Ghost, we are able to walk upright before the Lord. Without the Holy Spirit, we are totally helpless in this sinful world. When we accept Jesus as Lord and Savior, we have been freed from the curse of sin and death. Therefore, from this day forward, let us praise and worship the Lord with a pure heart toward him, resisting and putting away those things that are displeasing in his sight. The born-again believer no longer condones sinful behavior. They will forever repent and turn back to the will of God.

25) Did you know that the Bible teaches us that a man believes in his own heart that he is right in all matters concerning him? This is something good to know. Since every man thinks he is right even when he is often wrong, we should avoid senseless arguments with one another.

Scripture

"There is a way which seemeth right unto a man; but the end thereof are the ways of death" (Proverbs 14:12).

"The way of a fool is right in his own eyes: but he that hearkeneth unto counsel is wise" (Proverbs 12:15).

"All the ways of a man are clean in his own eyes; but the Lord weigheth the spirits" (Proverbs 16:2).

Let us learn to do it God's way and lean not to our own understanding. This will cause us to walk uprightly before God at all times. This should teach us as spirit-filled Christians never to argue with one another, especially over the word of God. The Bible tells us all the ways of a man are clean in his own eyes. This is a dangerous way to think or feel. This means that whatever one chooses to do in life, he thinks its okay or even justified just for him. When our deeds are righteous, this is a good thing. However, when our deeds are sinful, they carry serious consequences. Take for example, any and all immoral acts whether they be legal or illegal, man will always justify his ways to himself. There are many sinful jobs that are legal by the world's standard; however, God frowns upon them. Then you have the illegal acts of employment that men justify in order to make a living. Their heart and conscience has been seered with a hot iron. The wrongfulness of their actions no longer bothers them. They have condoned their sinful behavior. Since their sin does not bother them any longer, they refuse to repent to God. Without repentance, there is no forgiveness of sin. This is the special provision from God given only to the saints of God. When we come into the family of God, we have to agree with the Lord that sinful behavior is just that, SIN!

26) Did you know that Jesus our Lord explained to his disciples how major events causing large numbers of casualties will often occur in life? Mankind over the years has often asked the question, "Why God allows things to happen causing death and destruction toward men." Jesus taught his disciples that sometimes people die in situations which are deemed tragic. This does not mean that they were greater sinners than the ones who survived. The Lord's disciples asked the question whether or not the tower of Siloam could have been avoided when it fell while Jesus was in the earth, killing eighteen souls. Jesus responded by saying to his disciples that the victims who died were not sinners above all. He further informed his disciples that unless they too also repent, they could likewise perish at anytime. The bottom line is this, tragedies can and sometime will occur. The important thing to remember is to always be ready to meet God in the event it happens to you.

Scripture

Jesus said, *"Or those eighteen, upon whom the tower in Siloam fell, and slew them, think ye that they were sinners above all men that dwelt in Jerusalem? I tell you, Nay: but except ye repent, ye shall all likewise perish"* (Luke 13:4, 5).

Remember; do not forget the characteristics of Satan, especially when tragedies occur. Jesus describes him as the thief that comes to steal, kill and destroy. Anytime there is mass death and destruction, look to the enemy. Never falsely accuse God at anytime. Be very careful when you throw the false blame on the one true God which came to give us life and life more abundantly. Let us not forget how Adam sinned in the Garden of Eden in the beginning. This sinful act introduced sin into this world which now has everything out of order. In the beginning there was peace and tranquility as Adam and Eve communed with God in the garden. Sin is responsible for throwing everything out of place. Now that sin has been let loose, the devil is always taking advantage of opportunities to cause death and destruction where he can. The only problem is, without the knowledge of God, the unbelieving soul has no clue what's going on around him. The word of God warns us that even God's people will perish without the knowledge of his word. What chance does the unbeliever stand? The answer is, not a chance in this world.

27) Did you know that everything God created has the ability to hear? That's right. Everything God created, he spoke into existence. Therefore, in order for us to even get results, we must use our words! Jesus, on at least two occasions demonstrated this principle. On one occasion Jesus spoke directly to a fig tree. The Lord cursed the tree that it would never bear fruit again. Hours later, the healthy fruitless fig tree had withered away and died. On another occasion, Jesus spoke to the elements. He talked directly to the wind and told the wind to be still. Immediately, when the winds obeyed the Lord, his disciples wondered what kind of man Jesus was that even the winds obeyed him. In order to respond to the voice of God, one has to have the ability to hear.

Scripture

"Now in the morning as he returned into the city, he hungered. And when he saw a fig tree in the way, he came to it, and found nothing thereon, but leaves only, and said unto it, Let no fruit grow on thee henceforward forever. And presently the fig tree withered away" (Matthew 21:18-20).

"And when he was entered into a ship, his disciples followed him. And behold, there arose a great tempest in the sea, in so much that the ship was covered with the waves: but Jesus was asleep. And his disciples came to him, and awoke him, saying Lord save us; we perish. And he saith unto them, Why are ye fearful, O ye of little faith? Then he arose, and rebuked the winds and the sea; and there was a great calm. But the men marveled,

saying, What manner of man is this, that even the winds and the sea obey him" (Matthew 8:23-27)*!*

All living things have ears! How many times have you heard of people talking to plants and flowers? This will sound strange to the one who has not recognized his or her own spirituality. Once we realize that we are spirit beings attempting to master this human experience, this is the time when we learn that everything God has created has life. We must realize the power that the Lord Jesus has given us when we were born again of the Spirit of God. We have been given the power to become the sons of God. The original sin stripped us of or dominion God originally gave man in the beginning. The salvation of the Lord Jesus Christ has restored unto us our original dominion and power. Let us remember this every time we speak words out of our mouth. Jesus teaches us whatever we ask for believing that we receive the same; those things will be given to us providing there is no doubt whatsoever found within us.

Scripture

Jesus said, *"For verily I say unto you, That whosoever shall <u>SAY</u> unto this mountain, Be thou removed, and be thou cast into the sea; and shall not DOUBT in his heart, but shall BELIEVE that those things which he <u>SAITH</u> shall come to pass; he shall have whatsoever he <u>SAITH</u>"* (Mark 11:23).

28) Did you know that the Bible warns us about racism, hatred and superiority complexes toward one another? Let us go on a little journey as we change the beginning of man, and place ourselves in the shoes of our great ancestors, Adam and Eve. Let us take a look from this perspective. If you and your spouse were the first humans God created instead of Adam and Eve. Then you were given the opportunity to populate this world. The next thing you knew, a thousand generations had been established. All of a sudden, after the thousand generations, your distant kinfolk became foolish in their minds and started to complain and develop hatred toward one another. Remember, these are the result of your offspring.

What would you say? Would you wonder how they became separated from each other to the point that now they feel in their mind, there is a difference between them?

What would you say? Then you discover that the reason they feel that there is a difference is because of their skin tone and their cultural differences.

What would you say? Then you try and explain to them that they all came from the same stock with no physical characteristics that vary.

What would you say? What would you say to them if you had an opportunity to come back from the grave and confront them?

What would you say? Would you let them know that the enemy of God known as Satan has tricked them into believing that there is a difference among them whom God created in his image and likeness?

What would you say? Would you tell them that they are all your descendants, making their current thought process both ludicrous and wicked?

What would you say? Would you let them know that they are HELL bound in the event they cannot shed the hatred before they die in the flesh?

What would you say? Would you tell them that they have cursed their young children to the gates of HELL by teaching them to hate without a legitimate cause?

What would you say? Remember, God hates those who sow discord among the brethren. It is even viewed as an abomination! Therefore, what ever you would tell your generation then; YOU NEED TO TELL YOUR GENERATION NOW!

Scripture

"For there is no respect of persons with God" (Romans 2:11).

Did you know when the Bible makes reference to the term brother or brethren; it's referring to the entire human race God created? God loves all his creation which includes every human being. Only mankind struggles with such foolishness as racism or separatism among men. We are all descendants of Adam, by way of Noah's three sons due to the great flood. Therefore, we are all related whether we like it or not. Knowing the truth will always make you free. Therefore, when you learn the truth, you will learn to love and embrace the family of God. Then we will no longer be in captivity in our mind thinking that there is a diference among us.

Scripture

> *"He that saith he is in the light, and hateth his brother, is in darkness even until now. He that loveth his brother abideth in the light, and there is none occasion of stumbling in him. But he that hateth his brother is in darkness, and walketh in darkness, and knoweth not whither he goeth, because that darkness hath blinded his eyes"* (1 John 2:9-11).

Therefore, it is pure ignorance of the truth that mankind has developed over the centuries convincing himself that ethnicity matters. This mindset has done nothing but cause distance from God and confusion and discord among the brethren. When it comes to sowing discord among men, this is the seventh of the deadly sins that God hates. Therefore, this behavior of hating one another because of skin color or ethnicity is worse than most realize. When the Lord hates something, the last thing you want to do is to be found doing that which the Lord hates. Let's explore the seven deadly sins which God hates and tells us that seven are an abomination unto him.

Scripture

> *"These six things doth the Lord hate; yea, seven are an ABOMINATION unto him:*
>
> *1) A proud Look,*
>
> *2) A lying tongue,*
>
> *3) and hands that shed innocent blood,*

4) A heart that deviseth wicked imaginations,

5) Feet that be swift in running to mischief,

6) A false witness that speaketh Lies,

7) And he that <u>SOWETH DISCORD</u> among brethren"

(Proverbs 6:16-19).

When we train our innocent children to hate for no reason, this robs them of their innocence before they are old enough to think for themselves. God gave us our children as a gift with a special purpose for his world. Yet we curse their very souls to hell because we have taught them a behavior that God hates. They grow up confused in their minds, and then they pass the same hatred onto their offspring. This is why racism is an epidemic that doesn't seem to want to go away. The devil sits back and LAUGHS because his will for mankind is being accomplished. God commanded mankind to love one another. On the other hand, the devil wants mankind to hate each other. Therefore, when we practice hatred, we have just taken on the will of Satan. Now we are helping him accomplish his agenda in the earth. When we study the word of God, we learn the truth about who we are. Once we learn the truth that we are all related through Adam and are the descendants of Noah's three sons after the flood. This is the time we can gladly come together and embrace one another, and stop thinking that God created us special just because our skin tone may vary and our hair texture may differ. There are only two sides when it comes to God concerning his creation. God has his side, and Satan unfortunately has the other side. You choose your father whom you will serve and let that be the end of it. If you choose God the Father, you will spend eternity in his perfect kingdom. If you choose Satan, you will spend all eternity in the lake of fire and brimstone full of torment. The sooner we educate ourselves to comply with the will of God, the better life will be for us in this present world. If you continue to refuse the will of God, let that be your final decision. Just stop wondering why your struggles are unending and you have no peace.

Scripture

"We know that we have passed from death unto life, because we love the brethren. He that loveth not his brother abideth in <u>DEATH</u>. Whosoever hateth his brother is a MURDERER: and ye know that no murderer hath eternal life abiding in him. Hereby perceive we the love of God, because he laid down his life for us: and we ought to lay down our lives for the brethren" (1 John 3:14-16)!

Jesus tells us that if we have loved one to another, then they (the world) will know that we are his disciples. Those who harbor hatred in their hearts are deceiving themselves. The truth will always make you free in everything. Remember, Jesus gave us this one additional commandment.

Scripture

Jesus said, *"This is my commandment, That ye love one another, as I have loved you. Greater love hath no man than this, that a man lay down his life for his friends"* (John 15:12, 13).

Men are not to dominate other men nor rule over them. God rules over mankind and all their affairs. God gave this earth and its dominion to his children. Those who choose not to acknowledge God as their Lord will always lose their possessions and their inheritance set forth in the earth. They will eventually fall into some sort of bondage. Let us never again think that a man created in the image and likeness of God is nothing more than common CHATTEL.

Scripture

"And God said, Let us make man in our image, after our likeness: and let THEM have dominion over the FISH of the sea, and over the FOWL of the air, and over the CATTLE, and over all the EARTH, and over EVERY creeping thing that creepeth upon the earth. God created man in his own

image, in the image of God created he him; male and female created he them. And God blessed them, and God said unto them, Be fruitful, and multiply, and replenish the earth, and SUBDUE it: and have dominion over the fish of the sea, and over the fowl of the air, and over every living thing that moveth upon the earth" (Genesis 1:26-28).

God tells us who we are and he also gives us an assignment here to be fulfilled in the earth. This was not given to any one particular nation. This assignment was given to the one human race in general. First of all, God blessed mankind. Secondly, he commanded that they be fruitful and multiply and replenish the earth. Thirdly, he commanded us to subdue the earth and have dominion over the things he mentioned. These commandments are very clear. The word subdue in the Webster's dictionary has several meanings.

Subdue—to put under subjection, to bring into subjection, to overcome, to bring under cultivation.

God's original assignment to Adam was to have him dress and keep his beautiful garden in Eden. Even after Adam sinned, God commanded him to be a tiller of the ground, and not a conqueror of his offspring. Later when mankind became wicked and turned from God, that's when the children of Israel or the chosen people of God were established. God called a faithful man named Abram out of the land of the Chaldeans in order to establish the people of faith. God knew that it would require faith to receive the Son of the living God whom he was about to send into the earth. God established a relationship with Abram due to his faithfulness of heart. The Lord knew that Abram would teach his generation to love and obey him. Once God had developed this chosen nation from the loins of Abram, who was now by this time renamed Abraham; he later allowed this nation to war against and destroy other nations who worshiped false idol gods. This was an offense to the almighty God as he watched his creation engulfed in wickedness as they gave God's personal glory to their false idols. Over the years, men began to conquer nation after nation to control territory and wealth. They did not understand God's concept of destroying those who turned from honoring him as Lord of all creation. Other nations were only concerned with total domination for the purpose of gaining control over a territory and their resources. Therefore, always remember to have love one to another which includes all nations, tongues and kindred's. This will cause you to be blessed and not cursed. Then you can preach the good news of the gospel with a clean heart to all nations, having love for all.

29) Did you know that the Christian born-again believer is not appointed to the wrath of God? The wrath of God will be poured out without mixture during the Great Tribulation Period on the children of disobedience. Christians have been spared from this great travesty.

Scripture

"But let us, who are of the day, be sober, putting on the breastplate of faith and love; and for a helmet, the hope of salvation. For God <u>hath not appointed us to wrath</u>, but to obtain salvation by our Lord Jesus Christ, who died for us, that, whether we wake or sleep, we should live together with him" (1 Thessalonians 5;8-10).

"He that believeth on the Son hath everlasting life: and he that believeth not the Son shall not see life; but the wrath of God abideth on him" (John 3:36).

Therefore, accept Jesus Christ as Lord and get covered with his precious innocent blood. Remember that Jesus died for us all and paid our debt he did not owe, so that we could receive eternal life at a price we could not afford to pay. We are blessed and fortunate that Jesus loved us even in the midst of our sinful lives to die for each and every one of us. Jesus is our only true redeemer of this world. Our souls belong exclusively to the Lord.

30) Did you know that we desperately need the word of God in our lives? There are some that will still not agree. They live their lives in a way they think is best for them. Whether they realize it or not, the word of God helps direct us along the right path. It allows us to judge the matters of life correctly so that they will all line up with God's perfect will. We have to study in the word because even the enemy has power to perform signs and wonders. Voices that men and women often claim they hear may not be the voice of God at all. The wrong voice can also speak to the mind of men and women in the earth. Any voice or thought we entertain, we must always check it against the word of God. You might be surprised who you have been listening to all this time. Some people feel like they are so spiritual that they do not have to read and study God's holy word. Those are the ones who feel that the Lord will tell them everything they need to hear. The problem with this theory is they purposely lack knowledge in the word of God. They have a tendency to make up in their own mind what sound good to their naked ear. They can be led either way because they lack knowledge in the Holy Bible. Remember, God himself said his people are destroyed for lack of knowledge. Why then would God encourage anyone of his children not to seek his holy word? Those who serve and seek the Lord will search out his holy word with all diligence. They are looking to learn more about the God who gave them life. Those who refuse to seek God's word will rely on their own thoughts. They are the first ones who always falsely accuse God when tragedies occur in their lives. The feelings and emotions we often experience can be wrong or even mislead at times. The ways of the Lord are different from our ways. Therefore, read and study the Holy Bible and believe what it says. Do not be one of the ones deceived by your own mind. When Jesus returns for his church body of believers, you do not want to be left behind. The only way you will not be deceived is if you know and believe what the Holy Bible says. We as men have to be higher than the enemies of God. Think on this, Satan knows and believes the word of God. He just hates God and resists everything about his Creator. Remember, Satan was once an archangel named Lucifer who was the worship Cherub for the Highest. Now he is just a rebellious evil wicked spirit that has already been sentenced to death in the lake of fire. When man knows what the word of God says and fails to obey the same, he is operating in the will of the enemies of God. It's not enough to just know what the word of God says; we must obey it if we want to be considered a believer. If we know it and choose not to obey it, then we have rejected the word of God, just like the devil.

Scripture

"For there shall arise false Christ's, and false prophets, and shall show great signs and wonders, insomuch that, if it were possible, they shall <u>deceive the very elect</u>. Behold, I have told you before. Wherefore if they

shall say unto you, Behold, he is in the desert; go not forth: behold, he is in the secret chambers; believe it not" (Matthew 24:24, 25).

Even the elect of God may be deceived during this time period of signs and wonders performed by the antichrist and the false prophet. We have to make sure everything we see and hear lines up with the word of God. Let us not think for one moment that we need not study the Holy Bible. There may come a time in the future where the Holy Bible is not readily available to be studied. If this was to occur, would you possess the knowledge to carry on? This is why we do not have time to waste. We have to study like there is no tomorrow. We must eat and digest the whole roll. This holy book is our measuring stick which helps us to see and judge matters properly. Men and women have prayed over the years for ungodly things because their feelings and emotions were involved. This is why we need to know and understand the word of God.

A Few Examples of Ungodly Prayers

Praying for God to bless an adulterous affair you are involved in.
Praying for God to bless wicked financial gain you have obtained.
Praying for God to bless your desire to gamble, this is coveteous behavior against others.
Praying for wicked ungodly works; asking for God to bless what clearly glorifies Satan.
Praying for God to punish others, while extending his wonderful grace to you.
Praying for God to bless your fornicating relationship you are having with the opposite sex.
Praying for God to bless your fornicating relationship you are having with the same sex.
Praying for God to hurt and judge those who have hurt and offended you.
Praying for God to bless anything outside his perfect will.

These are only a few examples of how carnal Christians mistakenly pray the wrong prayers. Being a carnal Christian, you don't realize that your prayers are outside the will of God. This is primarily due to lack knowledge in the word of God. These Christians are being led by their feelings and emotions. The reason they feel this way is because they do not read and spend intimate quality time in the word of God. There are just some things in life that we cannot have according to the word of God. We just have to get over it and stop wrestling with our emotions when it comes to sin and lustful desires. When we take on the will of God, this is an easy task. However, when we try and cater to our own agenda, we struggle in the flesh something terrible. Always remember, we will remain lost without God's direction and guidance found in his holy word.

31) Did you know that the blood has life, power and a voice? There is life in the blood. For this reason, we should never eat any form of blood. God promises to set his face against any soul that consumes the blood. We must never forget that the life is in the blood.

Life
Scripture

> *"And whatsoever man there be of the house of Israel, or of the strangers that sojourn among you that eateth any manner of blood; I will even set my face against that soul that <u>eateth blood</u>, and will cut him off from among his people. For the life of the flesh is in the blood: and I have given it to you upon the alter to make an atonement for your soul: for it is the blood that maketh an atonement for the soul"*(Leviticus 17:10, 11).

> *"For it is the life of all flesh; the blood of it is for the life thereof: therefore I said unto the children of Israel, Ye shall eat the blood of no manner of flesh: for the life of all flesh is the blood thereof: whosoever eateth it shall be cut off"* (Leviticus 17:14).

Power
Scripture

> *"But if we walk in the light, as he is in the light, we have fellowship one with another, and the blood of Jesus Christ his Son cleanseth us from all sin"* (1 John 1:7).

> *"Whoso sheddeth man's blood, by man shall his blood be shed: for in the image of God made he man"* (Genesis 9:6).

The blood of Jesus covers the saints of God from head to toe concerning the sin stain inherited from Adam. This precious blood of Jesus has the power to even change the focus on death in the flesh. The above verse of scripture deals with man shedding the blood of another human being. God wants us to know how precious every man's life is to him. Since every man and woman was made in the image and likeness of God, this means their souls are extremely valuable to the Father. To take a human life is a serious offense against mankind. Innocent blood has power in its self; therefore, we should never shed innocent blood. Even animal blood has power. God used the blood of an innocent lamb on the day of pass-over in order to save the children of Israel from the death angel. This death angel came to destroy the first born population of Egypt. This was the last plague brought against the Egyptians due to the captivity of God's people. Since the children of Israel were in bondage in Egypt, this included their first born as well. However, God developed what is called the Lord's pass-over which saved the nation of Israel's first born from being destroyed along with the first born of Egypt. This death to the first born included both man and beast. God provided his people with a provision which involved the killing of an innocent male lamb of the first year. The blood of this lamb was to be placed in a basen, dipped with hyssop and stuck against the door post of the Israelites dwelling places. They were instructed to stay inside until morning, roast with fire the lamb, eat all of it with unleaven bread and bitter herbs. This day was to be a memorial forever through out all future generations. This is a reminder of how powerful the blood of life can be. The blood of that innocent lamb caused the death angel to pass over and spare the lives of God's covenant people. When God give us a provision, we must make sure we follow it according to his perfect will.

Scripture

> *"For the Lord will pass through to smite the Egyptians; and when he seeth the blood upon the lintel, and on the two side posts, the Lord will pass over the door, and will not suffer the destroyer to come in unto your houses to smite you"* (Exodus 12:23).

This reminds us of another provision God has made for his chosen people in a time of need. The Lord's provision he made for his people at the pass-over meal could not protect those who were outside the ark of safety. No one was permitted to go outside until the following morning after the death angel had passed over. Any Israelite dwelling where the door post was not marked by the blood of the innocent lamb, death of the frist born came to that house. Listen very careful people of God. The same provision given by God applies in this day and age. Anyone who is not cover with the blood of Jesus in the day of the Lord will likewise perish. Remember, Jesus is the Lamb of God who came to take away the sins of the world. John the Baptist proclaimed this truth. Just like in the day of the Lord's pass-over, anyone not covered with the blood will receive the second death, which is the lake of fire.

Leading up to the tribulation period, there will come a day when there will be a sign of blood in the heavens during the great outpouring of God's Spirit. This sign involves the moon turning to blood just before the great tribulation period. We must pay close attention to the word of God as it warns us of the future things to come.

Scripture

> *"And I will show wonders in the heavens and in the earth, blood, and fire, and pillars of smoke. The sun shall be turned into darkness, and the moon into blood, before the great and terrible day of the Lord come"* (Joel 2:30-31).

Voice

The Bible tells us that the blood cried out from the ground. This blood is the blood of Abel, the second son of Adam and Eve. When his elder brother Cain slew him, his blood spilled out and soaked into the earth. God heard the voice of Abel's blood crying out from the ground. Were you aware that everything God created has a way of communicating with him?

Scripture

"And Cain talked with Abel his brother: and it came to pass, when they were in the field, that Cain rose up against Abel his brother, and slew him. And the Lord said unto Cain, Where is Abel thy brother? And he said, I know not: Am I my brother's keeper? And he said, What hast thou done? the voice of thy brother's blood crieth unto me from the ground. And now art thou cursed from the earth, which hath opened her mouth to receive thy brother's blood from thy hand" (Genesis 4:8-10).

When a man or woman commits a murder, this act of violence is in full view of the eyes of God. Just so we are all on the same page, every sin you have ever committed, God had a ring side seat. This may sound elementary to the Christian scholar, however, unbelievers do not have a clue they are being watched and recorded by God. There is nothing in this world we have ever done that was not written down and recorded. All the murders, all the rapes, all the thefts, all the adultery and sexual sins, all the violence, all the true intentions of the heart have been both observed and recorded by God. The funny thing is there are some of you who thought you had got away with something. Hiding your sins from man is of no value. Man cannot put you in heaven nor send you to hell. Neither can he sentence you to the lake of fire and brimstone for all eternity. Only the true and living God can pronounce this sentence upon his creation. Therefore remember, God sees everything and knows everything that goes on in the earth. His eyes are in every place at the same time watching the behavior of all he has created.

Scripture

"The eyes of the Lord are in every place, beholding the evil and the good" (Proverbs 15:3).

Now that we know this, we can stop acting like our sins are hidden. Think on this the very next time you commit a wrongful act in the earth. Know that God has a ring side seat beholding the very act and the intent of your heart at the time. One thing we can be sure of, God doesn't misunderstand anything or anyone. He knows our true intention concerning all things. There will not be any misunderstanding on Judgment Day! Saying that you misunderstand may work here in the earth among those who are in cahoots with one another; however, it does not work with God.

32) Did you know that God wants his people to prosper and live an abundant life while in the earth? There are many occupations in this world today that produce wealth. Some of these occupations are good and some are not. Just because a business is legal by the worlds standard does not make it honorable in the sight of God. For example you have entertainers, athletes, dance club and strip club owners, the adult entertainment business, corporate america, the gambling industry and all sort of businesses both large and small just to name a few. All of these businesses mentioned are legal establishments however; all of them mentioned are not considered morally right. Society as a whole normally doesn't have a problem honoring wealth in these areas. However, men who dedicate their lives to serving the Lord and walking with God seem to be looked down upon when prosperity is in their home. Society in general will even complain when God's churches are blessed and overflowing with wealth. Why is it that the world system in general doesn't want the man of God blessed? The general population can yell, scream and shout at any sporting even or concert paying homage to world celebrities. However, when this behavior is practiced in a church, it is said to be both unnecessary and cultic. There is only one logical name behind this twisted way of thinking, and that name is Satan. Anytime you value what is bad or ordinary verses what is right and good, you can rest assure, the enemy of God will always be nearby.

Scripture

The Bible tells us, *"And it shall come to pass, if thou shalt hearken diligently unto the voice of the Lord thy God, to observe and to do all his commandments which I command thee this day, that <u>the Lord thy</u>*

God will set thee on high above all nations of the earth" (Deuteronomy 28:1).

The book of Deuteronomy, chapter 28, verses 1 through 14 lists the blessings of obedience. Servants of God have a right to live the abundant life because they have a covenant with the almighty God. Therefore, it is a true blessing to see a man of God prospering on the face of the earth. For it is the will of God.

Scripture

"Keep therefore the words of this covenant, and do them, that ye may prosper in all that ye do" (Deuteronomy 29:9).

God wants us to prosper and be in good health here in the earth. We have got to be careful with wealth without God. Any form of ungodly wealth received without God will eventually lead to destruction.

Scripture

*"But they that will be rich fall into temptation and a snare, and into many foolish and hurtful lusts, which drown men in destruction and perdition. **For the love of money is the root of all evil**: which while some coveted after, they have erred from the faith, and pierced themselves through with many sorrows"* (1 Timothy 6:9, 10).

God is warning us to be careful with wealth because it can cause us to fall away from him and ultimately end up in hell. All believers are covenant men and women of God and should be good stewards over the Master's goods. God said the heavens belong to him and the earth he has given to men. As covenant men and women of God, we co-own this earth with God the Father. He has entrusted us with his holy tithe and offering to be released into his kingdom. The man, who honors God, releases his holy tithe to be brought into the storehouse (church). Then he gives offerings to the Lord and sees about the poor, needy, widows and orphans. When you are obedient to what God has placed in your hands, you too will live a life of bountiful blessings and not be ashamed. If we are experiencing lack concerning our stewardship, we should examine ourselves closely. God blesses those who have shown they can be trusted not only over their own goods, but over the goods of others. Therefore, when you receive your blessing, remember your covenant with the Lord and do not be ashamed.

Scripture

"The blessing of the Lord, <u>it maketh rich</u>, and he addeth no sorrow with it" (Proverbs 10:22).

33) Did you know when Jesus died on the cross at Calvary; the veil in the temple tore itself from the top downward? The Bible also tells us that the graves were open and saints came forth out of them!

Scripture

"Jesus when he had cried again with a loud voice, yielded up the ghost. And behold, the veil of the temple was rent in twain from the top to the bottom; and the earth did quake, and the rocks rent, <u>and the graves were opened</u>; and many bodies of the saints which slept arose, <u>and came out of the graves after his resurrection</u>, and went into the holy city, and appeared unto many" (Matthew 27:50 - 53).

The temple veil tore itself from the top downward which indicates the Spirit of the Lord tore his veil, not the temple Pharisees. This means that we no longer have to rely on the Priests, Ministers, Pharisees, Sadducees, or any other leader to go to God on our behalf. We now can boldly go before the throne of grace for ourselves. Jesus made this all possible when he freed us from the curse of the law. No more animal sacrifices for sin. Jesus sacrificed himself for the sins of the entire world with royal blood shed on that rugged cross. The blood of God was shed for all souls who willing accepted Jesus as Lord. Now, concerning the dead souls that came up out of the graves, the Holy Bible lets us know that only the <u>saints</u> that were <u>asleep</u> came forth. This makes it clear in reference to what Jesus taught us about Christians asleep in Christ. When Jesus rose from the dead, Old Testament saints came out of their graves after his resurrection. This is a witness of how strong the power of God was and will be again concerning the resurrection of souls. It caused some to resurrect out of their graves and walk toward the holy city for all to see. The Bible also teaches us that since Jesus rose from the dead, absent in the body is now to be present with the Lord. Does this mean that our spirits are ushered into the presence of the Lord and our bodies go in the grave? Notice that according to the word of God, when Jesus returns for his Church body of believers, the dead in Christ shall rise first. Then all that remain alive in the earth will be caught up to be with Jesus in the clouds. There are three areas of belief concerning sleeping in Christ Jesus.

1) The first area of belief is that those who are asleep in Jesus are with him. Then when Jesus returns to the earth, they will return also.

2) The second area of belief is that all who sleep in Jesus can be viewed as being put to sleep by the Lord in a restful state awaiting his return for the Church.

3) The third area of belief is that Jesus puts his precious souls to sleep by taking them off the earth and reserving them until he returns to reconnect their spirits with their new resurrected bodies. If this theory is true, it shows that God knows exactly when to take his souls from this earth.

Either way, all resurrected saints will receive a new resurrected body to dwell in when Jesus returns for his Church body of believers. Therefore, whether you were cremated, returned to dust, cast at sea, it really doesn't matter. Jesus promises to reconnect our new resurrected body with our soul and spirit. How the Lord plans to perform this miracle is his business. Death in the flesh allows us to step over into eternity, which is the spirit realm where God is. One thing we can surely look forward to is the judgment of the Lord. The saints of God will go before the Judgment Seat of Christ to receive their rewards. The unsaved sinner who rejected the blood of the Lamb will appear before the Great White Throne Judgment of God. Always remember, Jesus truly cares for all souls. The time is now to receive the salvation of the Lord. Once death in the flesh occurs, the door to the free gift of salvation will be closed and sealed by God, just like in the days of Noah's flood. The living mourns the souls of the dead not realizing that Jesus knows best. Since God controls our departure date from this earth, let us trust in the Lord and believe that he knows what's best concerning death. The Lord calls us home at the appropriate time. Our job is to make sure we know the Lord Jesus Christ in the pardoning of our sins before we answer this call. Therefore, when it's our time to leave this world, we will forever be with the Lord. This news is worth celebrating over. This is why Christian funerals now days are often referred to as home goings. We recognize that God has called us home where we can now enter into his rest. As a child of God, we have a special appointment to meet the Lord when he returns.

Scripture

"For the Lord himself shall descend from heaven with a shout, with the voice of the archangel, and with the trump of God: and the dead in Christ shall rise first: Then we which are alive and remain shall be caught up together with them in the clouds, to meet the Lord in the air: and so shall we ever be with the Lord. Wherefore comfort one another with these words" (1 Thessalonians 4:16-18).

Be encouraged, be comforted and preach the good news of the gospel of Jesus Christ to all nations. Keep the faith and hope in the Lord, always looking forward in anticipation of his return.

34) Did you know that when God breathed breath into Adam's nostrils, man became a living soul? God created man in his own image and likeness for a reason. God wants us to enjoy eternal fellowship with him one day real soon in his Holy City. We were also created for God's own pleasure. The Lord even refers to man as little gods who were created by the one true and living God. We are all children of the Most High God.

Scripture

"Thou art worthy, O Lord, to receive glory and honour and power: for thou hast <u>created all things</u>, and <u>for thy pleasure they are and were created</u>" (Revelation 4:11).

"I have said, Ye are <u>gods</u>: and all of you are children of the Most High" (Psalm 82:6).

"Jesus answered them, Is it not written in your law, I SAID, Ye are gods? If he called them gods, unto whom the word of God came, and the scripture cannot be broken" (John 10:34, 35).

Notice how Jesus told the Jews that HE SAID they are gods? This is another area in the Holy Scriptures where Jesus exposed his deity and sovereignty to the Jews and temple leaders. Since the Lord calls us gods with the little g, we too have the power given by God to speak things into existence. So therefore, if you don't want to see it manifest, don't speak it. Believe me; your words have power—both good and bad. Be careful how you speak or prophesy concerning your life and the lives of your children. You can speak a blessing or a curse against you, your family, or others. If it's healing you want, speak words of healing from the word of God over your situation. Never speak doubt into your situation. You will find that negative speech will always produce a negative response. You will have whatever you say with your spoken words. Remember, the Bible teaches us that death and life is in the power of the tongue.

Scripture

"Death and Life are in the power of the tongue: and they that love it shall eat the fruit thereof" (Proverbs 18:21).

"And the tongue is a fire, a world of iniquity: so is the tongue among our members, that it defileth the whole body, and setteth on fire the course of nature; and it is set on fire of hell" (James 3:6).

"The preparations of the heart in man, and the answer of the TONGUE, is from the Lord" (Proverbs 16:1).

The Bible tells us that death and life is in the power of the tongue. This means that death and life are in the words we speak. Therefore, we must be careful what we say at all times. The Bible further teaches us that the tongue will also set on fire the course of nature. This means that our words can carry us to and fro. Wrong words can defile our whole body; likewise, right speech can create a positive path. The Bible also teaches us that God answers the words spoken from our heart. This means that anything we can think of and speak, God can make it happen. As long as we take care of our part which is the thinking and speaking, God will surely take care of his part which is the manifestation. Then we can rest assure while God takes care of his end. All we have to do is trust in the Lord and lean not to our own understanding. When we acknowledge God in all of our ways, he will direct our path. When we connect with the Lord, he gives us power to become his anointed sons and daughters in the earth. Even though the Bible refers to us as little <u>gods</u>, by no means are we anywhere close to the level of God. We have exactly what God has given us. His ways are higher than our ways. His thoughts are higher than our thoughts. Therefore, do not allow your chest to be puffed up because the Lord calls you a god. Instead, recognize this as you being fearfully and wonderfully made by the supreme God.

Scripture

"I will praise thee; for I am fearfully and wonderfully made: marvelous are thy works; and that my soul knoweth right well" (Psalm 139:14).

King David acknowledges that God made mankind with a certain degree of knowledge and power. Even though mankind was fearfully and wonderfully made by God, he still doesn't come close to the greatness of the Almighty. God is the King of kings and the Lord of lords. Above him there is no other.

Scripture

Jesus tells us, **"Which in his times he shall show, who is the blessed and only Potentate, the KING of kings, and LORD of lords"** (1 Timothy 6:15).

Jesus had to remind the Jews what the scriptures said when they accused him of being the Son of God. Jesus explained to the Pharisees that his word, which is the word of God tells man he is a god, with a small 'g.' The mention of the King of kings and Lord of lords in the above scripture is referring to the sons and daughters of God. There are references made also to the kings and the earth. Jesus Christ is the highest King and Lord over everything and everyone in this world. God's children have been deemed ambassadors, royal priest, kings and lord's over everything that God has made. They too share status with the kings and lords of the earth. The only difference is, the children of God fully surrender and accept God's sovereign rule over their lives. The appointed kings in the earth at the hands of man have exhalted themselves, some even to the point of placing themselves above God. However, the children of God know their proper place of sonship.

Scripture

"Now then we are ambassadors for Christ, as though God did beseech you by us: we pray you in Christ's stead, be ye reconciled to God" (2 Corinthians 5:20).

AMBASSADOR—the highest ranking diplomatic representative appointed by one country or government to represent it in another; a special representative or official agent with a special mission.

You must remember, those of us who accept Jesus Christ as Lord and Savior, our new citizenship is in heaven with God. This earth is no longer our home. We have defected from this world and entered into a new kingdom. Our new kingdom comes with a new citizenship. Now we belong exclusively to the Lord. Just like an Embassy in a foreign land, that patch of ground becomes home land. There is safety there. There is protection there. There is authority there. There is peace there. This is the same concept with the Christian born-again believers. All blood washed believers carrier around with them God's precious Holy Spirit and access to his royal kingdom. Now we represent the kingdom of God here in the earth. We have been bought and paid for by God with the precious blood of the Lamb. Jesus said we are little gods. Everything produces after its own kind. God created man in his own image and likeness. Therefore, it took a God in order to create little gods. This proves that God gave mankind a piece of himself during his creation process.

Scripture

"But as many as received him, **(Jesus)** *to them gave he power to become the sons of God, even to them that believe on his name"* (John 1:12).

All we have to do is seek the kingdom of God and his righteousness, and believe in our heart that Jesus is Lord. Then, we have that power that the Holy Scriptures speaks of which transforms us into the sons and daughters of God.

35) Did you know that the Bible tells us that God does not hear sinners? We as Christians must cry out to the Lord and he will hear us. This is what the Holy Scripture says concerning the sinners prayer.

Scripture

"Now we know that God heareth not sinners: but if any man be a <u>worshiper</u> of God, and doeth his will, him he heareth" (John 9:31).

When we become followers of the Savior Jesus the Christ, we are made the righteousness of God. This righteousness we did not earn ourselves, it was automatically given by God to the followers of Christ. This righteousness is granted based on what Jesus did for us on the cross at Calvary. This act of love in its self demonstrates once again how the true and living God loves his creation unconditionally. This is why we have to wake up and believe in the Son of the living God whose name is Jesus. Then we have the right to call on him and expect an answer. When we choose to disregard what the Lord says in his holy word, our prayers are hindered. Therefore, if you want to be heard by the true and living God and you are tired of having your prayers unheard, sanctify yourselves before the Lord. Prepare yourself realizing that there is a way to properly come before the Lord. When you choose to do it your way, you end up ignoring and rejecting the perfect will of God. Remember what the Bible says, if any man <u>be a worshiper</u> of God, and doeth his will, him God will hear. This means, in order to cause the ears of God to be opened to your prayer request, you must become a worshiper of him.

Scripture

"But the hour cometh, and now is, when the <u>true worshipers</u> shall worship the Father in spirit and in truth: for the Father seeketh such to worship him. God is a Spirit: and they that worship him must worship him in spirit and in truth" (John 4:23, 24).

Now that you fully understand how to start getting your prayers answered with confidence, there is one more important piece of information you need to know. This information is vital to the born-again Christian believer. Never be ashamed of the Lord Jesus Christ. This will prove to be your test time after time whether or not you are willing to lay down your life for what you truly believe. Jesus warns us himself if we are ever ashamed of his gospel, he too will be ashamed of us before God the Father and his heavenly host of angels.

Scripture

"For whosoever shall be ashamed of me and my words, of him shall the Son of man be ashamed, when he shall come in his <u>own glory</u>, and in his Father's and of the holy angels" (Luke 9:26).

Therefore, now that you have pledged your allegiance to the only true and living God, be not ashamed to confess the only begotten Son of God to this sinful world.

Scripture

"For the scripture saith, whosoever believeth on him shall not be ashamed. There is no difference between the Jew and the Greek: for the same Lord over all is rich unto all that call upon him. For whosoever shall call upon the name of the Lord shall be saved" (Romans 10:11-13).

"Even the righteousness of God which is by faith of Jesus Christ unto all and upon all them that believe: for there is no difference: For all have sinned, and come short of the glory of God; Being justified freely by his grace through the redemption that is in Christ Jesus: Whom God hath set forth to be a propitiation through faith in the blood, to declare his righteousness for the remission of sins that are past, through the forbearance of God" (Romans 3:22 - 25).

Remember, Jesus died on the cross for our sins while we were yet sinners. All we have to do is accept what Jesus has already done for us and God will hear us! Jesus died a horrible death for the sins of this world. Once we realize that Jesus took our place on that rugged cross, we will be more than glad to live our remaining days in the flesh serving him. The lake of fire is going to be a terrible place for those who arrogantly reject God.

36) Did you know that the Bible teaches us that Satan has blinded this world from being able to see the glory of God? Everyone who has not accepted the free gift of God's salvation is spiritually blinded to the glory God wants you to see. This is viewed as deception before coming into the knowledge of Jesus Christ. Satan has blinded the world which causes us to focus on the world's system and not the Creator of the heavens and the earth. Our day-to-day routine can become so burdened with responsibilities, that there is no time left to think about the Lord.

Scripture

"But if our gospel be hid, <u>it is hid to them that are lost</u>: In whom the god (Satan) of this world hath <u>blinded the minds of them which believe not</u>, lest the light of the glorious gospel of Christ, who is the image of God, should shine unto them. For we preach not ourselves, but Christ Jesus the Lord; and ourselves your servants for Jesus sake. For God, who commanded the LIGHT to shine in our hearts, to give the LIGHT of the knowledge of the glory of God in the face of Jesus Christ" (2 Corinthians 4:3-6).

As long as we are distracted by this world and the things of this world, our focus is taken off our precious Lord. Until we realize and are able to see the magnificent glory of God, we will never be able to put him first, or even know to do so. Therefore, listen to the men and women of God as they proclaim the gospel of Jesus Christ. Listen to them as they cry out and spread the word of the Lord to all nations. As witnesses of the gospel of Jesus Christ, we are the modern day John the Baptist for the church age. We have the spiritual keys to God's kingdom. Our mission is to go, teach all nations, baptizing them in the name of God the Father, God the Son, and God the Holy Spirit. All souls that have an ear to hear will freely receive the gift of salvation. Don't be deceived any longer by the mask Satan has placed on this world. Be willing to receive in your heart the message of salvation that God has freely given to a dying world. Remember, those who believe not are blinded by the enemy of God. Show this verse of scripture found in 2 Corinthians 4:3-5 to those who are not convinced. It will help them realize the state of mind they are in without the knowledge of God. This will also help shed light on the truth in the event they still insist on rejecting the gospel of Jesus Christ in their heart. Just remember, God will remove the blinders off the eyes of the lost souls when they turn to him and seek him diligently. Therefore, there is no excuse for anyone to perish in this world overridden with sin. Once we turn to God and accept him as Lord, our eyes will be opened to his marvelous glory, and we too, will serve Jesus Christ with a willing heart and mind. Always remember, there are two types of people in this world, those who have Jesus, and those who don't. One thing is for sure. The ones without the Lord Jesus may even know what the Holy Bible says, however, their only problem is they do not believe it. They have seen the word; they just do not believe what it says. This is the same problem that the Pharisees had when Jesus walked the earth. They knew the word; they just did not believe the word. Jesus told them that if they believed the word of God, then they would accept him. Therefore, if you know not the Son Jesus, neither do you know God the Father.

37) Did you know that God addresses the behavior of the married and unmarried individuals? Take this thought into consideration. Learn how to be single first before you enter into marriage. How you are as a single person, is what you will bring into your marriage covenant. Therefore, if you got it going on as a single individual, you will have it going on as a spouse. Marriage exposes the true you. All of your dirty little secret things that only you and God knew before will now be exposed. Ask yourself this question, "Would you marry yourself, if you knew in advance what you know about you?" If the answer is no, then you are not quite ready for marriage. Take the time to properly prepare yourself so that you can compliment your selected soul mate. Get rid of the old hurt and pain of your past. God developed marriage and he alone knows what makes it work, not the philosophers of our time. Marriage is a sacred oath made to God the Creator and is not to be taken lightly. This joins a male and female together until death do part them from this world. Therefore, be careful when taking these vows. We should plan to do it God's way, or not do it at all. Remember, be willing to submit yourself one to another. The Bible teaches us that the wife must honor and submit to her own husband. The Bible further teaches us that the man must love his wife as Jesus Christ loved the church and gave his life for it. These are the spiritual keys that unlock the formula to a successful marriage. Without these keys, you are doomed before you even get started.

Scripture

> *"Wives, submit yourselves unto your own husbands, as unto the Lord. For the husband is the head of the wife, even as Christ is the head of the church: and he is the Savior of the body. Therefore as the church is subject unto Christ, so let the wives be to their own husbands in everything. Husbands, love your wives, even as Christ also loved the church, and gave himself for it; That he might sanctify and cleanse it with the washing of water by the word, That he might present it to himself a glorious church, not having spot, or wrinkle, or any such thing; but that it should be holy and without blemish. So ought men to love their wives as their own bodies. He that loveth his wife loveth himself"* (Ephesians 5:22-28).

This formula will cause you to have a successful marriage. If you listen to man and his limited thought process, you will be told that you have a choice in the matter. You will be told that you can end your marriage regardless of what God has commanded. The problem occurs when you choose to believe man over God. You never want to be found placing your trust in man over God. The Bible teaches us that there is a curse for those who place their trust in man instead of God.

Scripture

> *"Thus saith the Lord; Cursed be the man that trusteth in man, and maketh flesh his arm, and whose heart departeth from the Lord"* (Jeremiah 17:5).

Never take man's word over the word of the true and living God. Honor the Lord with all of your heart, mind and soul. Select a spouse and plan on being joined together for the remainder of you days in the earth. When death doeth part either one of you, then you are privileged to be joined to another. If you have already made this mistake, repent for your sin, turn back to the Lord and do not repeat the process. This means, if you are blessed to marry again, do not repeat the same mistake you made the first time. The bottom line is, if you want to have a successful marriage, listen to the voice of the Lord.

Scripture

"Now concerning the things whereof ye wrote unto me: It is good for a man not to <u>touch a woman</u>. Nevertheless, to avoid fornication, let every man have his own wife, and let every woman have her own husband. Let the husband render unto the wife due benevolence: and likewise also the wife unto the husband. The wife hath not power of her own body, but the husband: and likewise also the husband hath not power of his own body, but the wife" (1 Corinthians 7:1-4).

This verse of scripture tells us that if one cannot abstain from sexual contact, let him take a spouse. This means, we should not touch anyone we are not married to. God knows whoever we link ourselves with sexually, the same becomes one flesh. This is how souls are spiritually joined together. That is why when we take on multiple partners, the results are devastating. The long-term effects cause us to struggle with issues like emotional stress, comparing partners one to another, no longer able to be satisfied with one person, risk and exposure to sexually transmitted disease and most importantly, the risk of being destroyed by God for defiling his holy temple (your body).

The prescription for peace in your home and holiness in your marriage is to remain in communion with God all of your days.

Scripture

"But if they cannot contain, let them marry: for it is better to marry than to burn. And unto the married I command, yet not I, but the Lord, Let not the wife depart from her husband: But and if she depart, let her remain unmarried, or be reconciled to her husband: and let not the husband put away his wife" (1 Corinthians 7:9 - 11).

"The wife is bound by the law as long as her husband liveth; but if her husband be dead, she is at liberty to be married to whom she will; only in the Lord" (1 Corinthians 7:39).

> *"But I would have you without carefulness. He that is unmarried careth for the things that belong to the Lord, how he may please the Lord: But he that is married careth for the things that are of the world, how he may please his wife. There is difference also between a wife and a virgin. The unmarried woman careth for the things of the Lord, that she may be holy both in body and in spirit: but she that is married careth for the things of the world, how she may please her husband"* (1 Corinthians 7:32-34).

Marriage is a blood covenant between God, a man (male) and a woman (female). No other union is to be sanctioned by God who created the heavens and the earth. Covenants require the spilling of blood. That's why both parties are required to be virgins when they enter into a marriage covenant. This is the way God commanded and intended it to be. The world changed the focus of marriage, and teaches that it is better to know a person sexually before marriage. This is called fornication which is still a sin in the eyes of God. God tells us that when we commit fornication, (unmarried sexual relationship) we sin against our own body. Sexual relations are only recognized between a husband (male) and a wife (female) in the eyes of God. This type of relationship requires a marriage covenant oath with the Lord. All other forms of sexual behavior are identified as forbidden sins. Therefore, you have a choice. You can either obey God, and be blessed, or ignore God and be cursed. The choice is up to you.

Scripture

> *"The word that came to Jeremiah from the Lord, saying, Hear ye the words of this covenant, and speak unto the men of Judah, and to the inhabitants of Jerusalem; and say thou unto them, Thus saith the Lord God of Israel; Cursed be the man that obeyeth not the words of this covenant, Which I commanded your father in the day that I brought them forth out of the land of Egypt, from the iron furnace, saying, Obey my voice, and do them according to all which I command you: so shall ye be my people, and I will be your God"* (Jeremiah 11:1-4).

The reason why there is a curse for not obeying the voice of the Lord is due to the principles of consequence set in place by God. Therefore, whatever God says being the sovereign ruler of the universe, it becomes world law. For this reason the entire Holy Bible which was inspired by God carries stiff consequences for non-compliance. This is why when it comes to marriage; we must take it very serious. As we take a look around this world, marriages are falling apart daily, especially in the church. This is what happens when man chooses <u>not</u> to obey the voice of the Lord.

Scripture

"Marriage is honorable in all, and the bed undefiled: but Whoremongers and Adulterers God will judge" (Hebrews 13:4).

The only sexual contact that is authorized and approved by God is that of a male and female who has entered into the bonds of holy matrimony. All other forms of sexual activity of any kind are DEFILED in the eyes of God. Even though mankind has taken it upon himself to make up his own rules that govern his life, he must one day come to the knowledge that God's way is the only way. The Bible teaches us that all sin with the exception of fornication is an outward sin. The act of fornication is the only sin that causes a man to sin against his own body, which is the temple of God where his Holy Spirit connects and dwells with man. God created mankind so that whosoever he joins himself too sexually, the same will become one flesh. The natural man cannot begin to understand nor believe this level of spirituality because he lacks spiritual discernment.

Scripture

"What? Know ye not that he which is joined to a harlot is one body? For two, saith he, shall be one flesh. But he that is joined unto the Lord is one spirit. Flee FORNICATION. Every sin that a man doeth is without the body; but he that committeth fornication sinneth against his own body. What? Know ye not that your body is the temple of the Holy Ghost which is in you, which ye have of God, and ye are not your own. For ye are bought with a price: therefore glorify God in your body, and in your spirit, which are God's" (1 Corinthians 6:16-20).

We belong to the Lord; let us never forget that. First, we must believe and understand what Jesus did on the cross for each and every one of us. The Lord Jesus sent us the Holy Ghost from God the Father whom he calls the COMFORTER. The Holy Ghost or Holy Spirit will be with us while we remain in the earth. For this Spirit is the Spirit of God. This is the same Holy Spirit Jesus talked about who leads us unto all truth. This Holy Ghost was sent to teach us and strengthen us in all matters concerning the perfect will of Jesus Christ. Therefore, let us obey the Lord and stop trusting in mankind. It is written in the word of God how to have a successful marriage. All we have to do is believe it and receive it in the name of the Lord.

38) Did you know that Christian fellowship is necessary for all who follow Christ? Fellowship with other born-again Christian believers will encourage and strengthen your walk with the Lord. Just like fellowship with unbelievers will weaken you to the point where eventually you will turn from God and be absorbed back into a sinful envorniment. We must fellowship together with those who believe likewise in the risen Savior.

Scripture

"Let us hold fast the profession of our faith without wavering; (for he is faithful that promised;) and let us consider one another to provoke unto love and to good works: Not forsaking the assembling of ourselves together, as the manner of some is; but exhorting one another: and so much the more, as ye see the day approaching" (Hebrews 10:23-25).

That great day approaching is referring to the return of Jesus for his church body. There is strength among numbers when you fellowship one to another. Jesus knows that we need to encourage one another in order to stay strong while running this Christian race. This helps us to grow and strengthen ourselves in the matters of the Lord. Coming together in the body of Christ, is very necessary. Many have said, "I don't have to go to church to worship God." When the body of believers gathers together on one accord, this provides strength. Fellowship encourages one another and sets an environment that is beneficial to everyone. Only those who choose to be an outsider will present themselves as an easy target for the devourer. The devil roams about like a roaring lion seeking whom he may devour. The enemy of God will always attack the easy prey first.

Scripture

"For whosoever shall call upon the name of the Lord shall be saved. How then shall they call on him in whom they have not believed? And how shall they believe in him of whom they have not heard? and how shall they hear without a preacher? And how shall they preach, except they be sent? As it is written, how beautiful are the feet of them that preach the Gospel, of peace, and bring glad tidings of good things! But they have not all obeyed the gospel. For Isaiah saith, Lord, who hath believed our report? So then faith cometh by hearing, and hearing by the word of God" (Romans 10:13 - 17).

The more we hear and read the word of God, the stronger our faith becomes. God sends us his anointed teachers and preachers to edify us. Our environment will eventually overtake us whether it is good or bad. That's why we have to be careful as Christians where we spend our quality time. There are areas where we may temporarily have to go for the purpose of spreading the gospel of Christ. But remember, God will strengthen and equip his servants for the task he has assigned them to perform.

Scripture

"Iron sharpeneth iron; so a man sharpeneth the countenance of his friends" (Proverbs 27:17).

"Make no friendship with an angry man; and with a furious man thou shalt not go; lest thou learn his ways, and get a snare to thy soul" (Proverbs 22:24-25).

The fact that iron sharpens iron shows us that our fellowship is very important. The warning concerning making friends with an angry man teaches us that people are going to be who they are. These scriptures teach us that an individual's ways will rub off on you in time. Only the power of Jesus can change the heart of a man. Therefore, let us never think that we can change a person ourselves. This is a big mistake that many have already made. Knowing this information, we can make better choices concerning our future selection of our friends and potential spouses. Since we know we cannot change the ways of another, let us no longer choose the wrong environment to dwell in. Only God can cause a man to change his ways. Therefore, choose wisely when it comes to selecting your spouse and your friends. Avoid isolation of yourselves when it comes to the assembling of the saints of God. God made us to care and love one another. No man is an island, and we are indeed our brother's keeper, whether we choose to accept it or not.

39) Did you know that salvation is not hereditary? Everyone must accept Jesus Christ as their personal Lord and Savior for themselves. The prayers of the righteous do avail much; however, no one can intercede on your behalf for the free gift of salvation offered to every soul in Christ Jesus. We can surely pray and intercede for one another concerning other matters, however salvation must be sought out and accepted one on one with the Lord Jesus Christ.

Scripture

"In whom ye also trusted, after that ye heard the word of truth, the gospel of your salvation: in whom also after that ye believed, ye were sealed with that Holy Spirit of promise" (Ephesians 1:13).

"Wherefore, my beloved, as ye have always obeyed, not as in my presence only, but now much more in my absence, work out your own salvation with fear and trembling. For it is God which worketh in you both to will and to do of his good pleasure" (Philippians 2:12-13).

"But we are bound to give thanks always to God for you, brethren beloved of the Lord, because God hath from the beginning chosen you to salvation through sanctification of the Spirit and belief of the truth: Whereunto he called you by our gospel, to the obtaining of the glory of our Lord Jesus Christ" (2 Thessalonians 2:13-14).

We must walk this road alone with the Son of the living God whose name is Jesus our Lord. Every knee shall bow to the Lord and every tongue shall confess to God that Jesus is Lord.

Scripture

Jesus tells us, *"For it is written, As I live, saith the Lord, Every knee SHALL bow to me, and every tongue SHALL confess to God. So then every one of us shall give account of himself to God"* (Romans 14:11-12).

Therefore, let us be obedient to the word of God and accept the Lord's plan for our salvation. This plan of God found in the Holy Bible covers us with the blood of Jesus who freely gave eternal life to all souls willing to accept him as Lord and Savior. Those who choose to develop their own imagination of what it takes to get to God's kingdom will all perish. There is only one way to God, and that is through Christ Jesus our Lord. This is not make-believe; it's a biblical fact. One day the glory of the Lord will shine unto all men and every soul will be convinced in their own heart that Jesus is God.

Scripture

"Thomas saith unto him, Lord, we know not wither thou goest; and how can we know the WAY? Jesus saith unto him, I AM the WAY, the TRUTH, and the LIFE: no man cometh unto the Father, but by me" (John 14:5, 6).

40) Did you know that the Lord's angels are waiting for the children of God to speak his holy written word over their earthly situations?

Scripture

The Bibles tells us, "To such as keep his covenant, and to those that remember his commandments to do them. The Lord hath prepared his throne in the heavens; and his kingdom ruleth over all. Bless the Lord, ye his angels that excel in strength, that do his commandments, hearkening unto the voice of his word. Bless ye the Lord, all his hosts; ye ministers of his that do his pleasure" (Psalm 103:18-21).

The word of God has all power. We as the righteousness of God through Christ Jesus have received power from the Holy Ghost. God's word comes alive in us when we place our faith in Jesus Christ. When we speak the word of God over our earthly situations, the heavenly host of angels will honor the voice of God. Therefore, every promise God has made to his people he will keep. All we have to do is speak the word and believe without doubt. Unfortunately, the same applies when we speak evil and wicked things. Satan's demonic host of spirit beings also ride upon the words spoken by the tongues of mankind. Therefore, be careful what you say at all times. Demonic spirits need a body to accomplish the will of their leader known as Satan. The willing earthen vessel of man causes Satan's will to also come alive in the earth's realm. The devil and his host cannot infiltrate the word of God when spoken by the tongue of man. However, we can give them power over us when we speak language they can use. This is how curses can be launched to and fro. Therefore, let us not open the door to demonic spirits. We must keep in mind that the Bible has already warned us that death and life is found in the tongues of man. Since we now understand the damage that our speech is capable of, let us always speak the words of the Lord and allow the heavenly host to operate in our lives.

41) Did you know that we as sons of God through Jesus Christ our Lord have more power than the devil? In this day and age, it appears that the presence of the devil causes fear to come upon this world. Whenever the subject arises, most people are not willing to entertain a conversation concerning this dreadful creature. Then you have those who believe that the devil does not exist at all. Satan and his demons are laughing at the souls of man that entertain this mentality. Then there is the born-again Christian that actually believes what the Holy Bible says. They know that Jesus has given the saints of God power over all the enemies of God. The original dominion that Adam lost to the devil in the Garden of Eden has been restored to all who believe in the risen Savior. Jesus tells us that not only did he behold Satan's fall from heaven as lightning, but he gave to the believers all power over this enemy.

Scripture

"And the seventy, (disciples) returned again with joy, saying, Lord even the devils are subject unto us through thy name. And he said unto them, I beheld Satan as lightning fall from heaven. Behold, I give unto you power to tread on serpents and scorpions, and over ALL THE POWER OF

THE ENEMY: and nothing shall by any means hurt you. Notwithstanding in this rejoice not, that the spirits are subject unto you; but rather rejoice because your names are written in heaven" (Luke 10:17 - 20).

Knowing this, we must recognize who we belong to here in the earth. We belong totally to God, and our citizenship is in the Lord's kingdom. This confirms what the Bible says about us being ambassadors for Christ. In order to be an ambassador, you must first be a loyal citizen of the kingdom you represent. Since our citizenship is now in heaven due to our rebirth, we are now servants and messengers of the most-high God. The earth is no longer our home. We died to this life when we accepted Jesus Christ as our Lord and Savior. Then we were born again by the Spirit of God. Now we have the total victory over this world.

42) Did you know that mankind must resist temptation at all cost? There are consequences either way—whether we resist or succumb to this thing called temptation.

Scripture

"Blessed is the man that endureth temptation: for when he is tried, he shall receive the crown of life, which the Lord hath promised to them that love him. Let no man say when he is tempted, I am tempted of God: for God cannot be tempted with evil, neither tempteth he any man: But every man is tempted, when he is drawn away of his own lust, and enticed. Then when lust hath conceived, it bringeth forth sin: and sin, when it is finished, bringeth forth DEATH" (James 1:14-15).

God knows that we live in a world of temptation to sin. The Lord is always looking out for his sons and daughters in the earth. The sin that is often successful at tempting man and woman is that one sin that each individual seems to have trouble with. In most cases, it varies from person to person. This is known as the BESETTING SIN. Therefore, avoid the avenue that leads to which ever besetting sin causes you to stumble. By doing so, you will cut temptation off at its path.

Scripture

The Bible tells us, *"There hath no temptation taken you but such as is common to man: but God is faithful, who will not suffer you to be tempted above that ye are able; but will with the temptation also make a way to escape, that ye may be able to bear it"* (1 Corinthians 10:13).

With this information, let us always look for the way of escape that our heavenly Father has faithfully provided for us. Remember, when Jesus was tempted in the wilderness, he resisted the devil by speaking the word of God as his chosen weapon. Since the weapons of our warfare are not carnal weapons to the pulling down of strongholds, we must use the preferred weapon of God to battle in this spiritual warfare. This weapon is called our sword, which is the holy word of God. We have to use the spoken word of God in order to be effective in this spiritual war. Jesus spoke to Satan every time he was tempted by saying, "IT IS WRITTEN," and then he quoted the Holy Scriptures. The devil had no choice at that point but to flee. There is Holy Ghost POWER in the word of God. This word is our sword that defeats the enemy of darkness. It is the <u>only weapon approved by God</u> that works against spiritual wickedness. All other worldly methods are useless and ineffective. They only caused mankind to be offended by one another and then ultimately separated. The devil likes it when men cannot come together. God said when mankind is on one accord, there is nothing they cannot accomplish.

Scripture

"And the Lord said, Behold, the people is one, and they have all one language; and this they begin to do: and now nothing will be restrained from them, which they have imagined to do" (Genesis 11:6).

This is the statement God made at the tower of Babel when man got together to build a tower to reach into the heavens. God recognized man's intent and felt it necessary to come down and confound their language. The Lord also scattered mankind across the whole earth. This was the true beginning of the different nations of men. The one human race of God's people was scatter due to their sinful nature inherited from Adam. Their power was quenched so that their evil imagination would not be accomplished. Man has power when there is unity. The devil knows this. Why do you think there is so much racism in the world today? Evil mankind has fed into the enemies plan to separate themselves. Even though, we all came from the loins of Adam, the first man. Today, some of us act as if God created each group of people separate for the purspose of building up oneself. Why else who anyone feel the need to purify their so called race? Anyone who feels this way has been deceived by the enemy and living in darkness ever now. Anyone who feels in their heart that they need to strengthen their particular race is fulfilling the will of Satan. Anyone who only cares for their particular ethinic group of people is serving the enemy of darkness and has no truth. We are our brother's keeper. Jesus commanded us to love one another, not just our respective groups. We must read and believe the word of God. There we will find the truth, and the truth will always make us free. Remember, when mankind fails to use his sword, which is the word of God, total deliverance will never come. Have you ever wondered why this world is still fighting the same issues centuries after centuries with no forward progress when it comes to peace in the Middle East? Man has forgotten about God. They act as if they are really going to solve the world's problems. Has it ever entered into your mind why the nation of Israel is still standing strong, dispite the many annihilation attempts made against them? It doesn't take a rocket scientist to figure out God is with the children of Israel. You really need to study the Holy Bible. The children of Israel cannot be destroyed by mankind as long as God has his precious hand upon them.

Scripture

"In that day will I make the governors of Judah like a hearth (hot spot) of fire among the wood, and like a torch of fire in a sheaf (bound together): and they shall devour all the people round about, on the right hand and on the left: and Jerusalem shall be inhabited again in her own place, even in Jerusalem" (Zechariah 12:6).

"In that day shall the Lord defend the inhabitants of Jerusalem; and he that is feeble among them at that day shall be as David; and the house of David shall be as God, as the Angel of the Lord before them. And it

shall come to past in that day, that I will seek to DESTROY ALL THE NATIONS that come against Jerusalem" (Zechariah 12:8, 9).

The Lord is forever with his chosen people. Regardless of the hatred expressed toward the nation of Israel over the centuries, the true and living God protects Jacobs's seed, which are the twelve tribes of Israel. Remember, there are only two sides when it comes to what God has created. The Lord has the right side and the devil has the wrong side. To all religions practiced in this world today, remember this important bit of information. This is called the acid test. Will your belief system stand up under the acid test?

Scripture

"Who is a liar but he that denieth that Jesus is the Christ? He is antichrist, that denieth the Father and the Son. Whosoever denieth the Son, the same hath not the Father: {but} he that acknowledgeth the Son hath the Father also" (1 John 2:22, 23).

"That all men should honour the Son, even as they honour the Father. He that honoureth not the Son honoureth not the Father which hath sent him" (John 5:23).

Those who oppose the Lord's side are automatically placed in the hands of the enemy. The true and living God being referred to here is the God of Abraham, Issac and Jacob. I am not referring to the many false gods worshiped among men in this day and age. Remember, the Holy Bible is the word of God he has given to us for our weapon of choice. Therefore, never leave home without it.

43) Did you know that some religions only honor the Old Testament version of the Holy Bible while disregarding the entire New Testament Scripture? However, those of us who trust and believe in the word of God also know how to recognize the many signs of the coming Messiah. Jesus the Christ is prophesied all through the Old Testament scriptures. The book of Isaiah even prophesied concerning his virgin birth. For this reason, no one should have doubted or disbelieved his appearance into the earthly realm.

The reason why the Pharisees during that time chose not to believe is because they had hatred in their hearts which blinded their eyes to the glory of God. The only way God will come unto men is when they accept his only begotten Son Jesus who was the living sacrifice for the sins of the world.

Scripture

Jesus said, *"He that hateth me hateth my Father also"* (John 15:23).

"Jesus answered and said unto him, If a man love me, he will keep my words: and my Father will love him, <u>and WE WILL COME UNTO HIM</u>, and make our abode with him" (John 14:23).

Therefore, you cannot have God the Father without having Jesus the Son. This statement is for the souls who feel in their heart and mind that they can separate the two. Here is another example of how great kings during the Old Testament spoke of seeing God in the form of the God-head while present in the earth's realm. The Lord Jesus was mentioned all through the Old Testament as the Son of God or the Son of Man. King Nebuchadnezzar spoke these words.

Scripture

"He answered and said, Lo I see four men loose, walking in the midst of the fire, and they have no hurt; and the form of the fourth is like the Son of God (Jesus)" (Daniel 3:25).

"I saw in the night visions, and, behold, one like the Son of man came with the clouds of heaven, and came to the ancient of days, and they brought him near before him. And there was given him dominion, and glory, and a kingdom, that all people, nations, and languages, should serve him: his dominion is an everlasting dominion, which shall not pass away, and his kingdom that which shall not be destroyed" (Daniel 7:13-14).

"Therefore the Lord himself shall give you a sign; Behold, a virgin shall conceive, and bear a Son, and shall call his name Immanuel" (Isaiah 7:14).

The name Immanuel is a symbolic name which means God with us—the incarnate Son of God walking in the flesh or was made flesh. Anyone seeking God with a pure heart, unlike the Pharisees, will clearly see that mankind had to be freed from sin in the same state in which he committed the act. Man sinned in the flesh; he had to be delivered in the flesh. This clearly explains why it was necessary for God to be manifested in an earthen vessel and appear unto men.

Scripture

"For unto us a child is born, unto us a Son is given: and the government shall be upon his shoulder: and his name shall be called Wonderful, Counselor, The Mighty God, The everlasting Father, The Prince of Peace" (Isaiah 9:6).

"Who hath believed our report? And to whom is the arm of the Lord revealed? For he shall grow up before him as a tender plant, and as a root out of a dry ground: he hath no form nor comeliness; and when we shall see him, there is no beauty that we should desire him. He is despised and rejected of men; a man of sorrows, and acquainted with grief: and we hid as it were our faces from him; he was despised, and we esteemed him not. Surely he hath borne our griefs, and carried our sorrows: yet we did esteem him stricken, smitten of God, and afflicted. But he was wounded for our transgressions, he was bruised for our iniquities: the chastisement of our peace was upon him; and with his stripes we are healed" (Isaiah 53:1-5).

The book of Isaiah was prophesied over 700 years prior to our Lord Jesus arriving on the scene. These scriptures were clearly written in the Old Testament prior to the birth of the Savior Jesus the Christ. The Bible further tells us in the first book of Psalms, Chapter 22 titled, "The Psalms of the Cross."

Scripture

"I am poured out like water, and all my bones are out of joint: my heart is like wax; it is melted in the midst of my bowels. My strength is dried up like a potsherd; and my tongue cleaveth to my jaws; and thou hast brought me into the dust of death. For dogs have compassed me: the assembly of the wicked have enclosed me: <u>they pierced my hands and feet</u>. I may tell all my bones: they look and stare upon me. They part my garments among them, and cast lots upon my vesture. But be not thou far from me, O Lord: O my strength, hast thee to help me" (Psalm 22:14-19).

The book of Psalms prophesied Jesus on the cross and how he would suffer over a thousand years before the actual event took place. Therefore, all religions that teach against Jesus as the Messiah and allegedly believe exclusively the Old Testament scriptures are deceived. They are depriving themselves of an opportunity to embrace the only true Savior of this world. It all boils down to this, if you do not know Jesus, you do not know God!

44) Did you know that we should never use the Lord our God's name in a vain way or vain expression? God is HOLY. When we speak concerning our Creator, we must reverence his Holy name anytime it rolls off our tongue. When we use God's name frivolously, we belittle the very God that holds our daily breath in his hand. We must always glorify the Lord and hold him in high regard. How many times have we heard someone refer to the Lord as the man upstairs? Remember, God is the Creator of the heavens and earth. He must be reverenced and glorified at all times. This is a clear indication that the person who refers to God in such a manner does not really know him intimately. We must magnify our Lord, always remembering that God is a holy God. He is entitled to all reverence, honor, glory and praise being the sovereign Creator of us all.

Scripture

"Thou shalt not take the name of the Lord thy God in vain: for the Lord will not hold him guiltless that taketh his name in vain" (Exodus 20:7).

This verse is the third commandment given by God to his servant Moses for the children of Israel. Be very careful when you speak concerning God and the use of his name. When the name of I AM, GOD, LORD, JESUS, JEHOVAH, ELOHIM, EL SHADDAD, EL EL YUN, or any name which refers to the Creator of the universe is spoken, we should remember he is HOLY. We should never forget it. Keeping in mind, God is the sustainer of life. Without him our life would be over. God is the one who redeemed our lives from death, hell and the grave when Jesus was resurrected. Remember, we must always come up to God's level. He should not be expected to come down to ours! When man creates a universe of his very own, then he can be the sovereign ruler over what he has created. However, until then, let us give God the respect and admiration that only he deserves as the true and sovereign Lord, maker of all things.

Scripture

"For my thoughts are not your thoughts, neither are your ways my ways, saith the Lord. For as the heavens are higher than the earth, so are my ways higher than your ways, and my thoughts than your thoughts" (Isaiah 55:8-9).

Let us exalt the Lord in all that we do as we continue to lift him up, for he is worthy to receive royal praise and honor from all nations, tribes and kindreds.

45) Did you know when we judge our brothers and sisters we condemn ourselves? There are so many individuals who enjoy being judgmental toward others. It's almost like a germ or a bad habit. The Bible warns us of this ungodly behavior. When Christians behave this way, it does more harm than good.

Scripture

"Therefore thou art inexcusable, O man, whosoever thou art that judgest: for wherein thou judgest another, thou CONDEMNEST thyself; for thou that judgest doest the same things. But we are sure that the judgment of God is according to truth against them which commit such things. And

thinkest thou this, O man, that judgest them which do such things, and doest the same, that thou shalt escape the judgment of God" (Romans 2:1-3).

Therefore, be wise, the Bible tells us when pertaining to false prophets, that we will know them by their fruits. This statement explains that one's behavior, speech, blessings and doctrine they proclaim will reveal the true nature of that person. We must show mercy and compassion toward our brothers and sisters. Remember we serve a God that shows us mercy and compassion even when we do not deserve it. God wants us to love one another, not judge one another. By loving each other, and praying for one another, this act of love causes unity among men. And when men unite, God is very well pleased. Remember, Satan wants to drive a wedge between the unities of mankind. Human beings are God's favorite creation. This makes the devil extremely mad because there is no hope for him. We are our brother's keeper here in the earth. When we dwell with our Lord in the new heaven, there will be one body of Christ. Man will no longer look down on his brothers and sisters. While in the earth, let us lift up one another instead of putting each other down and pointing our fingers. When we behave like this, we act like the devil. Remember, he is the accuser of the brethren, the original finger pointer. All men are in need of Jesus the Savior. Those who still continue to judge others have chosen not to walk in obedience to God. When we are eager to point out the sins of others, this means we are blinded to our own sins. There will come a time when the saints will judge the world. We must first be transformed from flesh to spirit. This will occur when we receive our glorified bodies in Christ Jesus. Then we will return with the Savior to judge the wickedness of this world, but not until then. Therefore, stop judging one another, for the Lord commanded it.

Scripture

"Do ye not know that the saints shall judge the world? And if the world shall be judged by YOU, are ye unworthy to judge the smallest matters? Know ye not that we shall judge angels? How much more things that pertain to this life" (1 Corinthians 6:2, 3)?

Jesus tells us, *"**But that which ye have already hold fast till I come. And he that overcometh, and keepeth my works unto the end, to him will I give power over the nations**"* (Revelation 2:25-26).

There are a few types of judgments that the children of God should be aware of. There is such a thing as judging the many situations that life has to offer. This is not judging with condemnation like the Bible speaks of, however, we have to judge everyday matters that concern us. For example, we have to judge whether things are good or bad for us.

We have to judge ones character based on the fruits that they bear.
We have to judge spoken words to make sure they line up with the word of God.
We have to judge behavior to determine whether or not its godly behavior.
We have to judge belief systems to determine whether or not fellowship can be established.

These are just a few examples of how we may have to judge small matters in order to remain strong in our Christian walk. This will keep us from being deceived by the enemy. Therefore, know that we do not judge to condemn our brother's deeds; however we do judge the many situations in life which will determine its true intention. This is accomplished when a born-again Christian believer has received spiritual discernment from God. Jesus lets us know that the obedient believer will also be given a reward of power and authority in the millennial kingdom as we reign with Christ.

46) Did you know if you shut God out of your mind, he may give you over to a reprobate mind? There are several definitions to describe the term reprobate. Webster's New World Dictionary defines the word reprobate in this manner. To disapprove of strongly; condemn, rejecting and abandoning as beyond salvation, rejected by God; excluded from salvation and lost in sin.

Without God, we are totally lost and dead to sin. If you have a reprobate mind, then you love and condone your sinful behavior. You want no part of the true and living God because it will interfere with your lustful desires. However, grace and mercy is available to the souls who are willing to turn back to God. God gives the invitation to turn to him, and he will then turn unto you.

Scripture

The Bible tells us, *"Professing themselves to be wise, they became fools"* (Romans 1:22).

"Wherefore God also gave them up to uncleanness through the lusts of their own hearts, to dishonor their own bodies between themselves: Who changed the truth of God into a lie, and worshiped and served the creature (Satan) more that the CREATOR (God), who is blessed for ever Amen" (Romans 1:24-25).

"And even as they did not like to retain God in their knowledge, God gave them over to a reprobate mind, to do those things which are not convenient; Being filled with all unrighteousness, fornication, wickedness, covetousness, maliciousness; full of envy, murder, debate, deceit, malignity; whisperers, backbiters, haters of God, despiteful, proud, boasters, inventors of evil things, disobedient to parents, Without understanding, covenant breakers, without natural affection, implacable, unmerciful: Who knowing the judgment of God, that they which commit such things are WORTHY of DEATH, not only do the same, but have pleasure in them that do them" (Romans 1:28-32).

These scriptures explain that God gave them all up. God will also give you up if you refuse to have faith in his holy word. God lets them do what they want to do which causes them to be lost and damned. God withdraws his gracious help because they rejected his mercy. They were blinded not because God withdrew his light, but because they loved darkness rather than light. Every ungodly act of behavior mentioned in the book of Romans, Chapter

1 verse 29 through 31 should never be named among the saints of God. The last thing you should ever want in life is to be given up on by your heavenly Father. The Lord gave them over to the natural result of their unbelief and their sinful lifestyles. When you choose to follow a lie, then you begin to walk in conformity to that lie. We have been given the truth in the holy word of God, therefore, turn from the lie that the enemy brings and receive eternal life in Christ Jesus.

God Gave Them Up to Three Kinds of Rejected Lifestyles

1) God gave them up to all forms of uncleanness and its consequences.
2) God gave them up to all forms of sexual depravity and its consequences.
3) God gave them over to a mind that would not retain him in its knowledge and its consequences.

Therefore, seek God with all of your heart now while he can be found. Remember, God will never leave us nor forsake us if we have faith in him. We are the ones who always end up leaving the presence of God. All we have to do is come to ourselves like the prodigal son. In other words, wake up and turn from our wicked ways, REPENT and come to Christ Jesus before it's too late. Remember, those who forsake and reject God from their lives have no hope beyond this life! Whatever state you are in whether you are rich or poor, when you take your last breath, will determine your destiny. Whatever you thought about during the time you had life will no longer matter anymore. The only thing that will matter is whether or not you accepted Jesus Christ as your personal Savior and Lord before you took your last breath. Therefore, seek the perfect will of God and not the lust of your flesh.

47) Did you know that the Bible tells us that angels occasionally appear and walk among men in the earth? The Bible tells us to be careful when entertaining strangers, for we just might have the opportunity to entertain an angel and not know it. This is a very valuable warning.

Scripture

"Let brotherly love continue. Be not forgetful to entertain strangers: for thereby some have entertained angels unawares" (Hebrews 13:2).

This verse reminds us that we have to be careful how we treat strangers. In the book of Genesis, Chapter 18 tells us that the patriarch Abraham was visited by three angels in the form of strangers, one being the Angel of the Lord.

Scripture

The verse reads, *"And the LORD appeared unto him in the plains of Mamre: and sat in the tent door in the heat of the day; And he lift up his eyes and looked, and lo, three men stood by him: and when he saw them, he ran to meet them from the tent door, and bowed himself toward the ground, And said, My Lord, if now I have found favor in thy sight, pass not away, I pray thee, from thy servant"* (Genesis 18:1-3).

Abraham showed hospitality toward these angels dressed as strange men with one being the Angel of the Lord. They stopped by to visit with Abraham on their way to destroy that sinful city known as Sodom and Gomorrah. While there with Abraham, the Lord promised Abraham's wife Sarah a male child according to the time of life. The Angel of the Lord eventually ended up by telling Abraham that nothing is too hard for God.

Scripture

"Is anything too hard for the Lord? At the time appointed I will return unto thee, according to the time of life, and Sarah shall have a son" (Genesis 18:14).

The Angel of the Lord after visiting with Abraham sent two angels to the city of Sodom to destroy both the cities of Sodom and Gomorrah. The cities wickedness was before the Lord. The two angels appeared and met Abraham's nephew Lot, who was sitting in the gate to the city. Lot showed hospitality toward the two angels who were in the form of men. Lot took the two angels to his home to show hospitality and protect them from the cities pretators.

Shortly afterwards, the wicked male pretators of the city wanted Lot to release the two men they had seen enter his house. The wicked men of the city wanted to have sex with the two male strangers. Lot attempted to protect the two angels by offering his two virgin daughters instead. The wicked perverted men of the city refused Lot's offer. Then the angels that were with Lot blinded the wicked men of the city as they tried to take them by force. The angels from the Lord instructed Lot to take his family and immediately leave the city and warned him and his family not to look back. Most of us know what happened next. Lot's wife could not leave sin behind, therefore, she looked back. The Bible tells us that she turned into a pillar of salt. This salt statue can probably still be seen today if we knew exactly where to look. As for the wicked twin cities, they were both totally destroyed by fire and brimstone which rained down from heaven. No one survived the destruction of Sodom and Gomorrah except Lot and his two daughters. Therefore, be careful how you treat strangers. You never know when the Lord will send you a ministering angel to assist you in whatever need you may be facing. God takes care of those who put their total trust in him.

48) Did you know that God hates divorce? When couples, male and female join their lives in holy matrimony, they establish a blood covenant with the Lord. All covenants require the shedding of blood in order to be enforced. That is why it is God's commandment that couples maintain themselves by abstaining from fornication prior to marriage. This will fulfill the shedding of blood once the marriage is consummated. God hates for his children to divorce and walk away from their marriage covenant. Ask yourself a question. Were you aware that you made a binding blood covenant with God when you entered into your marriage?

Scripture

"Yet ye say, Wherefore? Because the Lord hath been witness between thee and the wife of thy youth; against whom thou hast dealt treacherously: yet is she thy companion, and the wife of thy covenant. And did not he make one? Yet had he the residue of the spirit. And wherefore one? That he might seek godly seed. Therefore take heed to your spirit, and let none deal treacherously against the wife of his youth. For the Lord, the God of Israel, saith that HE HATETH PUTTING AWAY: for one covereth

violence with his garment, saith the Lord of Hosts: therefore take heed to your spirit that ye deal not treacherously" (Malachi 2:14-16).

The scriptures tell us that the Lord witnesses our joining to one another from above. In other words, God remembers our covenant spouse, even when we may want to forget. He warns us about dealing treacherously with the wife of our youth. God reminds us of the blood covenant we made with him and how he made us one flesh. We are to offer up godly seed unto the Lord by teaching our children about his saving grace. God tells us he HATES DIVORCE, which is the putting away of one another. Let us look to the Lord and stop attempting to develop our selfish individuality. God has joined two souls together as one. We can no longer be concerned with just ourselves any longer. Thank God for his grace and mercy he extends to the ones who have committed sin in this area. Those who repent and turn back to the Lord shall be forgiven.

Scripture

Jesus tells us, *"It hath been said, whosoever shall put away his wife, let him give her a writing of divorcement: But I say unto you, That whosoever shall put away his wife, saving for the cause of fornication, causeth her to commit adultery: and whosoever shall marry her that is divorced committeth adultery"* (Matthew 5:31,32).

The Bible tells us that from the beginning divorce was never authorized. Moses suffered them to put away their wives due to the hardness of their own hearts, as Jesus says in Matthew 19:8, but from the beginning it was not so.

Scripture

Jesus said, *"For there are some eunuchs, which were so born from their mother's womb: and there are some eunuchs, which were made eunuchs of men: and there be eunuchs, which have made themselves eunuchs for the kingdom of heaven's sake. He that is able to receive it, let him receive it"* (Matthew 19:12).

Jesus explains that it is God's intention for us to marry only once and remain with the wife of our youth. Those who cannot fulfill this should remain unmarried as eunuchs. Divorce should never be encouraged or suggested as a solution to what appears to be a problem. Remember, the devil is a deceiver. If we are not careful, we will ignore the word of God and cater to the desires of our flesh. We must realize that some should marry and others should not. All men cannot receive this truth that some are called to be married and remain married; others who cannot accept this are called not to marry at all. Remember, what causes a spouse to throw in the towel and want the marriage ended is the hardness of their heart. When you have two people wanting to go in different directions, a marriage cannot stand. Always remember, together we stand, divided we fall. We all have the same choice to walk together in agreement. Whenever a marriage fails, there will always be consequences to pay. Divorce never affects just the husband and the wife. All family members and even some relatives feel the pain when a divorce occurs. Whatever goes wrong in this world, God can fix it. The problem in most cases, people do not want their lives fixed. They want to start over with someone new. More than likely they have already picked out their new mate prematurely. They have chosen sin rather than looking to the Lord for the right solution. When one person wants a divorce and the other person does not, there is always sin in the midst. This generally indicates that one is willing to listen to the voice of God, and the other is rejecting what the holy word says.

Scripture

"Can two walk together, except they be agreed" (Amos 3:3)?

Married couples are deemed one flesh in the eyes of God. Therefore, they must walk together and come to an agreement on all matters. The word of God must be their guide. When a man and a woman share divine love toward one another, their relationship seems effortless. Only when selfishness is allowed to fester, will situations get to the point of no return. Divine love for one another will always cause us to put others before ourselves, just as Christ did when he hung on that rugged cross on our behalf.

49) Did you know that God can do any and all things? The one and only God of the universe, the God of all creation, the God of Abraham, Isaac and Jacob, our heavenly Father, the same God spoken of in the Holy Bible. That is the God I am referring to. God is bigger than any problem we could ever have or face. God takes care of his children here in the earth. Any form of sickness and disease, God can heal us. Any type of problem, God can solve it. Any level of captivity, bondage, or addiction, God can deliver us. Any need we may be facing, God will provide for us. God is our source. He provides all of our needs according to his riches in glory. Therefore, nothing is too hard for God. Is the Lord your Shepherd?

Scripture

"But my God SHALL supply all your needs according to his riches in glory <u>by Christ Jesus</u>" (Philippians 4:19).

The most important thing we can do for God is to obey his holy word. God can do anything but fail. God was merciful to mankind in the midst of a sinful world. God thought enough of his creation to freely give us the gift of salvation through Jesus Christ our Lord and Savior.

Scripture

"For I am not ashamed of the gospel of Christ: for it is the power of God unto salvation to everyone that believeth; to the Jew first, and also to the Greek" (Romans 1:16).

Therefore, based on what our Lord and Savior did for us on the cross, let us be very willing to proclaim the gospel of Jesus Christ to every nation. Let us make it our mission to bring all souls to the kingdom of God. The Lord God will wash and clean up the souls of man. All they have to do is believe in their heart and confess with their mouth that Jesus is Lord. This is called the good news of the gospel of Jesus Christ.

50) Did you know that God forbid the children of Israel to marry and link themselves up with other heathen nations? Many ethnic groups misunderstood this information to mean protect your heritage. The only thing God is interested in protecting is brotherly love for his covenant people. There is nothing in the Holy Bible that encouraged racism when it comes to marriage or interacting with one another. The devil is a liar. Only evil wicked men with hatred in their heart chose to teach something so sinister. God tells us not to be unevenly yoked with unbelievers. This clearly means do not marry heathens who worship idols. They will lead you from the presence of the Lord and cause you to be drawn to their perverted way of thinking. God knows that man whom he created is easily influenced by others. The Lord wanted the children of Israel to stay separated from other nations due to the influence of learned behavior. For example, if you hang around cannibals, the next thing you know, you, too, will soon place human beings on your menu. Even today, we must understand, you have the church, and then there is the world. We have a choice who we will serve. The meaning of church in the Greek language is, THE CALLED-OUT ONES. What it really boils down to is believers and nonbelievers—God's side or Satan's side. When it comes to the Lord, there are only two sides—good and evil. Race, ethnicity, nations, tribes and tongues have nothing to do with it. God the Father knows what all Christians eventually learn. We as human beings quickly adapt to our environment and whatever surroundings we choose for ourselves. God knows that if we allow ourselves to associate with worshipers of idols and false gods, it's just a matter of time that we too will adapt to their belief system. This is referred to as the monkey-see-monkey-do syndrome. Therefore, we have to be careful where we go, who we associate with, and what we practice. Let us desire to be like our Savior Jesus the Christ. Then we can learn to properly lead and make correct decisions for ourselves.

Scripture

"Let this mind be in you, which was also in Christ Jesus" (Philippians 2:5):

We must learn all the ways of God. We must seek to be different from the crowd/world. When we learn to have the same mind as our Lord and Savior, then we will be able to walk upright before God without stumbling. Pay no attention what the world thinks as a whole. Jesus reminds us that, "He that is not with me is against me; and he that gathers not with me scatters abroad."

All the ways of man seems right in his own mind, even when his ways are completely wrong.

Scripture

"He that is not with me is against me; and he that gathereth not with me scattereth abroad" (Matthew 12:30).

"All the ways of a man are clean in his own eyes; but the Lord weigheth the spirits" (Proverbs 16:2).

"There is a way which seemeth right unto a man; but the end thereof are the ways of death" (Proverbs 14:12).

The truth is man is wrong most of the time. If you are reading this, then it's talking about you. That can be real sad when a person is dead wrong and they do not have a clue. This is why we have to trust in the Lord and lean not to our own limited understanding. The bottom line is it only matters in the end what God has to say. The sooner we are awakened to this truth, the faster we will grow in our Christian walk.

51) Did you know that history has taught us over the years that it is <u>not</u> always safe in following the crowd? If the majority of people are doing one thing, be leery, it may be safer to try something different. Time has taught us over the years that normally when God is involved, there are usually only a few in numbers. Remember the Lord's servant Noah, the builder of the ark. He was a preacher in his day. The fact that it had never rained before on the earth, no one believed that it was going to rain in a dry desert. Noah, a righteous preacher, and a servant of the Lord had very little influence over the masses of people inhabiting the earth. God ended up saving Noah's immediate family which consisted of eight souls, plus all the specified animals God brought into Noah's ark. All other creation on the earth was destroyed, with the exception of the fish and sea creatures that were in the water. They were not destroyed according to the word of God. No one but Noah's family, the specified animals inside the ark and the fish of the sea survived the great flood. Noah's church congregation never got larger than eight souls. During the 120 years that it took to complete the ark, Noah did not convert one soul outside his immediate family. This goes to show you that it's not always about the size. Therefore, when you see large crowds of souls gathered together in fellowship, this does not necessary mean that the God is there. It's not always about the size of the congregation. For this reason, Men of God should stop allowing themselves to be puffed up by asking the vain question of, "How many are you running?" This statement is often referring to how many members are in ones congregation. It sort of reminds you of the question, "What type of car do you drive?" Often prideful men will ask the question in an attempt to size each other up. We should never compare ourselves with other, for this is the work of the enemy. The only one we should emulate is JESUS! Anyone who would ask such a thing should examine themselves very closely because pride has crepted in. Remember the trouble King David got into when he counted the children of Israel when his kingdom was enlarged. King David's count was probably considered an opportunity to establish ground for boasting. This is why it was wrong in the eyes of God.

Scripture

> *"For the king said to Joab the captain of the host, which was with him, Go now through all the tribes of Israel, from Dan even to Beer-sheba and number ye the people, that I may know the number of the people. And Joab said unto the king, Now the Lord thy God add unto the people, how many soever they be, a hundredfold, and that the eyes of my lord the king may see it: but WHY doth my lord the king delight in this thing"* (2 Samuel 24:2, 3)?

The response of King David's captain should have given him a clue that what he was requesting was oddly strange. Joab inquired to the king why he wanted to know such a thing. However, for whatever reason, King David was persistent. After the count which took nine months and twenty days to complete. The final numbers were given to King David. By this time, King David really felt bad in his heart. What he did not anticipate was the punishment that the Lord was about to inflict.

Scripture

"And David's heart smote him after he had numbered the people. And David said unto the Lord, I have sinned greatly in that I have done: and now, I beseech thee, O Lord, take away the iniquity of thy servant; for I have done very foolishly. For when David was up in the morning, the word of the Lord came unto the prophet Gad, David's seer saying, Go and say unto David, Thus saith the Lord, I offer thee THREE things; choose thee one of them, that I may do it unto thee. So Gad came to David, and told him, and said unto him, Shall seven years of famine come unto thee in thy land?

Or wilt thou flee three months before thine enemies, while they pursue thee?

Or that there be three days pestilence in thy land?

Now advise, and see what answer I shall return to him that sent me. And David said unto Gad, I am in a great strait: let us fall now unto the hand of the Lord; for his mercies are great: and let me not fall into the hand of man. So the Lord sent a pestilence upon Israel from the morning even to the time appointed: and there died of the people from Dan even to beer-sheba SEVENTY THOUSAND MEN. And when the angel stretched out his hand upon Jeruslaem to destroy it, the Lord repented him of the evil, and said to the angel that destroyed the people, IT IS ENOUGH: stay now thine hand. And the angel of the Lord was by the threshing place of Araunah the Jebusite. And David spake unto the Lord when he saw the angel that smote the people, and said, Lo, I have sinned, and I have done wickedly: but these sheep, what have they done? Let thine hand, I pray thee, be against me, and against my father's house" (2 Samuel 24:10-17).

King David offered a plea for his people and asked the Lord to harm his house instead. God heard David's plea and told the prophet Gad to tell David to build an altar. Gad gave David instruction to build the altar where the angel of the Lord stayed his hand. This happened to be at the house of Araunah the Jebusite, which was the king's servant. King David purchased the land and built an altar unto the Lord. David offered a burnt offering and a peace offering which satisfied the Lord. We must avoid pride at all cost. King David was reminded by God that his job was to care for the sheep placed under his control. Not to be so concerned about his level of greatness. Therefore, let us not be so concerned with the number of followers, as oppsed to whom and what they have chosen to follow! The Bible describes the way of the Lord as being straight. However, the way of the sinner is described as being very wide. Let us be careful who we follow and for what reason we follow them.

Scripture

> *"Enter ye in at the strait gate: for wide is the gate, and broad is the way, that leadeth to destruction, and many there be which go in there at: Because strait is the gate, and narrow is the way, which leadeth unto life, and __FEW__ there be that find it"* (Matthew 7:13,14).

The Bible confirms this theory. Always be leery of large crowds. When the majority is in agreement, be cautious. Seek the true and living word of God and learn the narrow way that leads to everlasting life.

52) Did you know that we have proof that demons knew who Jesus Christ was while he was in the earth's realm? Many souls in the earth whether they are Christians or not take pride in knowing the word of God. We must realize that Satan knows the word of God better than we do. As a matter of fact, he knows it very well. Before he got kicked out of heaven, he lived by the will of God. Therefore, just knowing what the word of God says means very little by itself. The question is do you believe the word of God enough to actually live by it? Satan loves to operate contrary to the will of God on purpose. He is the adversary. He despises everything about the Lord. If we want to be counted special in the eyes of God, we have to love his word and take pleasure in obeying the same. It is not enough to just know the word of God; you must have an understanding and a willingness to obey his word. Therefore, never brag on yourself regarding how much you know about the Holy Bible. If you know what it says and refuse to obey, you have a spirit of rejection, similar to the enemies of God. Remember, they reject the will of God by choice. We as men and women in the earth are created in the image and likeness of God; therefore, we at least want to be above God's enemies.

This next verse of scripture described how a demon that possessed a man recognized Jesus as God in his earthen vessel.

Scripture

"And in the synagogue, there was a man which had a spirit of an unclean devil, and cried out with a loud voice, Saying, Let us alone; what have we to do with thee, thou Jesus of Nazareth? <u>ART THOU COME TO DESTROY US? I KNOW THEE WHO THOU ART; THE HOLY ONE OF GOD.</u> And Jesus rebuked him, saying, <u>HOLD THY PEACE</u>, and come out of him. And when the devil had thrown him in the midst, he came out of him, and hurt him not" (Luke 4:33-35).

Notice in this scripture, the unclean devil referred to Jesus as the Holy One <u>OF</u> God. Notice that the devil did not say the Holy One <u>FROM</u> God. The Bible tells us Jesus is the only one which came from heaven. Jesus explained to the Pharisees in this next verse that they were of the earth and could not comprehend where he was from. Jesus had the blood of God in his veins when he walked among men in the earth.

Scripture

Jesus said, *"And he said unto them, ye are from beneath; I am from above: ye are of this world; I am not of this world"* (John 8:23).

Apostle John said, *"He that cometh from above is ABOVE ALL: he that is of the earth is earthly, and speaketh of the earth: he that cometh from heaven is ABOVE ALL"* (John 3:31).

The Pharisees knew that only God has the power to forgive sin. This just confirms who the Lord Jesus was when he was here in the earth and who he currently is now. The Pharisees had much trouble with this truth due to the hatred and pride lodged deep within their hearts.

Jesus told the Pharisees, **"Whether is easier to say, Thy sins be forgiven thee; or to say, rise up and walk? But that ye may know that the**

Son of Man hath power upon earth to forgive sins, he said unto the sick of the palsy, I say unto thee, Arise, and take up thy couch, and go into thine house. And immediately he rose up before them, and took up that whereon he lay, and departed to his own house, glorifying God" (Luke 5:23-25).

We must remember that demons and devils know Jesus as the Holy One, which is God Almighty. Mankind can and will be influenced by evil spirits from time to time. However, when we serve the Lord with our whole heart, mind and soul, we leave no room for anything demonic to enter in.

53) Did you know that this beautiful world God spoke into existence is still a spiritual mystery to all who reject him? In order to learn the truth which Jesus said would set us free, we must be willing to receive the wisdom and knowledge only found in the Holy Bible. The Holy Scriptures teach us that unless we believe and seek the Lord, we cannot know his perfect will. The Bible describes such a person as a NATURAL MAN—one who lacks the knowledge, wisdom and belief in God.

Scripture

"But the NATURAL MAN receiveth not the things of the Spirit of God: for they are foolishness unto him: neither can he know them, because they are spiritually discerned" (1 Corinthians 2:14).

"But we speak the wisdom of God in a mystery, even the hidden wisdom, which God ordained before the world unto our glory. Which none of the princes of this world knew: for had they known it, they would not have crucified the Lord of Glory" (1 Corinthians 2:7, 8).

In this particular verse, princes of this world refer to Satan, his demonic host and all souls influenced by him. In the book of Genesis, the Angel of the Lord referred to Jacob as a prince having power with the Lord and men. The spirit of Satan influenced the hearts and minds of the wicked temple Pharisees. If Satan had only known God's plan, he would not have been so eager to crucify the Son of God. This act of grace and mercy given by God allowed mankind to be free forever from the stain of sin. All we have to do is believe in our heart and confess with our mouth the risen Savior who is Jesus the Christ, and we all will be saved. The devil is extremely mad about this, however, there is nothing he can do about it.

54) Did you know that if we seek the kingdom of God and all his righteousness, he will add all things unto us? The scripture that refers to this statement lets us know that the more we seek things, and not God, we will never be satisfied. This is very true in the world we currently live in. There is only one thing that can fill that empty void that we all have, and that is the love of God. When we seek God above all things, keeping him first, he gives us all the things that the world seeks—in other words, the desires of our heart will overtake us. The key is, when we delight ourselves in the things of God, all of our godly desires are provided by the Lord.

Scripture

"Therefore take no thought, saying, What shall we eat? Or, What shall we drink? Or, Wherewithal shall we be clothed? (For after all these things do the Gentiles seek :) for your heavenly Father knoweth that ye have need of all these things? But seek ye first the kingdom of God, and his righteousness; and all these things shall be added unto you. Take therefore no thought for the morrow: for the morrow shall take thought for the things of itself. Sufficient unto the day is the evil thereof" (Matthew 6:31-34).

The Lord Jesus is telling us that we should not put much thought into what we should eat, drink, or wear. The world seeks all of these things first. God knows what we are in need of and he cares for the needs of those who love him. God reminds us to seek him first and foremost. This is the order of the Lord. When we seek God and his righteousness, he showers us with many blessings. When we do the opposite by seeking the things before seeking God, those things get farther and farther away from us. Haven't you noticed? Then we have the verse of scripture that tells us not to worry about tomorrow because tomorrow will take care of itself. Each day has its share of evilness within. We are to address it as it comes and not worry about it prematurely.

Scripture

"The eyes of the Lord are in every place, beholding the evil and the good" (Proverbs 15:3).

"For the eyes of the Lord are over the righteous and his ears are open unto their prayers: But the face of the Lord is against them that do evil" (1 Peter 3:12).

God sees everything mankind does in the earth. There is nothing hidden from his eyes. The righteous souls God watches over and hears every word when they pray. To the evil doer, God sets his face against them. Remember, God is always watching us wheresoever we are and whatsoever we are doing. There are no hiding places from the eyes of the Lord. Remember this truth the very next time you call yourself being secretive when it comes to sinful behavior.

55) Did you know that man was created by God for his own pleasure? Mankind was created to worship the Lord. God told us to be fruitful and multiply. God wanted us to train up godly seed in order to continue the practice of holy worship toward him. When we fail to train our seed in the admonition of the Lord, we hand deliver them right over to the enemies camp. There are those who worship the Lord, and those who choose not to serve him. Mankind will always find himself struggling with something. Most of the time it will involve worship issues contrary to the will of God. Whether they are good or bad, mankind desperately needs something to worship. You will either worship God, or you will find yourself worshiping the enemies of God. There is no middle ground. The deception shows up when you think that there is. All worship that does not belong to the Lord is empty and unfulfilled. God is the only one that can totally fulfill and satisfy that empty void that all men have until they come into the knowledge of Jesus Christ. Instead, mankind always seems to seek other avenues of fulfillment. This causes snares and traps to come upon men. The next thing you know, strongholds and addictions will have you bound up so tight you can't move. Then you have been totally captivated and taken over by sin, which by now is in full control of your life. Take a good look at the world today. Look at how many people are serving and worshiping the Lord Jesus Christ. The truth is there are not as many souls worshiping God as there should be. This world is full of souls that disbelieve and mock God on a regular basis. The devil has them totally under his spell. Hopefully this is not describing you.

Scripture

"Submit yourselves therefore to God. Resist the devil, and he will flee from you. Draw nigh to God, and he will draw nigh to you. Cleanse your hands, ye sinner; and purify your hearts, ye double minded. Be afflicted, and mourn, and weep: let your laughter be turned to mourning, and your joy to heaviness. Humble yourselves in the sight of the Lord, and he shall lift you up" (James 4:7-10).

If you find yourself in this predicament, surrender yourself and return unto the Lord. God will be extremely glad to take you back. As long as you have breath in your body and a willing heart, there is still time to be delivered and set free from sin.

56) Did you know that whatever you need from God is in your PRAISE? Anything you need from the Lord, praise his holy name. When we sing and make melody unto the Lord, he hears from heaven. Just make sure that your heart is pure, or else your melody will not be pleasing to the ears of the Lord. Honoring God for who he is on the throne is pleasing to him. First of all, it shows him that we truly believe. Secondly it shows we acknowledge him on his heavenly throne. God loves when we glorify and magnify him as sovereign ruler and Lord of all. The nonbelievers cannot worship the Lord, nor give praise and honor to his holy name because they disbelieve. Regardless of what we are going through day-to-day, God loves to be praised and worshiped by his people. The Bible tells us that God inhabits the praises of his people.

Scripture

The Holy Scripture reads, *"But thou art Holy, O thou that inhabitest the praises of Israel"* (Psalm 22:3).

The tribe of Israel is referring to Abrahams seed which is the household of faith. All born-again believers have been adopted into the family of God through faith in Jesus Christ our Lord. These souls are the seed of Abraham, God's covenant people. God will dwell in the midst of our praises. Therefore, we should praise and worship the Lord in good times and in bad times. Remember, we are special in the eyes of the Lord. He will come down and inhabit the praises of his people.

Scripture

"But ye are a chosen generation, a royal priesthood, a holy nation, a peculiar people; that ye should show forth the praises of him who hath called you out of darkness into his marvelous light: Which in time past were not a people, but are now the people of God: which had not obtained mercy, but now have obtained mercy" (1 Peter 2:9-10).

God blesses those who are willing to praise and worship him for his goodness and mercy. Therefore, always be quick to offer up praises and worship unto the Lord and remember this fact. When praises go up, the BLESSER comes down!

57) Did you know we have a responsibility to hear the word of God whether we accept it or not? The word of God tells us that we are responsible for ourselves. We are also responsible for knowing that a man of God or a prophet has been in our midst. We are held accountable.

Scripture

"And they, whether they will hear, or whether they will forbear, for they are a rebellious house, yet shall know that there hath been a prophet among them" (Ezekiel 2:5).

"And thou shalt speak my words unto them, whether they will hear, or whether they will forbear, for they are most rebellious" (Ezekiel 2:7).

Therefore, we as witnesses for the Lord have an obligation to minister the word of God to all that have an ear to hear. It is the responsibility of the hearer to hear and not avoid or reject God's precious word when it is being preached. Let us stay on course and continue in the will of God with all of our heart—ministering the good news of the gospel everywhere and to everyone. Those who reject the word of God when it is preached pray for them and go on to the next soul. The Lord's work is never done.

58) Did you know that God said, "My people are destroyed for lack of knowledge?" God wants us to spend time in his holy word and learn of him. This will cause us to know the will of God and learn all of his valuable principles and wisdom. The more knowledge we have concerning the word of God, the more successful we will be at emulating him in the earth. Some have claimed to have a direct relationship with God without feeling the need to read or study his holy word. This manner of thinking is not in line with what the word of God teaches us.

Scripture

"My people are destroyed for lack of knowledge: because thou hast rejected knowledge, I will also reject thee, that thou shall be no priest to me: seeing thou hast forgotten the law of thy God, <u>I will also forget thy children</u>" (Hosea 4:6).

So, according to God's holy word, if we ignore him, he will reject us and our children. The good news is that if we turn back and serve him, he will also turn and embrace us once again. Seek God with all of your heart, mind and soul. Study the word of God to show yourself approved so that you may rightly divide the word of truth. Do not take God for granted by failing to learn all you can about him. Seek him early while he may be found. There will come a time when the presence of the Lord will be taken from this world. Therefore, strengthen your faith while there is still time.

Scripture

"So then faith cometh by hearing, and hearing by the word of God" (Romans 10:17).

Our faith is strengthened by hearing the word of God and spending time studying his holy word. When we refuse to read the word of God as some of us do, we reject the very knowledge God intented for us to be blessed by. The word of God provides us with wisdom, knowledge and an understanding. This teaches us how to walk with God according to his way and not ours. It's not in the feeling; it's in the knowing. We are not to try to follow God according to how we feel inside. Our feelings and emotions can and most often will deceive us. We have to perform the will of God according to his way and not ours. God has given us specific instructions in his holy word that addresses every situation imaginable. All we have to do is read it and believe it.

Scripture

"Study to show thyself approved unto God, a workman that needeth not to be ashamed, rightly dividing the word of truth" (2 Timothy 2:15).

If a person will not read the word of God yet considers them self as a Christian, what happens is, they tend to rationalize every concern they face in life with what sounds good to their intellect. For some reason, they call this spiritually minded. In essence, it is a standard that will always justify their actions to themselves. This type of person is referred to as a carnal Christian. Until they seek God where he can truly be found, they will continue to error and ultimately be destroyed because they lack knowledge. Remember, God said, "My people are destroyed for lack of knowledge." How else will you ever receive the knowledge of the Lord without studying to show yourself approved?

59) Did you know that we as servants in the ministry are separate but equally important to one another? We all have different roles in the body of Christ that are equally important to God. Our main attribute is to be faithful in our assignment while the Master and Lord (Jesus) is away. So when he returns for his church body of believers, we will have put our God-given talents to full use here in the earth while he was away. Let us not get caught sleeping on the job when we should be ministering to lost souls about the good news of the gospel of Jesus Christ. The same way it felt the first time a witness of the Lord spoke to you concerning the will of God. Think back how your natural mind was not receptive to the idea at first. It took some time. This is the same way others hearing the gospel for the first time will probably react to you. Therefore, be not discouraged and continue to press your way through. Let the good news of the gospel flow directly out of your heart. Let us never forget that the holy word of God has power. It has a way of getting deep down into the heart of a man's spirit. After this type of experience, every time a messenger ministers the love of Jesus Christ, something will start to happen on the inside of that person. That first message that was planted will start to grow. It will be like a seed that is now receiving water for the first time. The desire to seek and learn more about the Lord will start to get stronger and stronger. The next thing you know, you too will be on the battlefield with other believers doing the work of the ministry. That's the wonderful thing about the word of God—it has supernatural Holy Ghost power. God's holy word never returns unto him void under any circumstances. Let us not praise man for his many titles and accomplishments that he has received here in the earth. God deserves all the praise and all the glory which should never be shared with anyone. We are equal and thankful servants who serve together in the army of the Lord. We all have an important part to play in the body of Christ. That makes us all equal members of a very important body of believers who belong exclusively to the Lord Jesus Christ.

Scripture

"For as we have many members in one body, and all members have not the same office. So we being many are one body in Christ, and every one member's one of another" (Romans 12:4-5).

God has something for each and every one of us to do for his wonderful kingdom. Therefore, make no big deal when it comes to titles or positions. Honor and respect all authority that has been placed over you. Do the work of the Lord that he has given you with a willing heart. God rewards diligent workers, not their titles. What good is it to have a title when you refuse to do the work? Serve the Lord with gladness, and in due season, God will exalt thee. Remember, too much is given, must is required.

Scripture

"But he that knew not, and did commit things worthy of stripes, shall be beaten with few stripes. For unto whomsoever much is given, of him shall be much required: and to whom men have committed much, of him they will ask the more" (Luke 12:48).

"Therefore judge nothing before the time, until the Lord come, who both will bring to light the HIDDEN THINGS of darkness, and will make manifest the counsels of the hearts: and then shall every man have praise of God" (1 Corinthians 4:5).

Therefore, let us not judge one another any longer, leaving the judgment up to the only one qualified to judge righteously. That holy one which is Jesus the Christ will make the final judgment of the world when he returns. He is the only one worthy to open the books which contain the names and deeds of every soul, whether they are righteous or unrighteous. For this reason, mankind was warned by God never to judge one another. This brings condemnation to the ones who have attempted to judge others when the Bible clearly says, they do the same things.

60) Did you know we should not curse nor swear out of the same mouth we pray to God with? Our prayers are sacred unto the Lord. Since this is so, why would anyone curse, swear, or use profanity with the same tongue used to pray holy prayers unto the Lord? We want God to hear us every time we pray and cry out for his help. Therefore, sanctify yourself in all that you do and say so that your prayers will never be hindered.

Scripture

The Bible tells us, *"But the tongue can no man tame; it is an unruly evil, full of deadly poison. Therewith bless we God, even the Father; and therewith curse we men, which are made after the similitude of God. Out of the same mouth proceedeth blessing and cursing. My brethren, these things ought not so to be"* (James 3:8-10).

The Bible is teaching us that we should never cruse our fellow man. The Lord created mankind in his own image and likeness. Therefore, we should not bless and curse with the same tongue. Remember, our words design our future. Therefore, be careful what you say and pray and how you say it and pray it. Always remember God created each and every one of us in his image and likeness. We as human beings are very valuable in the eyes of God. No man should ever put down another or view himself higher than his brother. The world we live in is influenced by Satan, who teaches us to categorize everyone. Unfortunately, this separates us. This type of judgment will always form different groups and classes of people. This is the trick of the enemy to cause strife among the children of God. The devil knows if he can cause mankind to hate one another, the act of sin will stay the hand of God. Anytime you have separation, the outcome will always be the same; men separated from God and one another. The Lord examines the true intention of every human being. When we pretend on the outside that we value someone, we only fool ourselves. Every man has unique value in the eyes of God. Only those who are blinded by the enemy cannot see the glory of the one who created them. Therefore, let every man prove himself by his deeds toward others. This is how ones true character will shine through. Good fruit will always come from a good tree; likewise, bad fruit will always come from a bad one. What a person looks like can be deceiving; it's what they are made of that really counts. Always remember, reputation is how the world sees you, and character is how God sees you! This is why integrity and character will always measure the value of a man. The world teaches a different lesson. They praise those who have material wealth, and look down upon those who don't. Examining the world's point of view, true character has no value. You can possess a wicked and evil nature and still be elevated above men. However, when it comes to the kingdom of God, nothing is hidden from the eyes of God. Everything is being recorded everyday of our lives. Nothing has ever been left out. Therefore, let us show love one to another and never put down our fellow man with our tongues. Always remember this, when we curse each other, we show very little respect for the image and likeness maker, which is God. The Lord has fashioned all souls in a unique way. Since we were all made in God's image and likeness, let us realize that God does not make junk.

61) Did you know that we have false prophets that exist in our world today? Those claiming to be prophets of God are deemed false prophets when they teach contrary to the Holy Bible. The Bible teaches us that these false prophets speak from their hearts and not from the word of God. They have failed and lost their privilege to be a spokesperson on God's behalf. They have chosen their own agenda. They prophesy lies from their own heart while ignoring the written word of God. The word of God is complete. There are no new doctrines. The Old Testament prophesied the New Testament. The New Testament manifested the Son of God who came and took sin away and gave mankind everlasting life. Jesus said it best in this next verse of scripture.

Scripture

"I AM Alpha and Omega, the beginning and the end, the first and the last" (Revelation 22:13).

There are no new doctrines. Therefore, beware of the false prophet. They have their own agenda. The Word of God will never contradict the words of a true prophet!

Scripture

"Thus saith the Lord of Hosts, hearken not unto the words of the prophets that prophesy unto you: they make you vain: they speak a VISION of their own hearts, and not out of the mouth of the Lord. They say still unto them that despise me, The Lord hath said, Ye shall have peace; and they say unto every one that walketh after the imagination of his own heart, No evil shall come upon you" (Jeremiah 23:16, 17).

"I have not sent these prophets; yet they ran: I have not SPOKEN to them, yet they prophesied. But if they had stood in my counsel, and had caused my people to hear my words, then they should have turned them from their evil way, and from the evil of their doings. Am I a God at hand, saith the Lord, and not a God afar off? Can any hide himself in secret places that I shall not SEE HIM? Saith the Lord. Do not I fill heaven and earth? Saith the Lord. I have heard what the prophets said, that prophesy

lies in my name, saying, I have dreamed, I have dreamed. How long shall this be in the heart of the prophets that prophesy lies? Yea, they are prophets of the deceit of their own heart" (Jeremiah 23:21-26).

The definition of a false prophet is one who claims to speak revelations that come from God, when in fact they are his own beliefs. These revelations are supposed to foretell future events. Some even claim to perform miracles, signs and wonders. This sounds like today's psychic hotline network. In the Bible, <u>false prophets</u> generally fall into three different categories:

1) Those who worship false gods and serve idols.
2) Those who falsely claim they receive messages from God almighty.
3) Those who stray from the truth and choose to be dishonest.

Scripture

"And that prophet, or that dreamer of dreams, shall be put to death; because he hath spoken to turn you away from the Lord your God, which brought you out of the land of Egypt, and redeemed you out of the house of bondage, to thrust thee out of the way which the Lord thy God commanded thee to walk in. So shalt thou put the evil away from the midst of thee" (Deuteronomy 13:5).

The Old Testament taught us that false prophets would be put to death for leading God's people away from his true and holy word. So, unless God has truly called you to be a prophet, take heed in making such a claim for yourself. The wicked souls will indeed be punished. Therefore, be careful, man of God, and stay with the teachings of the Holy Bible. Speak from the word of God and not from your own heart. God has said everything he needed to say in his holy word. His holy word called the Holy Bible is the alpha and the omega, the first and the last, the beginning and the end. There is no other authentic word know to man that was truly inspired by God himself. The Lord sent his Holy Word into the earth through his chosen people to be shared among all men.

Scripture

"All scripture is given by <u>inspiration of God</u>, and is profitable for doctrine, for reproof, for correction, for instruction in righteousness" (2 Timothy 3:16):

Therefore, always remember, we are God's true messengers held responsible to God for teaching his holy word to a sinful world. The holy word of God will free the mind of any soul willing to believe and receive it. No one has the right to change any part thereof, nor add anything to God's holy word. God has said everything he plans to say to the children of men. The Holy Bible gives a stiff warning to anyone brave enough to take it upon themselves to add, subtract or re-write any part thereof concerning the spoken word of God.

Scriptures

"For I testify unto <u>EVERY MAN</u> that heareth the words of the prophecy of this book, If <u>ANY MAN</u> shall add unto these things, God shall add unto him the plagues that are written in this book: And if <u>ANY MAN</u> shall take away from the words of the book of this prophecy, God shall take away his part out of the Book of Life, and out of the Holy City, and from the things which are written in this book. He that testifieth these things saith, Surely I COME QUICKLY, Amen. Even so, come, Lord Jesus. The grace of our Lord Jesus Christ be with you all, Amen" (Revelation 22:18-21).

Mankind should take this harsh warning very seriously. Jesus lets us know that his return for his church body of born-again believers will occur quickly. Not only is the time very near to the return of Christ, but every soul only has until the end of their life to make the choice. They will either choose everlasting life in Christ, or settle for everlasting damnation with the devil. No one knows how much time they have in the flesh. The only one who controls both our birthday and our deathdate is God almighty. Therefore, either you will accept the salvation of the Lord through Jesus Christ while you are alive, or choose to perish with the enemies of God after you are dead. The choice is up to you. This is another one of those biblical truths that a person must possess knowledge in or else they will be destroyed. Remember, God is the one who said <u>HIS PEOPLE</u> are destroyed for lack of knowledge.

62) Did you know that anyone who believes in evolution and not the God of all creation is cursed? When we choose to believe the theories of man over the almighty word of God, it's the same as rejecting God himself. This false theory and thought process from man came directly from the enemies of God. The devil wants the children of men to reject the grace of God so that they will join him in the lake of fire. There is no hope for the devil and his crew. Even though he knows this, he still plans to fight until the very end. He is already defeated and will be destroyed by Christ Jesus at the battle of Armageddon. The ending has already been determined and spoken in the word of God. The holy word of God is very clear on this. Those who believe in man and depart from God are cursed. Those who believe and trust in the Lord are blessed.

CURSED

Scripture

"Thus saith the Lord; Cursed be the man that trusteth in man, and maketh flesh his arm, and <u>whose heart departeth from the Lord</u>. For he shall be like the heath in the desert, and shall <u>not see</u> when good cometh; but shall inhabit the parched places in the wilderness, in a salt land and not inhabited" (Jeremiah 17:5, 6).

BLESSED

Scripture

"Blessed is the man that trusteth in the Lord, and whose hope the Lord is. For he shall be as a tree planted by the waters, and that spreadeth out her roots by the river, and shall not see when heat cometh, but her leaf shall be green; and shall not be careful in the year of drought, neither shall cease from yielding fruit" (Jeremiah 17:7, 8).

God's word is true. Therefore, if you insist on believing man's theory on how the earth was formed, just know when things in your life are not going so well, you now have your explanation. God created the heavens and the earth and all that is within. Mankind was created by God to be caretakers and lords over what he has created. Instead, there are those who have attempted to take credit for what God has made. This is called stealing the glory of the Lord. No one truly gets away with this form of theft. They only think they do. Everyone has to die and every one will be judged by the true Creator. The thought of some big bang theory is certainly preposterous. Anytime the truth is not involved, a lie will always find its way into the midst.

63) Did you know that Jesus said it is not what goes in a man's belly that defiles the man? The scripture that addresses this issue dealt with the Pharisees pointing the finger at the Disciples of Christ when they failed to wash their hands before eating bread. This was a good opportunity for Jesus to explain to the Pharisees the lack of importance concerning their many traditions. These temple leaders were not spiritually discerned at all. The funny thing is when you think about it, man was fashioned from the dust of the ground. Since God made man from dust, no small amount of dust or dirt is going to have that much of an effect on what a man consumes. Everything we consume has some amount of bacterial attached to it if it's a living organism. Therefore, dirty hands are the last thing we should be concerned with when it comes to self defilement.

Scripture

> Jesus said, *"Ye hypocrites, well did Isaiah prophesy of you, saying, This people draweth nigh unto me with their mouth, and honoreth me with their lips; but their heart is far from me. But in vain they do worship me, teaching for doctrines the commandments of men"* (Matthew 15:7-9).

Jesus lets us know that the hearts of men must be involved in true worship to God. The hypocrite is described here as a phony, ostentatious, insincere individual who speaks the words as a form of tradition, however, does not have it deep down in his heart to obey the will of God. This type of behavior will always result in a judgmental attitude toward others. Jesus informed the Pharisees what really defiles a man.

Scripture

Jesus said, *"Not that which goeth into the mouth defileth a man; but that which cometh out of the mouth, this defileth a man"* (Matthew 15:11).

Jesus told his disciples to leave the Pharisees alone after it was discovered that they were offended at what Jesus had said.

Jesus said, *"Let them alone: they be blind leaders of the blind. And if the blind lead the blind, both shall fall into the ditch"* (Matthew 15:14).

Jesus sums it up by saying, *"Do not ye understand that whatsoever entereth in at the mouth goeth into the belly, and is cast out into the draught? But those things which proceed out of the mouth come forth from the heart; and they defile the man. For out of the heart proceed evil thoughts, murder, adulteries, fornications, thefts, false witness, blasphemies: These are the things which defile a man: but to eat with unwashen hands defileth not the man"* (Matthew 15:17-20).

Jesus our Lord and Savior looks at the heart of a man to examine the purity therein. Let us also seek to be Christ-like when examining the hearts of our brothers and sisters. This will also prevent us from valuing an individual based solely on his or her outward appearance.

64) Did you know that the decisions we make based on the lust of our flesh will never last? Even though something may feel right, we still have to rely on God's word to do what's right. By doing so, it keeps us from facing terrible consequences later on in life.

Scripture

"For all that is in the world, the <u>Lust</u> of the flesh, and the <u>Lust</u> of the eyes, and the <u>Pride</u> of life, is not of the Father, but is of the world. And the world passeth away, and the lust thereof: but he that doeth the will of God abideth forever" (1 John 2:16, 17).

Therefore, let us stop trying to rationalize everything concerning our lives just because deep down inside, we want to satisfy our personal lust. We must walk in the spirit to avoid walking in the flesh. When we walk in the flesh, we will always stumble into sin.

Scripture

"Blessed is the man that endureth temptation: for when he is tried, he shall receive the CROWN OF LIFE, which the Lord hath promised to them that love him. Let no man say when he is tempted, I am tempted of God: for God cannot be tempted with evil neither tempted he any man: But every man is tempted when he is drawn away of his OWN LUST, and enticed. Then when lust hath conceived, it bringeth forth sin: and sin, when it is finished, bringeth forth DEATH. Do not err, my beloved brethren. Every GOOD gift and every PERFECT gift is from above, and cometh down from the Father of lights, with whom is no variableness, neither shadow of turning. Of his own will begat he us with the word of truth, that we should be a kind of first fruits of his creatures" (James 1:12-18)

God does not tempt man according to the word of God. The LUST of man and woman will always tempt them and draw them away if they are not rooted and grounded in the faith. Be very careful, men and women of God not to yield to the devil's temptation. Remember the teachings found in the word of God. All good and perfect gifts come from the Father of lights, which is God. Therefore, if it's not good and perfect, run from it. Remember, God speaks to the spirit of man. Whenever there is no peace involving the many situations we face in life, this means something is not right. We should proceed with caution, always willing to consult the word of God for answers. The Holy Bible answers every question in life we could ever imagine. This is why we must study and become very familiar with the Holy Bible. This biblical knowledge truly has the power to save our lives.

65) Did you know that once you accept Jesus Christ and become SAVED, your sanctification will also save your household? God has given his children the power to become the sons and daughters of God. With this power, your very home will be sanctified by God. This is manifested by the behavior of the

righteous souls. The Bible explains to us that whether or not our household serves God, we must continue to serve him with our whole heart. This causes the glory of the Lord to be seen by others. God's precious anointing becomes contagious toward other souls. On many occasions, God made sure that his servants were alone when he blessed them. When God blesses his people, any one close by will benefit and experience the affects once the blessings start to flow.

Scripture

Apostle Paul tells us, *"But to the rest speak I, not the Lord: If any brother hath a wife that believeth not, and she be pleased to dwell with him, let him NOT put her away. And the woman which hath a husband that believeth not, and if he be pleased to dwell with her, let her NOT leave him. For the unbelieving husband is sanctified by the wife and the unbelieving wife is sanctified by the husband: else were your children UNCLEAN; but now are they HOLY. But if the unbelieving depart, let him depart. A brother or sister is not under bondage in such cases: but God hath called us to peace"* (1 Corinthians 7:12-15).

God is telling us when we live upright in his sight; we provide a living example for those around us. This is another example of environmental control, and how it has power over those living in the midst. As long as we keep living for the Lord, our household will eventually come under subjection to the will of God. It is only when we turn away from God that our faith tends to fail. That's when we run the risk of losing the Lord's special favor he gives to the born-again believers. The Lord is looking for consistency when it comes to his special creation called man. We are the family of God, the called out ones who will spend eternity with Jesus. Therefore, let us continue in the work of the kingdom, knowing very well that are good deeds will always influence others to do the same.

66) Did you know when our Lord Jesus the Christ walked the earth he experienced all manners of temptation known to man? Knowing this, Jesus knows how difficult it is to walk in the flesh since he was both fully man and fully divine. The Bible teaches us once we become born-again believers; Jesus gives us power to become the sons of God.

Scripture

"Wherefore let him that thinketh he standeth take heed lest he fall. There hath no temptation taken you but such as is common to man: but God is faithful, who will not suffer you to be tempted above that ye are able; but will with the temptation also <u>make a way to escape</u>, that ye may be able to bear it" (1 Corinthians 10:12, 13).

"Seeing then that we have a great High Priest, that is passed into the heavens, Jesus the Son of God, let us hold fast our profession. For we have not a High Priest which cannot be touched with the feeling of our infirmities; but was in all points tempted like as we are, yet without SIN. Let us therefore come boldly unto the throne of grace, that we may obtain mercy, and find grace to help in time of need" (Hebrews 4:14-16).

The Lord Jesus is gracious and merciful. Not only was he tempted in all points without sin, he also promises to provide a way for us to escape when temptation comes knocking. All we have to do is look for that escape route. Every time we overcome temptation, we land intact on the other side of the test. When we yield to the tempter, we take a major setback. Therefore, be careful when temptation shows up. Never forget that God has made a way for us to escape, we just have to find it. This next verse of scripture found in the book of James greatly applies to this situation as well.

Scripture

"Blessed is the man that endureth temptation: for when he is tried, he shall receive the Crown of Life, which the Lord hath promised to them that love him. Let no man say when he is tempted, I am tempted of God: for God cannot be tempted with evil, neither tempteth he any man: But every man is tempted when he is drawn away of his own lust and enticed. Then when lust hath conceived, it bringeth forth sin: and sin, when it is finished, bringeth forth death" (James 1:12-15).

The Lord Jesus knows what our temptation feels like. The Bible tells us that Jesus experienced all manners of being tempted and prevailed every time.

He is the only perfect being ever born of a woman. Jesus lets us know that it is possible to resist temptation. We have to first be willing to resist, and then we have to act on it. Remember, Jesus used the word of God to battle Satan every time he came forth to try and tempt him. We, too, must use the same method in order to be successful against this wicked enemy of God. No other method will prevail. The word of God is our fighting sword that has been anointed by God to defeat his enemy. When we fail to use God's weapon of choice, we too will fall into temptation every time.

67) Did you know the Bible teaches us when we hear the word of God and fail to comply, we are deceived? We have to read and study God's holy word and apply it to our lives. We must be obedient to all matters concerning the Lord. Once we know the word, we are held accountable by God to obey his commands.

Scripture

> *"Wherefore, my beloved brethren, let every man be swift to HEAR, slow to SPEAK, slow to WRATH: For the wrath of man worketh not the righteousness of God. Wherefore lay apart all filthiness and superfluity of naughtiness, and receive with meekness the engrafted word, which is able to <u>SAVE YOUR SOUL</u>. But be ye doers of the word, and not hearers only, deceiving your own selves"* (James 1:19-22).

This scripture teaches us that we must be swift to hear, slow to speak and slow to wrath. This is not typically how most people operate. James, the apostle of Jesus Christ taught us a valuable lesson on all three of these reactions. Reference being swift to hear, James lets it be known that it is of very little value just to hear only and not act upon the word of God. We must remember, the devil himself hears and knows the word of God better than mankind. That is why the devil has to react to the word of the Lord when spoken against him. This enemy just enjoys rebellion and rejecting the will of God every chance he gets. We have to be on a different level than this defeated foe. That is why Christians know it is of little value to just hear the word and not act upon it. We must swiftly be willing to hear all issues pertaining to God and then obey those commands in order to be pleasing to our Father who art in heaven. In regards to being slow to speak, James taught us the dangers of the tongue. Once words go out, they will help design a man's future. The Bible tells us that anyone who offends not in words; the same is a perfect man. This is how important the tongue is, therefore, choose your words wisely. Regarding being slow to wrath, James taught us that we are to submit ourselves to God and take not revenge over our situations. This is why we must react slowly. When we release our wrath, it is always the inappropriate measure. This is why God tells us that vengeance belongs to him and him alone. God will repay our offender for our offense. Remember, we belong to the Lord which makes us his responsibility. Mankind has a tendency of always taking the matter too far. Be careful not to release your wrath. Show mercy and compassion toward one another and leave the rest up to the Lord.

68) Did you know that God gives us daily benefits and new mercies that start fresh every morning? The Lord truly loves each and every one of us. When we serve the Lord and trust in him, we become partakers of all the great benefits of God.

Scripture

"Bless the Lord, O my soul; and forget not all his benefits:

1) Who forgiveth all thine iniquities;

2) Who healeth all thy diseases;

3) Who redeemeth thy life from destruction;

4) Who crowneth thee with loving-kindness and tender mercies;

5) Who satisfieth thy mouth with good things; so that thy youth is renewed like the eagles" (Psalm 130:2-5).

The Bible tells us that as high as the heaven is above the earth, so great is God's mercy toward them that fear and reverence him. We serve a loving and merciful God. He gives us his mercy out of his shear goodness. We must also remember that God is a just God as well. This means that in addition to God showing unconditional love toward his creation, he must also punish sin. This is why he sent Jesus to be a living sacrifice for whosoever will believe. Without this innocent blood which cancels the penalty of sin, no man or woman could be saved. This is a free gift from a loving God. This is the kind of God we serve. Since God has spared our lives and shown mercy to all who believe, we must likewise do the same. The Bible clearly tells us to show mercy and forgiveness toward others if we expect the same from God.

Scripture

Jesus said, *"Blessed are the merciful: for they shall obtain mercy"* (Matthew 5:7).

"For if ye forgive men their trespasses, your heavenly Father will also forgive you: But if ye forgive not men their trespasses, neither will your Father forgive your trespasses" (Matthew 6:14, 15).

We must never forget, mercy and forgiveness was not earned nor deserved by any man. This is primarily due to the sinful nature we all inherited being descendants of the first man Adam. We must understand sin is dirty, wicked and evil in the eyes of God. The true and living God is HOLY; this means nothing can enter into his presence unclean. Everything must be perfect. This is why upon the return of Jesus; the saved souls will be given new resurrected bodies before entering into the presence of the Lord. The corruptible will put on incorruption, and the mortal must put on immortality. This is how Paul the apostle explained it in the word of God.

Scripture

"Behold, I show you a mystery; We shall not all sleep, but we shall all be changed, in a moment, in the twinkling of an eye, at the last TRUMP: for the trumpet shall sound, and the dead shall be raised incorruptible, and we

shall be changed. For the corruptible must put on incorruption, and this mortal must put on immortality. So when this corruptible shall have put on incorruption, and this mortal shall have put on immortality, then shall be brought to pass the saying that is written, DEATH IS SWALLOWED UP IN VICTORY" (1 Corinthians 15:51-54).

This is the mystery of God that will usher the saints of God from earth into his glorious kingdom. Always remember that mercy and forgiveness is freely given by God. The Lord loves mankind with his unconditional love known as AGAPE. God truly made mankind in his image and likeness for a reason. This is why we thank God for his mercy and goodness that endures forever.

69) Did you know that your soul is so important to God that even the angels rejoice in heaven over one sinner who repents? God loves us more than we will ever know. We are his only creation made in his image and likeness. When we admit that we are a sinner, and confess Jesus Christ as Lord with our mouth, this pleases God and his entire heavenly host. For they know, that soul has believed and accepted the provisions set forth by God which provides eternal life in Christ Jesus.

Scripture

Jesus tells us, *"Either what woman having ten pieces of silver, if she lose one piece, doth not light a candle, and sweep the house, and seek diligently till she find it? And when she hath found it, she calleth her friends and her neighbors together, saying, Rejoice with me; for I have found the piece which I had lost. Likewise, I say unto you, there is JOY in the presence of the angels of God over one sinner that REPENTETH"* (Luke 15:8-10).

Angels rejoice because they know that one more soul has been spared from the wrath of God and that horrible judgment in the lake of fire. This mighty wrath of God will be poured out onto the earth without mixture during the Great Tribulation Period. Trust me; you definitely want to escape this terrible time to come in the near future. The long list of distractions in this world has truly caused mankind to be setback. These same distractions are designed to take our concentration off the only thing that truly matters in life, which is the salvation of the Lord. Everything left can easily fall into the category of world deception. Although, when the light of Christ illuminates our heart, this causes us to seek the truth. And we all know that the truth will set us free from all forms of yokes and bondages.

70) Did you know that God commands us to teach and train our children in the admonition of the Lord? This will not only protect and shield them from the evils of this world, but it will also cause them not to stray too far away from the almighty God.

Scripture

"A foolish son is a grief to his father, and bitterness to her that bare him" (Proverbs 17:25).

"Chasten thy son while there is hope, and let not thy soul spare for his crying" (Proverbs 19:18).

"Train up a child in the way he should go: and when he is old, he will not depart from it" (Proverbs 22:6).

"Foolishness is bound in the heart of a child; but the rod of correction shall drive it far from him" (Proverbs 22:15).

"The father of the righteous shall greatly rejoice: and he that begetteth a wise child shall have joy of him. Thy father and thy mother shall be glad, and she that bare thee shall rejoice" (Proverbs 23:24, 25).

God knows exactly what it takes to produce righteous children. He wrote the book on it called the Holy Bible. The problem with mankind is that he wants to always do things his own way. God knows what's best for his creation because he is the Master Builder of man. When are we going to start listening to the voice of the Lord? When we fail to train our children according to the word of God, we are held accountable. Remember the High Priest Ely and his two sons, Hophni and Phinehas. The sons of Ely were made priests and abused their priestly positions by taking advantage of the people of God. The sons of Ely did evil in the sight of the Lord causing the people of God to transgress. God removed Ely and his sons and their whole generation from the priesthood forever because of this. The priest Ely after knowing about his son's wicked behavior refused to punish them according to the law. At the least, Ely could have removed his sons from the priesthood since they were not willing to follow the will of God. The priest Ely did nothing but counsels his sons and continued to ignore the situation.

Scripture

"Now Ely was very old, and heard all that his sons did unto all Israel: and how they lay with the women that assembled at the door of the Tabernacle of the congregations. And he said unto them, why do ye such things? For I hear of your evil dealings by all this people. Nay my sons; for it is no good report that I hear: ye make the Lord's people to transgress" (1 Samuel 2:22-24).

Ely the high priest had a discussion with his sons about their wicked behavior which did no good. Nor did they change their ways. Ely failed to properly judge and punish his sons, showing them special treatment before God and the children of Israel. Ely tried to reason with his sons, which was not good enough. This is a perfect example of putting your children before the Lord. Many parents of today pet their children instead of applying the proper discipline. Ely's two sons were not children but fully grown men, yet their father still failed to take the appropriate action toward them.

Scripture

Ely asked the question, *"If one man sin against another, the judge shall judge him: but if a man sin against the Lord, who shall entreat for him? Notwithstanding they hearkened not unto the voice of their father, because the Lord would slay them"* (1 Samuel 2:25).

Both of Ely's sons were slain along with 30,000 Israelites in a battle against the Philistines. Now Ely was ninety-eight years old and his eyes were dim that he could not see. Ely heard the report of the Philistine defeat over Israel and the death of his two sons. But when they made mention of the <u>Ark of the Covenant being captured</u>, Ely fell backward off his seat and broke his neck and died. This serves as an example that we must chastise our children and never condone their sins. God will hold us responsible, especially to those who hold leadership position in the kingdom of God. Sinful behavior among leaders will always cause the people of God to transgress. Leaders in the church have great influence over the people of God. However, as children of the Highest, we must never give our worship to man. God is the only one worthy to be praised and worshiped. Therefore, if a man falls, we can help restore that man by picking him back up and remembering that he too was born with a sin nature. We have to pray for one another everyday that our faith fail not. Sin can be repented for, but when a man or woman's faith fails, they will return back to the clutches of Satan. This should be avoided at all cost. Therefore, teach your children to always believe and trust in the Lord. Train them to fully understand that God will always be there for them.

Scripture

"Let your conversation be without covetousness; and be content with such things as ye have: for he hath saith, I WILL NEVER LEAVE THEE, NOR FORSAKE THEE" (Hebrews 13:5).

There is nothing in this world that we should every put before the love of God. This statement includes anybody and everybody. That's right, even our precious children whom God blessed us with. There is no exception to this biblical truth. However, we must teach our children that God will never leave them nor forsake them. This is true regardless of whether we can see him or not. Once we understand that the Lord will never leave us nor forsake us, our focus can then remain solely on what we must do for God.

71) Did you know that the Bible tells us that if we have no love for the Savior Jesus Christ, then we should be accursed? The Apostle Paul, who wrote the majority of the New Testament Gospel of Jesus Christ made this statement during his salutation and benediction.

Scripture

"The salutation of me Paul with mine own hand. If any man love not the Lord Jesus Christ, let him be Anathema (**accursed**) *Maranatha* (**The Lord is coming**)*"* (1 Corinthians 16:22).

Apostle Paul is letting us know that Jesus is coming back for his church before the Great Tribulation Period. All true believers will be caught up to be forever with the Lord when the last trump of God sounds. Therefore, unless you believe in your heart, and have love for the Lord and in the appearance of his coming, you will not be saved. Jesus made a tremendous sacrifice for our salvation. Please don't wait; get on board while there is still time and hope. Jesus loves all the souls he created!

72) Did you know that repentance means more than just saying I'm sorry? Repentance means a turning away from sin, disobedience, or rebellion and a turning back to the will of God. The more general meaning is to have a change of mind. True repentance does cause us to regret and feel remorse for our sinful conduct. This will bring on what is commonly referred to as a godly sorrow for the committed sinful act. This is what will compel us to turn and go in the opposite direction, which cause us to have a greater relationship with the Lord. John the Baptist preached to the people to REPENT as he baptized them with water for the remission of their sins. Jesus told us to REPENT of our sins to God, and to be baptized because the kingdom of God is at hand.

Scripture

Jesus said, *"And saying, the time is fulfilled, and the kingdom of God is at hand: REPENT ye, and believe the gospel"* (Mark 1:15).

"Then Peter said unto them, REPENT, and be baptized every one of you in the name of Jesus Christ for the remission of sins, and ye shall receive the gift of the Holy Ghost" (Acts 2:38).

So remember, when we repent for our sin to the Lord, be prepared to turn and go in the opposite direction. Jesus tells us that when we become the righteousness of God, he also empowers us to become the sons of God. The precious Holy Spirit gives us power to walk upright before the Lord. And if by chance you happen to fall, don't stay down there on the ground. Remember, the devil in the form of the serpent in the Garden of Eden. God cursed him to crawl on his belly and eat dust all of his days. Do not be like the serpent. Get up and continue the race for salvation. Keep running the Christian race set before you. Jesus Christ wants every one of us to be a winner in this lifetime marathon. The only way mankind can loose in this race is to give up and turn back.

Scripture

"And Jesus said unto him, No man having put his hand to the plough, and looking back is fit for the kingdom of God" (Luke 9:62).

"My little children, these things write I unto you, that ye sin not. <u>And if any man sin</u>, we have an advocate with the Father, Jesus Christ the Righteous: And he is the propitiation for our sins: and not for ours only, but also for the <u>sins of the whole world</u>" (1 John 2:1, 2).

Propitiate according to Webster's New World Dictionary means to cause to become favorably inclined; win or regain the goodwill of; appease or conciliate—sacrifices made to propitiate the gods—to pacify.

This tells us that Jesus has fully covered us. He is the appeasement for all of our sins ever committed. Jesus keeps the peace and satisfies the requirement between God and man. Without Jesus our Lord and Savior dying in our place, we would all be lost to sin forever. This is the good news of the gospel of Jesus Christ. All men should gladly accept this free gift of eternal life God has made available to all nations, tongues and kindreds. No one has been excluded unless they have chosen it for themselves.

73) Did you know that God gave us all special gifts and talents to be used for the edifying of his church? Some have received many while others

have received few. These talents were placed inside of us to be used for the kingdom of God. When raising children, we must pay very close attention to them. If we do this, we will see their talents unfold right before our very eyes. Parents have a responsibility to push or feed these talents in order to help develop their children in life. So many of us grow up and never discover our God given purpose. The Lord has equipped every soul with specific gifts and talents. That's right; God has fully equipped each and every one of us with a purpose to contribute to his world. That's why it's so important to train up your child in the admonition of the Lord. When this is <u>not</u> done, the world system—influenced by Satan—will overwhelm and overtake our children. This evil force in the world today is so strong, that without the knowledge of God, our children don't stand a chance of survival.

Scripture

"In whom the <u>god</u> (Satan) of this world hath blinded the minds of them which believe not, lest the light of the glorious gospel of Christ, who is the image of God, should shine unto them" (2 Corinthians 4:4).

The world system influenced by Satan and his demonic forces has blinded the unbelieving children of God. Satan causes men and women to be distracted with the many lusts of this world. The trick of the enemy is to cause mankind to seek after their own desires, regardless of how wicked they may seem. By doing so, it tends to put all of our focus on pleasing ourselves. This type of selfish wicked desire pleases the enemy instead of God. This takes the focus off the Lord and the God-given purpose he gave us to fulfill. Then, we spend a lifetime chasing our own selfish lustful desires. From the outside, our life looks great. Our outer self is being temporarily satisfied and clouded with a disguise as we seek the things of the creature instead of the CREATOR. When we come into the knowledge of Jesus Christ, our purpose and gifts God placed inside of us will start to shine through clearly. When we operate in our God-given talents, our life immediately starts to prosper. We become good and faithful servants of our Lord Jesus Christ. The words we will then hear from our Lord at his return are, "Well done, thou good and faithful servant." Remember, you have both talents and gifts. Be sure not to waste them by burying them in the earth.

74) Did you know that when demons are cast out of a person, they come back reinforced to try and re-enter their old dwelling place? Demonic spirits, once they set up house in a human body, they need to be cast out in the name of Jesus. Once cast out, they will come back. It is very important that you fill that space or void with the word of the almighty God. If this is not done, demons have a way of forcing their way back inside the person to once again regain access to their soul. This may sound frightening to an unbeliever; however, it is very true to the born-again believer who honors the word of God.

Scripture

"When the unclean spirit is gone out of a man, he walketh through dry places, seeking rest; and finding none, he saith, I will return unto <u>MY HOUSE</u> whence I came out. And when he cometh, he findeth it swept and garnished. Then goeth he, and taketh to him SEVEN OTHER SPIRITS more wicked than himself; and they enter in, and dwell there: and the last state of that man is worse than the first" (Luke 11:24-26).

This lets us know that when we get delivered from a stronghold, or have demonic spirits cast out; we must sin no more and conform to the will of God. We must fully engulf ourselves in the Holy Bible. By doing so, when the demons return, they will not be able to penetrate our walk with the Holy Spirit. The Lord has to give us power through the Holy Spirit to overcome demonic spirits. Once this power has been received, do not look back from whatever you were released from. Remember, Lot's wife looked back and she turned into a pillar of salt. In today's society, this could be any form of addiction. When Jesus delivers you from a stronghold, there is a window of opportunity for total deliverance. Some are recaptured and reclaimed by demonic spirits because they did not allow themselves to be filled with the Holy Spirit. The ones who replaced their empty void with the precious word of God experienced total deliverance. Their minds were completely renewed. Jesus told the parable of the ten lepers that he healed and only one returned to give him thanks. Always remember to give thanks unto the Lord.

Scripture

"And they lifted up their voices, and said, <u>Jesus, Master,</u> have mercy on us. And when he saw them, he said unto them, Go show yourselves unto the priests. And it came to pass, that <u>as they went,</u> they were cleansed. And one of them, when he saw that he was healed, turned back, and with a loud voice glorified God, and fell down on his face at his feet, giving him thanks: and he was a Samaritan. And Jesus answering said, Were there not TEN cleansed? But where are the nine? There are not found that returned to give glory to God, save this stranger. And he said unto him, Arise, go thy way: <u>thy FAITH hath made thee whole</u>" (Luke 17:13-19).

The question is, if the faith of this one stranger has made him whole for returning to give thanks unto the Lord, what about the nine lepers that were also cleansed. Did they have the measure of faith to make them whole, or were they temporarily cleansed? Will they fall back into the clutches of leprosy, or will some other sickness afflict them? This is why when God delivers us from a stronghold, always give thanks and get yourself connected to the Lord. As long as you are connected to the VINE which is Christ Jesus, we as the BRANCHES have power and protection over the enemy's devices. There iseverlasting life in the VINE. Many have been recaptured in this world and returned to their slave dens. Don't let this happen to you.

75) Did you know that Jesus gave us an additional commandment? Yes, this would be the eleventh commandment given by God. Jesus tells us that not only will this commandment determine whether or not we have discipleship, but this very important commandment gives man the capability of fulfilling and keeping the other Ten. The Bible tells us that without charity/love, what we do for God is meaningless. This very important commandment also connects us all one to another. In order to be received by Christ, we must all be members of one body.

Scripture

Jesus said, *"A new commandment I give unto you. That ye love one another; as I have loved you, that ye also love one another. By this shall ALL MEN know that ye are my disciples, if ye have love one to another"* (John 13:34, 35).

When we have unconditional love toward our brothers and sisters, we will not commit any ungodly offense toward them. You will not hurt the ones you truly love. Jesus knows that once we realize we are all his children and are loved by God the Father, that truth alone will set us free and cause us to likewise love one another unconditionally. Love is easier once we realize we are all related to one another. We all came from the loins of Adam by way of Noah's three sons. Whether you agree or disagree, we are all kinfolk. Never let us forget the great flood that destroyed all mankind with the exception of eight souls. After the flood the Bible tells us that Noah's sons repopulated the entire earth.

Scripture

"Which sometimes were disobedient, when once the longsuffering of God waited in the days of Noah, while the ark was a preparing, wherein few, that is __EIGHT SOULS__ were saved by water" (1 Peter 3:20).

"And all flesh died that moved upon the earth, both of fowl, and of cattle, and of beast, and of every creeping thing that creepeth upon the earth, and __EVERY MAN__" (Genesis 7:21).

"And the sons of Noah that went forth of the ark were Shem, and Ham, and Japheth: and Ham is the father of Canaan. These are the three sons of Noah: and of them was the __WHOLE EARTH OVERSPREAD__" (Genesis 9:18, 19).

This truth dispels any and all theories that Adam was not the first man created by God. Unfortunately, there are ministers who teach that Adam was created separate from other men already occupying the earth. How foolish this unsupported theory is. This is one of the belief systems that destroy unity among men. When a person does not know who they really are, they will forever walk in darkness. Unless other ethinic groups have no souls, then you may want to pay close attention to the false prophet's theory. The Holy Scriptures tell us that only eight souls survived the flood and the entire world was re-populated by Noah's three sons. We have a choice to either believe a Holy God, or a sinful wicked man. Remember, God is sovereign, just and holy. Every man is born with a sin nature, which means every third word that comes out of the mouth of man is questionable. The question is, who will you put your trust in? The bottom line is we must love one another at all cost. This is an easy task when we know and understand the truth about who we really are. Therefore, believe the report of the Lord over what mankind has to say. Without the word of God, man would not have a clue how he came into existence.

76) Did you know Jesus made a promise that the Holy Spirit would come and abide in us forever? The Holy Spirit will strengthen, teach and guide us unto all truth. He is our present help in our hour of need. Jesus said he would not leave us comfortless when he ascended back onto the throne of God.

Scripture

>Jesus tells us, *"If ye love me, keep my commandments. And I will pray the Father, and he shall give you another Comforter, that he may abide with you forever. Even the Spirit of truth; whom the world cannot receive, because it seeth him not, neither knoweth him: <u>but ye know him</u>; for he dwelleth with you, and shall be <u>**IN YOU**</u>. I will not leave you comfortless: I will come to you. Yet a little while, and the world seeth me no more; <u>but ye see me</u>: because I live, ye shall live also"* (John 14:15-19).

These scriptures teach us that our love for Jesus causes us to walk in obedience. The Comforter (HOLY SPRIT) will come and dwell inside of the born-again believer. The Holy Spirit will show us all truth. Only we as born-again Christian believers can know him. The world cannot know him nor receive him. It requires a revelation from the Lord in order to recognize the presence of the Holy Spirit. When Jesus rose from the dead and ascended into the heavens to take his royal seat on the right hand of the throne of God, the world would not see him again in this life. But the believers will forever see him through the mighty works of the Holy Spirit. God knew that we would need help in this world dealing with the sin nature we inherited from our ancestor Adam. The Holy Spirit will power us up to perform many marvelous works all in the name of Jesus. We as believers must truly be comforted with this knowledge and truth.

77) Did you know that God's servant, Moses, was not allowed to go into the promise land due to his disobedience to God? The Lord gave Moses specific instructions to SPEAK to a rock in the wilderness so that it would produce water. The purpose of speaking to the rock to cause water to flow was to convince the children of Israel once again of the mighty power and glory of the Lord. There was another valuable lesson God wanted to demonstrate to his chosen people. This lesson was to show the children of Israel the mighty power of God's spoken words, even when spoken by the mouth of man. The Bible tells us death and life is in the power of the tongue. If Moses had just spoken to the rock as God instructed, instead of striking it twice out of anger at the tribes, he would have been able to enter into the promise land. Instead, Moses was prohibited from going in because he lost control of his tempter. The children of Israel could have learned a valuable lesson earlier than they did. They could have learned how powerful the spoken words of God are, and also how to use those words to overcome any and all obstacles they would soon face. Unfortunately, they did not learn this lesson until later. Now when Moses and the children of Israel were in the wilderness desert of Zin and abode in the land of Kadesh, the Bible tells us that the people complained because there was no food or water there.

Scripture

> *"And the Lord spake unto Moses, saying, Take the rod, and gather thou the assembly together, thou, and Aaron thy brother, and SPEAK ye unto the rock before their eyes; and it shall give forth his water, and thou shalt bring forth to them water out of the rocks: so thou shalt give the congregation and their beast drink"* (Numbers 20:7,8).

Moses received God's instructions, but when he carried them out, he failed to follow them as God had spoken. Instead of just SPEAKING to the rock as God commanded, Moses decided to use his rod and STRIKE the rock not once, but twice. Moses let his anger get the best of him.

Scripture

> *"And Moses lifted up his hand, and with his rod he smote the rock TWICE: and the water came out abundantly, and the congregation drank, and their beast also. And the Lord spake unto Moses and Aaron, <u>Because ye believed me not, to SANCTIFY me in the eyes of the children of Israel,</u> therefore ye SHALL not bring this congregation into the land which I have given them"* (Numbers 20:12).

This passage of scripture teaches us how important it is to follow the word of God. Our Lord Jesus Christ had to later teach this valuable principle of SPEAKING to our situations in order for our mountains to move. This lesson that was later taught helped the children of God avoid the many obstacles and stumbling blocks life had to offer.

Scripture

Jesus tells us, *"For verily I say unto you, That whosoever <u>SHALL SAY</u> unto this mountain, Be thou removed, and be thou cast into the sea; and shall not doubt in his heart, but shall believe that those things which he saith shall come to pass; he SHALL have whatsoever he saith. Therefore I say unto you, what things so ever ye desire when ye pray, believe that ye receive them, and ye shall have them"* (Mark 11:23,24).

The scriptures teach us that we must have faith in God, and learn to open our mouth. We have to speak the godly things we desire. Our words design our future and provide the things we need when we open our mouth to speak. Just like our Lord Jesus tells us we can move mountains if we only <u>SPEAK TO IT</u> and doubt not what we say. The same applies if we choose to create and build mountains with our negative speech. The building process is the same. Therefore, watch what you say and always believe and live according to the word of God.

78) Did you know that some non-Christians are slow to come to the knowledge of Jesus because they observe the carnal lifestyle of fellow Christians? We as Christian believers have a responsibility to minister the word of God to all nonbelievers. In doing so, we must equip ourselves with the word of God and practice walking in the spirit to avoid walking after the lust of the flesh. When Christian believers stumble, nonbelievers are right there to observe it. This will cause the nonbeliever and even some believers to sin and break the law. Some nonbelievers feel they are better off than the born-again Christian believer. These nonbelievers feel this way because they don't struggle with the same sins they observe Christian born-again believers succumb to. In the mind of the non-Christian, even though they don't know the Lord in the pardoning of their sins, they are deceived in believing that they do not need a Savior. This is a trick of the enemy—that old devil called Satan. As long as Satan can convince mankind to stay blinded to the need of a Savior, mankind will forever be lost. We have to seek God while he may be found. Then the blinders will be removed and the glory of God will shine through. Man must first agree and believe that he is a sinner, and then he will realize his desperate need for a Savior. We only have up until the time we take our last breath to enter into the Lord's sheepfold. Don't get caught in the wilderness!

Scripture

"Seek ye the Lord while he may be found, call ye upon him while he is near: Let the wicked forsake his way, and the unrighteous man his thoughts: and let him return unto the Lord, and he will have mercy upon him; and to our God, for he will abundantly pardon" (Isaiah 55:6, 7).

Remember, once we accept the Lord Jesus as our Savior, we become the righteousness of God. We are so desperately in need of a Savior, and we have one in Christ Jesus. The Lord Jesus died on the cross at Calvary for our past, present and future sins. Once we come into the knowledge of Christ, we must surrender our total life to him and live the remainder of our days serving and worshiping the Lord. We should take our salvation very serious!

Scripture

> *"Wherefore, my beloved, as ye have always obeyed, not as in my presence only, but now much more in my absence, work out your own salvation with <u>fear</u> and <u>trembling</u>"* (Philippians 2:12).

This verse of scripture does not mean that we have to labor to enter into the kingdom of God. Jesus Christ has already paid the ultimate price. This verse of scripture means we must continue in the work of the ministry. If we have accepted Jesus Christ as Lord, we have obtained our salvation. Now we have to carry it to its logical conclusion. We become responsible for other souls that need to hear the gospel message as well. This is when the born-again believers start to see others more valuable than themselves. Their living sacrifice has now become their reasonable service to God. When we realize we are to value others more than ourselves, this is when we really start to walk in the anointing of God.

79) Did you know that some born-again Christians still struggle in the flesh? This is commonly referred to as a carnal Christian. One of the main reasons Christians become carnal is due to selfishness. Selfishness appears when we cater to the desires of our own flesh. In other words, we choose our selfish lustful desires over the word of God. After we receive Jesus Christ as Lord and Savior, we have to let go of sin. This is now possible since Jesus died on the cross at Calvary for the sins of the entire world. Christians must be willing to exercise their new God-given power received from the Holy Ghost. We have to walk in the spirit to avoid walking in the flesh. We must no longer be carnally minded or fleshly in our thinking. The main change in our life involves us making a decision within ourselves to serve the Lord with our whole heart.

Carnal is defined as SENSUAL, WORLDLY, NON-SPIRITUAL, and relating to or given to the crude DESIRES and appetites of the FLESH or BODY. These are individuals who let their flesh control them.

Scripture

"And thou shalt love the Lord thy God with all thy HEART, and with all thy SOUL, and with all thy MIND, and with all thy STRENGTH: this is the first commandment" (Mark 12:30).

When we obey and love God first and foremost, putting him ahead of everything and everybody, we are now walking in the spirit. The minute we put things, or our selfish fleshly wants and desires before the Lord, we stumble, we fall, we faint, and we miss the mark. In other words, we commit sin and walk contrary to the word of God. Let us be convinced as believers and serve the Lord with all of our might. Remember what the Bible says about the whole duty of man.

Scripture

"Let us hear the conclusion of the whole matter: FEAR God, and keep his commandments: for this is the whole duty of man. For God shall bring every work into judgment, with every secret thing, whether it be good, or whether it be evil" (Ecclesiastes 12:13, 14).

The Bible addresses the carnal mind and what it means to God. This is why we so desperately need the Savior Jesus the Christ. Without the blood of Jesus covering our sins, we would be totally exposed.

Scripture

"Because the carnal mind is enmity **(Hostility/Enemy)** *against God: for it is not subject to the law of God, neither indeed can be. So then they that are in the flesh cannot please God. But ye are not in the flesh, but in the spirit, if so be that the Spirit of God dwell in you. Now if any man have not the Spirit of Christ, he is none of his"* (Romans 8:7-9).

The Bible tells us when we walk in the flesh, we cannot please God. Likewise, when we walk in the spirit, we will not sin. Therefore, whether you feed the spirit man or the flesh man, this will determine who reins over your life. For we know that the spirit man cannot sin just like the flesh man will always sin. This is why we need to renew our mind with the word of God daily in order to see this new creature that the Bible speaks of. The Bible also addresses what types of behavior we perform while in the carnal state.

Scripture

"For ye are yet carnal: for whereas there is among you ENVYING, and STRIFE, and DIVISIONS, are ye not carnal, and walk as men" (1 Corinthians 3:3)?

This scripture tells us that carnality will cause envy, strife, divisions, or confusion among the brethren. We lack spiritual maturity as Christians when we act in such a manner toward one another. Remember, Jesus commands us to love one another. Jesus describes in this next verse of scripture the greatest form of love known to this world.

Scripture

"Greater love hath no man than this, that a man lay down his life for his friends" (John 15:13).

By loving our fellow man as we love ourselves, it becomes very easy and very possible to fulfill all of the commandments of God.

80) Did you know that Jesus spoke a curse in the book of Revelation pertaining to anyone who takes away or adds to any part of his Holy Bible? For those that will, or have attempted to rewrite, change, distort, take away, or add to the message of God, the same will receive a curse upon his or her life. God will add all the plagues written in the Holy Bible to the lives of them who violate this command. God will also take away their part in the book of life, which is the Lamb's Book of Life. This is a very serious penalty to come upon a person just because they do not agree with the word of God. Therefore, never attempt to change anything that is written in the word of God. The Lord said it how it needed to be said!

Scripture

"For I testify unto every man that heareth the words of the prophecy of this book, If any man <u>shall add unto these things</u>, God shall add unto him the plagues that are written in this book . And if any man <u>shall take away from the words of the book</u> of this prophecy, God shall take away his part out of the book of life, and out of the Holy City, and from the things which are written in this book" (Revelation 22:18,19).

This severe warning is aimed toward those who distort, change or rewrite the God given message he placed in his Holy Book. The speaker here is the Lord Jesus Christ himself who proclaims canonicity over this precious book. These genuine official scriptures are inspired by the almighty God.

Scripture

"All scripture is given by INSPIRATION of God, and is profitable for doctrine, for reproof, for correction, for instruction in righteousness" (2 Timothy 3:16).

The New Testament is equally as important as the Old Testament. Anyone who willfully changes or distorts the message of the book of Revelation proves that they are not a genuine born-again believer of the gospel of Jesus Christ. The soul of that individual will not receive eternal life or the blessings of the Holy City. Jesus makes a final promise that his return is forth-coming and will be without delay.

81) Did you know as believers in Christ, we have a responsibility to seek and learn all we can about the Lord? By doing so, we become a true worshiper of God. The last thing you want to do is accept Christ as Lord, get covered with his precious blood and just sit down on your salvation. We all have work to do for the kingdom of God. The last thing you want to do is not utilize your God given talent while in the earth. Once you learn to praise and worship the Lord, then you are on your way to discipleship. When you become a disciple of Christ, you are to teach and train up other disciples in the knowledge and admonition of God. Jesus said people will know that we are his disciples when we have loved one to another. We are in training for the New Jerusalem, which is the Holy City of God. In the kingdom, we will worship our Lord in his glory and will forever be with him. Let us learn to magnify the Lord while we are still here in the earth. Then we will learn the ways of the kingdom before we enter into the presence of the Lord. Jesus gave us his great commission to GO and TEACH all NATIONS. In order for us to fulfill the command Jesus gave us, we must fully equip ourselves with the truth.

Scripture

"And Jesus came and spake unto them, saying, All power is given unto me in heaven and in earth. Go ye therefore, and TEACH all nations, BAPTIZING them in the name of the Father, and of the Son, and of the Holy Ghost: Teaching them to observed all things whatsoever I have commanded you: and, lo, I am with you always, even unto the end of the world, AMEN" (Matthew 28:18-20).

"Then saith he unto his disciples, The harvest truly is plenteous, but the laborers are few; Pray ye therefore the Lord of the harvest, that he will send forth laborers into his harvest" (Matthew 9:37, 38).

We must get serious and busy about our training in the various matters of God. There is work to be done spreading the good news of the gospel of Jesus Christ our Lord. God needs us now! We are his ambassadors here in the earth. The HARVEST is ready right now! Therefore, prepare and equip yourselves to go into God's vineyard and minister to the lost souls. Someone cared enough to take the time to tell us of the goodness of Jesus the Savior. Should we not do the same? If we do not tell them, they will never know.

82) Did you know that every believer needs a shepherd to watch over their soul? God sends and assigns the shepherds to his many flocks in the earth. In other words, God sends the pastors to the congregation. They are appointed and anointed by God to edify the church and to walk upright before the congregation as an example to the people of God. Men and women who are called by God to be preachers and teachers of the gospel are well equipped for the task. Unfortunately, there are some who choose to become ministers of the gospel for the wrong reasons. These false prophets will have to answer to the almighty God one day real soon. We pray that such things should never occur, however it does. The best way to avoid this type of false prophet is to study the word of God for your self. There have been false leaders in the history of this world who have led congregations astray causing the death of many. In order to do this, these false leaders had to teach contrary to the Holy Bible. This is how you discover their falsehood. Never take a pastor's word without checking the Holy Scriptures for yourself. The Holy Bible teaches us that we need a shepherd; however, make sure he is in agreement with the word of God. Let God be true, and every man a liar when it comes to the Holy Bible.

Scripture

"For whosoever shall call upon the name of the Lord shall be SAVED. How then shall they call on him in whom they have not believed? And how shall they believe in him of whom they have not heard? <u>And how shall they hear without a Preacher?</u> And how shall they preach, <u>except they be SENT</u>? As it is written, How beautiful are the feet of them that preach the Gospel of Peace, and bring glad tidings of good things" (Romans 10:13-15)!

"And Moses spake unto the Lord, saying, Let the Lord, the God of the Spirits of all flesh, <u>set a Man over the congregation,</u> Which may go out before them, and which may go in before them, and which may lead them out, and which may bring them in; that the congregation of the Lord <u>be not as sheep which have no shepherd</u>" (Numbers 27:15-17).

God knows that sheep without a shepherd will soon go astray and become easy prey to their enemy. Sheep are very vulnerable animals. We as Christians are referred to as sheep because we have the same characteristics. As Christians, we need a shepherd to teach, cover, and protect us while looking out for our best interests, which is our very soul. When we try to walk alone, we have no covering or protection. We are not being fed the word of God. This is the shephards responsibility, to feed the flock of God. Therefore, without spiritual bread, we become careless and hungry for the wrong things. Remember, Satan the adversary, is like a roaring lion that walks about seeking whom he may devour. This enemy of God is always on the prowl. He will stop at nothing when given a chance to devour one of God's children. The best way to devour prey is when they are alone and helpless. Therefore, stay connected to the sheepfold; there is safety in the hands of the shepherd whom God has placed over you.

83) Did you know that God wants to bless his children and show forth his goodness to those who walk upright? We are not waiting on God, God is waiting on us!

Scripture

"For the eyes of the Lord run to and fro throughout the whole earth, to show himself STRONG in the behalf of them whose heart is perfect toward him" (2 Chronicles 16:9a).

The scriptures here tell us that God is looking for someone to bless in the earth. He wants to show himself mighty toward men and allow the world to see the blessings of the Lord manifested in the life of his faithful servants. All God requires us to do is to have a perfect heart toward him. Let us obey and serve the Lord with our perfect heart, mind and soul. We must keep God first and foremost in our daily affairs and resist all manner of evil. This will position us to be blessed abundantly.

Scripture

"And it shall come to pass, if thou shalt hearken diligently unto the voice of the Lord thy God, to observe and to do all his commandments which I command thee this day, that the Lord thy God will set thee on high above all nations of the earth. And all these blessings shall come on thee, and overtake thee, if thou shalt hearken unto the voice of the Lord thy God" (Deuteronomy 28:1, 2).

The Lord is telling us that if we listen to his voice and obey his word, our lives will be very fruitful, and he will set us above all the nations of the earth to represent his kingdom. The Lord will bestow so many blessings upon us that we will be overwhelmed. God truly wants to bless his children. When God blesses us in this manner, we become the envy of the ungodly.

Scripture

> *"Blessed be the God and Father of our Lord Jesus Christ, who hath blessed us with all spiritual blessings in heavenly places in Christ"* (Ephesians 1:3).

The Bible is telling us, being children of God in Christ Jesus; we have all spiritual blessings in heavenly places available to us. This is based on our belief and acceptance of our risen Savior Jesus the Christ. There is an opposite side to these blessings. If we will not obey and hear the voice of God and walk perfect in our hearts, there are consequences to face.

Scripture

> *"If ye will not hear, and if ye will not lay it to heart, to give glory unto my name, saith the Lord of Host, I will even send a <u>CURSE</u> upon you, and I will <u>CURSE</u> your <u>BLESSINGS</u>: yea, I have <u>CURSED</u> them already, because ye do not lay it to heart"* (Malachi 2:2).

The blessings come when we give glory to the Lord with our service while acknowledging his sovereignty. The curse comes when we reject the Lord, serve him not and fail to give him glory. Remember God wants us to have our blessings that are stored up waiting for our compliance in his word. Be not among those who are cursed already for not acknowledging and obeying the word of God.

84) Did you know that all born-again believers were chosen by God before the foundation of the world? God knew before the foundation of the world who would accept his plan for our salvation and likewise, who would reject him. God knew exactly who would harden their hearts and reject his free gift of salvation. We have always had men of God preaching God's message here in the earth. Some were prophets, some were priest, some were apostles, some were servants, some were judges, and some were even kings. But they all were anointed and sent by God. Some will have an ear to hear, and some will not. Then you have those that flat out reject anything having to do with God, sort of like what Satan has done. They are described as the ones who choose to be cut off from the Lord. The love of God should be passed down through generation after generation. This will preserve the faith and trust we have in the true and living God.

Scripture

> *"According as he has chosen us in him before the foundation of the world, that we should be holy and without blame before him in love. Having predestinated us unto the adoption of children by Jesus Christ to himself, according to the good pleasure of his will, to the praise of the glory of his grace, wherein he hath made us accepted in the beloved. In whom we have redemption through his blood, the forgiveness of sins, according to the riches of his grace."* (Ephesians 1:4-7).

There are three areas of concern here. The first area of concern is the predestination. The second area of concern is the adoption. The third area of concern is the forgiveness of sins. Let's take a closer look at each one of these categories that God has given us.

PREDESTINATION

The word predestination used in this content means to mark off or choose beforehand. This is what the Lord did before the foundation of the world. He knew who would receive him as well as who would reject him. This is called the foreknowledge of God. Once we realize that God has chosen us, we then must also realize that we have been ordained to do good works—just like Paul the apostle before he was chosen. Also, Saul/Paul was a blasphemer and persecutor of the church. God chose him out of darkness, and placed him in the light of Christ. God knew before the foundation of the world that Saul now called Paul would accept his call into the ministry. Likewise, God foreknew that Judas; the son of perdition would also betray Jesus, even though he walked with Christ. God knew beforehand that Judas would deceive the Son of God. Therefore, if you have not heard the call of God, be very concerned because you are not listening. Then on the other hand, you may be one of the ones with a hardened heart. God does not want anyone to miss out on his free gift of salvation.

ADOPTION

Paul the apostle used the word ADOPTION five times to describe how important the salvation experience will be. In today's society, the term adoption means to take one into a family and become legally responsible for that person or persons. This is what God did for all born-again believers. He adopted us into the family of God through a new spiritual birth. This birth involves being born again of the Spirit of God. We are transferred from our natural father to the authority of our new Spiritual Father who is God. We are now the sons of God and joint heirs with Christ Jesus. All born-again Christians are adopted sons and daughters of God who can now enjoy a special intimacy with the heavenly Father for all eternity.

FORGIVENESS OF SINS

Since the word forgiveness means to send off or send away, this is exactly what God does to our sins when we confess them to him. The Lord separates us from our sin as far as the east is from the west. If you know anything about direction, then you understand that these directions never meet up with each other. When you start off whether east or west, you will always be going in the same direction. Unlike north and south, if you travel north, as soon as you reach the North Pole, your direction will change back toward the South Pole. This gives you a general idea of how far God throws our sins away from us. God is the only one with the power to forgive sin. For this reason alone, the Pharisees should have recognized Jesus Christ for who he was in the flesh when he forgave the sins of many. When an individual receives Jesus Christ as Savior and Lord, that individual is forgiven of sin by means of this transfer from death onto life. One thing we must also remember, since God has forgiven us of all our transgressions, we must also forgive our brethren of all their transgressions committed, even when they are against us. This is the only way we can remain in the favor of God.

85) Did you know that God notices and pays special attention to all good deeds performed by man? God does not let one good deed go unnoticed in the earth. The Lord sees all the deeds of mankind at the same time. This includes both the good and the bad.

Scripture

"The eyes of the Lord are in every place, beholding the evil and the good" (Proverbs 15:3).

Our heavenly Father is omnipresent. He sees all things—good or bad. He is always watching the deeds being performed by men in his earth. There is nothing we can hide from the eyes of the Lord. When we do well for our brethren, or perform any act of kindness, God pays very close attention. The same occurs when we do bad or become an offense to our brethren, God will judge those matters as well. The souls of mankind waste time ducking and dodging one another while attempting to hide their sins in the earth. We must understand that mankind has no heaven or hell to put any of us in, nor the power to keep any of us out. Only God has this kind of power and authority over what he has created. Remember, the heavens, the earth, hell and the lake of fire all belongs to God. Only he can decide who ends up there. Therefore, our loyalty should be to God and not man. Let us make sure that we are playing by the Lord's rules. God has given us his plan of salvation through his Son Jesus Christ, the risen Savior of this world. Either we will freely receive the Savior of this world, or we will freely reject Jesus as Lord. This alone will determine where we will spend all eternity. The Lord sends no man or woman to hell or the lake of fire. It is those who reject the salvation of the Lord who will end up there.

86) Did you know that whatever thoughts capture the mind will also capture the man? In the Bible when dealing with the HEART, this is most often synonymous with the MIND. Therefore, we must protect our heart and mind at all costs. This is the area that Satan goes after. The Bible tells us that the issues of life come forth out of the heart. This also can be viewed as the mind or thought process.

Scripture

> *"Keep thy heart with all diligence; for out of it are the issues of life. Put away from thee a froward mouth, and perverse lips put far from thee. Let thine eyes look right on, and thine eyelids look straight before thee. Ponder the path of thy feet, and let all thy ways be established. Turn not to the right hand nor to the left: remove thy foot from evil"* (Proverbs 4:23-27).

Therefore, protect your mind, guard your words, watch what you look at, be careful where you go, and walk not toward the path of temptation. By observing and doing all these things, it will keep your feet from stumbling into sin.

87) Did you know that a good and prudent wife comes from the Lord? The Bible tells us that a man that finds a wife finds a good thing. The Bible also tells us that a prudent wife comes from the Lord. Therefore, seek the Lord for your spouse. Don't be lead by your personal lust. Personal lust will always ware off in a short period of time. Be patient and allow the Lord to bless you with a spouse that is suitable for you. He will divinely bring someone into your life. Remember, God knows what's best for his creation concerning all things. Remain obedient and tell the Lord what you desire in a help-mate and he will give you the desires of your heart. There is a difference between finding a wife and finding a woman to wed. Since God said a man that finds a wife, finds a good thing. Women must prepare and make themselves ready to be found. Make your petition know to God and prepare yourself in the meantime. Start cleaning out your worldly closet. Get rid of as much unwanted baggage as you can. This will tend to lighten your load. There is such a thing as being ready to receive a spouse. The question we should all ask is this. Would you marry you if you knew about yourself in advance? If the answer is no, then you still have work to do. If the answer is yes, then get ready, God too knows all about us. If you are a woman, do not search or hunt down a man. This will often end up causing you to make rash decisions as you settle for something God did not give you. God desires to bless those who desire a spouse. This brings the favor of God to all souls willing to form a blood covenant with the Almighty.

Scripture

"Whoso findeth a wife findeth a good thing, and obtaineth favor of the Lord" (Proverbs 18:22).

"House and riches are the inheritance of fathers: and a <u>prudent wife</u> is from the Lord" (Proverbs 19:14).

We as believers must consult the Lord God on all matters concerning our lives. This will prevent us from stumbling and making bad decisions toward our future. This also lets God know we totally place all of our trust in him. Therefore, consult the Lord before you choose a spouse and let him place the right person in your life. Marriage is sacred and requires our patients. Remember, marriage is not meant to be interchangeable, it is meant to last a life time.

88) Did you know that mankind SHALL not live by bread alone? This is an interesting verse found in the Holy Scriptures. Jesus tells us that we must live by every written word of God. Surely we need food to provide nourishment which will sustain our flesh bodies. This keeps our flesh from being hungry and worn down. Jesus also lets us know that we cannot function nor survive in this world without the written word of God. The word of God will help us survive, both in this earth, and when we enter into God's precious kingdom.

Scripture

Jesus said, *"Heaven and earth shall pass away: but my <u>WORDS</u> shall not pass away"* (Luke 21:33).

Without the word of God, mankind will be consumed like a fire in this wicked world we live in. Without the word of God, mankind has no protection in the earth. When we come to know Jesus as Lord and Savior, we are under the ark of God's safety net. Angels encamp around us. The Holy Spirit dwells within us. We are completely covered by the Lord on all four sides. We need our daily dose of the word of God which will help instruct our lives daily to be fruitful in all things. Remember to give God glory everyday for his wonderful bread of life.

Scripture

> Jesus tells us, ***"But he answered and said, It is written, Man SHALL not live by bread alone, but by every word that proceedeth out of the mouth of God"*** (Matthew 4:4).

The Lord tells us that we are to live by every word that came out of the mouth of God. This command applies whether we agree or disagree, like or dislike; eventually we must learn to do it according to what pleases God. This will prove that we fully trust the Lord God with our whole heart when it comes to the obedience of his word. Therefore, if you are serving in a religious group that does not honor the entire Holy Bible, but chooses bits and pieces, you are in the wrong place. Remember, Jesus said every word that proceedeth out of the mouth of God. This means the whole roll! You may not like it but who cares, God said it and therefore we must obey him. When we choose to reject the word of God, we rebel against the Almighty, just like Satan did. No one in their right mind wants to be categorized with this devil. This is why we must be very careful desiring to do our own will, over the will of the one who Creator us. No stubborn, rebellious, hard-hearted soul will inherit the kingdom of God. When Adam and Eve chose to listen to the devil in the Garden of Eden, it appears Satan imparted a part of himself into mankind. This part of the enemy is often referred to as the sin nature of Adam. Before Adam and Eve met the serpent who was influenced by the devil, they knew no sin. Therefore, let us recognize those rebellious, wicked, stubborn, selfish feelings when they arise. Since we understand where they came from, let us be willing to cast them down in the name of Jesus when they surface. The Lord Jesus who is God manifested in the flesh has given us the POWER and the ABILITY to recognize the enemies devices. Therefore, cast it down, regardless of what it feels like. Sometimes PRIDEFUL feelings may feel good to our flesh; however, it doesn't make it right in the eyes of God. The same principle applies to sin. There are times when sin feels good to our flesh, although it doesn't make it right. Every sin that a man commits is an offense to the almighty God. The Bible warns us that the wages of sin is still death. This is why we must surrender and humble ourselves before the Lord. This is why we must seek the Lord with all of our heart. We must read God's word daily so that all that junk will be purged from within us. Then we will not be so overly concerned about ourselves. Instead, our commitment and concern will be to our loving God. Therefore, when the traits of the enemy rise up within us like rebellion, rejection and selfishness, we can cast them down in the name of the Lord. Then we can move forward continuing to study the word of God. This will help prevent the unnecessary stumbling blocks and struggles that would normally hinder us. When we fail to equip ourselves with the word of God, we stumble and struggle through this life every step of the way. Once we come to the realization that we are a sinner in need of a Savior, that's when the light comes on in our spirit. God's word has been there all the time. The problem is <u>WE</u> have not always been there. Therefore, let us receive our daily dose of spiritual food everyday and be blessed forevermore.

89) Did you know that the Bible is very specific on how we are to enter into God's house of worship? For some, this may be a church, a temple, a synagogue, or whatever you call the location where you worship the true and living God. However, the Holy Bible is crystal clear on what we must do. We must be careful and not allow ourselves to fall victim to old and new traditions made up of men. Some religions require silence in their place of worship. You may feel like you can worship God in silence, however, to praise him, that's going to require the fruit of your lips. The word PRAISE is defined as the expression of approval or admiration. When we sing songs to the glory of God, this glorifies and magnifies his name. We must always use our mouth in order to accomplish this act of praise.

Scripture

"<u>Make a joyful noise</u> unto the Lord, all ye lands. Serve the Lord with gladness: <u>come before his presence with singing</u>. Know ye that the Lord he is God: it is he that hath made us, and not we ourselves; we are his people, and the sheep of his pasture. ENTER INTO HIS GATES WITH <u>THANKSGIVING</u>, AND INTO HIS COURTS WITH <u>PRAISE</u>: BE THANKFUL UNTO HIM AND BLESS HIS NAME. For the Lord is good; his mercy is everlasting; and his truth endureth to all generations" (Psalm 100:1-5).

Let us therefore praise the Lord and not be ashamed to open our mouth. Remember, God spoke this world into existence with his mighty words. The words we speak are also important as well, thanks to the Lord. Whether we are singing praises and magnifying God, or speaking good things into our future, let us never forget how important our spoken words are.

90) Did you know your attitude will establish your mood swing and determine whether or not your life will be peaceful, or dreadful? How you choose to deal with the situations of life that come your way will determine how long you experience there cycle. Two individual can be faced with the same problem. One may perceive it one way and the other another way. One chooses to worry, whereas the other chooses not to worry. Attitude will determine your state of mind as well as your course of action. Worry will cause stress to come upon you like a storm. Stress will then cause sickness to occur in your body. The Bible tells us not to worry because it doesn't change anything. If you examine your life and look back in the past, most of the things you worried over never occurred. All this proves is that we worry for nothing. The Lord clearly teaches against worrying.

Scripture

> *"Be careful for nothing; but in everything by prayer and supplication with thanksgiving let your requests be made known unto God. And the peace of God, which passeth all understanding, shall keep your hearts and minds through Christ Jesus"* (Philippians 4:6, 7).

The phrase 'be careful for nothing' means don't worry about anything. This is not to suggest that we dismiss legitimate concerns. It simply suggests that we rid our lives of unnecessary anxiety that tries to come against our mind. We must remember, by prayer and supplication and giving thanks unto the Lord, all of our burdens will be lifted off our shoulders. The way to be free of all anxiety is to be prayerful concerning all things. Apostle Paul knew that God was eager to hear our request accompanied with thanksgiving in advance. This shows the Lord that we trust in him to completely take care of all of our needs. When we worry as born-again believers, this proves we do not totally trust in the Lord. Worry creates doubt in the mind of all who choose to worry. Therefore, don't let your attitude ruin your day, knowing that as long as we hold onto ill feelings, we will stunt our spiritual growth.

91) Did you know that Christians are sinners saved by the grace of God? I say this because some Christians so easily forget where they began. Unfortunately, there are immature Christians who still turn their nose up at those who remain under the curse of the law. This is not the way we should view our brothers and sisters who are still lost in a world of sin. We should love them as Christ loved the church which is how we received salvation in the first place. Without the sacrifice made from the Lord Jesus Christ, mankind would be lost in sin forever. Mankind was unable to pay its own sin debt, therefore, God sent his only begotten Son to die in our place. This is why accepting the blood of Jesus in the pardoning of sin is crucial. Once we have been washed in the blood of the Lamb, that's the moment we become the righteousness of God. This righteousness is not earned by works or deeds, but by our own submission to Christ for how he died on the cross for us all. By faith and belief alone in Christ Jesus are we saved? This is what re-classifies us as saints of God.

Scripture

> *"For by grace are ye SAVED through faith; and that not of yourselves: it is the gift of God: Not of works, lest any man should boast. For we are his workmanship, created in Christ Jesus unto good works, which God hath **BEFORE ORDAINED** that we should walk in them"* (Ephesians 2:8-10).

This means that no part of salvation is because of our own doing or our own works. Salvation in its entirety is a special precious gift from God. No man can take credit for the sacrifice Jesus made for us on that rugged cross. There is a distinct difference between sinners and sinners saved by grace. The difference is that sinners are lost in their sins by choice because they refuse to believe. The Bible calls them condemned. Sinners saved by the grace of God have made a choice and chose to be convicted in their heart by the word of God. They have come to acknowledge their sins and have made the choice to REPENT to God. They have accepted the Lord's free gift of salvation which God has provided for the entire world through his Son Jesus. Their sins have been washed away with the innocent holy blood of Jesus Christ which was shed on the cross at Calvary. By faith they have been saved from eternal damnation. The bottom line is that they have come to themselves like the prodigal son and realized they were in desperate need of a Savior. They chose to believe God's word over man's theories concerning the whole matter. Unfortunately, there are those who choose not to believe the Holy Bible which is the inspired true word of God. For this reason, these unbelieving souls have decided to make the lake of fire their final resting place after the judgment of God. God sends no man or woman to this dreadful place called the lake of fire. Mankind is responsible for making that decision all by themselves. We can choose to believe God's report by accepting his free gift of salvation he has provided for us all. The other alternative is to not believe, which will make you a NONBELIEVER. This reserves your spot in the lake of fire by your own choice. That's one lake you do not want to take a swim in. The decision is left totally up to you. Remember, the lake of fire was developed by God for Satan and his demonic host which includes the beast, the false prophet, and the final destruction of the spirits bearing the name of death and hell. Unfortunately, some men and women will end up there because they have allowed their hearts to harden which led them to reject the grace of God. Wake up nation and realize who you are in Christ Jesus, knowing that your very soul is priceless. If you do not know Jesus Christ in the pardoning of your sins, Satan has possession of you. God has paid the price in order to purchase all souls into his eternal possession. That is why God sent Jesus to die on the cross which purchased every soul back to God the Father. Only the ones who want to stay with their wicked father who is Satan will not enter into the kingdom of God. They will spend all eternity with their chosen daddy the devil. Do not be one of them!

Scripture

"And death and hell were cast into the lake of fire, this is the second death. And whosoever was not found written in the BOOK OF LIFE was cast into the lake of fire" (Revelation 20:14, 15).

The name of the souls who choose to remain with the enemy of God will not be found written in the Lamb's Book of Life. Their names will be blotted out by God. They have chosen this form of punishment and torment for themselves. It is the only other alternative there is. Therefore, stop blaming God for sending souls to hell or the lake of fire. God has made the provision and has extended the invitation to all souls who will believe on his Son Jesus. Those who are stubborn and have hatred for God will reserve their spot in the lake of eternal damnation. Do not continue to be deceived by the deceiver. Stop listening to man when they choose to teach another doctrine. Many religions have been formed by men in the earth after God has sealed his book through his only begotten Son named Jesus. The Old and New Testament of the Holy Bible is the alpha and the omega concerning the true word of God. There are no other books to be considered a part of God's message to the church. Therefore, get covered with the blood of the Lamb, and spend eternity with God instead of his enemies. For this is the true plan of God unto our salvation. There is no other way into God's heavenly kingdom but through Jesus Christ out Lord.

92) Did you know that we did not choose God, but he has chosen each one of us with a holy calling? Despite what one may think, God has ordained those that he has chosen. God causes us to be spiritually brought together into the body of Christ. Just like in the days of Noah during the great flood. God has intervened and caused all elected souls to come into the body of Christ, just like the ark in Noah's day. One thing born-again believers have in common with one another is UNITY. Christian fellowship is the key that unlocks the unconditional love of God the Father. True agape love allows us to worship together and to see no divisions among the nations of men. The Bible says God has chosen and ordained us to go and bring forth fruit.

Scripture

Jesus tells us, *"Ye have not chosen me, but I have chosen you, and ORDAINED you, that ye should go and bring forth fruit, and that your fruit should remain: that whatsoever ye shall ask of the Father in my name, he may give it you. These things I command you, that ye love one another. If the world hate you, ye know that it hated me before it hated you. If ye were of the world, the world would love his own: but because ye are not of the world, but I HAVE CHOSEN YOU OUT OF THE WORLD, therefore the world hateth you"* (John 15:16-19).

Jesus clearly tells us that men are specifically chosen for the work of the Lord. As a result of this selection, the world will hate all chosen men of God just as they hated our Savior Jesus the Christ. Therefore, be not deceived when the hatred of the world comes upon you suddenly like a storm. Just remember, they hated Jesus first, which means they will eventually hate you next.

Scripture

"All that the Father giveth me SHALL come to me, and him that cometh to me I will no wise cast out" (John 6:37).

Jesus said, *"No man can come to me, except the Father which hath sent me DRAW HIM: and I will raise him up at the last day. It is written in the prophets, and they shall be all taught of God. Every man therefore that hath heard, and hath learned of the Father, cometh unto me"* (John 6:44, 45).

Pray that the Lord is tugging at your life. The Bible says the Lord is knocking at the door of our heart. Make sure you open the door and welcome him to come in freely and be the Lord over your life.

Scripture

Jesus says, *"Behold, I stand at the door, and knock: if any man hear my voice, and open the door, I will come in to him, and will sup with him, and he with me. To him that overcometh will I grant to sit with me in my throne, even as I also overcame and am set down with my Father in his throne"* (Revelation 3:20, 21).

God wants all souls to be SAVED. Unfortunately, there are going to be some who will refuse to repent and insist on rejecting the grace of our Lord. The Lord knows exactly who will, and who will not come to him before it is too late. God knows the heart and mind of every soul. Just like in the days of Noah, those called will come into the body of Christ and the doors to salvation will be shut and sealed. Remember, when God sealed the ark and shut Noah and his family inside, all souls that did not enter in perished in the great flood. In this case, the great tribulation is what awaits the souls who refuse to enter into the body of Christ. This will be a time of great terror and judgment.

Scripture

"And as it was in the days of Noah, so shall it be also in the days of the Son of Man" (Luke 17:26).

The Bible makes reference to the days of Noah when mankind chose not to believe the preacher Noah until his message came to pass. The same will happen in the day of the Lord's return. The saints of God will be taken up to be with the Lord Jesus because they chose to believe God's gospel concerning the Savior. Then you will have those who choose not to believe. They will be headed for the great tribulation period to face and drink the wrath of God without mixture. This is going to be a horrible eventful time to occur in the near future. Please do not be there if you know what's good for you!

93) Did you know that the Bible tells us that there will come a day when hailstones will fall from the sky in the weight of sixty to one-hundred pounds? These large hailstones will fall on man during the time the wrath of God is poured out onto the earth.

Scripture

> *"And there fell upon men a great hail out of heaven, every stone about the weight of a talent: and men BLASPHEMED God because of the plague of the hail; for the plague therefore was exceeding great"* (Revelation 16:21)!

The large hail is described as a talent in weight. The weight of a talent weighs sixty to one-hundred pounds. Surely the size and weight of these hailstones will destroy cities as well as men. During this time, unbelieving mankind will still choose to BLASPHEME God. They will still refuse to REPENT before the Lord. This time period is during the wrath of God when it is poured out on the lost souls of men. These lost souls will curse God because of his great wrath. These men and women will be the ones who chose not to believe God's report (the Holy Bible) when they had the chance. This is the unfolding of those who refused to answer the call of God while his presence was still in the earth. This is the same call that the scriptures spoke of when Jesus was standing at the door of their hearts knocking. All those who answered the call, Jesus came unto them and supped with them. They are safe and protected in his loving arms and their eternal life is secure in the New Jerusalem that Christ has prepared. This is just one of the many wraths that will be poured out on the earth during that great and terrible day of the Lord. Don't be among the souls who get struck by these great hailstones.

94) Did you know that the Bible tells us when we accept Jesus as Lord and are born again of the Spirit of God, we become a NEW CREATURE? The Bible further teaches us that old things have passed away, and behold, all things become new.

Scripture

> *"Therefore if any man be in Christ, he is a NEW CREATURE: old things are passed away; behold, all things are become new. And all things are of God, who hath reconciled us to himself by Jesus Christ, and hath given to us the ministry of reconciliation"* (2 Corinthians 5:17).

"And be not conformed to this world: but be ye transformed by the renewing of your mind, that ye may prove what is that good, and acceptable, and perfect, will of God" (Romans 12:2).

The word of God teaches us in order for our mind to be both renewed and transformed; we must change our thought process. We have to develop a new way of thinking. This is done by studying and absorbing the word of God in our mind daily. Then we will have received this day our daily bread. Our new way of thinking has to line up with the Holy Bible. This is what brings us into agreement with our heavenly Father. We can no longer do things our own way. When our mind has been renewed, transformed and changed, then our life will be changed to conform to the will of God. When we think different, we act different and become new creatures in Christ Jesus. The Lord Jesus sent us the Comforter which is the Holy Spirit from our heavenly Father. The Holy Spirit gives us power to walk upright before God. The Lord has addressed all matters concerning mankind and how we are to live here in the earth. Until we line ourselves up with the will of God, we will continue to struggle finding no peace in the earth.

Scripture

"But as many as received him, to them gave he power to become the sons of God, even to them that believe on his name" (John 1:12).

When we receive Jesus, this is when he becomes our Savior and Lord. We are then transformed into the sons of God here in the earth and given all power needed to complete our task. The word 'power' literally means authority in this particular verse. We have been given the authority to become the sons of God. Our new birth in Christ Jesus is not of human origin but rather it is spiritual and supernaturally received of the Lord. Therefore, recognize who you are in Christ Jesus and rise up in the earth and take your rightful position. There is assigned work for you to complete here in the earth to the glory of God the Father. All who believe in the risen Savior and accept him as Lord are members in the body of Christ. We have a unique purpose to fulfill for the kingdom of God. Do not let the devil rob you of your purpose.

95) Did you know that we as Christians have been entrusted with our Master's goods here in the earth? First of all, who is our Master? The Master and Lord is Jesus the Christ. He has entrusted us with the talents he has given us. Our job is to take our God given talents placed inside of us and multiply them unto good works while Christ is away preparing the Holy City for his people to dwell in. Jesus gave us scripture in the form of a parable to help us understand the use of our God-given talents. The talents God gave us are to be used for the building up and the edifying of the body of Christ. When we waste our talents by not using them, they will be taken away and given to another.

Scripture

Jesus tells us, *"For the kingdom of heaven is as a man traveling into a far country, who called his own servants, and delivered unto them <u>HIS GOODS</u>. And unto one he gave five talents, to another two, and to another one; to every man according to his several ability; and straightway took his journey. Then he that had received the five talents went and traded with the same, and made them other five talents. And likewise he that had received two, he also gained other two. But he that had received one went and digged in the earth, and hid his Lord's money. After a long time the Lord of these servants cometh, and reckoneth with them. And so he that had received five talents came and brought other five talents, saying, Lord, thou deliveredst unto me five talents: behold, I have gained beside them five talents more. His Lord said unto him, Well done, thou good and Faithful Servant: thou hast been faithful over a few things, I will make thee ruler over many things: enter thou into the joy of thy Lord. He also that had received two talents came and said, Lord, thou deliveredst unto me two talents: behold, I have gained two other talents beside them. His Lord said unto him, Well done, good and faithful servant; thou hast been faithful over a few things, I will make thee ruler over many things: enter thou into the joy of thy Lord."*

THE LESSON

Scripture

"Then he which had received the one talent came and said, Lord, I knew thee that thou art a hard man, reaping where thou hast not sown,

and gathering where thou hast not strewed. And I was afraid, and went and hid thy talent in the earth: lo there thou hast that is thine. His Lord answered and said unto him, THOU WICKED AND SLOTHFUL SERVANT, thou knewest that I reap where I sowed not, and gather where I have not strewed. Thou oughtest therefore to have put my money to the exchangers, and then at my coming I should have received mine own usury. Take therefore the talent from him, and give it unto him which hath ten talents. For unto every one that hath shall be given, and he shall have abundance: but from him that hath not shall be taken away even that which he hath. And cast ye the unprofitable servant into outer darkness: there shall be weeping and gnashing of teeth" (Matthew 25:14-30).

This parable explains what we should be doing here in the earth with the talents and gifts provided for us while our Lord Jesus is away preparing a place for us. This parable of the talents stresses the importance of faithful service while Jesus Christ is away. The Lord Jesus is only gone away for a little while. He gave us a commission to go and teach all nations, baptizing them in the name of the Father, of the Son and of the Holy Spirit. The Lord Jesus said to teach them to observe all things he has commanded us and he would be with us, even until the end of the world. Therefore, let us not get caught sleeping on the job. Let us make use of the talents and gifts God has placed inside every soul. Let us keep in mind that these talents have been given by God for the edifying of the church body and not for our personal bragging rights. When our Lord Jesus returns for his church, we want to hear him say, "Well done, thou good and faithful servant." We also want to hear him say that we have been faithful over a few things, and that he will now make us ruler over many things. Then we will have completed our mission here in the earth. Jesus will have rewarded some and burned up the works of others at the Judgment Seat of Christ. Therefore, let us get busy doing the work of the Lord. Time is truly running out as each day passes. I pray that all souls have spiritual eyes to see and spiritual hear to hear what "**Thus saith the Lord!**

96) Did you know that we must seek the Lord while he may be found? The Bible tells us to seek the Lord while he is near. This warning we must take very seriously. While we are alive in the land of the living, this is the time to seek the Lord with all of our might. When the breath of life leaves your body,

THE LAMB'S BOOK OF LIFE:

if you have not found Jesus Christ by then, it will be too late. This is neither a threat nor a scare tactic, it is a fact!

Scripture

> *"Seek ye the Lord while he may be found, call ye upon him while he is near: Let the wicked forsake his way, and the unrighteous man his thoughts: and let him return unto the Lord, and he will have mercy upon him; and to our God, for he will <u>abundantly pardon</u>"* (Isaiah 55:6, 7).

Once we die in the flesh, according to the true and living word of God, we can do no more from the grave. Let us seek the Lord before it's too late. The time to believe is now. The Bible tells us the story of the poor man Lazarus and the rich king. The rich king chose not to believe until it was too late. He lived his life in riches. His destiny was decided based on his decision not to believe nor follow the will of God. This is a perfect example of a man gaining the whole world and losing his own soul. However, the poor man named Lazarus on the other hand chose to believe in the God of salvation while he was yet alive, causing him to have a glorious ending. Lazarus was the poor beggar that lay at the rich man's gate, full of sores and desired the crumbs which fell from the rich man's table. In addition, scripture tells us that the dogs came and licked his sores. Let us no longer take the Lord for granted while we are alive, realizing that one day our soul too will be required of us. The way the story ends, Lazarus was carried by angels into paradise when he died and was comforted in the bosom of father Abraham to await the coming Messiah. The rich man was not so fortunate. He had a spirit of disbelief which caused him to go into the pit of hell where he lifted up his eyes. Once there, the rich man wanted someone to go back to the land of the living to warn his five brothers. Father Abraham yelled from across the great gulf from paradise to the pit of hell and replied the living have Moses and the prophets of God. If they will not believe them, they will not believe the dead even if they returned. Father Abraham was not just talking way back then, this fact holds true even today. Jesus is the risen Savior of the entire world who conquered death, hell and the grave, yet many souls still wonder in disbelieve. The Bible tells us that our breath is in the very hand of God. Therefore, let us recognize who the Lord is and what he truly means to us while we have breath in our bodies. Then we can put our thoughts in proper alignment to acknowledge the glory of the Lord. This will give us the right frame of mind and a willing heart to offer up praises unto the God of all creation. From this day forward, we must SEEK the Lord while there is still time left. Don't be like the rich man who waited until it was too late and then tried to make what he thought was a logical excuse for his kinsmen. The time is now!

97) Did you know that DEATH is an enemy to mankind? After sin was introduced into the world with the disobedience of Adam and the deception of Eve in the garden, death received power in the earth. Death and Hell are both spiritual beings that the Bible speaks of. Many have thought that certain death comes from God. The Bible signifies death as a spiritual personality with a physical bodily form. The Bible depicts death as a spiritual person riding on a pale horse with hell closely following him. This account can be found in the book of Revelation 6:8. If we as human beings could see in the spirit realm as John the apostle did in the book of Revelation, we would see angels, demons, and spirits of all kind. We would probably even see the spirit of death and hell as John the apostle had seen. These are the overseeing spirits that have been given charge over their assignments. The scriptures describe these two forces of evil known as death and hell just like their name represents. Their job is to cause death while committing souls into the pit of hell.

Scripture

> *"And when he had opened the fourth seal, I heard the voice of the fourth beast say, COME AND SEE. And I looked, and behold a Pale Horse: and his name that sat on him was <u>DEATH</u>, and <u>HELL</u> followed with him. And POWER was given unto THEM over the fourth part of the earth, to kill with SWORD, and with HUNGER, and with DEATH, and with the BEAST of the earth"* (Revelation 6:7, 8).

Death or hell could not hold Jesus after he died on the cross and descended into the deep. The Bible tells us Jesus descended into the deep and ministered to the souls in paradise. While there, Jesus took the keys of hell from the enemy of God who had possession of them. King David prophesied that

Jesus' soul would not be left in hell; neither would the holy one see corruption. Ultimately, the Lord would be raised from the dead and would ascend into heaven where he is seated on the right hand of the throne of God. The spirits of death and hell could not hold Jesus the Messiah in that place called Hell.

Scripture

"Because thou wilt not leave my soul in hell, neither wilt thou suffer thine Holy One to see corruption. Thou hast made known to me the ways of life; thou shalt make me full of joy with thy countenance. Men and brethren, let me freely speak unto you of the patriarch David that he is both dead and buried, and his sepulcher is with us unto this day. Therefore being a prophet, and knowing that God had sworn with an oath to him, that of the fruit of his loins, according to the flesh, he would raise up Christ to sit on his throne: he seeing this before spake of the resurrection of Christ, that his soul was not left in hell, neither his flesh did see corruption. This Jesus hath God rose up, whereof we all are witnesses" (Acts 2:27-32).

The Lord Jesus now holds the keys to death and hell. They both will be destroyed and thrown in the lake of fire together in the last days. Death will be the last enemy of God to be destroyed in the lake of fire.

Scripture

"The last enemy that shall be destroyed is DEATH" (1 Corinthians 15:26).

"And DEATH and HELL were cast into the Lake of Fire, This is the second death. And whosoever was not found written in the book of life was cast into the lake of fire" (Revelation 20:13-15).

The book of Revelation here again is describing death and hell as spiritual persons. At the Great White Throne Judgment, the dead were delivered up for judgment without the protective blood of Jesus. The Holy Bible also mentions death and hell delivered up their dead which they held captive since the beginning. The Bible referred to death and hell as them! Death is referred as him (male gender) and hell is referred to as her (female gender). We know that hell is a holding place awaiting the Great White Throne Judgment. But remember this, the Bible tells us that hell was following death who was riding on the pale horse about to commit death and destruction throughout the land. In other words, these two evil forces work together. Death kills the souls and Hell collects them!

Scripture

> *"Therefore hell has enlarged <u>HERSELF</u>, and opened <u>HER</u> mouth without measure: and their glory, and their multitudes, and their pomp, and he that rejoiceth, shall descend into it"* (Isaiah 5:14).

This proves that hell is a place and is perceived as the female gender, similar to how the Bible speaks about wisdom in the female sense. This is a big spiritual world we live in and unfortunately, unbelievers do not have eyes to see or ears to hear all the spiritual matters concerning God. Only the Lord can open the eyes of the blinded souls of this world. The spirit world of God is the true reality, not the earth's dimension where everything is temporary and view as make believe. Even mankind fits into this temporary mode. All men and women are born into this world, and then they die in the flesh. After death occurs, then will every man be judged by God? This is why it's so important to live according to the will of God. The children of the righteous are protected by the shed blood of Jesus the Christ. Just like at the Pass-over when Moses instructed the children of Israel to place the lamb's blood over their door post. This provision from God protected them from the Death Angel which came to destroy the first born. Jesus is the Pass-over Lamb. This too is God's provision he has given to this world. Just like in the days of old, some will receive it, others will not. I am sure there were those who doubted that the lamb's blood would be affective at the first pass-over. To the ones who fail to follow the instructions of God, they were killed by the Death Angel. This was not God's fault they chose to be hard headed. This was based on their own stubbornness. They have forgotten who God is verses who they are. Sort of like when a parent allows their children to assume their honored role of the home. All the respect leaves. This is the same disrespect we show toward God when we reject his holy word. We attempt to strip God of his sovereign position. The created soul dishonors the one who created them. Think about that for a moment because this could be describing you! The devil influences the mind of mankind causing them to feel prideful and self righteous in how they view themselves. This is that same feeling one gets when they reject the word of God. This same feeling will cause a person to not want to hear anything concerning the true and living God. They reject this teaching because it interrupts their current sinful lifestyle and causes shame to come upon them based on how they choose to live. The children of the wicked will be judged without the protective blood of the Lamb of God. They will be condemned unto everlasting damnation, just like the ones who fail to apply the blood at the first pass-over. When we fail to listen and honor the Lord, there will always be stiff consequences to pay. There are two primary benefits for accepting Jesus as Lord and Savior. The first benefit deals with believing God, and his plan for our salvation which saves our soul. This shows that we trust the word of God and believe what the Lord says. Secondly, we become the righteousness of God just by accepting Jesus as our Lord and Savior through faith. We are made righteous, not based on our works but based on what Jesus did for us on the cross. He is the living sacrifice for sin. We are viewed by God the Father as a parent views his beloved sons and daughters. God views us this way because of how his Son Jesus made us his righteous seed when he went to the cross. The wicked unbelievers are not so fortunate. They have hardened their hearts and rejected the grace of God of their own freewill. Even though they have chosen to use the out of sight, out of mind theory, the word of God will always stand forever. When this world passes away, the word of God will still be here.

Scripture

"Heaven and earth shall pass away, but my words shall not pass away" (Matthew 24:35).

This causes the wicked to be viewed in the eyes of God as a judge would view someone he is about to sentence harshly. We as believers have been cleansed by the innocent blood of our Savior, but the wicked shall be judged because they have rejected God, his grace, and his mercy. Jesus has paid the price for sin for all mankind with his innocent bloodshed. Even though the price was paid in full, some souls will insist on believing they can make it into God's kingdom their own way. This is a trick of the enemy he uses to deceive false religions. They are given a sense of PRIDE and REBELLION which keeps them from receiving God's free gift. The God we love and worship, who is Jesus our Lord and Savior, is not a religion. We as Christians have developed a RELATIONSHIP with the God of salvation. Jesus said if we love him, we will keep his commandments. For this is the word and will of God.

98) Did you know that animals can sometimes see in the spiritual realm? Mankind is not certain how often this occurs, although, it has taken place according to the Holy Scriptures. What mankind knows for certain is that animals do instinctively what God programmed them to do. Even in the midst of a sinful world, animals react out of instinct. In the book of Numbers, it tells us that a donkey saw an Angel of the Lord. The donkey also spoke words to his master after he was continuously struck three times for avoiding the Angel of the Lord. This Angel of the Lord is said by some scholars to have been the pre-incarnate Christ. He appeared to Balaam the soothsayer/magician and blocked his way with an avenging sword. God had already warned Balaam against making the journey and he failed to take heed.

Scripture

"And Balaam rose up in the morning, and saddled his ass and went with the prince of Moab. And God's anger was kindled because he went: and the Angel of the Lord stood in the way for an adversary against him. Now he was riding upon his ass, and his two servants were with him. And the ass saw the Angel of the Lord standing in the way, and his sword drawn in his hand: and the ass turned aside out of the way, and went into the field: and Balaam smote the ass, to turn her into the way. But the Angel of the Lord stood in a path of the vineyards, a wall being on this side, and a wall on that side. And when the ass saw the Angel of the Lord, she thrust herself unto the wall, and crushed Balaam's foot against the wall: and he smote her again. And the Angel of the Lord went further, and stood in a narrow place, where was no way to turn either to the right hand or to the left. And when the ass saw the Angel of the Lord, she fell down under Balaam: and Balaam's anger was kindled, and he smote the ass with a staff. And the Lord opened the mouth of the ass, <u>and she said</u>

unto Balaam, What have I done unto thee, that thou hast smitten me these three times? And Balaam said unto the ass, because thou hast mocked me: I would there were a sword in mine hand, for now would I kill thee. <u>And the ass said unto Balaam,</u> Am not I thine ass, upon which thou hast ridden ever since I was thine unto this day? Was I ever wont to do so unto thee? And he said nay. Then The Lord <u>OPENED THE EYES OF BALAAM,</u> and he saw the Angel of the Lord standing in the way, and his sword drawn in his hand: and he bowed down his head, and fell flat on his face. And the Angel of the Lord said unto him, wherefore hast thou smitten thine ass these three times? Behold, I went out to withstand thee, because thy way is perverse before me. <u>And the ass saw me</u>, and turned from me these three times: unless she had turned from me, surely now also I had slain thee, and saved her alive. And the Angel of the Lord said unto Balaam, Go with the men: but only the word that I shall speak unto thee that thou shalt speak. So Balaam went with the princes of Balak" (Numbers 22:21-35).

The ass saw the Angel of the Lord about to slay Balaam as he blocked their way. The ass kept Balaam from the point of death; he just didn't know it. After Balaam continued to beat his animal, the Lord opened the mouth of the ass and they had a conversation. This is the kind of true and living God we serve. Then eventually, the Lord opened the blinded eyes of Balaam so he could see into the spirit realm briefly to obtain understanding. The Lord gave him instruction and sent him on his way. The Lord reminded Balaam not to curse, but to <u>BLESS ISRAEL</u> with the exact words God gave him. This is another example of how spiritual beings are all around us. We just can't see them with our naked eye. This is a perfect example that shows God can use whoever or whatever he chooses to accomplish his will in the earth. There is no limit to what God can do.

99) Did you know there is a difference between Christianity and other forms of religion? Christianity is a relationship with the Savior of the world whose name is Jesus, the Messiah sent from God. Other religions are just that, religions. The Holy Bible teaches us that God reaches out to man. God loved his creation first, even when we were yet lost in sin. The Holy Bible teaches us that man is incapable of reaching out to God. Almost all other religions believe that mankind can reach God through his or her own efforts. This is the same way the Pharisees thought during the time Jesus walked the earth.

In the culture we now live in, many teach that there is no God and that man is alone in this universe. The world is left to think that this life is all that there is, and then you die. How wrong they are. The problem with thinking that you are alone will cause you to have no hope in the future. This philosophy will elevate one to the position of thinking or feeling like he or she are <u>gods</u> over themselves. This mindset makes you not fear and reverence the one and only true God of this world. That is why man continues to try and develop theories that will attempt to explain how he came to exist.

Scripture

> *"The FEAR of the Lord is the beginning of KNOWLEDGE: but fools despise wisdom and instruction"* (Proverbs 1:7).

We as Christians must learn to properly FEAR the Lord. This type of fear involves love, respect, and reverence for God's sovereignty—remembering that he is the Creator of the heavens and the earth and all that is contained therein. Religions that teach mankind can get to God and into his kingdom without the Savior Jesus the Christ have been deceived by the devil. While man believes that his state of being is okay with God, Satan continues to laugh because he knows that time is running out for he and thee. Satan also knows that whosoever feels this way is rejecting the very will of God. Sin and its nature made us all worthy of death. God gave us his plan for our salvation. There is nothing in the Bible that says we can choose our own way to enter into the kingdom of God. We have a choice to believe God and accept his only begotten Son, or disbelieve God and reject his will for our lives. The devil knows that if he can keep us blind to the will of God found in his holy word, we automatically join him in the lake of fire. Remember, there is no hope at all for Satan and his demonic host. Therefore, let us come back to the Holy Bible, the one and only inspired word of God. The word of God lets us know two very important things pertaining to having a relationship with Jesus. These two important bits of information are spelled out in the next two verses of scripture.

Scripture

Jesus tells us, *"He that believeth on him is not condemned: but he that believeth not is condemned already, because he hath not believed in the name of the only begotten Son of God"* (John 3:18).

"Neither is there <u>SALVATION IN ANY OTHER</u>: for there is none other name under heaven given among men, whereby we <u>MUST BE SAVED</u>" (Acts 4:12).

100) Did you know that HOPE is a beautiful thing? We as Christians have learned to have the best kind of hope there is—the hope in the Lord Jesus Christ and all he has promised to those who believe on his name. A man without hope is a man who has no future. The definition of hope involves having an expectation of something that's going to happen, take place or unfold. Hope is something that we learn to put all of our trust in. We as believers come to rely and depend upon the things we have hope for. This is why we believe and trust in a God we cannot see with our naked eye. We feel the Lord's presence in our spirit and we experience his manifestations when he blesses our lives. The glory of the Lord is all around us. We trust in the holy word of God and believe that it show us the way to his kingdom. The Lord calls men and women into his sheepfold to become servants to accomplish his will in the earth. The Bible describes this as God drawing believers unto his sheepfold which is his holy kingdom. The word of God lets us know that everyone who hears the call of God will answer. However, there are those who cannot hear the voice of the Lord. In the last days, there will be men and women who refuse to repent and turn from their wicked ways. God depends on men and women in the earth to accomplish and fulfill his will. When we obey the Lord and accept his call, we make ourselves available for the Master's use. The hope in the Lord is the most beautiful thing we have in this world to look forward to. The disciples had the privilege of being with Jesus who was God manifested in the flesh. They experienced every form of humanism with the Savior of the world.

Scripture

"Jesus saith unto him, Thomas, because thou hast seen me, thou hast believed: blessed are they that have not seen, and yet have believed" (John 20:29).

The beautiful thing about faith in hope is that it causes us to BELIEVE in God's plan for our salvation. This belief in the word of God causes us to trust in the Savior Jesus Christ who redeemed our lives from the second death which is the lake of fire. This final judgment brings eternal damnation to all who find themselves caught up without hope. Therefore, have faith, believe, and trust in the Lord, continuing in the blessed hope of his return for his church body of believers. Christ will be looking for a church without spot or wrinkle. Will you be included in this family of blood washed believers?

Scripture

"That he might present it to himself a glorious church, not having spot, or wrinkle, or any such thing: but that it should be holy and without blemish" (Ephesians 5:27).

The ultimate purpose of Jesus' divine love for his church is to present the church back to him as a chaste bride. As a man wants an untainted virgin as his bride, Jesus wants his church without moral flaw. Keep hoping for the promised things of God. The blood of the Lamb both preserves and presents the born-again believer spotless unto God. This is the <u>ONLY WAY</u> we can be presented clean enough in order to enter into the New Jerusalem also called the Holy City where God will be. Therefore, if you want to be with the Lord for all eternity, get covered with the blood of Jesus and receive the salvation of God. God will be waiting for you!

DAY FOUR

THE TEN COMMANDMENTS

Two Tables of Stone

Scripture

> *"And he gave unto Moses, when he had made an end of communing with him upon Mount Sinai, two tables of testimony, tables of stone, written with the FINGER OF GOD"* (Exodus 31:18).

The Ten Commandments of God are the laws written by the finger of God and given to his servant Moses on Mount Sinai. God gave Moses instructions to give his laws to the children of Israel for a guideline to their daily living. These commandments are the law of God which provide a standard and establishes a covenant between the Lord and his people. Moses gave the Ten Commandments to the children of Israel over 3,000 years ago. The same commandments of God are still relevant today. These laws have an abiding significance because God's character and word never changes. The Lord Jesus upheld the same laws 1,300 years after God gave them, calling them <u>HIS</u> commandments. The Lord Jesus placed these laws on a higher plane. Jesus demanded that the spirit as well as the legal aspects of the law be kept. Jesus let the people know that he did not come to destroy the law, but he came to fulfill the law.

Scripture

> *"And God spake all these words, saying, I AM the Lord thy God, which have brought thee out of the land of Egypt, out of the house of bondage.*

1) THOU SHALL HAVE NO OTHER gods BEFORE ME.

2) THOU SHALL NOT MAKE UNTO THEE ANY GRAVEN IMAGE, OR ANY LIKENESS OF ANY THING THAT IS IN HEAVEN ABOVE, OR THAT IS IN THE EARTH BENEATH, OR THAT IS IN THE WATER UNDER THE EARTH.

"Thou shalt not bow down thyself to them, nor serve them: for I the Lord thy God am a jealous God, visiting the iniquity of the fathers upon the children unto the third and fourth generation of them that hate me; And showing mercy unto thousands of them that love me, and keep my commandments.

3) THOU SHALL NOT TAKE THE NAME OF THE LORD THY GOD IN VAIN:

"Thou shall not take the name of the Lord thy God in vain: for the Lord will not hold him guiltless that taketh his name in vain.

4) REMEMBER THE SABBATH DAY TO KEEP IT HOLY.

"Six days shalt thou labor, and do all thy work: But the seventh day is the Sabbath of the Lord thy God: in it thou shalt not do any work, thou, nor thy son, nor thy daughter, thy manservant, nor thy maidservant, nor thy cattle, nor thy stranger that is within thy gates: For in six days the Lord made heaven and earth, the sea, and all that in them is, and rested the seventh day: wherefore the Lord blessed the Sabbath day, and hallowed it."

5) HONOR THY FATHER AND THY MOTHER: THAT THY DAYS MAY BE LONG UPON THE LAND WHICH THE LORD THY GOD GIVETH THEE.

6) THOU SHALL NOT KILL.

7) THOU SHALL NOT COMMIT ADULTERY.

8) THOU SHALL NOT STEAL.

9) THOU SHALL NOT BEAR FALSE WITNESS AGAINST THY NEIGHBOR.

10) THOU SHALL NOT COVET THY NEIGHBOR'S HOUSE, THOU SHALL NOT COVET THY NEIGHBOR'S WIFE, NOR HIS MANSERVANT, NOR HIS MAIDSERVANT, NOR HIS OX, NOR HIS ASS, NOR ANYTHING THAT IS THY NEIGHBOR'S" (Exodus 20:1-17).

Everytime we break one of God's commandments, it greatly displeases him. God sent his only begotten Son Jesus into this world to be our advocate and rescue us from his coming judgment. God's wrath will be poured out without mixture upon this wicked world. Unfortunately, this will include the unsaved, uncovered children of disobedience. When we repent and accept Jesus as Lord and Savior, he forgives all of our sins. Then we become followers of Jesus Christ—the King of all kings and Lord of all lords. No one is above the Creator of all things, for he is the sovereign God of all. The enemy Satan thought he would try and exhalt himself above God once and you see where it got him! Don't be like the devil. For him there is no hope at all.

WHAT IS FORNICATION

Fornication is defined by Webster's New World Dictionary as voluntary sexual intercourse generally forbidden by law between an unmarried woman and an unmarried man; any unlawful sexual intercourse including adultery. Notice that the dictionary described fornication as intercourse generally forbidden by law. The Bible goes even further. Fornication is any sexual contact outside the realm of marriage. Fornication is also considered any and all forms of sexual immorality. This covers all sexual perversions that mankind has introduced over the centuries. The Bible teaches us that we as born-again Christians are married to our Lord Jesus Christ. Therefore, there is no room for infidelity because we belong exclusively to God. When the Lord ordains a marriage between a male and female, that marriage bed is undefiled. All other forms of sexual activity are defiled in the eyes of God. The Lord knows that whoever a man or woman becomes intimate with; they are connecting their spirits one to another. This means when their spirits are joined together, they become one flesh. When this behavior is practiced among the unmarried individuals, it leaves them in a state of confusion. No matter what society has said concerning sex outside of marriage, it is still a sin. The world system teaches that it is acceptable to have sexual activity with the same or opposite sex partners as long as there is legal consent. This is sinful behavior in the eyes of God and considered morally wrong. When it comes to 'same' sex partners, this act within itself is an abomination to God. Even though this particular act is considered an abomination, God still loves his children dearly who struggle in this area. The Lord is looking for souls who love him enough to agree with him that sin is sin. Then God <u>can</u> and <u>will</u> deliver you from whatever sin has you bound. However, as long as you are willing to condone whatever sin or abomination that has latched on to you, then you have just surrendered your will to the enemy known as Satan. Always remember, it is the devils will and purpose to oppose the will of God.

Scripture

> *"**Thou shalt not lie with mankind, as with womankind: it is ABOMINATION**"* (Leviticus 18:22).

Here is a list of sexual activities to avoid so that you remain in the will of God. Remember, even if you find yourself struggle in any of these areas, know that God loves you and he can and will deliver you. Therefore, REPENT and turn from your wicked ways, and then turn back to God. He has his arms stretched out wide anxiously awaiting to receive you!

1) Sexual intercourse or activity—any form of sexual activity outside of marriage.
2) Homosexual activity—same sex intercourse or activity practiced at

any time.
3) Masturbation—self-manipulation of one's genitals to achieve sexual gratification.
4) Bestiality—sexual intercourse or activity with any form of beast or animal.
5) Exhibitionism—the act of exposing one's self for the purpose of sexual gratification.
6) Voyeurism—an exaggerated interest in viewing sexual images or activity for the purpose of sexual gratification.
7) Pornography—sexually explicit material or activity viewed either in a magazine, on a computer, or in a movie, or even practiced in the flesh.

These are seven types of sexual behavior to avoid as a child of God. These behaviors are very perverse in nature. They are very habit-forming if practiced. When a person feels like this is normal behavior, they have been totally deceived by the enemy which is the devil. They now condone this behavior as normal. There has been no repentance for their actions. The perverse-minded soul will eventually end up despising the Lord. They feel they have a right to their own likes and dislikes regardless of how perversed it may seem.

Scripture

"He that walketh in his uprightness feareth the Lord: but he that is perverse in his ways despiseth him" (Proverbs 14:2).

You must remember that you belong to the Lord. Everyone who accepts Jesus Christ as their Lord and Savior has been bought and paid for in full. Your body belongs to the Lord where his Spirit now dwells inside of you. When a soul cannot refrain from sexual activity, it is better for that soul to marry. A soul that continues to burn in the lust of their flesh will be tempted to sin often. Therefore, refrain from the many acts of sexual sin and strengthen your relationship with the Lord. Remember, God loves the sinner, but hates the sin!

Scripture

"For if they cannot contain, let them marry: for it is better to marry than to burn" (1 Corinthians 7:9).

"Nevertheless, to avoid fornication, let every man have his own wife, and let every woman have her own husband. Let the husband render unto the wife due benevolence: and likewise also the wife unto the husband. The wife hath not power of her own body, but the husband: and likewise also the husband hath not power of his own body, but the wife" (1 Corinthians 7:2).

At all cost, Christians are to avoid fornication. The Bible tells us to flee fornication at all cost. The Bible teaches us that fornication is the only sin where a man sins against his own body. All other sins are considered outward sins.

Scripture

"Flee fornication. Every sin that a man doeth is without the body; but he that committeth fornication sinneth against his own body" (1 Corinthians 6:18).

Since fornication sins against the body, this means the consequences we must reap will involve corruption toward the body. Once married, surrender to one another when it comes to sexual intimacy. This way, the desires of the flesh will be satisfied between one another. Those who are not married, pray for strength from the Lord to continue in the work of the ministry. All who belong to the Lord is of one spirit.

Scripture

"But he that is joined unto the Lord is one spirit. Flee FORNICATION. Every sin that a man doeth is without the body; but he that committeth fornication sinneth against his own body. What? Know ye not that your body is the temple of the Holy Ghost which is in you, which ye have of God, and ye are not your own? For ye are bought with a price: therefore glorify God in your body, and in your spirit, which are God's" (1 Corinthians 6:17-20).

Did you know that the body you possess belongs to God? All this time we have claimed our bodies as our own. Let us come into the knowledge of God and embrace the truth so that from this day forward, we can take better care of our temple (the body).

CLEAN AND UNCLEAN ANIMALS

Food Consumption Authorized by God

Did you know that God has given us knowledge on maintaining a healthy lifestyle concerning our food source? This knowledge can be found in the book of Leviticus 11:1-47. God reveals the difference between clean and unclean animals. Unclean animals have a specific purpose, either to clean up the dead carcasses to prevent the spread of bacteria and/or perhaps to control the food chain. Clean animals can serve as a food source for both man and beast, or other purposes that God may deem necessary.

The scriptures read,

1) *"And the Lord spake unto Moses and Aaron, saying unto them,*
2) *Speak unto the children of Israel, saying, These are the beasts which ye shall eat among all the beast that are on the earth.*
3) *Whatsoever parteth the hoof, and is cloven footed, and cheweth the cud, among the beast, that shall ye eat.*
4) *Nevertheless these shall ye <u>NOT</u> eat of them that chew the cud, or of them that divide the hoof: as the CAMEL, because he cheweth the cud, but divideth not the hoof; he is unclean unto you.*
5) *And the CONEY, because he cheweth the cud, but divideth not the hoof; he is unclean unto you.*
6) *And the HARE, because he cheweth the cud, but divideth not the hoof; he is unclean unto you.*
7) *And the SWINE, though he divideth the hoof, and be cloven footed, yet he cheweth not the cud; he is unclean to you.*

8) *Of their flesh shall ye not eat, and their carcass shall ye not touch; they are unclean to you.*
9) *These shall ye eat of all that are in the waters: <u>whatsoever hath fins and scales</u> in the waters, in the seas, and in the rivers, <u>them shall ye eat</u>.*
10) *And all that have <u>NOT</u> fins and scales in the seas, and in the rivers, of all that move in the waters, and of any living thing which is in the waters, <u>they shall be an abomination unto you</u>:*
11) *They shall be even an abomination unto you; ye shall <u>NOT</u> eat of their flesh, but ye shall have their carcasses in abomination.*
12) *Whatsoever hath no fins nor scales in the waters, that shall be an abomination unto you.*
13) *And these are they which ye shall have in abomination among the fowls; they shall <u>NOT</u> be eaten, they are an abomination: the EAGLE, and the OSSIFRAGE, and the OSPRAY,*
14) *And the VULTURE, and the KITE after his kind;*
15) *Every RAVEN after his kind;*
16) *And the OWL, and the NIGHT HAWK, and the CUCKOW, and the HAWK after his kind,*
17) *And the LITTLE OWL, and the CORMORANT, and the GREAT OWL,*
18) *And the SWAN, and the PELICAN, and the GIER EAGLE,*
19) *And the STORK, the HERON after her kind, and the LAPWING, and the BAT.*
20) *All fowls that creep, going upon all four, shall be an abomination unto you.*
21) *Yet these may ye eat of every flying creeping thing that goeth upon all four, which have legs above their feet, to leap withal upon the earth;*
22) *Even these of them ye may eat; the LOCUST, after his kind, and the BALD LOCUST, after his kind, and the BEETLE after his kind, and the GRASSHOPPER after his kind.*
23) *But all other flying creeping things, which have four feet, shall be an abomination unto you.*

24) *And for these ye shall be unclean: whosoever toucheth the carcass of them shall be unclean until the even.*
25) *And whosoever beareth aught of the carcass of them shall wash his clothes, and be unclean until the even.*
26) *The carcasses of every beast which divideth the hoof, and is not cloven footed, nor cheweth the cud, are unclean unto you: every one that toucheth them shall be unclean.*
27) *And whatsoever goeth upon his paws, among all manner of beasts that go on all four, those are unclean unto you: whosoever toucheth their carcass shall be unclean until the even.*
28) *And he that beareth the carcass of them shall wash his clothes, and be unclean until the even: they are unclean unto you.*
29) *These also shall be unclean unto you among the creeping things that creep upon the earth; the WEASEL, and the MOUSE, and the TORTOISE, after his kind,*
30) *And the FERRET, and the CHAMELEON, and the LIZARD, and the SNAIL, and the MOLE.*
31) *These are unclean to you among all that creep: whosoever doth touch them, when they be dead, shall be unclean until the even.*
32) *And upon whatsoever any of them, when they are dead, doth fall, it shall be unclean; whether it be any vessel of wood, or raiment, or skin, or sack, whatsoever vessel it be, wherein any work is done, it must be put into water, and it shall be unclean until the even; so it shall be cleansed.*
33) *And every earthen vessel, whereinto any of them falleth, whatsoever is in it shall be unclean; and ye shall break it.*
34) *Of all meat which may be eaten, that on which such water cometh shall be unclean: and all drink that may be drunk in every such vessel shall be unclean.*
35) *And everything whereupon any part of their carcass falleth shall be unclean; whether it be oven, or ranges for pots, they*

shall be broken down: for they are unclean, and shall be unclean unto you.

36) *Nevertheless a fountain or pit, wherein there is plenty of water, shall be clean: but that which toucheth their carcass shall be unclean.*

37) *And if any part of their carcass fall upon any sowing seed which is to be sown, it shall be clean.*

38) *But if any water be put upon the seed, and any part of their carcass fall thereon, it shall be unclean unto you.*

39) *And if any beast, of which ye may eat, die; he that toucheth the carcass thereof shall be unclean until the even.*

40) *And he that eateth of the carcass of it shall wash his clothes, and be unclean until the even: he also that beareth the carcass of it shall wash his clothes, and be unclean until the even.*

41) *And every creeping thing that creepeth upon the earth shall be an abomination; it shall <u>NOT</u> be eaten.*

42) *Whatsoever goeth upon the belly, and whatsoever goeth upon all four, or whatsoever hath more feet among all creeping things that creep upon the earth, them ye shall NOT eat; for they are an abomination.*

43) *Ye shall not make yourselves abominable with any creeping thing that creepeth, neither shall ye make yourselves unclean with them, that ye should be defiled thereby.*

44) *For I am the Lord your God: ye shall therefore sanctify yourselves, and ye shall be HOLY; for I am HOLY: <u>neither</u> shall ye defile yourselves with any manner of creeping thing that creepeth upon the earth.*

45) *For I am the Lord that bringeth you up out of the land of Egypt, to be your God: ye shall therefore be HOLY, for I am HOLY.*

46) *This is the law of the beast, and fowl, and of every living creature that moveth in the waters, and of every creature that creepeth upon the earth:*

47) To make a difference between the unclean and the clean, and between the beast that may be eaten and the beast that may not be eaten" (Leviticus 11:1-47).

BLESSINGS OF OBEDIENCE
(Deuteronomy 28:1-14)

The Bible specifically tells us what the blessings of obedience are. Let us receive this knowledge and benefit from what God has taught us about obedience.

1) *"And it shall come to pass, if thou shalt hearken diligently unto the voice of the Lord thy God, to observe and to do all his commandments which I command thee this day, that the Lord thy God will set thee on high above all nations of the earth.*

2) *And all these blessings shall come on thee, and overtake thee, if thou shalt hearken unto the voice of the Lord thy God.*

3) *Blessed shalt thou be in the city; and blessed shalt thou be in the field.*

4) *Blessed shall be the fruit of thy body (thy seed), and the fruit of thy ground, and the fruit of thy cattle, the increase of thy kine, and the flocks of thy sheep.*

5) *Blessed shall be thy basket and thy store.*

6) *Blessed shalt thou be when thou comest in, and blessed shall thou be when thou goest out.*

7) *The Lord shall cause thine enemies that rise up against thee to be smitten before thy face: they shall come out against thee one way, and flee before thee seven ways.*

8) *The Lord shall command the blessing upon thee in thy storehouses, and in all that thou settest thine hand unto; and he shall bless thee in the land which the Lord thy God giveth thee.*

9) *The Lord shall establish thee a holy people unto himself, as he hath sworn unto thee, If thou shalt keep the commandments of the Lord thy God, and walk in his ways.*
10) *And all people of the earth shall see that thou art called by the name of the Lord; and they shall be afraid of thee.*
11) *And the Lord shall make thee plenteous in goods, in the fruit of thy body, and in the fruit of thy cattle, and in the fruit of thy ground, in the land which the Lord sware unto thy fathers to give thee.*
12) *The Lord shall open unto thee his good treasure, the heavens to give the rain unto thy land in his season, and to bless all the work of thine hand: and thou shalt lend unto many nations, and thou shalt not borrow.*
13) *And the Lord shall make thee the head, and not the tail; and thou shalt be above only, and thou shalt not be beneath; if that thou hearken unto the commandments of the Lord thy God, which I command thee this day, to observe and to do them:*
14) *And thou shalt not go aside from any of the words which I command thee this day, to the right hand, or to the left, to go after other gods to serve them."*

Notice that there are only fourteen verses that apply to the blessings of the Lord. These fourteen verses cover the entire spectrum of all that man could possibly want and desire of the Lord.

CONSEQUENCES OF DISOBEDIENCE (Deuteronomy 28:15-68)

The Bible specifically tells us what the consequences of disobedience are. Let us obey God so that we will not have to face the terrible consequences listed in these next fifty-four verses.

15) *"But it shall come to pass, if thou wilt not hearken unto the voice of the Lord thy God, to observe to do all his commandments and his statutes which I command thee this day; that all these curses shall come upon thee, and overtake thee:*

16) *Cursed shalt thou be in the city, and cursed shalt thou be in the field.*
17) *Cursed shall be thy basket and thy store.*
18) *Cursed shall be the fruit of thy body (thy seed), and the fruit of thy land, the increase of thy kine, and the flocks of thy sheep.*
19) *Cursed shalt thou be when thou comest in, and cursed shalt thou be when thou goest out.*
20) *The Lord shall send upon thee cursing, vexation, and rebuke, in all that thou settest thine hand unto for to do, until thou be destroyed, and until thou perish quickly; because of the wickedness of thy doings, whereby thou hast forsaken me.*
21) *The Lord shall make the pestilence cleave unto thee, until he have consumed thee from off the land, whither thou goest to possess it.*
22) *The Lord shall smite thee with a consumption, and with a fever, and with an inflammation, and with an extreme burning, and with the sword, and with blasting, and with mildew; and they shall pursue thee until thou perish.*
23) *And thy heaven that is over thy head shall be brass, and the earth that is under thee shall be iron.*
24) *The Lord shall make the rain of thy land powder and dust: from heaven shall it come down upon thee, until thou be destroyed.*
25) *The Lord shall cause thee to be smitten before thine enemies: thou shalt go out one way against them, and flee seven ways before them: and shalt be removed into all the kingdoms of the earth.*
26) *And thy carcass shall be meat unto all fowls of the air, and unto the beast of the earth, and no man shall fray them away.*
27) *The Lord will smite thee with the botch of Egypt, and with the emerods, and with the scab, and with the itch, whereof thou canst not be healed.*
28) *The Lord shall smite thee with madness, and blindness, and astonishment of heart.*

29) *And thou shalt grope at noonday, as the blind gropeth in darkness, and thou shalt not prosper in thy ways: and thou shalt be only oppressed and spoiled evermore, and no man shall save thee.*

30) <u>*Thou shalt betroth a wife*</u>*, and* <u>*another man shall lie with her:*</u> *thou shalt build a house, and thou shalt not dwell therein: thou shalt plant a vineyard, and shalt not gather the grapes thereof.*

31) *Thine ox shall be slain before thine eyes, and thou shalt not eat thereof: thine ass shall be violently taken away from before thy face, and shall not be restored to thee: thy sheep shall be given unto thine enemies, and thou shalt have none to rescue them.*

32) *Thy sons and thy daughters shall be given unto another people, and thine eyes shall look, and fail with longing for them all the day long: and there shall be no might in thine hand.*

33) *The fruit of thy land, and all thy labors, shall a nation which thou knowest not eat up; and thou shalt be only oppressed and crushed always:*

34) *So that thou shalt be mad for the sight of thine eyes which thou shalt see.*

35) *The Lord shall smite thee in the knees, and in the legs, with a sore botch that cannot be healed, from the sole of thy foot unto the top of thy head.*

36) *The Lord shall bring thee, and thy king which thou shalt set over thee, unto a nation which neither thou nor thy fathers have known; and there shalt thou serve other gods, wood and stone.*

37) *And thou shalt become an astonishment, a proverb, and a byword, among all nations whither the Lord shall lead thee.*

38) *Thou shalt carry much seed out into the field, and shalt gather but little in; for the locust shall consume it.*

39) *Thou shalt plant vineyards, and dress them, but shalt neither drink of the wine, nor gather the grapes; for the worms shall eat them.*

40) *Thou shalt have olive trees throughout all thy coasts, but thou*

shalt not anoint thyself with the oil; for thine olive shall cast his fruit.

41) *Thou shalt begat sons and daughters, but thou shalt not enjoy them, for they shall go into captivity.*

42) *All thy trees and fruit of thy land shall the locust consume.*

43) *The stranger that is within thee shall get up above thee very high; and thou shalt come down very low.*

44) *He shall lend to thee, and thou shalt not lend to him: he shall be the head, and thou shalt be the tail.*

45) *Moreover all these curses shall come upon thee, and shall pursue thee, and overtake thee, till thou be destroyed; because thou hearkenedst not unto the voice of the Lord thy God, to keep his commandments and his statutes which he commanded thee:*

46) *And they shall be upon thee for a sign and for a wonder, and upon thy seed for ever.*

47) *Because thou servedst not the Lord thy God with joyfulness; and with gladness of heart, for the abundance of all things;*

48) *Therefore shalt thou serve thine enemies which the Lord shall send against thee, in hunger, and in thirst, and in nakedness, and in want of all things: and he shall put a yoke of iron upon thy neck, until he have destroyed thee.*

49) *The Lord shall bring a nation against thee from far, from the end of the earth, as swift as the eagle flieth; a nation whose tongue thou shalt not understand;*

50) *A nation of fierce countenance, which shall not regard the person of the old, nor show favor to the young:*

51) *And he shall eat the fruit of thy cattle, and the fruit of thy land, until thou be destroyed: which also shall not leave thee either corn, wine, or oil, or the increase of thy kine, or flocks of thy sheep, until he have destroyed thee.*

52) *And he shall besiege thee in all thy gates, until thy high and fenced walls come down, wherein thou trustedst, throughout all thy land: and he shall besiege thee in all thy gates throughout all thy land, which the Lord thy God hath given thee.*

53) *And thou shalt eat the fruit of thine own body, the flesh of thy sons and of thy daughters, which the Lord thy God hath given thee, in the siege, and in the straitness, wherewith thine enemies shall distress thee:*

54) *So that the man that is tender among you, and very delicate, his eye shall be evil toward his brother, and toward the wife of his bosom, and toward the remnant of his children which he shall leave:*

55) *So that he will not give to any of them of the flesh of his children whom he shall eat: because he hath nothing left him in the siege, and in the straitness, wherewith thine enemies shall distress thee in all thy gates.*

56) *The tender and delicate woman among you, which would not adventure to set the sole of her foot upon the ground for delicateness and tenderness, her eye shall be evil toward the husband of her bosom, and toward her son, and toward her daughter.*

57) *And toward her young one that cometh out from between her feet, and toward her children which she shall bear: for she shall eat them for want of all things secretly in the siege and straitness, wherewith thine enemy shall distress thee in thy gates.*

58) *If thou wilt not observe to do all the words of the law that are written in this book, that thou mayest fear this glorious and fearful name, The Lord Thy God;*

59) *Then the Lord will make thy plagues wonderful, and the plagues of thy seed, even great plagues, and of long continuance, and sore sicknesses, and of long continuance.*

60) *Moreover he will bring upon thee all the diseases of Egypt, which thou wast afraid of; and they shall cleave unto thee.*

61) *Also every sickness, and every plague, which is not written in the book of this law, them will the Lord bring upon thee, until thou be destroyed.*

62) *And ye shall be left few in number, whereas ye were as the stars of heaven for multitude; because thou wouldest not obey the voice of the Lord thy God.*

THE LAMB'S BOOK OF LIFE:

63) And it shall come to pass, that as the Lord rejoiced over you to do you good, and to multiply you; so the Lord will rejoice over you to destroy you, and to bring you to nought; and ye shall be plucked from off the land whither thou goest to possess it.

64) And the Lord shall scatter thee among all people, from the one end of the earth even unto the other; and there thou shalt serve other gods, which neither thou nor thy fathers have known, even wood and stone.

65) And among these nations shalt thou find no ease, neither shall the sole of thy foot have rest: but the Lord shall give thee there a trembling heart, and failing of eyes and sorrow of mind:

66) And thy life shall hang in doubt before thee; and thou shalt fear day and night, and shalt have none assurance of thy life:

67) In the morning thou shalt say, would God it were even! And at even thou shalt say, would God it were morning! For the fear of thine heart wherewith thou shalt fear, and for the sight of thine eyes which thou shalt see.

68) And the Lord shall bring thee into Egypt again with ships, by the way whereof I spake unto thee, Thou shalt see it no more again: and there ye shall be sold unto your enemies for bondmen and bondwomen, and no man shall buy you."

Notice that there are fourteen verses that apply to the blessings of the Lord and fifty-four verses that apply to the consequences of disobedience. The last thing you want to experience is the many curses written in the word of God. After reading all fifty-four verses, I'm sure you found several curses that perhaps you may have already experienced in your life time. Take heed and beware, every choice we make has consequences. When we obey the word of God we receive his wonderful blessings written in his holy word. If we choose to separate ourselves and walk in disobedience, we will experience that long list of curses. Therefore, honor the Lord and surrender to his will which is holy. Then your life will forever be blessed.

WHO WROTE THE SIXTY-SIX BOOKS OF THE BIBLE?

First of all, I want to establish that the HOLY BIBLE is the inspired word of God. The sixty-six books of the Bible were written by handpicked servants of God selected and inspired by the Angel of the Lord also known as the Holy Spirit of God. This is what the holy word of God says regarding its authenticity.

Scripture

"<u>All scripture is given by inspiration of God</u>, and is profitable for doctrine, for reproof, for correction, for instruction in righteousness. That the man of God may be perfect, thoroughly furnished unto all good works" (2 Timothy 3:16-17).

God almighty visited and anointed men in the spirit to compel them to scribe his holy word for the purpose of edifying the church in the many mysteries involving the kingdom of God. No man had any sole imput in scribing these writings which came from God. The Holy Spirit of God controlled the process of bringing things to the writer's memories. All Holy Scriptures is given by inspiration of God and not of any private interpretation of man.

Scripture

The Apostle Peter wrote, *"Knowing this first, that no prophecy of the scriptures is of any private interpretation. For the prophecy came not in old time by the <u>will of man</u>: but holy men of God spake as they were moved by the Holy Ghost"* (2 Peter 1:20, 21).

When the Holy Bible was scribed by these anointed men of God, the Holy Spirit moved upon them to ensure that they recorded the precise Word of God. No man was allowed to have personal imput when it came to the writing of God's love letter to his beloved creation. Mankind cannot survive on his own without the holy spirit of God to guide his life. When a man is left to himself, he will just about worship anything he can imagine in his mind. This statement holds true based on all the many different forms of worship that are practiced in this world today. The Holy Bible was given to the many nations of this world by God's chosen covenant people. These men of the earth were personally selected by God to perform this specific service so that mankind would know and understand the very nature and character of the true and living God. They were inspired what to write by the Angel of the Lord so that other men would have a lantern to light their way to the hidden kingdom of God. Remember, Jesus brought the kingdom of God with him when he came into the earth. Prior to that, the kingdom of God was hidden from man. The information contained in the Holy Bible is designed to guide us and teach us all the beautiful things pertaining to the Lord. The wisdom of the Lord can only be found written in the Holy Bible. The Bible teaches us that wisdom is the principle thing. Once we have obtained wisdom, we then need understanding to go along with it. Every situation in life has been addressed in this great love letter called the Holy Bible which God gave to his children. Now let us explore all the great prophets, priest, servants, kings, apostles who actually were inspired by God to write these wonderful words of wisdom known as the books of the Bible.

The Authors of the Sixty-Six Holy Books

MOSES 1400 BC—wrote the books of Genesis, Exodus, Leviticus, Numbers and Deuteronomy.
JOSHUA 1350 BC—wrote the book of Joshua.
SAMUEL/NATHAN/GAD 1000-900 BC—wrote the books of Judges, Ruth, 1 Samuel and 2 Samuel.
JEREMIAH 600 BC—wrote the books of 1 King and 2 King.
EZRA 450 BC—wrote the books of 1 Chronicles, 2 Chronicles, Ezra and Nehemiah.
MORDECAI 400 BC—wrote the book of Esther.
MOSES 1400 BC—wrote the book of Job.
KING DAVID—the book of Psalm was written over a period from 1400-400 BC. King David wrote the majority of this precious book. There are others who also contributed to the writing of this blessed book.
- **MOSES**—Psalm 90
- **ASAPH**—Psalm 50, 73-83
- **KING SOLOMON**—Psalm 72, 127.

- **HEMAN**—Psalm 88.
- **ETHAN**—Psalm 89.

KING SOLOMON 900 BC—wrote the books of Proverbs, Ecclesiastes, and Song of Solomon.

ISAIAH 700 BC—wrote the book of Isaiah.

JEREMIAH 600 BC—wrote the books of Jeremiah and Lamentations.

EZEKIEL 550 BC—wrote the book of Ezekiel.

DANIEL 550 BC—wrote the book of Daniel.

HOSEA 750 BC—wrote the book of Hosea.

JOEL 850 BC—wrote the book of Joel.

AMOS 750 BC—wrote the book of Amos.

OBADIAH 600 BC—wrote the book of Obadiah.

JONAH 700 BC—wrote the book of Jonah.

MICAH 700 BC—wrote the book of Micah.

NAHUM 650 BC—wrote the book of Nahum.

HABAKKUK 650 BC—wrote the book of Habakkuk.

ZEPHANIAH 650 BC—wrote the book of Zephaniah.

HAGGAI 520 BC—wrote the book of Haggai.

ZECHARIAH 500 BC—wrote the book of Zechariah.

MALACHI 430 BC—wrote the book of Malachi.

MATTHEW 55AD—wrote the book of Matthew.

JOHN MARK 50 BC—wrote the book of Mark.

LUKE 60 AD—wrote the book of Luke.

JOHN 90 AD—wrote the book of John.

LUKE 65 AD—wrote the book of Acts.

PAUL 50-70 AD—wrote the books of Romans, 1 Corinthians, 2 Corinthians, Galatians, Ephesians, Philippians, Colossians, 1 Thessalonians, 2 Thessalonians, 1 Timothy, 2 Timothy, Titus and Philemon.

PAUL, LUKE, BARNABAS or **APPOLLOS**—wrote the book of Hebrews. These authors more than likely wrote this know as, "The book of Better Things." The true author is still somewhat of a mystery.

JAMES 45 AD—wrote the book of James.

PETER 60 AD - wrote the books of 1 Peter and 2 Peter.

JOHN 90 AD—wrote the books of John, 1 John, 2 John and 3 John.

JUDE 60 AD—wrote the book of Jude.

JOHN 90 AD—wrote the final book of REVELATION.

FIVEFOLD MINISTRY

The fivefold ministry is identified as five spiritual gifts given by God to the church. These spiritual gifts are described as abilities given to Christian leaders to function in five different spiritual areas.

1) Apostles
2) Prophets
3) Evangelists
4) Pastors
5) Teachers

These five areas ordained by God are gifted abilities that serve and glorify the Lord for the purpose of edifying the body of Christ. However, the pastor's and the teacher's position have a dual function. They serve together as an overseer and an instructor. The pastors and teachers are responsible for overseeing the parishioners' spiritual lives while at the same time instructing them in the word of God. Jesus referred to this action as feeding his flocks or feeding his sheep. Keep in mind that the Bread of Life is the Word of God. This is the food Jesus is referring to that his sheep require.

Scripture

"But unto every one of us is given grace according to the measure of the gift of Christ. Wherefore he saith, when he ascended up on high, he led captivity captive, and gave gifts unto men. Now that he ascended, what is it but that he also descended first into the lower parts of the earth? He that descended is the same also that ascended up far above all heavens, that he might fill all things. And he gave some, APOSTLES; and some, PROPHETS; and some, EVANGELISTS; and some, PASTORS and TEACHERS; For the perfecting of the saints, for the work of the ministry, for the edifying of the body of Christ: Till we all come in the unity of the faith, and of the knowledge of the Son of God, unto a perfect man, unto the measure of the stature of the fullness of Christ" (Ephesians 4:7-13).

The purpose and responsibility of the gifted individuals are for the perfecting of the saints. They are assigned to train and equip the body of

Christ to finish the work of the ministry. In doing so, the church body will increase in number and spirituality. This will continue until we all come into the unity of the faith. This means there will only be one church and one body of born-again believers who Jesus is coming back for. Denominations overall are pointless. Anyone who focuses solely on their particular denomination often looses sight on the importance of their relationship with Jesus. Only the relationship we establish with the risen Savior will matter in the very end. The Lord Jesus and the Word of God go hand in hand. Therefore, if you accept Jesus as your Lord and personal Savior while obeying the word of God, you will not go wrong. Only when we focus all of our attention on rituals and traditional matters will we often get side-tracked.

SPIRITUAL GIFTS

The spiritual gifts are of the same spirit. The manifestation of the Spirit is given to every man to profit withal.

1) *"For to one is given by the SPIRIT the word of WISDOM;*
2) *To another the word of KNOWLEDGE by the same SPIRIT;*
3) *To another FAITH by the same SPIRIT;*
4) *To another the gifts of HEALING by the same SPIRIT;*
5) *To another the working of MIRACLES;*
6) *To another PROPHECY;*
7) *To another DISCERNING of SPIRITS;*
8) *To another divers kinds of TONGUES;*
9) *To another the interpretation of TONGUES;*

"But all these worketh that one and the selfsame SPIRIT, dividing to every man severally as he will" (1 Corinthians 12:8-11).

The emphasis on these gifts is on the results, not the process. In other words, the gift of healing does not produce DIVINE HEALERS but DIVINE HEALING. These spiritual gifts are diversities of operation, but it is the same God which worketh all in all. The Lord uses men to bless with his gifts to accomplish his wonderful works here in the earth. These gifts are not for men to shine, but for God to be glorified as his gifts are manifested through men. Every gift God gives to man is strictly for the purpose of edifying the body of Christ.

Scriptures

"Now concerning spiritual gifts, brethren, I would not have you ignorant. Ye know that ye were Gentiles, carried away unto these <u>dumb idols</u>, even as ye were led. Wherefore I give you to understand, that <u>no man speaking by the SPIRIT of God called Jesus accursed</u>: and that <u>no man can say the Jesus is Lord, but by the HOLY GHOST</u>. Now there are diversities of gifts, but the same SPIRIT. And there are differences of administrations, but the same Lord" (1 Corinthians 12:1-5).

All spiritual gifts are given by God to be used to benefit the body of Christ. Therefore, let us never allow ourselves to feel high-minded concerning what God has blessed us with. This is strickly for the Lord's purpose and not ours. We should refrain from boasting in front of men, especially when it was God who elevated us in the first place. We must keep our thoughts on the purpose which God has called us to perform.

Scripture

"Now ye are the body of Christ, and members in particular. And God hath set some in the church, first APOSTLES, secondarily PROPHETS, thirdly TEACHERS, after that MIRACLES, then gifts of HEALINGS, helps, governments, diversities of TONGUES. Are all APOSTLES? Are all PROPHETS? Are all TEACHERS? Are all workers of MIRACLES? Have all the gifts of HEALING? Do all speak with TONGUES? Do all interpret? But covet earnestly the <u>best gifts</u>: and yet show I unto you a more excellent way" (1Corinthians 12:27-31).

Apostle Paul is not trying to instruct his readers in the best way to use their spiritual gifts. The apostle is teaching them how to keep their priorities straight. Spiritual gifts are indeed a blessing to the church and ministry. Without love of the church, their spiritual value weakens. The church was showing strife instead of love when it came to the use of their spiritual gifts. Without love, our blessed spiritual gifts will be misused. Therefore, do not brag on the gifts God has given you, understanding that they are specifically for the body of Christ. Here are an additional twelve gifts of the Spirit that also play an important role in completing the work Christ commissioned.

Scripture

"He that DESCENDED is the same also that ASCENDED up far above all heavens, that he might fill all things. And he gave,

10) some, apostles; and

11) some, prophets; and

12) some, evangelists; and

13) some, pastors and

14) teachers:

"For the perfecting of the Saints, for the work of the ministry, for the edifying of the body of Christ: <u>Till we all come in the unity of the faith</u>, and of the knowledge of the Son of God, unto a perfect man, unto the measure of the stature of the fullness of Christ" (Ephesians 4:10-13).

"Having then gifts differing according to the grace that is given to us,

15) Whether prophecy, let us prophesy according to the proportion of faith;

16) Or ministry, let us wait on our ministering:

17) Or he that teacheth, on teaching;

18) Or he that exhorteth, on exhortation:

19) He that giveth, let him do it with simplicity;

20) He that ruleth, with diligence;

> *21)   He that showeth mercy, with cheerfulness.*

"*Let love be without dissimulation. Abhor that which is evil: cleave to that which is good. Be kindly affectioned one to another with brotherly love; in honor preferring one another; Not slothful in business; fervent in spirit; serving the Lord*" (Romans 12:6-11).

There are a total of twenty-one gifts of the Spirit mentioned that qualify as works to be performed in the ministry of Jesus Christ our Lord. Every one of them has an important function which contributes to the need of the church. Jesus made sure that we had everything we needed to continue in the work of the ministry. Whatever gift God has blessed you with, do it with all of your heart knowing that the Lord is counting on you.

QUALIFICATIONS OF BISHOP, ELDER AND DEACON

Qualification of Bishop
Scripture

"*This is a true saying, If a man desires the office of a bishop, he desireth a good work. A bishop then must be blameless, the husband of one wife, vigilant, sober, of good behavior, given to hospitality, apt to teach; Not given to wine, no striker, not greedy of filthy lucre; but patient, not a brawler, not covetous; One that ruleth well his own house, having his children in subjection with all gravity; For if a man know not how to rule his own house, how shall he take care of the church of God? Not a novice, lest being lifted up with pride he fall into the condemnation of the devil. Moreover he must have a good report of them which are without; lest he fall into reproach and the snare of the devil*" (1Timothy 3:1-7).

Duty to Elders

Scripture

"Let the elder that rule well be counted worthy of double honor, especially they who labor in the word and doctrine. For the scriptures saith, Thou shalt not muzzle the ox that treadeth out the corn. And the laborer is worthy of his reward. Against an elder receive not an accusation, but before two or three witnesses. Them that sin rebuke before all, that others also may fear. I charge thee before God, and the Lord Jesus Christ, and the elect angels, that thou observe these things without preferring one before another, doing nothing by partiality. Lay hands suddenly on no man, neither be partaker of other men's sins: keep thyself pure" (1 Timothy 5:17-22).

Qualification of Deacon

Scripture

"Likewise must the deacons be grave, not double tongued, not given to much wine, not greedy of filthy lucre; Holding the mystery of the faith in a pure conscience. And let these also first be proved; then let them use the office of a deacon, being found blameless. Even so must their wives be grave, not slanderers, sober, faithful in all things. Let the deacons be the husbands of one wife, ruling their children and their own houses well. For they that have used the office of a Deacon well purchase to themselves a good degree, and great boldness in the faith which is in Christ Jesus" (1 Timothy 3:8-13).

Pastoral Office Responsibilities

The pastor who shepherd's today's church fulfills the role of either an elder, pastor or bishop which means overseer. He is responsible to the Lord for the spiritual welfare of the church. When Jesus returns, he will judge and reward the pastors (elders) according to how they have led the church to accomplish the will of God. The title of elder is used to emphasize wisdom and spiritual maturity. The title of bishop is used to emphasize administrative capabilities necessary to operate and function in today's church office. The title of pastor is used to emphasize the responsibility of caring for the church as a shepherd cares for his flock of sheep. The title of preacher is used to emphasize the public proclamation of the gospel of Jesus Christ found in the word of God. The title of teacher is used to emphasize the ability and willingness to teach what thus saith the Lord. We as Christians have a responsibility to support our spiritual leaders as they fulfill their assignment in the ministry of God.

DAY FIVE

LOVE AND CHARITY

Love is the one thing that the Bible teaches us that all of God's laws and principles hang on. Jesus commands us to love one another in order to be recognized as one of his disciples. Love puts all things into motion. Without love, the Bible teaches us we have not the Father. Jesus said, if we love him, we will keep his commandments. Love was such an important principle that Jesus gave us an eleventh commandment concerning this.

Scripture

Jesus said, *"This is my commandment, that ye love one another, as I have loved you. Greater love hath no man than this, that a man lay down his life for his friend"* (John 15:12, 13).

Charity—defined as LOVE—the type of love God has for man and the type of love man has for one another.

This description explains that true love and charity have everything in common. Other forms of affection cannot be compared to love the way God describes it. We must understand that there are other forms of affection known to man. These other forms of affection are often mistaken for true love. The truth is, what many call love, is nothing more than fleshly lust. What the world calls love is no comparison to God's written description of what love truly is. Since God cannot lie, we as Christians have an obligation to believe what, "Thus saith the Lord" before embracing the world's point of view.

The Way of Love—Book of 1 Corinthians
Scripture

"Though I speak with the tongues of men and of angels, and have not CHARITY, I am become as sounding brass, or a tinkling cymbal.

"And though I have the gift of prophecy, and understand all mysteries, and all knowledge; and though I have all faith, so that I could remove mountains, and have not CHARITY, I am nothing.

"And though I bestow all my goods to feed the poor, and though I give my body to be burned, and have not CHARITY, it profiteth me nothing.

"CHARITY suffereth long, and is kind; CHARITY envieth not; CHARITY vaunteth not itself, is not puffed up.

"Doth not behave itself unseemly, seeketh not her own, is not easily provoked, thinketh no evil.

"Rejoiceth not in iniquity, but rejoiceth in the truth.

"Beareth all things, believeth all things, hopeth all things, endureth all things.

"CHARITY never faileth: but whether their be prophecies, they shall fail; whether there be tongues, they shall cease; whether there be knowledge, it shall vanish away.

"For we know in part, and we prophesy in part.

"But when that which is perfect is come, then that which is in part shall be done away.

"When I was a child, I spake as a child, I understood as a child, I thought as a child: but when I became a man, I put away childish things" (1 Corinthians 13:1-11).

> *"And now abideth **FAITH, HOPE, CHARITY**, these three; <u>but the greatest of these is **CHARITY**/</u> (**LOVE**)"* (1 Corinthians 13:13).

This is a clear description of what true LOVE/CHARITY is. When love is not the motivating force, especially concerning the issues of God, these issues will mean absolutely nothing. Relationships can benefit greatly from this type of true love. This verse deals with CHARITY/LOVE being longsuffering, kind, not envying others, not boasting or bragging and puffing one's self up; not easily provoked, thinking no evil at all; choosing to rejoice in only truthful things, never in sinful things; bearing all things, believing all things and enduring all things. These are excellent qualities we must learn to possess when dealing with God or involving ourselves in marriages and loving relationships. Having this frame of mind, forgiveness must always be readily available. We have to be willing to extend forgiveness quickly to those who may offend us in this life. This will keep evil thoughts from overtaking us. All of our relationships would be wonderful if we followed these important principles of God. Love allows us to possess the qualities necessary to fulfill the commandments of the Lord. Loving our brothers and sisters more that we love ourselves will keep us from intentionally offending them. This special kind of AGAPE love requires us to love God first in order to experience this divine type of love. Once this occurs, we will begin to look at each other with value, realizing that all souls have been made in the image and likeness of the almighty God. Then we will learn to put others before ourselves. When we focus solely on the outer appearance of our brothers and sisters, we will always have trouble loving them according to God's standard. Looking at the outward appearance causes us to notice the flesh and not the spirit of man. We will then see drunks, drug addicts, the poor and rich, racial barriers, thieves, whoremonger's, homosexuals and all manners of sin when we focus our vision on the outer flesh. Only pagans have preferences when it comes to mankind. When we look at our brothers and sisters for <u>WHO</u> they are inside, we see the children of God. We realize each and every man and woman was made in the image and likeness of the almighty Creator. All souls are valuable in the eyes of the Lord. We must view others like God views us. This is indeed the unconditional kind of love that the Lord gives and requires.

THE LAMB'S BOOK OF LIFE:

THE BEATITUDES OF JESUS CHRIST

This section reveals the great Sermon on the Mount spoken by Jesus Christ himself. This sermon deals with the inner state of mind and heart that is essential for true Christian discipleship. Jesus taught us what type of character and conduct as genuine true believers we should have as a disciple, or student of God. The life of the Christian believer was described by Jesus as a life of grace and glory. This grace and glory only comes from God and God alone. Knowing and learning these principles of the Lord Jesus Christ will truly bless the lives of the born-again believers. When we are blessed by God, we are privileged to walk in his favor all of our days in the earth.

The Eight Character Blessings Taught by Jesus

These blessings will teach us how to have peace in our heart. Jesus was freely teaching the souls who were willing to follow him about the necessary character and conduct required for the Christian believer. Jesus explained the benefit and the outcome of all characteristics mentioned. This is how a trueChristian believer should walk. Then they will experience a blessed life as a result of the Lord's knowledge and wisdom.

Scripture

"And seeing the multitudes, he went up into a mountain: and when he was set, his disciples came unto him: And he opened his mouth, and taught them, saying,

1) Blessed are the poor in spirit: for theirs is the kingdom of heaven.

2) Blessed are they that mourn: for they shall be comforted.

3) Blessed are the meek: for they shall inherit the earth.

4) Blessed are they which do hunger and thirst after righteousness: for they shall be filled.

5) Blessed are the merciful: for they shall obtain mercy.

6) Blessed are the pure in heart: for they shall see God.

7) Blessed are the peacemakers: for they shall be called the children of God.

8) Blessed are they which are persecuted for righteousness sake: for theirs is the kingdom of heaven. Blessed are ye, when men shall revile you, and persecute you, and shall say all manner of evil against you falsely, for my sake. Rejoice, and be exceeding glad: for great is your reward in heaven: for so persecuted they the prophets which were before you" (Matthew 5:1-12).

The word 'blessed' is synonymous with being happy. This is a basic description of the Christian believer's inner condition as a result of the word of God. The beatitudes described here do not show you how to be saved, but describes the character of those who have been saved.

1) The first blessing talks about the poor in spirit. The poor in spirit is the opposite of the proud and haughty in spirit. They have been humbled by the grace of God and have acknowledged their sin and therefore, their dependency is upon the Lord.
2) The second blessing deals with those that mourn shall be comforted. Those who mourn over sin shall be comforted in their confession. Those who mourn for human distress of the lost shall be comforted by the compassion of God.
3) The third blessing describes how the meek shall inherit the earth. Those who are meek have been humbled before God and will inherit the kingdom of God. They will also ultimately share in the kingdom of God on earth. The kingdom of which Jesus preached is both in us and is yet to come.
4) The fourth blessing tells us that those who hunger after righteousness shall be filled. These are the ones who have a deep desire for personal righteousness. This in itself is proof of their spiritual rebirth or conversion. Those who are poor and empty in their own spiritual poverty understand the depth of their need. This causes a hunger and thirst for that which only God can give.

5) The fifth blessing deals with the merciful who will obtain mercy. Those who are merciful have been born-again by the mercy of God. Divine love which comes from God has been extended to them. They have the work of the Holy Spirit in them producing a mercy that many cannot comprehend. Jesus became the ultimate example of mercy when he cried out on the cross. Jesus asked God the Father to forgive mankind for they know not what they do.

6) The sixth blessing explains the pure at heart. The scripture tells us that they are the ones who will see God. Those who are truly saved shall see God. Their lives have been transformed by the grace of God. They are not yet sinless, but their position before God has been changed. They have a new birth, a saving faith, and holiness. They are experiencing the process of sanctification which is constantly changing them to the image of Jesus Christ.

7) The seventh blessing addresses the peacemaker. These are the ones who are at peace with God and desire to live in peace with all men. It is the peace which Jesus equips men and women with to become ambassadors of the kingdom of God. Then they can go forth with the message of the gospel to a troubled and dying world. This qualifies them to be called the children of God.

8) The eighth blessing is for those who are persecuted for righteousness sake. All who will live godly in Christ Jesus shall suffer persecution. The Lord Jesus forewarns us concerning this, therefore be not discouraged when it comes. This type of persecution is twofold. The first involves a physical pursuing of the persecuted Christian believer. The second involves a personal attack of slander against the Christian believer. Jesus tells us to rejoice and be exceedingly glad either way. Jesus further tells us that great is our reward in the kingdom of heaven. We must learn to set our focus on our eternal destiny concerning all spiritual things. Once we know and understand the truth concerning eternal life, nothing can steal our joy ever again. Our hope and trust is in the Lord and all that he has promised us concerning eternal life with him. This knowledge in the word of God teaches us <u>not</u> to focus all of our attention on the matters of this world. Therefore, regardless of what we go through in this life, understand that God has promised us a beautiful ending.

GRACE AND MERCY

This blessing from God is not to be overlooked. The grace of God goes all the way back to the Garden of Eden as God dealt with Adam and Eve. The word grace can also be found mentioned in the Bible during the time of the great patriarch Noah. The mercies of God can also be associated with the wonderful acts of kindness God bestowed on the children of men—namely to mention during the time of Sodom and Gomorrah how God spared Abraham's nephew Lot from destruction. Every one of these patriarchs received the Lord's favor because they chose to believe and was willing to serve God. Despite Adam and Eve were created blameless, even after the sin of Adam, God still showed them grace and mercy when he cover their nakedness with animal skins. However, blood had to be shed for the sin that was committed in the garden by Adam. For this reason, Jesus willingly left his heavenly glory to visit mankind in the earth in order to die for the remission of sin. Jesus made his appearance into the earth after fourty-two generations which starting with Abraham and ended with the birth of the Messiah. This was the point where total salvation entered into this world.

Scripture

"But if we walk in the light, as he is in the light, we have fellowship one with another, and the <u>blood of Jesus Christ</u> his Son cleanseth us from all sin. If we say that we have no sin, we deceive ourselves, and the truth is not in us" (1 John 1:7, 8).

Noah was a preacher during the time he built the ark for the Lord. Lot was Abraham's nephew who later became faithful unto the Lord when God rescued him from the twin cities of Sodom and Gomorrah. The Lord ordered the destruction of Sodom and Gomorrah by raining down fire and brimstone from heaven. Mankind has always received God's unmerited favor, even when they found themselves lacking in their good works. The Lord saw the inner heart of these chosen servants and through his unconditional love granted grace and mercy to them both. This is just to name a few.

Scripture

"But Noah found GRACE in the eyes of the Lord" (Genesis 6:8).

God gave Noah grace because he was a righteous man and a servant unto the Lord. Grace is that unmerited favor from God that he gives us because he loves us. This grace is undeserved, unearned, unworthy and given only because of the goodness of God alone. Now concerning Lot, the two angels sent from the Lord ushered Lot and his family away from the sin city before the destruction took place.

Scripture

"And while he lingered, the men laid hold upon his hand, and upon the hand of his wife, and upon the hand of his two daughters: the Lord being merciful unto him: and they brought him forth, and set him without the city" (Genesis 19:16).

"It is of the <u>Lord's mercies</u> that we are not consumed, because his compassions fail not. They are <u>new every morning</u>: great is thy faithfulness" (Lamentations 3:22, 23).

Thank God man does not always get what he deserves. The wages of sin is still death. Thank God for his grace and mercy. God's mercy is new every morning and he is faithful in all that he does. Grace and mercy comes from our Lord just because he is loving and good toward mankind. The Bible tells us that God's mercy endures forever. The Lord's mercy lifts us up and always seems to provide us with a protective shield.

Grace

Grace is favor or sheer kindness shown to mankind without regard to merit or worth. This grace is totally undeserving. What causes God to show this kind of favor toward men? God loves his people whom he created. God is merciful, gracious, longsuffering, compassionate, and full of goodness and truth. The grace of God given to mankind was further revealed in the finishing work of Jesus Christ our Lord. When Jesus died on the cross and was resurrected, the broken fellowship was restored between God and his people, both the Jews and the Gentiles. God does not wish that any of his children should perish.

Scripture

"The Lord is not slack concerning his promise, as some men count slackness; but is longsuffering to us-ward, <u>not willing that any should perish</u>, but that all should come to repentance" (2 Peter 3:9).

Grace is the love of God that causes him to forgive the undeserved. In case you are wondering who the undeserved individuals are, do yourself a favor. The next time you pass by a mirror, say hello to him or her for me. Remember, by grace are we saved and not of works.

Scripture

"For by grace are ye saved through faith; and that not of yourselves: it is the gift of God: Not of works, lest any man should boast. For we are his workmanship, created in Christ Jesus unto good works, which God hath before ordained that we should walk in them" (Ephesians 2:8-10).

The scripture clearly tells us that by faith are we saved. There is nothing that mankind did to receive this special favor from God. Once we accept salvation through Christ Jesus, our lives will definitely change. This is when the struggle between the spirit and the flesh really begins. The Lord said we are his workmanship created in Jesus unto good works. Therefore, we have been foreordained that we should walk in these good works. Our lives should line up with the word of God. We should walk in righteousness or else something is out of place. God knows who will be called into his good works. The scripture tells us that God planned our assignments before the foundation of the world. This means, God also knew who would be saved before the world began. To all the souls that God has chosen from the beginning, receive the necessary grace from the Lord and be holy. God knows exactly who will answer his call.

Scripture

"Who hath saved us, and called us with a HOLY CALLING, not according to our works, but according to his own purpose and GRACE, which was given us in Christ Jesus before the world began" (2 Timothy 1:9).

That's right, God ordained us holy before the world began. This was accomplished when God chose us before the foundation of the world to be saved. Our holiness comes from God through his grace given unto us. This is such a wonderful blessing to receive out of sheer love from God. Now we know and understand that when we accept Jesus Christ as Lord and Savior, we are made RIGHTEOUS and HOLY unto the Lord. This is the gift of God, not from the works of mankind. We now understand that if man was able to work or earn his way to God, he would think too highly of himself. The scriptures clearly express this point in the book of Ephesians.

Scripture

"For by grace are ye saved through faith; and that not of yourselves: it is the gift of God: Not of works, <u>lest any man should boast</u>. For we are his workmanship created in Christ Jesus unto good works, which God hath before ordained that we should walk in them" (Ephesians 2:8-10).

The Lord saved us by his grace and beforehand ordained that we walk in his good works. In other words, our ordained good works have been waiting on us to come to our senses since the beginning. This means your life will change when you come into the knowledge of Jesus Christ as Lord. There are good works with your name written on them just waiting to be fulfilled by you, and only you. God has work for us to do here in the earth. We all start out as prodigal sons and daughters in this journey called life. When we come to ourselves, that's when we receive our assignment which has always been right there waiting on us. Let us wake up out of darkness and enter into the marvelous light of Jesus Christ.

Mercy

Mercy is the love from God that he gives to those who have sinned and broken his law. God is merciful and full of love. The mercy of God through Jesus Christ healed all manner of sickness and disease, and even delivered us from all manner of captivity. These things were out of man's control and required the mercy of God to intervene. The sheer mercy of God caused him to send his only begotten Son to die for the sins of all mankind. This is what you call sheer mercy. God visited the earth to see about his creation and to make a way for us to enter into his precious kingdom. Finally, because God is merciful, he commands his children to be merciful also toward each other.

Scripture

"Blessed are the merciful: for they shall obtain mercy" (Matthew 5:7).

Those who give mercy shall receive mercy. Those who refuse to give mercy will likewise not receive it in return where it counts the most, which is from the almighty God. There is an additional thought here. If the so-called born-again believer allows their heart to be hardened toward forgiveness, is their eternal salvation in jeopardy? Remember, when the Lord speaks, his words are not up for discussion. This means everything in the Holy Bible has to be obeyed without question. If God says forgive thy neighbor that is exactly what we must do. Remember, God is the sovereign ruler, not man. When you take it upon yourself and choose not to walk with the Lord, this is called REBELLION and DISOBEDIENCE toward God. When you choose to have a problem with the written word of God, you have taken on the spirit of God's enemy known as Satan. This defeated foe bears the only spirit that purposely lives contrary to the word of God. When we imitate the enemy, we accomplish his will through our life. This is not a good thing. You did know that Satan too has an agenda? Therefore, let us as Christians show mercy toward all mankind, realizing this is the only way God will show mercy toward us.

WISDOM

Webster's dictionary defines wisdom as the quality of being wise; power of judging rightly and following the soundest course of action, based on knowledge, experience, understanding, and good judgment. This definition is fine, but the Bible tells us more. We must remember to always operate in the gracious wisdom of God, and then the answers will come to life's difficult questions. Wisdom also is the key that unlocks the good treasures to the kingdom of God!

(What the wise king had to say)

King Solomon gave us an example of why wisdom is the most important thing.

Scripture

> *"And Solomon went up thither to the brazen altar before the Lord, which was at the tabernacle of the congregation, and offered a thousand burnt offerings upon it. In that night did God appear unto Solomon, and said unto him, Ask what I shall give thee. And Solomon said unto God, Thou hast showed great mercy unto David my father, and hast made me to reign in his stead. Now, O Lord God, let thy promise unto David my father be established: for thou hast made me king over a people like the dust of the earth in multitude. Give me now <u>WISDOM</u> and <u>KNOWLEDGE</u> that I may go out and come in before this people: for who can judge this thy people that is so great. And God said to Solomon, because this was in thine heart, and thou hast not asked riches, wealth, or honor, nor the life of thine enemies, neither yet hast asked long life; but hast asked WISDOM and KNOWLEDGE for thyself, that thou mayest judge my people, over whom I have made thee king: Wisdom and Knowledge is granted unto thee; and I will give thee riches, and wealth, and honor, such as none of the kings have had that have been before thee, neither shall there any after thee have the like"* (2 Chronicles 1:7-12).

King Solomon learned how important it was to have wisdom. He found out in all his wisdom that it also unlocks the door to the multitude of treasures from God. King Solomon had an opportunity to ask for anything his heart was capable of desiring and he chose wisdom to properly lead God's people. This pleased God so much that he made King Solomon's name go down in history as the world's riches and wisest king. Wisdom will always cause you to make the right choices and avoid life's many pitfalls. Once the pitfalls have been eliminated, then your life will soar to the top.

Scripture

"But whosoever hearkeneth unto me **(the Lord)** *shall dwell safely, and shall be quiet from fear of evil"* (Proverbs 1:33).

Wisdom comes from God, and when we find it, we should lay hold of it like unto precious jewels or hidden treasure. Wisdom allows us to dwell safely and not fear the evil that is ready to pounce around every dark corner.

Scripture

"Wisdom is the principal thing; therefore get wisdom: and with all thy getting get understanding. Exalt her, and she shall promote thee: she shall bring thee to honor, when thou dost embrace her. She shall give to thine head an ornament of grace: a crown of glory shall she deliver to thee" (Proverbs 4:7-9).

Wisdom teaches us how to properly fear and reverence God. This will cause us to obey the Lord's commandments while making wise decisions which will establish our future. When we seek God's wisdom, remember to operate therein with a pure, peaceably, gentle, and self-controlled heart. This will help us humble ourselves before the Lord as we establish the right frame of mind. Then your decisions will be wise and your consequences will produce the good treasures from God.

FAITH VS FEAR

Faith is what gives the born-again believers a confident attitude in knowing and trusting in the Lord Jesus Christ. This same faith causes those chosen before the foundation of the world to be committed to the will of God. On the other hand, fear is a spirit which comes from Satan himself.

The evil one knows that if he can cause fear to come upon the people of God, they will forever be tormented in their minds having no rest. Satan knows that fear causes a man to be a prisoner of his thoughts. God tells us that he gave us not the spirit of fear. God first of all lets us know that fear is indeed a spirit. Secondly, he lets us know that this spirit does not come from him. We must understand that this spirit called fear is the opposite of faith. Both faith and fear have expectations of future things to come. Faith is the substance of things hoped for, and the evidence of things not seen, while fear anticipates frightful events both now and in the immediate future. We now have a choice to make. We can either choose faith which pleases God, or we can choose fear and live the remainder of our lives in torment. The final decision is up to each and every one of us.

Faith Pleases God
Scripture

"Now FAITH is the substance of things hoped for, the evidence of things not seen. Through FAITH we understand that the worlds were framed by the word of God, so that things which are seen were not made of things which do appear" (Hebrews 11:1, 3).

Apostle Paul prayed," *Wherefore I also, after I heard of your Faith in the Lord Jesus, and love unto all the saints, Cease not to give thanks for you, making mention of you in my prayers; That the God of our Lord Jesus Christ, the Father of glory, may give unto you the spirit of wisdom and revelation in the knowledge of him"* (Ephesians 1:15-17).

Faith does not coincide with common sense. Faith requires spiritual vision to see and believe in the things we cannot see and believe in the natural. Faith applies to the things we hope and long for. The things which we can see with our natural eyes require no faith because they are present before us. The thing we cannot see is what requires our hope and belief. The God of salvation has given us power to call those things that we cannot see into our present existence. The Bible says it like this.

Scripture

"As it is written, I have made thee a father of many nations, before him whom he believed, even God, who quickeneth the dead, and <u>CALLETH THOSE THINGS WHICH BE NOT AS THOUGH THEY WERE</u>. Who against hope believed in hope, that he (Abraham) might become the father of many nations, according to that which was spoken, <u>SO SHALL THY SEED BE</u>.

This means calling resources into the earthly realm from the heavenly realm. God has caused everything we need to come forth for our use in the earth. All visions and ideas are divinely placed in the thoughts of man by God himself. All this time you thought it was you alone. The Bible teaches us that all we have to do is allow ourselves to think of an idea and speak forth the words; God will take over from there and cause the manifestation to occur.

Scripture

"The preparation of the heart in man, and the answer of the tongue, is from the Lord" (Proverbs 16:1).

The heart and mind is considered the same when it comes to our thought process. The Lord has likewise blessed the righteous words we speak. Remember, death and life is still in the power of our tongue. This same principle applies when we speak our thoughts into existence. God takes over and causes everything in the earth to manifest. This is why everything belongs to God. If you feel differently about this, try taking something from this world when you die. By then, it will be too late to give God his rightful glory he was due. This is why we must praise and worship the Lord right now! He is worthy to be praised. We as children of God have been given power to become the sons of God. Therefore, we can believe by faith, and have anything we believe and ask God for in Jesus' name. But remember, all things that are given have consequences, so be careful what you ask of God.

Scripture

Jesus said, *"And whatsoever ye shall ask in my name, that will I do, that the Father may be glorified in the Son. If ye shall ask any thing in my name, I will do it"* (John 14:13, 14). *"For we walk by FAITH, not by sight"* (2 Corinthians 5:7).

The first part of this verse lets us know that whatever we ask of God the Father in the name of Jesus we can have—as long as it brings glory to God. If what we ask does not glorify God, then it's not from God. The Bible tells us that all good and perfect gifts come from the Lord.

Scripture

"Every good gift and every perfect gift is from above, and cometh down from the Father of LIGHTS, with whom is no variableness, neither shadow of turning" (James 1:17).

If this is true, where do the wicked gifts come from? Satan is always looking for evil men to raise us in the earth so that his kingdom of darkness can increase. This will cause those super-stars of Satan to attract the lost souls of this world as they are ushered into the enemy's camp. Satan copies everthing that God the Father does. Nothing that Satan ever does is original. Notice that wealthy wicked men in some way or another always end up mocking the will of God. This glorifies the devil whether they realize it or not. This is why you see wicked and evil manifestations appearing prosperous all over the world. This sinful wealth all around us is only temporary and will shortly be transferred into the hands of the righteous saints of God. For example, God is not blessing the billion dollar pornography industry, however, its everywhere you look tempting our nation. Likewise, the Lord is not blessing the promotion of harmful things sold whether legal or illegal in this country. Everything that a man does is not always blessed by God. I guarantee you that the enemy of God known as Satan has influenced all wicked and evil behavior known to man. The scripture that deals with faith and sight explains to us that we should trust in the Lord at all times. This type of trust is necessary regardless of how our situation may look or feel. It's not in the feeling; it's always in the knowing. That is why it is imperative that we study and grow to love the word of God. Once we begin to know better, we can certainly expect to do better. The Lord has addressed every problem and concern we will ever face in life in his precious love letter to this world. All we have to do is read and spend time in the Holy Bible in order to receive the revelation knowledge God intends for us to have. When we know and understand the will of God, we can live in harmony and fellowship under the protection of the Almighty. If we continue to live selfishly, always satisfying the sinful needs of our flesh, we will continue to suffer and struggle in this life.

Scripture

"But the just shall live by FAITH" (Habakkuk 2:4b).

This scripture deals with the fact that once we are justified in Christ Jesus, from that moment on, we should live by FAITH. Anything that is not of faith is sin!

Scripture

"For whatsoever is not of faith is sin" (Romans 14:23b).

We should live according to the word and will of the almighty God. Faith causes us to rely and commit ourselves totally to our Lord Jesus Christ. Once we dedicate our lives to our Lord and Savior, we can then believe by faith and place our trust in the finished work of Christ. That is why we must be about our Father's business while we are yet alive. Jesus said that we would do greater works than he once he ascended back to the right hand of the throne of God. Therefore, let us stay busy doing the work of the kingdom as we look forward to spending eternity with God. The Lord is preparing a beautiful kingdom so that he may dwell with his precious saints forever. Therefore, work out your salvation with fear and trembling as you prepare yourselves to meet God.

Faith Healing

Faith in God and belief in his promises will always manifest healing in our lives. Jesus died on the cross for the sins of the entire world. Therefore, we no longer have to accept sickness when it attacks our body. Remember, our body is the temple of God where he dwells. When we become the righteousness of God in Christ Jesus, the Lord says that the afflictions will be many. Although, be not discouraged, God has made a way for his righteous souls to overcome all things by faith.

Scripture

"Many are the afflictions of the righteous: but the Lord delivereth him out of them all" (Psalm 34:19).

This lets us know when we follow Jesus, and afflictions come, we must know in our heart that the Lord has forewarned us concerning this. So rest assured that God will keep his word and deliver us out of the many afflictions we will have to face. Therefore, worry not—just trust and believe God's report, regardless of how the situation may look. The scriptures further tell us that Jesus paid the price on the cross for sin, sickness, iniquities, peace and healing. There is nothing that our Savior Jesus the Christ failed to cover with his precious blood when he died on that rugged cross.

Scripture

"But he was wounded for our transgressions, he was bruised for our iniquities: the chastisement of our peace was upon him; and with his stripes <u>WE ARE HEALED</u>" (Isaiah 53:5).

"For she said within herself, If I may but touch his garment, I shall be whole. But Jesus turned him about, and when he saw her, he said, Daughter, be of good comfort; <u>THY FAITH</u> hath made thee whole. And the woman was made whole from that hour" (Matthew 9:21, 22).

This scripture deals with our FAITH which is required for the manifestation of God to work on our behalf. If we can believe it, we can receive it. Jesus himself said in the Bible that he did very few miracles in his hometown due to their UNBELIEF! It's not that Jesus our Lord was incapable of healing whomever and wherever he pleased. Jesus would often ask a question to those he confronted. One of the questions the Lord often asked was, "Will thou be made whole?" Another statement Jesus would often make as he encounted those in need was, "Thy faith has made thee whole." There are even scriptures in the Bible where Jesus observed ones faith and immediately informed them that their sins are forgiven. We must understand that the sin issue has to always be dealt with first! Thank God for repentance. There is another verse of scripture that comes to mind where Jesus asked a blind man this question. "Believe you that I am able to do this?" All these questions asked by the Lord challenged the faith of all who sought something from God. The people that came to Jesus had an expectation of deliverance, or else they would not have come. Therefore, they had strong faith and hope to expect and receive exactly what they were seeking from the Lord. Knowing that the God we serve is almighty, we must worship him at all times in spirit and in truth. When we trust and believe that the word of God will do exactly what God said it will do, that's when we will witness the many manifestations come to life. Any form of doubt will always cancel out faith. The Bible teaches us that faith is a key element which connects us to God.

Scripture

"But without faith it is IMPOSSIBLE to please him: for he that cometh to God must believe that he is, and that he is a REWARDER of them that DILIGENTLY seek him" (Hebrews 11:6).

This scripture lets us know that God requires us to have FAITH and BELIEF in order to please him. In order to believe, we must first believe in our heart and know in our mind that God is who he says he is. The final point here is God blesses and rewards those of us who seek him with all diligence. God loves that intense, passionate, zeal, enthusiastic, devotion that we have when we are on fire for him. Let us never forget that we belong exclusively to God. Only faith can reveal this unto us. Let us never forget the sacrifice Jesus Christ made for each one of us when he laid down his sinless life on that rugged cross.

Scripture

"For ye are the children of God by faith in Christ Jesus. For as many of you as have been baptized into Christ have put on Christ. There is neither Jew nor Greek, there is neither bond nor free, there is neither male nor female: for ye are all one in Christ Jesus" (Galatians 3:26-28).

Let us never allow ourselves to forget that Jesus voluntarily took our place when he laid down his life for the sins of the world. Jesus the Christ never committed sin while he walked in the flesh. Therefore, he hung on that cross for you and I. Ask youself a question? Would you endure pain, suffering and ultimately lay your life down for a crime someone else clearly committed?

Since the answer is already NO. We should be very thankful for what the Lord has done on our behalf. This is the kind of God we serve.

Fear is from Satan

The ACRONYM we like to use in the church body for fear is:

FALSE
EVIDENCE
APPEARING
REAL

Scripture

"For God hath not given us the Spirit of Fear; but of power, and of love, and of a sound mind" (2 Timothy 1:7).

"There is no Fear in love; but perfect love casteth out Fear: because FEAR hath TORMENT. He that Feareth is not made perfect in love" (1 John 4:18).

The above scripture explains that fear is a SPIRIT not given by God. Let us understand that fear is first of all a spirit. Then we must understand that if fear does not come from God, it has to come from the enemy of God. The enemy of God known as the devil sends this spirit to torment the people of

God. Do you realize whatever you fear will eventually come upon you? Fear has a way of controlling your entire life. Fear will also make you a prisoner in your own mind. Anyone not knowing Jesus Christ in the pardoning of their sins fear DEATH! This common fear causes torment in the mind of men and women everywhere, especially when they start to age. When we get over the fear of death, the torment that fear produces will also leave. The Bible teaches us that the fear of death also causes one to be in bondage.

Scripture

"Forasmuch then as the children are partakers of flesh and blood, he also himself likewise took part of the same; that through death he might destroy him that had power of death, that is, <u>the devil</u>; And deliver them who through FEAR of DEATH were all their lifetime subject to bondage" (Hebrews 2:14, 15).

When we come into the knowledge of Jesus Christ as Lord and Savior, we then understand that he died on the cross to save us from the second death. This second death is known as the lake of fire that will open its mouth to receive all unsaved souls on the Day of Judgment. Christian believers know and trust the scripture that deals with being absent from the body is to be present with the Lord. When the saints die in the flesh, they are ushered at some point into the presence of God to face the Judgment Seat of Christ. This is where the rewards will be given to the saints for their faithful service during their work in God's vineyard. Those who appear at this judgment of Christ will have their salvation assured. Only their works will be burned if they were not profitable unto the Lord.

Scripture

"We are confident, I say, and willing rather to be absent from the body, and to be present with the Lord" (2 Corinthians 5:8).

This reassures the Christian believer of where their destiny will be when they die in the loving arms of Christ Jesus. Therefore, let us no longer have fear concerning death. The Bible also teaches us never to fear situations that occur in the earth. The Lord places a shield of protection around us while he personally fights all of our battles. This next verse of scripture reminds us not to be afraid of anything at any giving time.

Scripture

> *Thou shalt not be afraid for the terror by night; nor the arrows that flieth by day; Nor for the pestilence that walketh in darkness; nor for the destruction that wasteth at noonday. A thousand shall fall at thy side, and ten thousand at thy right hand; but it shall not come nigh thee"* (Psalm 91:5-7).

> "*Because thou has made the Lord, which is my refuge, even the Most High, thy habitation; There shall NO EVIL befall thee, neither shall any plague come nigh thy dwelling. For he shall give his angels charge over thee, to keep thee in all thy ways. They shall bear thee up in their hands, lest thou dash thy foot against a stone"* (Psalm 91:9-12).

The Lord tells us not to be afraid of anything. He reassures us that he is our protector. Regardless of what the situation looks like, or how bad it seems, the Lord is always there to protect his followers. When we make the Lord our God, he gives his angels charge over us. Their assignment is to watch over us and make sure we are not harmed. The Lord cares so much for us, that he is concerned over the smallest to the greatest needs of his children. We serve a God that is even concerned over his children dashing their foot against a tiny stone. The Lord is so concerned that before he will let you stub your toe, his angels have been instructed to lift you up. Remember, fear not and trust in the Lord with all of your might. Realizing the value of the salvation Jesus died to give us. This same salvation spares the born-again believer from the wrath of God and the second death known as the lake of fire. Therefore, fear death no longer knowing that absent in your flesh body is to be present in the Spirit with the Lord. The soul and spirit of man will indeed live forever; the choice is totally up to you where your soul and spirit will spend eternity.

Your Worse Fear Will Come upon You

We must remember to be very careful allowing fear to come upon us. Let us not forget, fear is from Satan and not from God. When we fear something, it sticks with us like a fungus. We worry about it night and day until it begins to torment our mind. The next thing you know, whatever fear you chose to worry about will manifest in your life. It's almost like you worry about a situation so much until it finally shows up. The reason the situation occurs this way is because you chose not to let it go. You worried about it, you talked about it, and you thought about it constantly. Remember, everything starts with a thought. Unless you take that thought captive, it will always come to pass. The Bible tells us in the book of Job that his worst fear came upon him. Job is letting us know that whatever we choose to constantly worry about will eventually show up. This is what the Bible had to say.

Scripture

"For the thing which I greatly FEARED is come upon me, and that which I was AFRAID of is come unto me. I was not in safety, neither had I rest, neither was I quiet; yet trouble came" (Job 3:25, 26).

Job is a true story and lesson provided for us in the Holy Bible. Satan had to receive permission from God to trouble Job. God, knowing his servant very well, granted Satan the permission to test Job. This test caused Job to loose everything he owned, including his ten children to the hands of the enemy. When Job fails to curse God like Satan had suggested, God granted Satan permission to further pursue Job by afflicting his body only for a short season. However, the Lord would not let Satan kill Job's flesh. The problem with this scenario is Job had no idea what was going on, nor how long his affliction would last. We as humans dwell in the earthly realm. This means that we are not privileged to see things in the spiritual realm unless we are invited by the Angel of the Lord. When we know and trust in the Lord and believe on his every word, we understand the trials when they come. We choose to believe God's report instead of what mankind thinks. Knowing the word of God prepares us for all obstacles when they come our way. You will never see Satan having a conversation with God about you, however, you can rest assure, it will occur. Satan has to obtain permission from God before he can cause harm to the people of God. What we do know and understand is that the Lord will protect and care for those who love him. Even if God has given the devil permission to test us, we must understand that God said he would not put anymore on us than we could bear. This means our Creator knows just how much we can take. No matter whether sickness or disease, or any other infirmity that may attack our flesh, Jesus said, "By his stripes, we <u>ARE</u> healed." No sickness or disease can remain among the saints of God. The holy word teaches us how Jesus has given the victory to all who believe in his holy name. If you do not believe in the risen Savior, do not worry about this section because it does not apply to you. Only those who believe can receive this word of truth.

Scripture

"But he was wounded for our transgressions, he was bruised for our iniquities: the chastisement of our peace was upon him; and with his stripes we are <u>HEALED</u>" (Isaiah 53:5).

Remember; fear nothing in this world knowing that we will attract what ever it is we stand in fear of. When afflictions come, remember that God may be discussing your good name and character with his enemy Satan. The book of Job has already given us instruction and a peek of what goes on in the spirit realm. Therefore, learn from this teaching. Trust in the Lord that he will do exactly what his holy word promises he will do. Then we can be made free from all things through the blood of Jesus Christ our Lord.

POWER OF PRAYER

Prayer is the ultimate communication initiated from man to God. The Lord is so gracious, anyone can offer up prayers. However, sinners who have not accepted Jesus Christ as Lord and received his free gift of salvation, remain alienated from God. Therefore, while unbelievers may offer up prayers to the Lord, they lack fellowship by not knowing Jesus in the pardoning of their sins. When we come into the knowledge of Jesus Christ as Lord, we go from being a sinner to a sinner saved by the grace of God. This is when we become the righteousness of God by faith based solely on how Jesus sacrificed his life for sin on the cross at Calvary.

Scripture

"Now we know that God heareth NOT sinners: but if any man be a worshipper of God, and doeth his will, him he heareth" (John 9:31).

Christians become stronger in the faith as they learn to lean more and more on the Creator of the universe. The Christian believer has every reason to express gratitude and thankfulness to God for his wonderful blessings. Christians often get excited and emotional over God for all the good deeds he performs in their lives. Since the born-again believer experiences the love of God, there is nothing in this world that can rob them of that relationship. Notice I did not say they could not give it away. What I did say is no one could take or rob the Christian of their relationship with the Lord. The great love of God was demonstrated to the entire world when he sent his only begotten Son to save the lost souls. Therefore, it is clear evidence that God loved us first. This Savior named Jesus offered to experience life, death, and the resurrection so that mankind could survive the judgment of a holy God. Prayer will help us get ready to do the will of God; as well as receive his wonderful blessings he has in store for us. Never let us assume that prayer is designed exclusively for the purpose of God doing our will. We must fully understand that prayer is designed to cause mankind to conform to the will of God. Then you will witness the will of God manifest itself in your personal life. We must be obedient to the word of God when we pray in order for his many blessings to flow freely. Always remember, when you pray, you will stop sinning, and when you sin, you will stop praying!

Pray in Faith

The most sincere and meaningful prayers come from a true heart that places its total trust in God. This is the God of the universe who created the heavens and the earth—the same God of the Bible who sent his only begotten Son named Jesus who is the Savior of the world. God speaks to his children through the Holy Bible. There are people who claim they hear the voice of

God audibly. Whether this is true or not can be easily determined. There is one thing that is for certain. If what they are hearing doesn't line up with the word of God, then you can rest assure it's not the voice of the Lord they are hearing? The question is…whose voice is it? Anything heard that is contrary to the word of God is of the devil, and that's a fact. The Bible tells us that the Holy Scriptures, also called the Holy Bible is the Alpha and the Omega, the beginning and the end, the first and the last. Everything we need is in the word of God. We speak to God in our faithful loving prayers. God is alive and all-knowing, full of power and righteous wisdom. God is the sustainer of our very being. Those who pray to God must believe and have faith that he is who the Holy Bible says he is.

Prayer in Worship

Worship deals with the level of praise to the only one worthy to receive it which is God almighty. Nothing or no one else compares to the Lord. Only God deserves our highest level of respect when it comes to our communication with him. The Bible tells us that angelic creatures (Seraphim) covered their faces as they gave God praise crying out Holy, Holy, Holy is the Lord of Host (Isaiah 6:2, 3). Christians love to worship the Lord with prayer and praise. It's our way of expressing gratitude and thanksgiving to the Lord for his mighty good works. Make sure when you offer worship through prayer and praise to God that you always sanctify yourself and clear your mind. God will only accept that which is pure in heart. The word of God teaches us that God is the sovereign Spirit, and they who worship him must worship him in spirit and in truth.

Prayer in Confession

As believers, once we become aware of God's holiness, then we are made conscious of our own sinful nature. When we sin in the flesh, we disappoint God by grieving the Holy Spirit. Then we hurt ourselves and those closest to us. We need to realize and understand that mankind still struggles with confidentiality and forgiveness. The Bible tells us to confess our sins to one another. However, be very careful who you trust with your confession. Not everyone is spirit-filled. Always confess your sins directly to God who promised to forgive you of all your sins and cleanse you from all unrighteousness (1

John 1:9). Therefore, during our prayer time with the Lord, always remember, never condone sin. Always openly admit any and all wrongdoing to the Lord. Remember, God is all-seeing and all-knowing. We cannot hide anything from the Lord. We have to agree with God on all sinful acts in order for him to accept our repented heart. Then we must pray that God takes the sinful desire from us. This involves a willing heart on our part to want to be free from anything contrary to the word of God. Find yourself a mature Christian to confide in. Then you can share your confessions with a soul that is mature enough to be an encourager and not one who tittle-tattles. This is very helpful when it comes to having someone you can be accountable to in the earth. God commanded us not to be judgmental toward one another. The sad truth is a large number of Christians are. Therefore, be very careful who you select to be accountable to.

Pray in Adoration

God has demonstrated his great love for the world by giving us the free gift of his only begotten Son Jesus for the redemption of mankind. God's greatest desire is that we all come to love him with all of our heart, mind and soul (Matthew 22:37, 38). We must realize that God first loved us right in the midst of our sinful state. Jesus refers to this type of love as the first and greatest commandment. And the second is like unto it, "Thou shalt love thy neighbor as thyself" (Matthew 22:39). We must always adore and reverence God every time we bow our knees to pray.

Pray in Praise

Praise includes faith, worship, confession and adoration. When we praise our Lord, we like to uplift and hold in high regard the one whom we respect and love above all others. We praise God for his mighty acts and his awesome greatness" (Psalm 150:2). God's children give sincere praise to his name for just being God all by himself. Never be afraid or ashamed when it comes to offering up praise unto God. This act often requires some form of sound. You may be able to worship God in silence, but when it comes to praising the God that has your very breath in his hand, never be ashamed or too proud to make a joyful noise. The Bible gives us this instruction on the matter.

Scripture

"Make a joyful NOISE unto the Lord, all ye lands. Serve the Lord with gladness: come before his presence with singing. Know ye that the Lord he is God: it is he that hath made us, and not we ourselves; we are his people, and the sheep of his pasture. Enter into his gates with thanksgiving, and into his courts with PRAISE: be thankful unto him, and bless his name. For the Lord is good; his mercy is everlasting; and his truth endureth to all generations" (Psalm 100:1-5).

Pray in Thanksgiving

We have to be thankful to God in all things. If we were unthankful and thought for a moment that we had not received what we rightfully deserved, then think again. If God gave us what we deserved, we would be condemned based on our act of sin alone. Born with a sinful nature doesn't qualify us to be children of God. By God's own grace and mercy, he has saved us. God's mercy and grace is available to all willing to accept Jesus the Messiah as Lord and Savior. This is God's plan for our salvation. Based on his plan, he has forgiven and covered our sins with the blood of Jesus. Therefore, we have been granted the right to be sons and daughters of the Highest. We now have righteous standing, a new heart, and the eternal kingdom of God awaiting us. That's why believers are so thankful and full of joy. In everything, whether it is in good times or bad, we as believers give thanks to God. Our prayers should never cease giving thanks unto the Lord.

Pray in Intercession

This is the time Christians take to intercede for others. When we pray to God the Father in the name of Jesus, the Bible tells us we can have whatsoever we ask. Remember, it is important to know the will of God. That way, we won't pray for anything outside his perfect will.

Scripture

Jesus tell us, *"Ye have not chosen me, but I have chosen you, and ordained you, that ye should go and bring forth fruit, and that your fruit should remain: That whatsoever ye shall ask of the Father in my name, he may give it you"* (John 15:16).

God hears the prayers of the righteous saints. The Bible tells us that righteous prayers are very important. This shows love and compassion for one another. Jesus commanded that we have love for one another in order to be recognized as one of his disciples.

Scripture

"Confess your faults one to another, and pray for one another, that ye be healed. The effectual fervent prayer of the righteous availeth much" (James 5:16).

God likes to hear our prayers of intercession on behalf of one another. This shows the Lord that we are becoming more like him. Since we are our brother's keeper, we should be concerned with the affairs of our neighbors when they require a helping hand.

Hindrance to Prayer

There are several hindrances to prayer mentioned in the Holy Bible. This next verse of scripture deals with the iniquity in the heart.

Scripture

"If I regard iniquity in my heart, the Lord will not hear me" (Psalm 66:18).

This next verse of scripture deals with refusal to hear God's Law. We all are required to seek and know the word of God for ourselves. It is our sole responsibility.

Scripture

"He that turneth away his ears from hearing the law, even his prayer shall be <u>abomination</u>" (Proverbs 28:9).

All who reject or refuse even to read the word of God have placed themselves in harm's way. The Holy Bible teaches us that the prayers of those who turn from hearing the word of God have brought an abomination upon them. Their very prayers have been deemed abominable to the Lord. This next verse of scripture deals with sinful separation from God.

Scripture

"But your iniquities have separated between you and your God, and your sins have hid his face from you, <u>that he will not hear</u>" (Isaiah 59:2).

God does not give ear to the sinner without his grace being upon them. Therefore, if you reject and refuse the grace of God, your very prayers he will not hear. However, God will listen to the prayer of repentance when the sinner is ready to turn from their wicked ways. This next verse of scripture deals with waywardness.

Scripture

"Thus saith the Lord unto this people, Thus have they loved to wander, they have not refrained their feet, therefore the Lord doth not accept them; he will now remember their iniquity, and visit their sins. Then said the Lord unto me, (Jeremiah) Pray not for this people for their good. When they fast, I will not hear their cry; and when they offer burnt offering and oblation, I will not accept them: but I will consume them by the sword, and by the famine, and by the pestilence" (Jeremiah 14:10-12).

God is looking for souls who are steadfast and unmoveable. To them that love to wander about aimlessly, they shall be cut off. These souls choose not to refrain from evil. The scripture says that even the prophet Jeremiah was not to pray for them. Nothing they attempted to do would cause the Lord to open his ears to their cry. This next verse of scripture deals with the prayer of the hypocrite. This type of prayer is only performed so that man can be seen of other men.

Scripture

> *"And when thou prayest, thou shalt not be as the hypocrites are: for they love to pray standing in the synagogues and in the corners of the streets, that they may be seen of men. Verily I (Jesus) say unto you, they have their reward. But thou, when thou prayest, enter into thy closet, and when thou hast shut thy door, pray to thy Father which is in secret; and thy Father which seeth in secret shall reward thee openly"* (Matthew 6:5,6).

When you pray, make sure you are praying from the heart and not for recognition from men. God knows the spirit and true intention of every soul. The Lord loves to see and hear secret prays. Then he is willing to bless that soul openly so that the whole world can witness the glory of God. This next verse of scripture deals with the lack of faith.

Scripture

> *"But without FAITH it is impossible to please him: for he that cometh to God must believe that he is, and that he is a rewarder of them that diligently seek him"* (Hebrews 11:6).

This last verse of scripture pertains to having your prayer hindered when asking improperly or in a wrongful manner.

Scripture

> *"Ye ask, and receive not, because ye ask amiss, that ye may consume it upon your lusts"* (James 4:3).

This verse of scripture deals with the unsatisfied and selfish lustful desires of men. Therefore, it is very important that we know what and how to make our prayer requests known unto God.

Answer to Prayer

God has promised to answer our prayer requests when we start helping the hungry and the afflicted. This next verse of scripture sheds light on dealing with those who help the hungry and afflicted.

Scripture

"Then shalt thou call, and the Lord shall answer; thou shalt cry, and he shall say, here I AM. If thou take away from the midst of thee the yoke, the putting forth of the finger, and speaking vanity: And if thou draw thy soul to the HUNGRY, and satisfy the AFFLICTED soul, then shall thy light rise in obscurity, and thy darkness be as the noonday: And the Lord shall guide thee continually, and satisfy thy soul in drought, and make fat thy bones: and thou shalt be like a watered garden, and like a spring of water, whose water fail not" (Isaiah 58:9-11).

This next verse of scripture deals with the forgiveness of others and how crucial it is that you forgive one another. This is the only way God the Father can and will forgive you.

Scripture

"And when ye stand praying, forgive, if ye have aught against any: that your Father also which is in heaven may forgive you your trespasses. But if ye do not forgive neither will your Father which is in heaven forgive your trespasses" (Mark 11:25, 26).

This next verse of scripture deals with believers receiving by faith exactly what they ask for.

Scripture

"And verily I say unto you, that whosoever shall say unto this mountain, Be thou removed, and be cast into the sea; and shall not doubt in his heart, but shall believe that those things which he saith shall come to pass; he shall have whatsoever he saith. Therefore I say unto you, What things so ever ye desire, when ye PRAY, believe that ye receive them, and ye shall have them" (Mark 11:22-24).

This next verse of scripture deals with asking whatsoever from God with confidence in the powerful name of the Lord Jesus. That name above every name. At the name of Jesus, everything and everyone must bow. For this reason, the name of Jesus can be applied to any and all situations in life. Therefore, trust in the Lord and believe that he overcame all obstacles on the cross at Calvary.

Scripture

"And whatsoever ye shall ask in my name, that will I do, that the Father may be glorified in the Son. If ye shall ask any thing in my name (**Jesus**), *I will do it"* (John 14:13, 14).

This next verse of scripture deals with the promises of God when we abide in Christ and his holy word, plus obeying all his commandments as well.

Scripture

"If ye abide in me, and my words abide in you, ye shall ask what ye will, and it shall be done unto you" (John 15:7).

This next verse of scripture deals with praying in the spirit.

Scripture

"Knowing that whatsoever good thing any man doeth, the same shall he receive of the Lord, whether he be <u>bond</u> or <u>free</u>" (Ephesians 6:6).

This next verse of scripture deals with obeying the Lord's commandments.

Scripture

"And whatsoever we ask, we receive of him, because we keep his commandments, and do those things that are pleasing in his sight" (1 John 3:22).

This next verse of scripture deals with asking according to the will of God.

Scripture

> *"And this is the confidence that we have in him, that, if we ask any thing according to his will, he heareth us: And if we know that he hear us, whatsoever we ask, we know that we have the petitions that we desired of him"* (1 John 5:14,15).

God wants to be able to trust us to respond properly to his word. When it comes to prayer, we have to trust the Lord that he knows what's best for us. God has ultimate wisdom and he will answer our prayers based on him knowing how to best handle our needs. Therefore, if you truly serve the Lord, then trust him and allow him to properly handle your situations in life.

FIVE SENSES OF MANKIND

Mankind is often quick to say that God has given him five senses! This statement is normally used the most when mankind wants to choose his own direction or do his own will. This statement is also used in an attempt to say to others or even sometimes to God, I have a mind; I can think, and I can handle this on my own. In other words, I can make good decisions all by my lonesome. What mankind fails to realize is when we pay too close attention to our senses, especially our sense of sight and touch, we can easily be lead astray. In the word of God, we are taught to walk by faith, not by our natural sight. We are taught to believe things because God said it, even if we cannot visually see it YET. Therefore, we have to be extremely careful when acknowledging our senses in this manner. We must learn that our senses are God-given and designed to help us communicate with one another and find our way here in the earth. In order to communicate with God the Father, this must be done in spirit and in truth. Our senses also have unique functions which help us to recognize the beauty and glory of our Lord and all his marvelous creation.

1) SIGHT

Our vision helps us to see the beauty of God's marvelous creation as we walk in the earth realm without stumbling in the natural. This wonderful sense of sight also allows us to read the precious word of God as we grow closer and closer to the Lord.

2) HEARING

Our ears allow us to hear the beautiful words coming from the mouth of men and women who stand boldly and proclaim the true inspired word of God. Our ears also allow us to communicate with one another and enjoy beautiful melodies in the earthly realm.

3) TOUCH

This powerful sense allows us to embrace one another once we recognize who we are in the family of God. The same embrace helps us to establish relationships with those we are responsible for. Touch teaches our children to feel and experience love. This sense allows us to feel our way through life touching all the beautiful things God has created.

4) SMELL

Our sense of smell allows us to recognize the lovely natural scents God has created in the creations of flowers, plants, and herbs, etc. This sense of smell lets us know we are alive as we walk in the earth experiencing all the many scents and fragrances—good and bad—that surround us.

5) TASTE

Our sense of taste allows us to experience all the many good treats God has given us in the earth to enjoy. There are many flavors to be enjoyed in the earthly realm. Let us be thankful for this sense realizing that it is truly a blessing from God. The Bible tells us that, "God satisfieth thy mouth with good things; so that thy youth is renewed like the eagle" (Psalm 103:5).

In all things give thanks to the Lord. We must give thanks to God for everything he has created with his spoken words, for it is good.

Scripture

Always remember, *"O give thanks unto the Lord; for he is good: for his mercy endureth for ever: O give thanks unto the God of gods: for his mercy endureth forever"* (Psalm 136:1, 2).

That's right, God calls us little <u>gods</u>, made in the image and likeness of him/them who created us.

Scripture

"And God said, <u>Let us</u> make man <u>in our</u> image, after <u>our likeness</u>: and <u>let them</u> have dominion over the fish of the sea, and over the fowl of the air, and over the cattle, and over all the earth, and over every creeping thing that creepeth upon the earth" (Genesis 1:26).

Hopefully, this verse of scripture will not confuse you. There are two points we can learn here. First of all, God is speaking in the plural sense concerning his own deity. Secondly, this verse of scripture describes how God was going to fashion Adam out of the dust of the ground and breathe his Spirit into him. When God spoke the words, 'let them' this also teaches us that the Lord planned for one man to develop into many nations. Therefore, understand that there is only one God in three distinct persons that operate independently to accomplish his will. This is just one of many areas in the Holy Scriptures that confirms the GOD-HEAD which is, God the Father, God the Son, and God the Holy Spirit. These three Holy Deities make up one Holy God known as Jehovah God. Remember, we as men are likewise triune beings similar to our Creator, having a spirit and a soul which dwells in a flesh body. The spirit of man is symbolic of God the Father. The soul of man is symbolic of the Comforter known as the Holy Spirit or Holy Ghost. The flesh body of man is symbolic of Jesus manifested in the flesh to commune with human beings in the earth. The flesh suit we all live in keeps each and every one of us attached to the earthly realm. Once our flesh bodies expire in the earth, our soul and spirit steps out of time over into eternity. All men were created in the image and likeness of the almighty God. We all have an eternal soul that will live forever somewhere. The question is, will your soul dwell with God in his eternal kingdom, or will your soul be among those who reject the grace of God. Anyone that chooses to seprate themselves from the love of God will have a place of their own to dwell. Unfortunately, in this place you will find Satan, the false prophet, the beast, death and hell, and the entire demonic host dwelling there. Therefore, let us stop living our lives like we will not be held accountable for our actions in the earth. This is why we should never forget to always acknowledge God and his marvelous creations set in the universe. The Lord is truly worthy to be praised by all living things.

Scripture

"Let everything that hath breath praise the Lord. Praise ye the Lord" (Psalms 150:6).

THE TRYING OF YOUR FAITH

Wrestle with God

When we wrestle with God, we wrestle alone. God does not care about our status that we have attained in this world. The only thing God cares about is us. He loved us enough to sacrifice his only begotten Son for the sins of the entire world. God painfully shows us who we really are. The Bible tells us that the Angel of the Lord wrestled with Jacob all night. The Angel of the Lord in the very end changed Jacob's name to Israel because he had been changed. Jacob had learned how his old nature of a trickster had to be mordified to conform to the will of God. He received the covenant blessing passed down from his grandfather Abraham to his father Isaac. After changing Jacob's character, God renamed him Israel because the twelve tribes were about to be birth from his loin. This was the birth of the children of Israel, God's covenant people in the earth. Through this covenant nation of people, God sent his Holy Word to all mankind living in the earth. This Holy Word is known as the Holy Scriptures and also called the Holy Bible. After the Lord wrestled with Jacob and touched the hollow of his thigh, he was made a prince in the earth and received the blessings of God.

Scripture

"And Jacob was left alone; and there wrestled a man with him until the breaking of the day. And when he saw that he prevailed not against him, he touched the hollow of his thigh; and the hollow of Jacob's thigh was out of joint, as he wrestled with him. And he said, Let me go, for the day breaketh. And he said, I will not let thee go, except thou bless me. And he said unto him, What is thy name? And he said, Jacob. And he said, Thy name shall be called no more Jacob, but <u>Israel</u>: for as a prince hast thou power with God and with men, and hast prevailed. And Jacob asked him, and said, Tell me, I pray thee, thy name. And he said, Wherefore is it that thou dost ask after my name? And he blessed him there" (Genesis 32:24-29).

The man which is the Angel of the Lord is identified by some as the pre-incarnate Christ, and by others as an angel—a special messenger from God. The context seems to favor the Angel being the pre-incarnate Christ. Only the Angel of the Lord will openly bless man. What we do know is that this Angel had the authority to change Jacob's name plus blessed him on top of that. This is an indication that this particular Angel was indeed the Angel of the Lord. The name Jacob means (heel catcher, sup planter or deceiver). This was the old character and nature of Jacob. When his named was changed by the Lord to Israel which means (may God prevail), the Lord revealed to Israel formally known as Jacob who he now was in God. Jacob to Israel had to step up to his rightful position to establish his covenant with the Lord—no more lies, tricks, and schemes. That was the old man before he wrestled with the Angel of the Lord. It's the same today when we accept Jesus as our Lord. He has to change who we were to who we now have become in Christ Jesus. When we are born-again of the Spirit of God, we have been marked by the Lord. This means we have been washed in the blood of the Lamb. The change is so significant that the whole world will take notice and recognize that God is in full control of our lives.

Your Test of Faith by Fire

When we choose to accept Jesus as Lord over our lives, unexplainable things may start to happen. These things are referred to as the trying of your faith. We go from living life our way, to being converted to living life God's way. You will be tested. You must understand that God cannot use you until you are tested with fire.

Scripture

> *"Wherein ye greatly rejoice, though now for a season, if need be, ye are in heaviness through manifold temptation: That the trial of your faith, being much more precious than of gold that perisheth, though it be tried with FIRE, might be found unto Praise and Honor and Glory at the appearing of Jesus Christ"* (1 Peter 1:6, 7).

We must remember that true faith can never be destroyed. This is the gift from God. When we go through trials for a season, this is God's way of refining our faith. That is why trials are not designed to last always. They are designed to last only for a short season. The Lord wants us to know who we are and how powerful he is. These trials will cause us to know and fully understand how valuable the salvation of the Lord truly is. When the trial comes upon you, will you still praise, worship and trust in the Lord? This is the test question that many of us will be faced with. Once deliverance is received, we will gladly be willing to share the good news of how God has blessed our life. This is what provides us with an everlasting testimony of the goodness of the Lord and his wonderful healing power. The Bible refers to this as a fiery trial. This is what the Holy Scripture had to say.

Scripture

> *"Beloved, think it not strange concerning the <u>FIERY TRIAL</u> which is to try you, as though some strange thing happened unto you: But rejoice inasmuch as ye are partakers of Christ's sufferings; that, when his glory shall be revealed, ye may be glad also with exceeding joy. Yet if any man suffer as a Christian, let him not be ashamed; but let him glorify God on this behalf. For the time is come that judgment must begin at the house of God: and if it first begin at us, what shall the end be of them that obey not the gospel of God? <u>And if the Righteous scarcely be saved, where shall the ungodly and the sinner appear?</u>"* (1Peter 4:12, 13 and 16-18).

Has something strange happened to you lately? Has your life taken a turn in a downward direction? Keep serving the Lord thy God. You may be experiencing strange occurrences for a reason. Stay strong in the Lord believing that God is still in control. Remember to rejoice as partakers of Christ's sufferings. Remember what happened to God's servant Job. Satan went to God and got permission to test Job's faithfulness. God allowed it because he knew in advance what Job could endure. Job was not privileged to attend this meeting between God and Satan, nor did he have knowledge that it even took place. The scripture tells us what went on behind the scenes pertaining to Job's fiery trial.

Scripture

"Now there was a day when the sons of God (**angelic beings**) *came to present themselves before the Lord, and Satan came also among them. And the Lord said unto Satan, Whence comest thou? Then Satan answered the Lord, and said, From going to and fro in the earth, and from walking up and down in it. And the Lord said unto Satan, Hast thou considered my servant Job, that there is none like him in the earth, a perfect and an upright man, one that feareth God and escheweth evil? Then Satan answered the Lord, and said, Doth Job fear God for nought? Hast not thou made a hedge about him, and about his house, and about all that he hath on every side? Thou hast blessed the work of his hands, and his substance is increased in the land. But put forth thine hand now, and touch all that he hath, and he will curse thee to thy face. And the Lord said unto Satan, Behold, all that he hath is in thy power, only upon himself put not forth thine hand. So Satan went forth from the presence of the Lord"* (Job 1:6-12).

These scriptures in the book of Job tell us what went on between God and Satan concerning God's servant Job. Once Satan received God's permission to tempt Job, the test was on. Satan came back to God to receive further permission when his plan failed. God granted Satan further permission to inflict Job's body when he would not curse God. Job held on and never cursed the Lord nor accused him falsely. Job learned a valuable lesson from God while enduring his temptation and fiery trial. The first thing Satan destroyed from Job was his ability to make a sacrifice to the Lord. This was accomplished by destroying all of Job's flocks. Once Job was unable to make a sacrifice to the Lord, the hedge came down around Job and Satan killed all ten of his children and most of his servants. God taught Job a valuable lesson about who he truly was during his trial period. Job had nothing left but his wife. The reason Satan failed to kill her is because he planned to use her later to come against her husband. Satan later influenced Job's wife to try and convince Job to curse God and die. The story tells us that Job held his ground and informed his wife that she spoke like a very foolish woman. God later instructed Job's friends to go to Job and offer up a sacrifice for themselves and have Job pray for them. For Job's friends had not spoken the right things as Job had. When Job's friends offered up their sacrifice and Job prayed for them, God accepted their sacrifice on Job's behalf. Then the Bible said God turned the captivity of Job when he prayed for his friends. God also gave Job twice as much as he had before. There was a blessing on the other side of Job's test and fiery trail. Therefore, always remember, God is always with us whether it seems that way or not. God hears the cry of his people. Always keep that in mind. Remember, when you come into the light of Christ, you are on the devil's hit list. This may sound bad, but actually this is good. This will establish your placement in the kingdom of God, verses the lake of fire.

Better to be on the devil's hit list because you serve the Lord, than on Satan's slow roller coaster ride to hell and not know it.

This way, you qualify for the blessings and the promises of God as his loyal servant. On the other hand, the devil's team qualifies you for eternal damnation in the lake of fire. Serving the creature instead of the Creator books you a first-class ticket to the fiery lake on the Day of Judgment.

Scripture

"For whom the Lord loveth he chasteneth, and scourgeth every son whom he receiveth" (Hebrews 12:6).

This verse teaches us that God chasteneth and scourgeth every son whom he receiveth. The word scourge means to punish, chastise or afflict severely.

This is necessary when God is training us for discipleship. The word of God teaches us not to spare the rod or else we have hatred for our own sons and daughters. This is the same principle God uses to try us in order to position our earthen vessels for his personal use. So therefore, fret not, faint not, and endure the chastisement when it comes, and God will use you. God is all-knowing and he will prepare and strengthen you for your test. God knows what is lurking around the corner that we as men cannot see with our natural sight. God sends angels to encamp around us for our own protection. Once we come into the knowledge of God and become his loyal servants, he will guide and direct our future steps. The test is designed to give you a great testimony of the power and goodness of the almighty God. This test is also designed to empower us. God stretches, fashions, tries, and impacts us so that we are changed and converted to be vessels of honor for the Master's use.

Scripture

> *"If ye endure chastening, God dealeth with you as with sons; for what son is he whom the father chasteneth not? But if ye be without chastisement, whereof all are partakers, then are ye <u>BASTARDS</u>, and not sons. Furthermore we have had fathers of our flesh which corrected us, and we gave them REVERENCE: shall we not much rather be in subjection unto the Father of Spirits, and live? For they verily for a few days chastened us after their own pleasure; but he for our profit, that we might be partakers of his Holiness. Now NO chastening for the present seemeth to be joyous, but grievous: nevertheless afterward it yieldeth the peaceable fruit of RIGHTEOUSNESS unto them which are exercised thereby"* (Hebrews 12:7-11).

> *"For if we would judge ourselves, we should not be judged. But when we are judged, we are chastened of the Lord, that we should <u>not be condemned with the world</u>"* (1 Corinthians 11:31, 32).

The Bible teaches us as Christians that if we judge ourselves, we should not be judged. When we as Christians are judged, we are chastened by the Lord quickly. We are not judged like the world. The Lord does not want us condemned like the world. Therefore, he corrects us quickly if we fail to correct ourselves. The Bible further tells us that if we pass our test and endure, God will use us or deal with us as sons. God lets us know that if we belong to him, he has to teach and train us to walk upright. But if God does not correct us, then we are viewed as bastards and not sons. God lets us know that everyone he corrects belongs to him. The Lord gave us the same instruction for raising our own children. If we spare the rod and refuse to chastise our children, they will grow up to disrespect and not honor us as parents. If we correct and chastise them when it is needed, they will not only grow to love and respect us, but they will honor and reverence us as well. It's something about the chastisement of a child that later lets them know that they were truly loved enough to be corrected. God knows this, and good parents realize this, but children can't see this at the time because they lack understanding. That's why they are the TRAINEES and we as parents are the TRAINERS. Those parents, who wish to do it their own way, get ready for the consequences, because they will arise.

Scripture

"FOOLISHNESS is bound in the heart of a child; but the rod of correction shall drive it far from him" (Proverbs 22:15).

The Lord teaches us that a few swift strikes on the soft backside will drive out all manners of wickedness and bad behavior bound up in a child. Therefore, be not afraid to chastise your children. It will save their very soul from the pits of hell. You may wonder what hell has to do with it. It's simple. If you raise an undisciplined child, they will grow up with no regard for others. They will rise up on every occasion and never allow themselves to be restrained. This will cause evil to come upon them. The principle of reaping what you sow will surely bring on whatever behavior they exemplify, only the harvest will be magnified. Thus, when your behavior is bad, the outcome is worst. Their near future either holds prison or the grave. Therefore, chastise them while they are yet young. This will save both their life, and their soul.

Scripture

"Chasten thy son while there is hope, and let not thy soul spare for his crying" (Proverbs 19:18).

Anytime you refrain from disciplining your child because of their crying, you have just been tricked by demonic influence. That child has learned that all they have to do is shed phony tears every time they misbehave and you will be fooled. This is how the wicked devices found in children manipulation the good nature found in parents. Think of it like this. When a child cries to keep the rod of correction from striking, ask yourself this question, "Has any pain been inflicted yet? What's causing the tears since the act of disobedience has already occurred? Therefore, when your children react this way, look at them very closely. Pay very close attention to their expression before and after the tears. If you are ever able to compare the two, you will see and recognize the demonic influence in their expression. You are being manipulated. If you succumb to it, you have just been made a fool of by wicked influence. If you ignore the phony act and chastise betimes like God teaches us in his holy word, then you are not only wise, but you have just did your child a huge favor. You've just imparted into them the knowledge of how bad behavior will always bring on severe consequences. This way, they will not be among those who think they can get away with their evil deeds done in the earth. This valuable lesson will protect and convince them to eschew evil all of their days.

JUDGMENT / CONDEMNATION

We were born in sin based on the nature we all inherited from our true and original ancestor Adam. Adam and Eve both were punished when they disobeyed God in the Garden of Eden which caused sin to enter into this world. Since we all have inherited Adam's sin nature, the Bible commands us never to judge one another while in the earth.

Scripture

> *"Therefore, thou art inexcusable, O man, whosoever thou art that judgest: for wherein thou judgest another, thou condemnest thyself; <u>for thou that judgest doest the SAME THINGS</u>. But we are sure that the judgment of God is according to truth against them which commit such things. And thinkest thou this, O man, that judgest them which do such things, and doest the same, that thou shalt escape the judgment of God"* (Romans 2:1-3)?

"Judge not, that ye be not judged. For with what judgment ye judge, ye shall be judged and with what measure ye mete, it shall be measured to you again. And why beholdest thou the <u>mote</u> that is in thy brother's eye, but considerest not the <u>beam</u> that is in thine own eye? Or how wilt thou say to thy brother, Let me pull out the mote out of thine eye, and, behold, a beam is in thine own eye? Thou HYPOCRITE, first cast out the beam out of thine own eye; and then shalt thou see clearly to cast out the mote out of thy brother's eye" (Matthew 7:1-5).

"Judge not, and ye shall not be judged: condemn not, and ye shall not be condemned: forgive and ye shall be forgiven" (Luke 6:37).

God's word teaches us when we judge our brothers and sisters, we do the same things. This is an interesting scripture. It informs us that we do exactly the same things that we tend to judge others on. The word of God lets us know that we will cause condemnation to come upon us when we do such things. The Holy Bible further teaches us that when we judge others and doest the same; don't think that we will escape the Lord's judgment. These scriptures focus on those who tend to be the self-righteous individuals dispite of how they live. This occurs when we are quick to judge the lifestyle of others, when in essence; we live exactly the same way they do. When we focus on our brothers and sisters, we fail to take into consideration our own faults and sinful behavior. The mature Christian no longer focuses on the sins of others, but learns to examine his or her own self. This way, we are quick to forgive and show mercy toward everyone. Remember how the Pharisees in the temple reacted during the time Jesus walked the earth? The Lord despised this type of hypocritical behavior. Jesus is the only righteous judge. When man attempts to do only what the Lord is qualified to do, he does it unjustly. For this reason, we should never point the finger at our brethren. The proper way to be Christ-like is to show love one to another. By doing so, we will encourage our brothers and sisters instead of passing judgment upon them. Judge not, lest you be judged with the same measure you judge others.

THE LAMB'S BOOK OF LIFE:
DEATH AND LIFE IS IN YOUR TONGUE

This is a very important principle taught in the Holy Bible. God warns us concerning the words we speak. There is power in our tongues to establish the course of our future. Whatsoever you say with your mouth, will come to pass, whether it is good or bad. The devil wants us to curse any and everything with our words because he knows the power they hold. Once words leave our mouth, we cannot take them back. The devil knows this as well. The fact is we live our life by design. Even though time and chance happens to every man, where we end up is totally up to us. This statement holds truth. Everything in life happens for a purpose. Even the words we speak will cause our future to be mapped out. The saints of God know that unseen things can be called into our present existence by faith. As long as you can see it, no faith is required. Therefore, we must also be careful letting others speak unprofitable words into our lives. We have to be on guard at all times ready to rebuke those who lack wisdom and knowledge in this area. Always be willing to speak positive words over all your situations, including your friends and family. Never curse anyone, regardless of how angry you may become. Remember, we must still reap whatsoever seed we sow, even when it comes to the fruit of our lips. All seed produces a harvest whether it is good or bad. The Bible tells us, "Seedtime and harvest will never cease as long as the earth remains" (Genesis 8:22). If we want blessings, let us sow blessings. If we want to be cursed, let us continue to curse others. God told the great patriarch Abraham, "And I will bless them that bless thee, and curse him that curse thee: and in thee shall all families of the earth be blessed" (Genesis 12:3). This scripture teaches us many things. The Bible lets us know that when we become the sons and daughters of God through faith in Jesus Christ our Lord, we become Abraham's seed. And being Abraham's seed, all promises of God apply to us as well. Remember, God established a covenant family with Abraham. The Pharisees thought it was enough to be the near kinsmen descendants of Abraham alone. What they did not fully understand is God was establishing a covenant family of faith believers. Jesus the Messiah was going to be manifested in the flesh real soon for the redemption of mankind. Therefore, the Lord knew that it would require faith in Christ Jesus in order to see the kingdom of God. Jesus answered the question pertaining to the identity of his true family. The answer the Lord gave did not reveal his nearest of kin. This next scripture reveals who Jesus' true kinfolk are.

Scripture

"Then came to him his mother and his brethren, and could not come at him for the press. And it was told him by certain which said, Thy mother and thy brethren stand without, desiring to see thee. And he answered and said unto them, My mother and my brethren are these which hear the word of God, and do it" (Luke 8:19-21).

Jesus clearly teaches us that if we want to be considered a member in the family of God, we must be willing to hear and obey the word of God. This is that faith covenant that overrides any type of family tree. Remember, we are all descendants of Adam. When God chose Abraham within the human race of his people, he knew that faith would cause his righteous family to emerge. This is the true seed of Abraham that the Lord is coming back for. Therefore, since you are the seed of Abraham, no one has the right to curse you without being likewise cursed by God. The same applies to us when we are foolish enough to curse one of our brothers in Christ. Expect God to honor his word, even concerning you!

Scripture

"Death and life are in the power of the tongue: and they that love it shall eat the fruit thereof" (Proverbs 18:21).

"If any man among you seem to be religious, and bridleth not his tongue, but deceiveth his own heart, this man's religion is VAIN" (James 2:26).

"For in many things we offend all. If any man offend not in words, the same is a perfect man, and able to bridle the whole body" (James 3:2).

The Bible gives the illustration of the bit used in a horse's mouth to control such a large animal. Another illustration used in the Bible is the example of a large ship, great in size, driven by fierce winds and controlled by a very small helm. These are examples of how powerful the tongue is. It's the smallest member of the body and yet the most dangerous and powerful member of all.

Scripture

"And the tongue is a fire, a world of iniquity: so is the tongue among our members, that it <u>defileth the whole body, and setteth on fire the course of nature</u>; and it is set on fire of HELL. For every kind of beasts, and of birds, and of serpents, and of things in the sea, is tamed, and hath been tamed of mankind: But the TONGUE <u>can no man tame</u>; it is an unruly evil, full of deadly poison. Therewith Bless we God, even the Father; and therewith curse we men, which are made after the similitude of God. Out of the same mouth proceedeth blessing and cursing. My brethren, these things ought not so to be" (James 3:6-10).

Jesus said, *"Ye have heard that it hath been said, Thou shalt LOVE thy neighbor, and HATE thine enemy. But I say unto you, LOVE your enemies, BLESS them that curse you, do good to them that HATE you, and PRAY for them which despitefully use you, and persecute you: That ye may be the children of your Father which is in heaven: for he maketh his sun to rise on the evil and on the good, and sendeth rain on the just and on the unjust"* (Matthew 5:43-45).

"For he that will love life, and see good days, let him refrain his tongue from evil, and his lips that they speak no guile: Let him eschew evil, and do good; let him seek peace, and ensue it" (1 Peter 3:10, 11).

We must learn to speak the right things out of our mouth at all times and we will receive the many blessings from God. Remember, you will have what you say based on the words you choose to speak. Without the knowledge and redemption of the Lord Jesus Christ, lost souls do not regard what they say. This is why we need Jesus to cleanse our souls free of sin. Only then can we look back and see the state of damnation we were once in. Once our eyes have been opened to the glory of God, then we too will learn to speak the words of life to ourselves and others. Remember, God said himself that his people are destroyed for lack of knowledge. When you do not know what is contained in God's Holy Bible, not only will you perish, but also it is impossible for you to speak correctly. Therefore, once you learn the will of God, you will also learn how to speak blessings instead of curses. Whatever you sow, you will also reap. This principle of God includes every word we sow with the fruit of our lips. We owe all thanks to the Lord Jesus Christ who gave us the power to become the sons of God.

PROPHECY VS SPEAKING IN TONGUES

The Bible tells us that prophesying and speaking in an unknown tongue is a gift of the Holy Spirit.

Scripture

> *"Follow after charity, and desire spiritual gifts, but rather that ye may prophesy. For he that speaketh in an unknown tongue speaketh not unto men, but unto God: for no man understandeth him; howbeit in the spirit he speaketh mysteries. But he that prophesieth speaketh unto men to edification and exhortation, and comfort. <u>He that speaketh in an unknown tongue edifieth himself;</u> but he that prophesieth edifieth the church. I would that ye all spake with tongues, but rather that ye prophesieth: for greater is he that prophesieth than he that speaketh with tongues, <u>except he interpret, that the church may receive edifying.</u> Now brethren, if I come unto you speaking with tongues, what shall I profit you, except I shall speak to you either by revelation, or by knowledge, or by prophesying, or by doctrine"* (1 Corinthians 14:1-6)?

Apostle Paul explains here that prophesy is preferred over speaking in tongues when it comes to church edification. Both are wonderful spiritual gifts from the Holy Spirit. However, prophesying edifies the entire church body. This is a form of enlightening the congregation. When speaking in tongues you are not speaking to men, you are speaking directly to God. This edifies the individuals own spirit. In the event there is an interpreter which is also one of the gifts of the Spirit, the translation can be made known to the church. There are some who have asked the question, "Do all speak in tongues?" Then you have others who seem to think that speaking in an unknown tongue is a thing of the past. This is what Jesus had to say concerning the matter.

Scripture

> *"And these signs shall follow THEM THAT BELIEVE; In my name shall they cast out devils; <u>they shall speak with new tongues</u>; They shall take up serpents; and if they drink any deadly thing, it shall not hurt them; they shall lay hands on the sick, and they shall recover"* (Mark 16:18).

Jesus clearly informs us that whosoever <u>believes</u>, these signs shall follow them. In the name of Jesus they shall cast out devils, <u>SPEAK WITH NEW TONGUES</u>, take up serpents, be immune to all poisonous things, and finally, they have been given the power from Christ to lay hands on the sick and recovery will take place. According to this scripture, the gift of tongues is addressed here. Those who believe shall receive a prayer language to communicate directly with God the Father. Notice that Jesus did not say that this gift was exclusive to the church leaders, or single any one position out. He said to all that BELIEVE. This sound like Jesus knew that there would be Christians who were not fully persuaded, or perhaps lack the necessary measure of faith required to perform the works. Therefore, if you believe, the gift of tongues will be given unto you. This gift has to come from the Holy Spirit who will give you utterance in your mind concerning your heavenly language.

Scripture

> *"And on the day of Pentecost was fully come, they were all with one accord in one place. And suddenly there came a sound from heaven as of a rushing mighty wind, and it filled all the house where they were sitting. And there appeared unto them cloven tongues like as of fire, and it sat upon each of them. And they were all filled with the Holy Ghost, and began to speak with other tongues, as the Spirit gave then utterance"* (Acts 2:1-4).

The word UTTER or UTTERANCE means to express audible words, thoughts or verbal sounds. The Holy Spirit will give us the language to speak. The Bible tells us that this language is unknown to us. We just have to be bold enough to speak it out of our mouth when it comes into our mind. This is not a gift from man; it comes from the Holy Spirit of God. Therefore, let us be careful trying to jump-start this gift which comes only from the Holy Spirit and not from man. In other words, there has been occasion where men have instructed the recital of repetitive words in order to try and issue this gift to men. This is not the way to receive this blessed gift from God. However, the Lord breathed on the disciples and Peter the apostle spoke words over them and men received this precious gift.

Scripture

"Then said Jesus to them again, Peace be unto you: as my Father hath sent me, even so send I you. And when he had said this, he BREATHED on them, and saith unto them, RECEIVE YE THE HOLY GHOST" (John 20:21, 22):

"Therefore let all the house of Israel know assuredly, that God hath made that same Jesus; whom ye have crucified, both Lord and Christ. Now when they heard this, they were pricked in their heart, and said unto Peter and to the rest of the apostles, Men and brethren, what shall we do? Then Peter said unto them, Repent, and be baptized every one of you in the name of Jesus Christ for the remission of sins, and ye shall receive the gift of the Holy Ghost" (Acts 2:36-38).

Jesus said, *"But ye shall receive POWER, after that the Holy Ghost is come upon you: and ye shall be witnesses unto me both in Jerusalem, and in all Judea, and in Samaria, and unto the uttermost part of the earth"* (Acts 1:8).

There is no doubt; we all desperately need the Holy Ghost operating in our lives. This is where our spiritual power comes from to walk upright before the Lord. This is where we receive our power to love like God, to forgive like God, and also to minister to the lost souls without ceasing. Ultimately, we gain the power to defeat all the enemies of God when they launch their vicious attacks. The power of the Holy Ghost also reveals the many mysteries of God. The Bible tells us that God will reveal his mysteries and wisdom during this process of communicating in this unknown spiritual language. The wonderful thing about this secret language is it cannot be penetrated by anyone. This includes the angels in heaven, the fallen angels beneath the earth, and every man and woman. Most importantly, it includes the devil. Any other time when man is speaking, the enemies of God are always listening to gain an advantage over mankind. However, this is one language you do not have to worry about the devil gaining access to.

Scripture

> *"Now we have received, not the spirit of the world, but the Spirit which is of God; that we might know the things that are freely given to us of God. Which things also we SPEAK, not in the words which man's wisdom teacheth, but which the HOLY GHOST teacheth; comparing spiritual things with spiritual. But the NATURAL MAN receiveth not the things of the Spirit of God: <u>for they are foolishness unto him: neither can he know them</u>, because they are spiritually discerned"* (1 Corinthians 2:12-14).

The Holy Scriptures are describing the born-again Christian being given the ability to communicate with God in an unknown heavenly language. This is called speaking with other or unknown tongues according to the Holy Bible. The Lord will teach and warn his servants of the spiritual mysteries through this language not taught of man's wisdom. This wisdom that God shares with his servants is taught by the Holy Ghost which dwells within the Christian born-again believer. Therefore, if you are an UNBELIEVER, do not worry about whether or not Christians speak in a language unknown to you. Since you choose to disbelieve, this precious spiritual gift does not apply to you, neither can you comprehend it. As a matter of fact, the Bible tells us that the NATURAL MAN which is the UNBELIEVER cannot receive at all the things of the Spirit of God. This person views this behavior as foolishness. The Bible further tells us that they cannot know the things of God because they are spiritually discerned. Therefore, if you have an opportunity to hear a born-again believer speaking in an unknown tongue, do not be alarmed. The Bible says man cannot understand this language, neither can the person speaking to the Lord understand himself. This is a faith language. Not even the angels of God have the ability to decipher this secret communication between God and man. This unknown language is a direct link to the almighty Creator. Then the Lord will translate his mysteries and precious wisdom to those who speak to him in their heavenly language. Think of it this way. The born-again Christian believer speaks his heavenly language which no one can understand but God. The Lord receives this language which the enemy Satan cannot decipher. God channels his wisdom, knowledge and mysteries back into the ear-gate of the one who speaks. When you have no idea what to do, or what to pray for, pray in your heavenly language that the Holy Spirit gave you. Then you will receive your answer from God concerning his mysteries and perfect will for your life.

THE LAST DAYS

The Last Days began with the birth of Jesus Christ and will reach its high point when Jesus returns to the earth to set up his kingdom. Apostle Paul wrote about the perilous times that indicate the great falling away and abandonment of the church that will lead up to the final days of the Church Age.

Scripture

"This know also, that in the last days perilous times shall come. For men shall be lovers of their own selves, covetous, boasters, proud, blasphemers, disobedient to parents, unthankful, unholy, Without natural affection, trucebreakers, false accusers, incontinent, fierce, despisers of those that are good, traitors, heady, high minded, lovers of pleasure more that lovers of God; Having a form of godliness, but denying the power thereof: from such turn away. For of this sort are they which creep into houses, and lead captive silly women laden with sins, led away with divers lust, ever learning, and never able to come to the knowledge of the truth" (2 Timothy 3:1-7).

All these things mentioned are not uncommon in this day and age. The time is nearer than we think. The RAPTURE or the CARRYING AWAY of the church body of Jesus Christ is at hand. The word 'rapture' does not appear in the Bible, however, the rapture means exactly what Jesus intends to do with his church body when he returns for it.

Definition

The word **RAPTURE** is defined as the state of being carried away with joy, love, and ecstasy; an expression of great joy, and pleasure; a carrying away or being carried away in body and spirit.

This definition describes in full detail what and how the Lord Jesus intends to do when he returns for his church body of Christian born-again believers. Understand that when Jesus returns for his church, this will take place prior to the Great Tribulation Period. Jesus is fulfilling God's plan for our salvation to all those who believe in the risen Savior by faith.

Scripture

> *"For the Lord himself shall descend from heaven with a shout, with the voice of the archangel, and with the trump of God: and the dead in Christ shall rise first: Then we which are alive and remain shall be caught up together with them in the clouds, <u>to meet the Lord in the air</u>: and so shall we ever be with the Lord"* (1 Thessalonians 4:16, 17).

OLD TESTAMENT—JUDGMENT OF GOD

Throughout scripture, God is the almighty Judge. The many judgments of God can be viewed through the great flood in Noah's day—the devastating destruction of the sinful cities of Sodom and Gomorrah; the various collapse of several nations, including Israel and Judah; and the judgments specifically placed on the children of Israel when they complained about the manna from heaven (angels food). The Bible tells us that they begged for meat and God gave them quails until it came running out of their nostrils. Let this be a lesson to be very careful what you ask for; you just might get it, and it may not be the way you want it.

Scripture

"And say thou unto the people, Sanctify yourselves against tomorrow, and ye shall eat flesh: for ye have wept in the ears of the Lord, saying, who shall give us flesh to eat? For it was well with us in Egypt: therefore the Lord will give you flesh and ye shall eat. Ye shall not eat one day, nor two days, nor five days, neither ten days, nor twenty days; But even a whole month, until it comes out at your nostrils, and it be loathsome unto you: because that ye have despised the Lord which is among you, and have wept before him, saying, Why came we forth out of Egypt" (Numbers 11:18-20)?

These are just a few judgments in the Old Testament to speak of. We must be very careful not to complain when God has surely taken great care of us. Even after the Lord delivered the children of Israel from over 400 years of bondage at the hands of the Egyptians, they were unappreciative. They began to whine, and the Lord sent his judgment once again. Let us learn from this passage of scripture. Be thankful and grateful to the almighty God that sustains us daily.

Scripture

"But my God shall supply all your need according to his riches in glory by Christ Jesus" (Philippians 4:19).

NEW TESTAMENT—JUDGMENT OF GOD

In the New Testament, judgment tends to occur in eight areas.

1) The Cross Judgment
Scripture

Jesus said, *"Of judgment, because the prince of this world is judged"* (John 16:11).

The work of the Holy Spirit is to convict us while pointing out faults and errors which will expose all things contrary to the word of God. The Holy Spirit reveals the reality of redemption. The prince (Satan) of this world is already judged. The power of Christ to judge Satan and overthrow his kingdom is not a future event. This judgment occurred at the cross during Christ resurrection. Satan will be sentenced real soon in the lake of fire. His ending has been determined and decided by God the Father.

2) The Believers' Self-Judgment Seat of Christ
Scripture

"For if we would judge ourselves, we should not be judged" (1 Corinthians 11:31).

As believers we are to judge ourselves; then God will not have to. This is why you may see lost souls in the earth prospering when Christian souls appear to be suffering and receiving persecutions. When the children of God commit sin in the earth, they are chastised by the Lord betimes. This is the same formula God gave man for the purpose of chastising their own offspring. The lost souls of this world observe the saints of God being chastised and think in their mind that they are getting away with their sinful acts. The truth is they are not getting away. The Christian is chastised on the spot because we serve a Holy God. Remember, God gave the same fomular to his children. Therefore, if we obey God and chastise our children, they will be blessed in the earth. They will learn that all sin has consequences. On the other hand, if we as parents treat our children like Satan treats the world, we will cause them to fall right into the hands of the enemies of God. Notice Satan does not chastise his followers. He allows them to walk in all manners of destruction because he knows hell awaits them. The same system applies to a parent who refuses to discipline their children. They either end up in prison or dead because the wicked world system will consume them. Anyone who has no discipline will be an offense to others. Therefore, the next time you see sinners who appear to get away with murder, while they are laughing in your face, understand that their destruction is already on the way, they just don't know it. They have just become numb to their sin, not knowing that one day they too will be judged by God. Their punishment is just prolonged for the final judgment. This judgment will take place at the Great White Throne Judgment of God. That is why when souls come to Jesus and receive the salvation of the Lord, they have to be often chastised and scourged. Once saved by Jesus Christ and washed in his blood, these same souls will be appointed to face a judgment of rewards, not condemnation. Their salvation has been assured and sealed. This judgment that will take place at the Judgment Seat of Christ will determine what crowns they will receive. The five crowns that Jesus has as gifts for his Christian born-again believers will be issued to the saints of God. These crowns are the gifts awaiting the righteous souls for the many good works performed in the ministry while in the earth.

3) The Chastisement by the Father
Scripture

> *"For whom the Lord loveth he chasteneth, and scourgeth every son whom he receiveth. <u>If ye endure chastening, God dealeth with you as with sons</u>, for what son is he whom the Father chasteneth not? But if ye be without chastisement, whereof all are partakers, then are ye <u>BASTARD'S</u> and not sons. Furthermore we have had fathers of our flesh which corrected us, and we gave them reverence: shall we not much rather be in subjection unto the Father of Spirits and live? For they verily for a few days chastened us after their own pleasure; but he for our profit, that we might be partakers of his Holiness. Now no chastening for the present seemeth to be joyous, but grievous: nevertheless afterward it yieldeth the peaceable fruit of righteousness unto them which are exercised thereby"* (Hebrews 12:6-11).

This scripture lets us know that we all must go through something during the cross over. This proves that we have been accepted into the family of God.

The Bible tells us that after we go through and endure the chastisement of the Lord, we will yield the peaceable fruit of righteousness.

4) The Bema (Judgment Seat) of Christ

Scripture

"For we must all appear before the Judgment Seat of Christ; that every one may receive the things done in his body, according to that he hath done, whether it be good or bad" (2 Corinthians 5:10).

This scripture tells us that we must all appear before the Judgment Seat of Christ. This judgment is for the BELIEVERS, not the UNBELIEVERS. It is true that for the Christian born-again believers, there is no condemnation to them that walk in the spirit and not in the flesh. The scripture tells us that every man may receive the things done in his own body. Whether these things are good or bad is how the scripture teaches us. Since this is so, let us focus on good deeds rather than the bad, knowing that one day we will be confronted with the same.

Scripture

"If any man's work abide which he hath built thereupon, he shall receive a reward. If any man's work shall be burned, he shall suffer loss: <u>BUT HE HIMSELF SHALL BE SAVED</u>; yet so as by fire" (1 Corinthians 3:14, 15).

To the saved souls who have received the salvation of the Lord, their deeds will be rewarded at the Judgment Seat of Christ. If the deeds were honorable, they will be rewarded with a crown of gold. In the event they were dishonorable to the edifying of the body of Christ, they will be burned up by fire. Thank God that the Judgment Seat of Christ is not for the purpose of determining whether or not that soul will receive eternal life. This decision has already been decided by the shed blood of Jesus if you are blessed enough to be present at the Judgment Seat of Christ.

5) The Tribulation

Scripture

> *"For then shall be great tribulation, such as was not since the beginning of the world to this time, no, <u>nor ever shall be</u>. And except those days should be shortened, there should no flesh be SAVED: but for the elect's sake those days shall be shortened"* (Matthew 24:21, 22).

This judgment of God will be the greatest that ever was, even since the beginning of the world. The timeframe will be shortened to avoid all men from being destroyed. The peace time will be the first portion of the seven-year peace treaty that the anti-christ will initiate. The antichrist will bring this temporary peacetime to deceive the nations. After three and a half years, he will break his own agreement and launch an all out attack on the world. Those who accept Jesus and reject the antichrist during this tribulation period will have to suffer for their newfound faith in Christ. God has even made provisions for them who have to endure this great tribulation period. The 144,000 chosen from the twelve tribes of Israel have been reserved for this particular moment in time by God the Father. They will serve as a beacon of LIGHT for the souls who are left in the earth during that time period. These are the souls who chose not to believe the men and women of God when they had the chance. Now that the saints of God have all been gathered and are now with Jesus Christ, the souls who were previously lost now will perhaps believe. For this reason, God has his precious servants in the earth to show them the way. Salvation will be available for all souls who refuse to receive Satan's mark of the beast in their hand or on their forehead. The souls refusing to accept Satan's mark will be outcast in a world overrun with sin and destruction. Remember, this same world overrun with sin will also have to face the many judgments of God poured out onto the earth without mixture. This is called the wrath of God. The souls who remain will have to suffer at the hand of God's enemy. However, they will receive eternal salvation once they step over into eternity after death has come in their flesh. Believe now in the risen Savior named Jesus who was sent by God the Father to be a living sacrifice for the sins of the world. This is the only way you can avoid the JUDGMENT and WRATH of the almighty God. Our God is a holy and just God; therefore, he must judge the world righteously. Based on his love for his creation, he has made a way for us to escape, and his name is Jesus!

Scripture

> *"And as it is appointed unto men once to die, but after this the JUDGMENT. So Christ was once offered to bear the sin of many; and <u>unto them that look for him shall he appear the second time</u>, without sin unto salvation"* (Hebrews 9:27, 28).

According to the precious word of God, you can be born twice and die once, or you can be born once and die twice. What this phrase signifies is that all souls who accept Jesus as Lord and Savior have been washed in the blood of the Lamb. Therefore, they have been born again. Since everyone has been born into this world, this means that the redeemed of the Lord have been born twice—first at birth of the womb, and secondly at birth by the Spirit of God. This second spiritual birth caused the spiritual adoption to occur into the family of God. The Holy Bible teaches us that the saved souls are the righteous saints of God. They are not appointed to God's wrath that will be poured out onto the earth without mixture. These saints have been spared from the judgment of the Lord that will be executed upon the earth. However, the unsaved souls are not that blessed. They have rejected the <u>free gift</u> of salvation from God. They are not born again; hence, they have only been born once. This means they have to die twice—once in the flesh, and then again when they are cast into the lake of fire and brimstone for rejecting the grace of God. The Holy Bible refers to the lake of fire as the second death, which the saints of God have been redeemed from. If you are reading this, it's not too late to receive the salvation of the Lord. Jesus has redeemed all mankind from the sins of the world. All you have to do is believe it and confess the same in Jesus' name; then you shall receive eternal life in the kingdom of God.

6) The Judgment of Gentile Nations

Scripture

"When the Son of Man shall come in his Glory, and all the holy angels with him, then shall he sit upon the throne of his glory: And before him shall be gathered <u>ALL NATIONS</u>: and he shall separate them one from another, as a shepherd divideth his sheep from the goats: And he shall set the sheep on his right hand, but the goats on the left. Then shall the King say unto them on the right hand, Come, ye blessed of my Father, inherit the kingdom prepared for you from the foundation of the world: For I was an hungered, and ye gave me meat: I was thirsty, and ye gave me drink: I was a stranger, and ye took me in: Naked, and ye clothed me: I was sick, and ye visited me: I was in prison, and ye came unto me.

Then shall the righteous answer him, saying, Lord, when saw we thee an hungered, and fed thee? Or thirsty, and gave thee drink? When saw we thee a stranger, and took thee in? Or naked, and clothed thee? Or when saw we thee sick, or in prison, and came unto thee? And the King shall answer and say unto them, <u>Verily I say unto you, Inasmuch as ye have done it unto one of the least of these my brethren, ye have done it unto me.</u>

Then shall he say also unto them on the left hand, Depart from me, ye cursed, into everlasting fire, <u>prepared for the devil and his angels</u>: For I was an hungered, and ye gave me no meat: I was thirsty, and ye gave me no drink: I was a stranger, and ye took me not in: sick, and in prison, and ye visited me not. Then shall they also answer him, saying, Lord, when saw we thee an hungered, or athirst, or a stranger, or naked, or sick, or in prison, and did not minister unto thee? Then shall he answer them saying, Verily I say unto you, Inasmuch as ye did it not to one of the least of these, ye did it not to me. And these shall go away into EVERLASTING PUNISHMENT: but the righteous into LIFE ETERNAL" (Matthew 25: 31-46).

The many scriptures mentioned here deal with the judgment of all nations living through the great tribulation on earth at the time of Christ's return—his second coming. This is a judgment of separation. This is a judgment to determine the 'saved' and 'lost' during the tribulation period—those who accept or refuse the mark of the beast. The Bible explains this judgment as living nations, whereas the great white throne judgment deals with the wicked dead whose bodies are resurrected to face the final judgment of the lost.

7) The Great White Throne Judgment

Scripture

"And I saw a Great White Throne, and him that sat on it, from whose face the earth and the heavens fled away; and there was found no place for them. And I saw the DEAD, small and great, stand before God; and the books were open: and another book was open, which is the BOOK OF LIFE: and the DEAD were judged out of those things which were written in the books, according to their works. And the sea gave up the DEAD which were in it; and DEATH and HELL delivered up the DEAD which were in them: and they were judged every man according to their works. And DEATH and HELL were cast into the Lake of Fire. This is the <u>SECOND DEATH</u>. And whosoever was not found written in the book of life was cast into the Lake of Fire" (Revelation 20:11-15).

This judgment explains how even the dead and the spiritual dead will not escape the judgment of God. Therefore, rid yourself of the mentality of when you are dead—you're just dead. This is the farthest thing from the truth. Every man or woman will face God when they die in their flesh. Whoever told you that when you are dead, you're just dead; you must find that person and tell them the truth. Then you just might be able to save their soul from a devils hell. Either you will believe what God said, or you will believe the lie man has told you which came from the enemies of God. This next verse of scripture will encourage you to make the right choice. The question is whose report you will believe?

Scripture

"Thus saith the Lord; CURSED be the man that trusteth in man, and maketh flesh his arm, and whose heart departeth from the Lord" (Jeremiah 17:5).

"And say thou unto them, thus saith the Lord God of Israel; CURSED be the man that obeyeth not the words of this covenant" (Jeremiah 11:3).

The first verse of scripture teaches us that anytime we put man before God, watch out because we have just been CURSED. God is a jealous God and he does not share his glory with anyone, nor should he. The second verse of scripture teaches us that God has established a covenant with his people. Anytime God's people disobey his commands, we have to repent in order to remain in covenant with God. If we fail to do so and continue to walk in disobedience, we are CURSED. We must obey the Lord at all costs. There is life more abundantly for those who will, and death and destruction for them who won't.

8) The Judgment of Angels

Scripture

"Do ye not know that the saints shall judge the world? And if the world shall be judged by you, are ye unworthy to judge the smallest matters? Know ye not that we SHALL judge angels? How much more things that pertain to this life" (1 Corinthians 6:2, 3)?

We as saints of God shall judge the world which includes angels. The question is…what angels?

Scripture

"And it shall come to pass in that day, that the Lord shall punish the host of the high ones that are on high, and the kings of the earth upon the earth. And they shall be gathered together, as prisoners are gathered in the

pit, and shall be shut up in the prison, and after many days, shall they be visited" (Isaiah 24:21, 22).

The host of the high ones (satanic powers) and the kings of the earth (earthly powers) will be gathered in the pit and shut up many days. After a period of time, they shall be visited. These angels that the saints of God will judge are the fallen angels that were cast out of heaven by God. They chose to likewise rebel against God and follow their leader Lucifer, now known here in the earth as the devil or Satan. The only difference is, Lucifer sinned against God on his own, the fallen angels made the choice to follow their leader the devil. This is why Lucifer, the devil, or Satan was judged at the cross when God resurrected Jesus from the dead. When the Holy Scriptures refer to the saints judging angels, they are referring to the fallen celestial beings. When the saints of God Judge the world with Christ Jesus, this is referring to those who have made their bed in hell because they refused the grace of God. This place called the pit where these individuals will be gathered and shut up in many days is also called hell. This place called hell is a temporary hold facility for those awaiting the Great White Throne Judgment of God. Therefore, this is the place being referred to as the awaiting PIT. The Bible tells us that Hell will empty out its dead at the Great White Throne Judgment of God.

Scripture

"For if God spared not the angels that sinned, but cast them down to hell, and delivered them into chains of darkness, to be reserved unto judgment" (2 Peter 2:4);

"The Lord knoweth how to deliver the godly out of temptations and to reserve the unjust unto the Day of Judgment to be punished" (2 Peter 2:9);

"And the angels which kept not their first estate, but left their own habitation, he hath reserved in everlasting chains under darkness unto the judgment of the great day" (Jude 6).

Based on these scriptures, it is crystal clear which angels this judgment is referring to. This judgment deals with the host of angels that were cast down by God. The kings of the earth include the wicked souls in positions of authority who refused the salvation of the Lord down through the centuries. They have also refused to repent and chose to reject the grace of God. Satanic and earthly souls that have taken on the nature of the devil will ultimately end up with him in the lake of fire. Remember, anything unlike God is of the devil.

WHAT IS THE WRATH OF GOD?

There are several wraths spoken of throughout the Holy Bible. The one we really need to be concerned about today is the wrath of God's judgments. These are the wraths of God that will be poured out on the earth during the Great Tribulation Period. The scriptures tell us about several wraths in the Old Testament that have already come to pass. The wrath that is to be poured out on the children of disobedience for rejecting the salvation of the Lord is still to come. The Bible tells us this wrath of God will be poured out without mixture. In other words, it will be an uncut judgment poured out on the earth.

Scripture

"If any man worship the beast and his image, and receive his mark in his forehead, or in his hand, the same shall drink of the wine of the Wrath of God, which is poured out without MIXTURE into the cup of his indignation; and he shall be tormented with fire and brimstone in the presence of the holy angels, and in the presence of the Lamb" (Revelation 14:9, 10).

The fire and brimstone judgment will be witnessed by the angels of the Lord and the Lamb of God who is Jesus Christ the King of kings and the Lord of lords over all. Therefore, remember, we must be concerned with this judgment. We must make sure, based on our belief in Christ Jesus as Lord and our hope in glory that salvation belongs to us.

Scripture

The Bible tells us, *"For God hath not appointed us to the wrath, but to obtain salvation by our Lord Jesus Christ, Who died for us, that, whether we wake or sleep, we should live together with him"* (1 Thessalonians 5:9, 10).

FINAL WRATH

The Bible tells us which souls have the wrath of God abiding on them. Are you one of the souls who have <u>not</u> been covered with the blood of Jesus for your many sins committed in your lifetime? If so, then you are the one being referred to in this section. The wrath of God abides on you. The only way to be delivered from death is to get covered with the blood of Jesus right now at this very moment. Jesus warns us that we must be born again.

Scripture

The book of John tells us, *"He that believeth on the Son hath everlasting life: and he that believeth not the Son shall not see life; but the WRATH of God adideth on him"* (John 3:36).

The book of Romans tells us, *"For the Wrath of God is revealed from heaven against all ungodliness and unrighteousness of men, who hold the truth in unrighteousness"* (Romans 1:18).

The book of Ephesians tells us, *"Let no man deceive you with vain words: for because of these things cometh the Wrath of God upon the children of disobedience. Be not ye therefore partakers with them"* (Ephesians 5:6, 7).

The book of Colossians tells us, *"For which things sake the Wrath of God cometh on the children of disobedience: In the which ye also walked some time, when ye lived in them"* (Colossians 3:6, 7).

The book of Colossians tells us, *"But now ye also put off all these; ANGER, WRATH, MALICE, BLASPHEMY, FILTHY COMMUNICATION out of your mouth. Lie not one to another, seeing that ye have put off the <u>OLD MAN</u> with his deeds; And have put on the <u>NEW MAN</u>, which is <u>renewed in knowledge</u> after the image of him that created him: where there is neither Greek nor Jew, circumcision nor uncircumcision, Barbarian, Scythian, bond nor free: but Christ is all, and in all"* (Colossians 3:8-11).

THE JUDGMENT

Scripture

The book of Revelation tells us, *"And the third angel followed them, saying with a loud voice, If any man worship the beast and his image, and receive his mark in his forehead, or in his hand. The same shall drink of the wine of the wrath of God, which is poured out without mixture into the cup of his indignation; and he shall be tormented with fire and brimstone in the presence of the holy angels, and in the presence of the Lamb. And the smoke of their torment ascendeth up forever and ever: and they have no rest day nor night, who worship the beast and his image, and whosoever receiveth the mark of his name. Here is the patience of the saints: here are they that keep the commandments of God, and the faith of Jesus. And I heard a voice from heaven saying unto me, Write, <u>Blessed are the dead which die in the Lord from henceforth</u>: Yea, saith the Spirit, that they may rest from their labors; and their works do follow them"* (Revelation 14:9-13).

The book of Revelation tells us in Chapter 15:1 that John the apostle saw another sign in heavens, great and marvelous. There were seven angels having the seven last plagues. For in these plagues were they filled up with the wrath of God? Chapter 16:1 tells us that John the apostle heard a great voice out of the temple saying to the seven angels, "Go your way, and pour out the vials of the wrath of God upon the earth." This will be a dreadful day for all who have to endure and witness this horrible end.

THE GREAT DAY OF GOD'S WRATH

The great day of God's wrath is called the Day of the Lord. This is the predicted time set for God's judgment toward the earth and its inhabitants. The day of God's judgment at that time is to be compared to the day of God's grace at this time. These two timeframes are in contrast to one another. We are living in the day of the wonderful grace of the Lord. God's judgment will be poured out on the earth without mixture. When the great day of the Lord comes, the earth and those who are left in it will experience three different forms of wrath. The seven seals will be opened. The seven trumpets will sound. The seven vials will be poured out upon the earth. The vials will be the last part of God's wrath to be emptied out upon the earth for its final judgment.

THE SEVEN SEALS

As a result of the judgment of the first six seals, many unbelievers will want to die. Many will try to hide from the face of God, but will be unable to hide. They will even attempt to commit suicide and will not be able to die. Can you imagine some one jumping off a cliff in an attempt to try and cause their death? Their body becomes all mangled; however, they continue to live on in that state of pain and disfigurement. Unable to die is what the word of God says. John the apostle witnessed these events when the Lord invited him to come up to the kingdom of God in order to reveal the Revelation of Jesus Christ to the churches.

Scripture

"And I saw when the Lamb opened one of the Seals, and I heard as it were the noise of thunder, one of the four beasts saying, COME AND SEE.

1) And I saw, and behold a WHITE HORSE: and he that sat on him had a bow; and a crown was given unto him: and he went forth conquering, and to conquer" (Revelation 6:1, 2).

"And when he had opened the second Seal, I heard the second beast say, COME AND SEE.

2) *And there went out another HORSE that was RED: and power was given to him that sat thereon to take peace from the earth, and that they should KILL one another: and there was given unto him a great sword*" (Revelation 6:3, 4).

"And when he had opened the third Seal, I heard the third beast say, COME AND SEE.

3) *And I beheld, and lo a BLACK HORSE; and he that sat on him had a pair of balances in his hand. And I heard a voice in the midst of the four beasts say, A measure of wheat for a penny, and three measures of barley for a penny; and see thou hurt not the oil and the wine*" (Revelation 6:5, 6).

"And when he had opened the fourth Seal, I heard the voice of the fourth beast say, COME AND SEE.

4) *And I looked, and behold a PALE HORSE: and his name that sat on him was DEATH, and HELL followed with him. And power was given unto them over the fourth part of the earth, to KILL with sword, and with hunger, and with death, and with the beast of the earth*" (Revelation 6:7, 8).

"And when he had opened the fifth Seal,

5) *I saw under the altar the souls of them that were slain for the word of God, and for the testimony which they held: And they cried with a loud voice, saying, How long, O Lord, Holy and True, dost thou not judge and avenge our blood on them that dwell on the earth? And white robes were given unto every one of them; and it was said unto them, that they should rest yet for a little season, until their fellow servants also and their brethren,

that should be KILLED as they were, should be fulfilled" (Revelation 6:9-11). *"And I beheld when he had opened the sixth Seal,*

> *6) And, lo, there was a great earthquake; and the sun became black as sackcloth of hair, and the moon became as blood. And the stars of heaven fell unto the earth, even as a fig tree casteth her untimely figs, when she is shaken of a mighty wind. And the heavens departed as a scroll when it is rolled together, and every mountain and island were moved out of their places. And the kings of the earth, and the great men, and the rich men, and the chief captains, and the mighty men, and every bondman, and every free man, hid themselves in the dens and in the rocks of the mountains; And said to the mountains and rocks, <u>FALL ON US</u>, and hide us from the face of him that sitteth on the throne, and from the <u>Wrath of the Lamb</u>. For the great day of his Wrath is come; and who shall be able to stand"* (Revelation 6:12-17).

Notice that the Holy Scriptures describe this great wrath of God as the wrath of the Lamb, which is Jesus the Christ. Hopefully, this will help clear up in the minds of the souls that often wondered how Jesus as God was manifested in the flesh for man's sake.

The 144,000 Sealed

This section will explain the 144,000 that were sealed by God before the Great Tribulation Period begins. The 144,000 are all Israelites from the twelve tribes of Israel. The number of 144,000 came from the 12,000 times twelve tribes of souls which were selected and sealed by God for his purpose. The word of God lets us know that they are from the tribes of Israel formulated out of the sons of Jacob. This is still a mystery as to where they are or how they will appear. But one thing we do know is that they are God's chosen people that will be selected to appear during the Tribulation Period. Their purpose is to be a beacon of LIGHT unto God in the earth for those who have to go through the Great Tribulation Period. The Bible tells us that God will remember his people and their children in that day. These 144,000 souls will be on assignment to recover the remnant of God's people during this Great Tribulation period. This 144,000 may be actual descendants of the twelve Tribes of Israel walking in the earth today. However, God will seal them with his mark and use them as a beacon of LIGHT unto the many nations that remain during that time period. There will be souls from all nations that failed to believe the preachers and the prophets in the earth today. They chose not to accept Jesus as the true Messiah when they had the chance. Now that the saints of God are gone on to be with the Lord, the ones who at one time did not believe see differently now. There will be souls who receive salvation during this awful period of time. Those who are left to suffer and be tormented will still have a chance to pledge their allegiance to Jesus as the Messiah under very harsh conditions. All souls who refuse to accept the mark of Satan's beast will still have a chance to come to the Lord Jesus. But be prepared to suffer a horrible death for your new found belief in Christ Jesus. Right now, you have a chance to be born-again into the loving family of Jesus Christ. Make a decision to live life eternally with God, knowing that Jesus is the one and only Savior of all mankind. The other choice is to keep putting it off and taking your chances. Once we die in the flesh, that's it. We will either sleep in Christ Jesus like the Bibles tells us, or we will go where the wicked are held in torment until that day of FINAL JUDGMENT. That day is called the Great White Throne Judgment—a place where you don't want to be, trust me.

Scripture

"For if ye turn again unto the Lord, your BRETHREN and your CHILDREN SHALL find compassion before them that lead them captive, so that they shall come again into this land: for the Lord your God is GRACIOUS and MERCIFUL, and will not turn away his face from you, if ye return unto him" (2 Chronicles 30:9).

"And in that day there shall be a root of Jesse, which shall stand for an ensign of the people; to it shall the Gentiles seek: and his rest shall be glorious. And it shall come to pass in that day, that the Lord shall set his hand again the second time to recover the REMNANT of his people, which shall be left, from Assyria, and from Egypt, and from Pathos, and from Cush, and from Elam, and from Shinar, and from Hamath, and from the Islands of the sea. And he shall set up an ensign for the nations, and shall assembly the OUTCASTS of Israel, and gather together the dispersed of Judah from the four corners of the earth" (Isaiah 11:10-12).

The four angels held back the four winds until an angel with the seal of God sealed the 144,000 children of Israel. Many nations and kindred's will be saved during this Great Tribulation Period. This will occur through the evangelistic ministry of the 144.000 sealed Jews.

The Numberless Multitude

John the apostle was shown another revelation pertaining to a great multitude which no man could number. This multitude stood before the throne and before the Lamb of God (Jesus).

Scripture

"After this I beheld, and, lo, a great multitude, which no man could number, of all NATIONS, and KINDREDS, and PEOPLE, and TONGUES, stood before the throne, and before the Lamb, clothed with white robes, and palms in their hands; And cried with a loud voice, saying Salvation to our God which sitteth upon the throne, and unto the Lamb" (Revelation 7:9, 10).

"And one of the elders answered, saying unto me, What are these which are arrayed in white robes? And whence came they? And I said unto him, Sir, thou knowest, And he said to me, These are they which came out of Great Tribulation, and have washed their robes, and made them white in the blood of the Lamb. Therefore are they before the throne of God, and serve him day and night in his Temple: and he that sitteth on the throne shall dwell among them" (Revelation 7:13-15).

These multitudes of nations are those who came out of the Great Tribulation period. Clearly, God has no respect of persons. Despite how humans get along here in the earth, heaven is not going to be segregated by any means. Anyone who allows their heart to feel this way cannot dwell in God's Holy City. Therefore, believe in the love of God and crucify the hatred of man that remains in your flesh.

Scripture

"For there is no respect of persons with God" (Romans 2:11).

7) And when he had opened the seventh Seal, <u>there was silence in heaven about the space of half an hour</u>. And I saw the seven angels which stood before God; and to them were given seven trumpets. And another angel came and stood at the altar, having a golden censer; and there was given unto him much incense, that he should offer it with the <u>prayers of all saints</u> upon the golden altar which was before the throne. And the smoke of the incense, which came with the prayers of the saints, ascended up before God out of the angel's hand. And the angel took the censer, and filled it with fire of the altar, and cast it into the earth: and there were voices, and thunderings, and lightnings, and an earthquake" (Revelation 8:1-5).

When these prayers were cast down to the earth with the fire from the altar of God, voices were heard upon the earth. The prayers of the saints could be heard over all the earth which was mingled with thunder, lightning, and an earthquake. Can you imagine hearing the prayers of the saints in the winds that blow through the skies? The voices of men and women clearly being translated by sound in the heavens. Blessed be the name of the Lord.

THE SEVEN TRUMPETS

"And the seven angels which had the seven trumpets prepared themselves to sounds.

1) The first angel sounded, and there followed hail and fire mingled with blood, and they were cast upon the earth: and the third part of the trees was burnt up, and all green grass was burnt up" (Revelation 8:6-7).

2) And the second angel sounded, and as it were a great mountain burning with fire was cast into the sea: and the third part of the sea became blood. And the third part of the creatures which were in the sea, and had life, died; and the third part of the ships were destroyed" (Revelation 8:7-9).

3) *And the third angel sounded, and there fell a great star from heaven, burning as it were a lamp, and it fell upon the third part of the rivers, and upon the fountains of waters; And the name of the star is called Wormwood: and the third part of the waters became wormwood: and many men died of the waters, because they were made bitter"* (Revelation 8:10, 11).

4) *And the fourth angel sounded, and the third part of the sun was smitten, and the third part of the moon, and the third part of the stars; so as the third part of them was darkened, and the day shone not for a third part of it, and the night likewise. And I beheld, and heard an angel flying through the midst of heaven, saying with a loud voice, Woe, woe, woe, to the inhabiters of the earth by reason of the other voices of the trumpet of the three angels, which are yet to sound"* (Revelation 8:12, 13).

5) *And the fifth angel sounded, and I saw a star fall from heaven unto the earth: and to him was given the key of the BOTTOMLESS PIT. And he opened the bottomless pit; and there arose a smoke out of the pit, as the smoke of a great furnace; and the sun and the air were darkened by reason of the smoke of the pit. And there came out of the smoke locusts upon the earth and unto them was given power, as the scorpions of the earth have power. And it was commanded them that they should not hurt the grass of the earth, neither any green thing, neither any tree;* <u>*but only those men which have not the Seal of God in their foreheads*</u>*. And to them it was given that they should Not kill them, but that they should be tormented five months: and their torment was as the torment of a scorpion, when he striketh a man.* <u>*And in those days shall men seek DEATH, and shall not find it; and shall desire to DIE, and DEATH shall flee from them*</u>*. And the shapes of the locusts were like unto horses prepared unto battle; and on their heads were as it were crowns like gold, and their faces were as the faces of men. And they had hair as the hair of women, and their teeth were as the teeth of lions. And they had breastplates, as it were breastplates of iron; and the sound of their wings was as the sound of chariots of many horses running to battle. And*

they had tails like unto scorpions, and there were stings in their tails: and their power was to hurt men five months. And they had a king over them, which is the angel of the bottomless pit, whose name in the Hebrew tongue is Abaddon, but in the Greek tongue hath his name Apollyon. One woe is past; and, behold, there come two woes more hereafter" (Revelation 9:1-12).

6) *And the sixth angel sounded, and I heard a voice from the four horns of the golden altar which is before God. Saying to the sixth angel which had the Trumpet, Loose the four angels which are bound in the great river Euphrates. And the four angels were loosed, which were prepared for an hour, and a day, and a month, and a year, for to slay the third part of men. And the number of the army of the horsemen were two hundred thousand thousand: and I heard the number of them. And thus I saw the horses in the vision, and them that sat on them having breastplates of fire, and of jacinth, and brimstone: and the heads of the horses were as the heads of lions; and out of their mouths issued fire and smoke and brimstone. By these three was the third part of men killed, by the fire, and by the smoke, and by the brimstone, which issued out of their mouths. For their power is in their mouth, and in their tails: for their tails were like unto serpents, and had heads, and with them they do hurt. And the rest of the men which were not killed by these plagues yet <u>REPENTED NOT</u> of the works of their hands, that they should not worship devils, and idols of gold, and silver, and brass, and stone, and of wood: which neither can see, nor hear, nor walk: Neither repented they of their MURDERS, nor of their SORCERIES, nor of their FORNICATION, nor of their THEFTS"* (Revelation 9:13-21).

The Angel and the Little Book

"And I saw another mighty angel come down from heaven, clothed with a cloud: and a rainbow was upon his head, and his face was as it were the sun, and his feet as pillars of fire: And he had in his hand a little book open: and he set his right foot upon the sea, and his left foot on the earth. And cried with a loud voice, as when a lion roareth: and when he had cried, seven thunders uttered their voices. And when the seven thunders had uttered their voices, I was about to write: and I heard a voice from heaven saying unto me,

THE LAMB'S BOOK OF LIFE:

<u>SEAL UP THOSE THINGS WHICH THE SEVEN THUNDERS UTTERED, AND WRITE THEM NOT.</u>

And the angel which I saw stand upon the sea and upon the earth lifted up his hand to heaven. And sware by him that liveth forever and ever, who created heaven, and the things that therein are, and the earth, and the sea, and the things which are therein, that there should be time no longer" (Revelation 10:1-6).

7) But in the days of the voice of the seventh angel, when he shall begin to sound, the mystery of God should be finished, as he hath declared to his servants the prophets. And the voice which I heard from heaven spake unto me again and said, Go and take the little book which is open in the hand of the angel which standeth upon the sea and upon the earth. And I went unto the angel, and said unto him, Give me the little book. And he said unto me, Take it, and eat it up; and it shall make thy belly bitter, but it shall be in thy mouth sweet as honey. And I took the little book out of the angel's hand, and ate it up: and it was in my mouth sweet as honey: and as soon as I had eaten it, my belly was bitter. And he said unto me, Thou must prophesy again before many peoples, and nations, and tongues, and kings" (Revelation 10:7-11).

THE VIALS OF WRATH

The seven vials of wrath are the last to be poured out by God in the earth.

Scripture

"And I heard a great voice out of the temple saying to the seven angels, Go your ways, and pour out the vials of the Wrath of God upon the earth.

1. And the first went, and poured out his vial upon the earth; and there fell a noisome and grievous sore upon men which had the mark of the beast and upon them which worshiped his image.

2. And the second angel poured out his vial upon the sea; and it became as the blood of a dead man; and every living soul died in the sea.

3. And the third angel poured out his vial upon the rivers and fountains of waters; and they became blood.

4. And the fourth angel poured out his vial upon the sun; and power was given unto him to scorch men with fire. And men were scorched with great heat, and blasphemed the name of God, which hath power over these plagues: and they repented NOT to give him glory.

5. And the fifth angel poured out his vial upon the seat of the beast; and his kingdom was full of darkness; and they gnawed their tongues for pain. And blasphemed the God of heaven because of their pains and their sores, and repented NOT of their deeds.

6. And the sixth angel poured out his vial upon the great river Euphrates; and the waters thereof was dried up, that the way of the kings of the east might be prepared.

7. And the seventh angel poured out his vial into the air; and there came a great voice out of the temple of heaven, from the throne, saying, It is done! And there were voices, and thunders, and lightnings; and there was a great earthquake, such as was not since men were upon the earth, so mighty an earthquake, and so great. And the great city was divided into three parts, and the cities of the nations fell: and great Babylon came in remembrance before God, to give unto her the cup of the wine of the fierceness of his wrath. And every island fled away, and the mountains were not found. And there fell upon men a great hail out of heaven, every stone about the weight of a talent: (sixty to one-hundred pounds), and men blasphemed God because of the plague of the hail; for the plague thereof was exceeding great" (Revelation 16:1-21).

The seventh vial is the very last of the twenty-one plagues poured out upon the earth. This concludes all the plagues that will be poured out with out mixture upon the earth during the tribulation period. You don't want to be there!

DESCRIPTION OF SATAN

When the devil was in the kingdom of God, his name was Lucifer. God created him full of wisdom and beauty. He had special pipes created in him to make beautiful worship music to glorify the Most High. This was before he sinned and was cast down to the earth. This is how the Holy Scriptures described Lucifer then.

Scripture

"Thus saith the Lord God; Thou sealest up the sum, full of wisdom, and perfect in beauty. Thou hast been in Eden the garden of God; every precious stone was thy covering, the sardius, topaz, and the diamond, the beryl, the onyx, and the jasper, the sapphire, the emerald, and the carbuncle, and gold: <u>the workmanship of thy tabrets and of thy pipes was prepared in thee in the day that thou wast created</u>. Thou art the anointed cherub that covereth; and I have set thee so: thou wast upon the holy mountain of God; thou hast walked up and down in the midst of the stones of fire. Thou wast perfect in thy ways from the day that thou wast created, til iniquity was found in thee. By the multitude of thy merchandise they have filled the midst of thee with violence, and thou hast SINNED: therefore I will cast thee as profane out of the mountain of God: and I will destroy thee, O covering cherub, from the midst of the stones of fire. Thine heart was lifted up because of thy beauty, thou hast corrupted thy wisdom by reason of thy brightness: I will cast thee to the ground, I will lay thee before kings, that they may behold thee. Thou hast defiled thy sanctuaries by the multitudes of thine iniquities, by the iniquity of thy traffic; therefore will I bring forth a FIRE from the midst of thee, it shall devour thee, and I will bring thee to ashes upon the earth in the sight of all them that behold thee. All they that know thee among the people shall be astonished at thee: thou shalt be a terror, and never shalt thou be any more" (Ezekiel 28:12b-19).

Now you have a clear picture of who Satan once was in the kingdom of heaven. He was created perfect by God with beauty, wisdom and the ability to makes sweet music. He served near the presence of God until he became guilty of the sin of PRIDE. The Bible says Lucifer was perfect in his ways until iniquity was found in him. Now he is a present day terror for just a little while longer. One of his strongest weapons is deception. That was who Lucifer was. His new name is now Satan and this is who he is today. The book of Revelation which is the last book of the Holy Bible described Satan as the <u>great</u> red dragon. By no means does this insinuate that Satan is great or anything to be adored. This enemy of God must never be worshiped by man. Remember, self-worship is what Satan wanted in the kingdom of heaven before he was cast down to the earth by God. He wanted the worship that belonged exclusively to the Creator of all things, which is God alone. Let us never forget, the devil is the enemy of God whose sentence has already been established and sealed. There is no hope for the devil, or anyone who is foolish enough to follow or associate with him. Unfortunately, even today there are many souls in the earth that worship this so-called great dragon. Man has even written a satanic bible and formed a church in the name of Satan that many have freely joined around the world. Therefore, be not deceived, Satan has men and women in the earth willing to follow him into the pit of hell to await the Great White Throne Judgment of God. The reason why these lost souls have chosen this foolish path is because deep in their heart, they really do not believe the word of God is true. This is how the devil has deceived them into thinking there is no God. This will be a said day when these rebellious souls realize that Satan whom they worshiped deceived their very soul. Just like in the days of Noah when they laughed, thinking that the rain would not appear in the desert. When the rains came, they realized it was too late. Every soul that has entered into the pit of hell over the centuries truly regrets not believing in God who was preached in the earth. Their fate awaits the Great White Throne Judgment where they will be judged without protection. Every one of these souls rejected the blood of Jesus which is the only protection from God's judgment against sin. When they are about to be cast into the lake of fire with their chosen father the devil, they will HATE the day deception took a hold of their soul.

Scripture

"And there appeared another wonder in heaven; and behold a great red dragon, having seven heads and ten horns, and seven crowns upon his heads. And his tail drew the <u>third part of the stars of heaven</u>, and did cast them to the earth" (Revelation 12:3, 4a).

The color red for the dragon portrays Satan's murderous character. His seven heads and seven crowns depict the completeness and universal power and influence he has over this earth. His ten horns show Satan's connection with the fourth beast spoken of in the book of Daniel and with the beast from the sea. The third part of the stars of heaven represents the fallen angels who followed Satan when he rebelled against God. At the time of the birth of Jesus Christ, Satan was ready to kill him. This can be found in the book of Matthew 2:13-18. Satan influenced the mind of Herod the king who ordered all male children slain from new birth up to two years of age. Herod the king was afraid of losing his throne to the newborn King Jesus. Herod the king had no idea that this king was the KING of the world, and not just over a province. King Herod lacked understanding causing the death of all the male children he slaughtered before he died and entered into his judgment. The male child born named Jesus the Christ was destined to rule all nations as the prophesied Messiah sent into this world by God. The dragon is identified as the devil and Satan in this final book of Revelation.

Scripture

"And the great dragon was cast out, that old serpent, called the devil, and Satan, which deceiveth the whole world: <u>he was cast out into the earth</u>, and his angels were cast out with him" (Revelation 12:9).

This Holy Scripture tells us that the dragon called the devil and Satan that deceived the whole world was cast out into the earth. God created man from the dust of the ground and breathed into his nostrils the breath of life. Man became a living soul that would be attached to the earth that God had formed. God gave man dominion over the earth so that he would rule as lord instead of the red dragon called Satan. The problem occurred when Satan tricked Eve to eat of the forbidden fruit and she gave also to Adam who willingly disobeyed God. This was the point where man lost his dominion over the earth. For this reason, God had to come into the earth in the form of flesh in order to redeem man back from the clutches of his enemy, the devil. Many who reject the word of God still have trouble accepting this truth. They refuse to believe that the Lord Jesus was 100 percent DIVINE, and at the same time 100 percent HUMAN. Those who have trouble with this truth do not understand that mankind had to be redeemed in the same state in which he fell. In this case, it was in the flesh that man sinned and fell out of fellowship with God. All this was done thanks to the deception of the devil that was eventually imposed upon all flesh. We have to be careful that the will of Satan does not impose himself upon us. Remember how Satan influenced Herod the king to attempt to destroy Jesus at his birth. The book of Revelation describes in this next verse of scripture how the virgin birth of Christ took place, also his ascension back to the throne of God.

Scripture

"And the dragon stood before the woman which was ready to be delivered, for to devour her child as soon as it was born. And she brought forth a man child, who was to rule all nations with a rod of iron: and her child was caught up unto God and to his throne" (Revelation 12:4b-5).

This verse of scripture reminds us how Jesus the Christ was born and the devil sought anxiously to destroy him. Satan did not understand God's plan at that time. For this reason he influenced the mind of Herod the king to carry out that decree of destroying all male children in the land under the age of two. This way, the devil figured he would kill the Christ child by process of elimination. The wise men appeared before Herod the king concerning the birth of the Messiah prior to the king's decision to destroy the children. Herod the king, not fully understanding the plan of God had wickedness in his heart and further felt his kingdom was being threatened. Having this in mind, he was a perfect vessel willing to be used by the enemy—Satan. That is why we should never harbor hatred in our hearts. Anytime we allow hatred to fester, it will always lead to murder. Many families lost their infant males during this time of great slaughter at the hands of the sword. After the command of destruction was carried out, shortly thereafter, the soul of Herod was required of him by God. The king died after his decree and he was succeeded by his son, king Archelaus who was wicked than his father. He only ruled from 4BC to 6AD.

ARE YOU STILL IN CAPTIVITY?

This is a very interesting question. This question is asking you if you are still the property of Satan. Many fail to realize that what our great ancestor Adam did in the Garden of Eden still affects us today. The blood of Jesus Christ takes care of the matter; however, many have still failed to accept the Savior's precious blood. Those who have not accepted God's plan for salvation are still in captivity. Now, let's talk about what captivity means. In order to do this, we have to go back to the Garden of Eden. Remember when Adam disobeyed God? He went from being created perfect to becoming imperfect. Sin entered into the heart of mankind. Every offspring of Adam inherited his sinful nature. The fact that babies are truly a gift from God, we must never forget they still come into the world with that same old sinful nature that Adam passed down through his bloodline. The only flesh-born individual who avoided this contaminated bloodline was Jesus Christ. The Lord and Savior of this world received his bloodline from the Holy Spirit of God who overshadowed the Virgin Mary. Since Jesus had no earthly father, his blood came directly from the Heavenly Father.

Scripture

> *"Then said Mary unto the angel, How shall this be, seeing I know not a man? And the angel answered and said unto her, The HOLY GHOST shall come upon thee, and the power of the HIGHEST shall <u>overshadow</u> thee: therefore also that Holy thing which shall be born of thee shall be called the Son of God"* (Luke 1:34, 35).

Since the Holy Ghost is part of the Godhead, this proves that Jesus had the blood of God the Father running through his veins. Therefore, when Jesus shed his blood on the cross at Calvary, this was the only thing valuable enough to pay our sin-debt in full. No other blood would do. This act of love from

Christ Jesus made salvation available to all who would receive his cleansing blood. No one can enter into the kingdom of God without first being covered with the blood of the Lamb, which is Christ Jesus. We are all born into sin and that's a fact. The problem with the lost souls living upon the earth is they cannot see their sin. This is why they feel in their heart that they have no sin and they need no Savior. However, the word of God says it like this.

Scripture

"Behold, I was shapen in iniquity; and in sin did my mother conceive me" (Psalm 51:5).

The good news of the gospel of Jesus Christ is that when we accept God's plan for our salvation, we are no longer in captivity. The Lord Jesus freed us from the clutches of the devil's grip by washing our sins away. Without our Lord Jesus the Christ, we would have remained in bondage for all eternity with Satan and his followers. Therefore, study and believe the holy word of God and be delivered and set free forever. Once we come into the knowledge of God, our minds are completely set free—no more deception. No more receiving lies from the enemy. No more spiritual blindness blocking the glory of God. No more lack of knowledge which causes the destruction of man. No more resentment toward the Savior who God sent to give us eternal life. We must realize that the precious Holy Spirit is the one who strengthens us to walk uprightly before God the Father. This makes it possible for us to walk in that newness that the word of the Lord speaks of. I will ask you the same question again as in the title of this section, "ARE YOU STILL IN CAPTIVITY?"

THE WILL OF SATAN

Satan was referred to as Lucifer while he dwelled in heaven before his fall. Lucifer was his name before sin was found within him. Once sin entered into him, God changed his name to Satan which means the accuser. This next section of scripture tells us exactly where Satan made his big mistake. Pride is what brought Lucifer down. What we know about our God is that he hates pride. God tells us that pride defiles a man.

Scripture

"A man's PRIDE SHALL bring him low: but honor shall uphold the humble in spirit" (Proverbs 29:23).

Jesus said, "And he said, that which cometh out of the man, that defileth the man. For from within, out of the heart of men, proceed Evil Thoughts, Adulteries, Fornications, Murders, Thefts, Covetousness, Wickedness, Deceit, Lasciviousness, an Evil Eye, Blasphemy, <u>PRIDE</u>, Foolishness: All these evil things come from within, and defile the man" (Mark 7:20-23).

"The fear of the Lord is to hate evil: <u>PRIDE</u>, and arrogancy, and the evil way, and the froward mouth, DO I HATE" (Proverbs 8:13).

God warns his children against PRIDE telling us that it will bring us low. The world's wicked system teaches us to be prideful in our hearts. Nations are taught to put themselves over other nations. Some parents teach their children that they are superior to other nations, tribes and kindreds. The rich look down on the poor. The smart despises the moronic. The bottom line is when pride is promoted, it produces hatred, and then hatred will always bring on murder in the end. God further tells us that pride defiles a person. God ends up in this last verse informing us that ultimately he hates pride. Pride overtook Lucifer when he desired to be like the Most High. Lucifer was originally created as one of God's highest angels, possessing all angelic attributes. Lucifer's name was changed by God to Satan as he led angels in rebellion against the Lord. Satan was cast down because of his will to be above God. He wanted to replace God on his holy mountain. Satan willed five times that he would be like the Most High. There is no salvation for Satan and his fallen angels who freely chose to leave their first estate in heaven. The heavenly host of the Lord's angels that followed Satan had a choice, and they chose to use their freewill to sin and rebel against God. Based on the sin of Adam, mankind after him was born into this world with the same sinful nature. Therefore, we as human beings did not will this sin nature against ourselves. We had no choice in the matter. God made atonement for us through his only begotten Son Jesus Christ the Messiah. Now let's hear what Satan said that got him kicked out of the kingdom of heaven.

Scripture

"How art thou fallen from heaven, O Lucifer, son of the morning! How art thou cut down to the ground, which didst weaken the nations! For thou hast said in thine heart,

1) *I WILL ascend into heaven*

2) *I WILL exalt my throne above the stars of God*

3) *I WILL sit also upon the mount of the congregation, in the sides of the north*

4) *I WILL ascend above the heights of the clouds*

5) *I WILL be like the most High.*

Yet thou shalt be brought down to hell, to the sides of the pit. They that see thee shall narrowly look upon thee, and consider thee, saying, Is this <u>the man</u> that made the earth to tremble, that did shake kingdoms; That made the world as a wilderness, and destroyed the cities thereof; that open not the house of his prisoners" (Isaiah 14:12-17)?

Notice that the Holy Scriptures referred to Satan as <u>a man</u> who made the earth tremble and caused the kingdoms to shake. There is no hope for Satan and his fallen angels who chose to rebel against God. The Lord knows how his enemy Satan is a threat to this world. He is the accuser of the brethren in the earth. Jesus is the one seated on the right hand of the throne of God making intercession for mankind as Satan accuses the brethren daily. Remember what happen to God's servant Job? Satan not only accused him to God, but suggested that he would curse God if his blessings were taken from him. Job ended up withstanding the test and was restored by God double for his trouble. Thank the Lord for sending his only begotten Son Jesus to save us from a world of sin and destruction. The entire world will be judged real soon. God made a way for his children in the earth to be rescued from his final judgment. The only way to avoid the wrath of God is through his only begotten, and his name is Jesus.

SPIRIT OF THE ANTICHRIST

Who has the spirit of the antichrist? Anyone who does not believe in the only begotten Son of God has that evil spirit upon him. Could this be you? There are those who have not read the Holy Bible, yet they've convinced themselves that God would never come to the earth. There are some religions that feel and teach that God has no Sons. When this type of belief is practiced, this person or group has chosen to rebel against God. They practice religion, and at the same time refusing the relationship offered by God to accept his only begotten Son Jesus the Christ. The problem is they never understood that the Holy Bible tells us that God sent Jesus into the earth. This was not man's idea. There are many who call Christianity a man made religion. This is because they refuse to read and believe what is written in the holy word of God. They accept other forms of non-canonized doctrines. They do not understand nor accept the doctrine of the gospel of Jesus Christ found in the Holy Bible. You still have certain religions that believe only in the Old Testament books of the Bible. They fail to read the entire Holy Bible which contains both the Old and the New Testament. They do not even pay closely attention to the Old Testament doctrine, because if they did, they would have developed an understanding of Jesus the Messiah. Anyone truly seeking God would have believed its prophecy of the coming Messiah which is mentioned all through the Old Testament. The Messiah was even prophesied in the book of Isaiah as IMMANUEL, which means '<u>God with us</u>.' This prophecy was proclaimed over seven hundred years before the Messiah's arrival. This clearly teaches the reader that God was going to show up in the earth. The reason why the Pharisees could not understand this is due to the hatred in their hearts. This is what blinded their eyes to the glory of the Lord. Hatred for Jesus the Christ made these temple leaders eventually become murderers, and murderers will have no place in the kingdom of God. We know that the book of Isaiah was written and prophesied over 700 years before the birth of Christ.

The book of Psalms was written over 1000 years before the birth of Jesus. Both books prophesy the coming of the Lord Jesus Christ as IMMANUEL, which means, 'God with us.' Therefore, if anyone does not believe that God sent Jesus to be atonement for the sins of the world, that person has a spirit of antichrist upon his or her life. Even the name Jesus means Savior of the world. You would have thought the religious leaders would have had a clue. Hatred causes a man to walk in complete darkness stumbling ever step of the way.

Scripture

"Whosoever hateth his brother is a MURDERER: and ye know that no MURDERER hath eternal life abiding in him" (1 John 3:15).

"But he that hateth his brother is in darkness, and walketh in darkness, and knoweth not whither he goeth, because that darkness hath blinded his eyes" (1 John 2:11).

"Little children, it is the last time and as ye have heard that antichrist shall come, even now are there many antichrist; whereby we know that it is the last time" (1 John 2:18).

"Who is a liar but he that denieth that Jesus is the Christ? He is antichrist that denieth the <u>Father</u> and the <u>Son</u>. Whosoever denieth the Son, the same hath not the Father: but he that acknowledgeth the Son hath the Father also" (1 John 2:22, 23).

These scriptures explain that all souls that are against Jesus the risen Savior have a spirit of antichrist inside of them. The next verse makes it even clearer.

"Beloved, believe not every spirit, but <u>try the spirits</u> whether they be of God: because many false prophets are gone out into the world. Hereby know ye the Spirit of God: <u>Every spirit that confesseth that Jesus Christ is come in</u>

the flesh is of God. And every spirit that confesseth NOT that Jesus Christ is come in the flesh is NOT of God: and this is that spirit of antichrist, whereof ye have heard that it should come; and even now already is it in the world. Ye are of God, little children, and have overcome them: because greater is he that is in you, than he that is in the world" (1 John 4:1-4).

Therefore, if you do not believe in Jesus as Savior and Lord, then you have a spirit of antichrist within you. Remember, the Lord gave us his plan for our salvation. This plan involved God sending his only begotten Son into the earth to be atonement for sin. If you fail to agree or believe God's word concerning this truth, you possess a spirit of antichrist. You might as well support the work of the devil because your spirit puts you in agreement with him.

Scripture

Jesus said, *"He that is not with me is against me; and he that gathereth not with me scattereth abroad"* (Matthew 12:30).

Either you are with Jesus, or you are against him. If you are against him, then you are likewise against God. Jesus said he and the Father are one. Therefore, if you are either against the Father or the Son, the spirit of antichrist has taken possession of your soul. Come to the knowledge of the Lord Jesus Christ and avoid eternal damnation in the lake of fire.

POWER OF DEMONS

Did you know that demons have power over those who refuse to accept Jesus as Lord? Unless you accept Jesus as Savior and Lord, and repent of your sins, demonic spirits will end up overtaking you! The reason is because you have no power. Jesus gave the saints of God power to become the sons of God. The Holy Spirit gives the born-again believer power over all the enemies of God.

Scripture

> "Then certain of the vagabond Jews, exorcists, took upon them to call over them which had evil spirits the name of the Lord Jesus, saying, We adjure you by Jesus <u>**WHOM PAUL PREACHETH**</u>. And there were seven sons of one Sceva, a Jew, and chief of the priests, which did so. <u>And the evil spirit answered and said, Jesus I Know, and Paul I Know; but who are ye?</u> And the man in whom the evil spirit was leaped on them, and overcame them, and prevailed against them, so that they <u>fled out of that house naked and wounded.</u> And this was known to all the Jews and Greeks also dwelling at Ephesus; and fear fell on them all, and the name of the Lord Jesus was magnified. And many that believed came, and confessed, and showed their deeds. Many of them also which used <u>curious arts</u> brought their books together, and burned them before all all men: and they counted the price of them, and found it fifty thousand pieces of silver. So mightily grew the word of God and prevailed" (Acts 19:13-20).

This is a perfect example of someone making an attempt to cast out evil spirits that has not come to know Jesus as their Lord. The Jew and the chief priest did so respond to the one with the evil spirit by saying, "<u>I adjure you by Jesus whom the Apostle Paul preaches</u>." It was obvious that the Jew and the chief priest were not born-again believers. They must have been into some other form of occult worship. They were just repeating what they had heard the disciples speak. This type of false attempt even occurs today when the unbelieving souls attempts to cast out demons, or lay hands on the sick without them recovering. Evil spirits have power over those who are not called of God. The books burned that were mentioned are said to be occult books which valued over one million dollars by current day standards. The scripture describes these books burned as curious arts, obviously having nothing to do with the Holy Bible. The power to overcome the enemies of God comes from Jesus once we are born again of the Spirit of God. This is when we are endured with power to become the sons of God. Jesus further tells us in the word of God that he witnessed Satan fall from heaven as lightning.

Scripture

Jesus said, *"And he said unto them, I beheld Satan as lightning fall from heaven. Behold, I give unto you power to tread on serpents and scorpions, <u>and over ALL the power of the enemy</u>: and nothing shall by any means hurt you. Notwithstanding in this rejoice not, that the spirits are subject unto you; but rather rejoice because your <u>names are written in heaven</u>"* (Luke 10:18-20).

Based on this scripture, it is obvious that the Jews who made the attempt to cast out the evil spirits did not have the power that only Jesus Christ could give. By true faith we believe unto salvation. This gives us the power to become the sons of God that Jesus had described. This happens only when we believe in our heart and confess the Lord Jesus with our mouth, not having any doubt at all.

Scripture

"He (Jesus) was in the world, and the world was made by him, and the world knew him not. He came unto his own, and his own received him not. But as many as received him, to them gave he POWER to become the sons of God, even to them that believe on his name" (John 1:10-12).

This scripture confirms that the born-again believers in Christ Jesus have power over the enemies of Satan. Without this power given by Jesus, demons will overtake and influence your life anytime they please. You are powerless without the Lord's Spirit which dwells inside the saints of God. Therefore, if you are not a born-again believer, this powerless individual is you!

Demons Recognize God and Know His Laws

Demons recognized Jesus in the flesh as the Holy One of God. They knew that God gave mankind dominion in the earth to rule. Demons know that God will not violate his own spoken word at any time. They understand how a heavenly kingdom operates. This next verse of scripture deals with a demon that recognized Jesus and attempted to expose his identity before man. This demon never expected God to be walking in the flesh. He knew that God in the Spirit would not interfere with the freewill of man in the earth. This is why the Lord always raises up a deliverer to free his people whenever they are in bondage. God uses faithful men and women in the earth to accomplish his will. We are his arms and legs to be used at his discretion. That is why God loves to bless his faithful servants abundantly.

Scripture

*"And when he (**Jesus**) was come out of the ship, immediately there met him out of the tombs a man with an unclean spirit. Who had his dwelling among the tombs; and no man could bind him, no, not with chains: Because that he had been often bound with fetters and chains, and the chains had been plucked asunder by him, and the fetters broken in pieces: neither could any man tame him. And always, night and day, he was in the mountains, and in the tombs, <u>crying</u>, and <u>cutting himself</u> with stones. <u>But when he saw Jesus afar off,</u> **HE RAN AND WORSHIPED HIM**, And cried with a loud voice, and said, <u>What have I to do with thee, Jesus, thou Son of the MOST HIGH GOD?</u> I adjure thee by God, that thou torment me not. For he said unto him, Come out of the man, thou unclean spirit. And he asked him, What is thy name? And he answered, saying, My name is Legion: for we are many. And he besought him much that he would not send them away out of the country. Now there was there nigh unto the mountains a great herd of swine feeding. And all the devils besought him, saying, Send us into the swine, that we may enter into them. And forthwith Jesus gave them leave. And the unclean spirits went out, and entered into the swine: and the herd ran violently down a steep place into the sea. (They were about two thousand ;) and were choked in the sea. And they that fed the swine fled, and told it in the city, and in the country. And they went out to see what it was that was done. And they come to Jesus, and see him that was possessed with the devil, and had the legion, sitting, and clothed, and in his right mind: and they were afraid"* (Mark 5:2-15).

Not only did the unclean spirit run to worship Jesus but he also tried to remind Jesus that according to the law of God, he could not interfere with him taking possession of a willing human being. The demon did not quite connect the fact that God was manifest into this earth realm when he saw Jesus standing in the flesh. Demons see in the spirit realm. Therefore, Jesus being God in Spirit made him divine and also being man in the flesh gave him the original dominion given to mankind in the beginning. This meant that the word of God was not violated. The unclean spirit felt that Jesus being the Holy One of God could not interfere with that man's freewill to be a willing vessel for Satan. However, the unclean spirit was wrong. Without a human body to dwell in, demonic spirits and devils have no place to dwell. They begged Jesus not to send them away and out of the country. Jesus granted them the right to enter into the body of a herd of swine grazing nearby. This was probably done so that man could witness the deadly effects of being under the influence of demonic spirits. Once the unclean spirits entered the swine, they caused the animals to run violently off of a steep place into the sea where they were drowned. This is how destruction will eventually come to the souls of man under the possession of demonic spirits. The same thing the unclean spirits did to the swine, they will do to mankind. They first cause you to harm yourself, and eventually you will self-destruct. The world will blame the person for the act of suicide or other forms of self-destruction, when all of the time, it was the devils will for your life. Let not the enemy's spirit infiltrate your soul and utilize your body. As mentioned earlier, this was an opportunity for Jesus to reveal to man what happens when unclean spirits take over the soul of a man. Witnessing the unclean spirits enter the nearby swine was an opportunity to teach man what demons and devils are capable of. The casting out of these evil spirits was a perfect opportunity to set the captive free and bring glory to the Lord.

DAY SIX

IS JESUS CHRIST THE ONLY WAY?

The answer to this profound question is **YES!** Many have said all religions are the same. There are even those who think all religions require equal respect. Some have said that we are all going in the same direction. Others have said we all serve the same God. Even some have asked the question, "How do you know that other religions are wrong?" Are any of these statements correct? The fact is, when dealing with RELIGION, these questions may make sense to the hearer. If its religion you are seeking, feel free to explore these other avenues. However, if it's a RELATIONSHIP with God that you seek, come to Jesus Christ right now. When you believe the entire word of God with all of your heart, then you will believe exactly what it says—Jesus Christ is Lord. Jesus himself tells us that no one can come to God the Father except through him. Therefore, when you come to know the Lord Jesus Christ, you realize your connection is a personal relationship with the Savior, not a religion. Let us remember why the Lord Jesus Christ came into the earth in the first place. The Holy Bible tells us that the Son of man came to save the lost souls and give his own life for a ransom for sin once and for all. The Bible also says it like this.

Scripture

"For the Son of man is come to SEEK and to SAVE that which is LOST" (Luke 19:10).

This verse of scripture helps explain the true purpose why Christ came to redeem mankind. There is only one way to the true and living God. Many religions will find out the hard way in the end when they finally realize they needed a Savior to wash away their unrepented sin. This is the only way sin could be covered by the blood in order to avoid the second death, which is the lake of fire. The Savior bears the name of Jesus, the only begotten Son of the true and living God. Whenever you have a question concerning life, learn not to ask it of men. Understand that the Holy Bible has all the answers to life's many questions. We know that mankind has many opinions about many things. The way to receive the correct answer is to see what God has to say about it.

Scripture

> Jesus said, *"Let not your heart be troubled: ye believe in God, believe also in me. In my Father's house are many mansions: if it were not so, I would have told you. I go to prepare a place for you. And if I go and prepare a place for you, <u>I will come again</u>, and receive you unto myself; that where I am, there ye may be also. And whither I go ye know, and the way ye know. Thomas saith unto him, Lord, we know not whither thou goest; and how can we know the WAY? Jesus saith unto him, I AM THE WAY, THE TRUTH, AND THE LIFE: <u>NO MAN COMETH UNTO THE FATHER, BUT BY ME</u>"* (John 14:1-6)*!*

Jesus explained in these verses that we are never to worry. Trust that he is preparing a place for his born-again believers in the New Jerusalem, which is the Holy City. There is only one kingdom of God. No other religion has different kingdoms that truly exist. The kingdom we are referring to is the kingdom of God, not the devils kingdom of followers. Jesus tells us that he is coming again to receive his believers, so that where he is, there we will be also. Jesus makes it crystal clear that he is the only <u>WAY</u>, the only <u>TRUTH</u>, and the only <u>LIFE</u> mankind will ever have. No man or woman can come, or find their way to God the Father unless they come through the King of kings and Lord of lords which is Christ Jesus. This is the almighty Son of the true and living God. He is the Messiah spoken of in the Old Testament by the mouth of the prophets of old. Do not feel bad if you choose not to believe this doctrine concerning Jesus the Christ. The Bible tells us that there will be those who are going to refuse to believe in the Son of the living God. Unfortunately, the lake of fire is waiting for all who have chosen not to believe in God's provision, which is Christ Jesus.

Scripture

Jesus tells us, *"Verily, verily, I say unto you, he that entereth not by the door into the sheepfold, <u>but climbeth up some other way</u>, the same is a thief and a robber. But he that entereth in by the door is the shepherd of the sheep. To him the porter openeth; and the sheep hear his voice: and he calleth his own sheep by name, and leadeth them out. And when he putteth forth his own sheep, he goeth before them, and the sheep follow him for they know his voice. <u>And a stranger will they not follow</u>, but will flee from him: for they know not the voice of strangers"* (John 10:1-5).

Jesus tells us that his disciples did not understand this parable he spoke concerning the true shepherd of the kingdom. One thing to remember—cows have to be herded; however, sheep must be led. They are passive animals which must be taught to follow. Once they recognize their shepherd, they will only follow him and not a stranger. This same principle applies to the church pastors. They are the undershephards of Jesus Christ. Their assignment is to feed and lead the flocks of God from earth to glory. They all have been sent divinely by God to an assigned group of souls in the earth. Have you ever wondered why some Christians go to church and never end up following the vision of the pastor? This is why we must look for our assigned shepherd instead of searching for a sanctuary to socialize. We are not there for our purpose, we are there to offer up praise and worship to God. It's his time, not ours. The scripture makes reference to being a thief and a robber if we attempt to find God some other way. The thieves and robbers in those days were the Pharisees in the temple which were false prophets misleading God's people. The sheep that know their shepherd's voice are the called out ones, commonly referred to as the people of God. This is why the Bible teaches that God sends his appointed shepherds to the sheepfold in the earth. These pastors and teachers are undershepherds with a calling from God upon their lives. They are the designated leaders called to properly instruct the people in the word of God. Their mission is to teach them how to follow the Lord from earth to glory. Jesus is the Chief Shepherd of the entire church body. He lets us know that all who came before him were thieves and robbers. Jesus further reminded us of the character and nature of his enemy known as Satan. This defeated enemy is always trying to gain an advantage over the people of God.

One thing is for sure, when God is the Chief Shepherd over your life, all of your daily needs will be met by him.

Scripture

"Then said Jesus unto them again, Verily, verily, I say unto you, I AM THE DOOR OF THE SHEEP. ALL THAT EVER CAME BEFORE ME ARE THIEVES AND ROBBERS: BUT THE SHEEP DID NOT HEAR THEM. I AM THE DOOR: BY ME IF ANY MAN ENTER IN, HE SHALL BE SAVED, AND SHALL GO IN AND OUT, AND FIND PASTURE. The thief cometh not, but for to STEAL, and to KILL, and to DESTROY: <u>I AM</u> come that they might have LIFE, and that they might have it more abundantly. <u>I AM the good Shepherd</u>: <u>the good Shepherd giveth his Life for the sheep</u>" (John 10:7-11).

Jesus is predicting his crucifixion in the latter part of this verse, letting the sheep know that he is about to lay down his life for the church. <u>No other religion has made such a claim to offer or sacrifice something so precious.</u> This is an act of true unconditional love from God. He made the provision for his only begotten Son to lay down his innocent life, and shed his innocent blood for the sins of a guilty world. That is why this relationship is very personal between Jesus and the church body of born-again believers. Religion has absolutely nothing to do with it!

Scripture

Jesus said, *"He that is not with me is against me; and he that gathereth not with me scattereth abroad"* (Matthew 12:30).

"If any man love not the Lord Jesus Christ, let him be ANATHEMA MARANATHA. The grace of our Lord Jesus Christ be with you. My love be with you all in Christ Jesus. Amen" (1 Corinthians 16:22-24).

These scriptures tell us that if we are not with Jesus, we are against him and God. Paul the apostle said, if we don't love Jesus Christ, let that man be Anathema (accursed) because Maranatha (the Lord is coming). Therefore, if you choose to think that you can earn your way by worshipping false gods, or by following doctrines that oppose the gospel of Jesus Christ, go right ahead. This is a straight-up denial of God's only plan for our salvation which is the same as rejecting the almighty God himself. Those who commit this act have refused the grace extended to all by the Holy Spirit of God. This behavior is called blaspheming the Holy Spirit, or rejecting what God has freely offered. Remember that salvation is still a free gift from the Lord. This great sacrifice that Jesus made for us, we could not have paid such a great debt ourselves. Jesus bore all of our sins on that rugged cross—enduring all the pain, all the shame, all the humility, and the suffering. The sins of the whole wide world were covered by the innocent blood of Jesus Christ. We can surely be thankful for the opportunity to enjoy eternal life in the kingdom that Jesus Christ has prepared for us. All this was made possible by the glorious, wonderful, and merciful Savior of the world. Jesus is the only way to the kingdom of God. This is God's plan written in his Holy Bible for his beloved people. Will you believe sinful man and their many made up religions, or will you believe the Holy Bible inspired by God, the almighty Creator? Remember, before you make your decision; understand that man does not have a heaven or a hell to put you in. Only God can assign this fate to your future. Therefore, never choose to follow man over God, or else you will welcome a curse to come upon your life.

Scripture

"Thus saith the Lord; Cursed be the man that trusteth in man, and maketh flesh his arm, and whose heart departeth from the Lord" (Jeremiah 17:5).

Jesus was Prophesied in the Old Testament

This section is dedicated to all nonbelievers in Jesus Christ who claim to believe in the Old Testament yet shun the New Testament. There are religions that cater to the Old Testament but doubt the New Testament gospel of Jesus Christ. Some religions argue whether or not Jesus or the virgin birth of his earthly mother is ever mentioned in the Old Testament. When nonbelievers refuse to read for themselves, they tend to make up what sounds good to their iching ears. The truth is both the virgin birth and the Son of God were prophesied clearly all through the Old Testament scriptures.

Scripture

> *"Therefore the Lord himself shall give you a sign; Behold, <u>a virgin shall conceive, and bear a Son</u>, and shall call his name IMMANUEL"* (Isaiah 7:14).

This verse of scripture found in the Old Testament book of Isaiah tells us that the Lord gave them a sign. The book of Isaiah was written over 700 years before Jesus was born into the earth. This prophecy not only tells us of the virgin birth of Mary, it also tells us what the Messiah's identity would represent. The name Immanuel means 'God with us' or 'with us the almighty God.' This should have told every reader that God himself was getting ready to make an appearance in the earth in the form of flesh. Instead of doubting Jesus as the true Messiah, the Jews should have been trying to understand why sin had to be dealt with in the flesh. They should have paid attention to the works of Jesus Christ, noticing that they were all done in love for mankind. Not one evil deed could be linked to the Savior Jesus the Christ. This next verse of scripture, also found in the book of Isaiah prophesies how the Messiah would come in the flesh, grow up among us, and endure much pain, suffering, and many afflictions on our behalf.

Scripture

> *"Who hath believed our report? And to whom is the arm of the Lord revealed? For he shall grow up before him as a tender plant, and as a root out of dry ground: he hath no form nor comeliness; and when we shall see him, there is no beauty that we should desire him. He is despised and rejected of men; a man of sorrows, and acquainted with grief: and we hid as it were our faces from him; he was despised, and we esteemed him not. Surely he hath borne our griefs, and carried out sorrows: yet we did esteem him stricken, smitten of God, and afflicted. But he was wounded for our transgressions, he was bruised for our iniquities: the chastisement of our peace was upon him; and with his stripes we are healed"* (Isaiah 53:1-5).

The scriptures describe how the Lord will grow up and appear among men. Every aspect of Jesus' outcome was prophesied in this scripture over 700 years prior to his birth. The Old Testament foretold every area of punishment that Jesus would endure for the sins of the world. Each form of punishment that Jesus endured blessed the people of God with a special gift. Therefore, to all the souls who choose to believe only in the Old Testament scriptures, think on this. Jesus Christ is prophesied all through the Old Testament scriptures. When reading the Bible for the distinct purpose of seeking more of God, the Lord will then reveal what you missed before. Then you will fully understand that the New Testament is indeed the manifestation of the Old Testament scriptures. Therefore, trust in the word of God and read very closely the entire Holy Bible with the right motive. You will be surprised what will be revealed unto you.

JESUS, THE HOLY SEED

Jesus often used the example of seed in the parables he taught. Here are three different parables involving the sowing of seed that Jesus used in teaching his disciples.

1) The parable of the Sower.

Scripture

"And he spake many things unto them in parables, saying, "Behold, a sower went forth to sow; and when he sowed, and the fowls came and devoured them up. Some fell upon stony places, where they had not much earth: and forthwith they sprung up, because they had no deepness of earth: And when the sun was up, they were scorched; and because they had no root, they withered away. And some fell among thorns; and the thorns sprung up, and choked them: <u>But others fell into good ground, and brought forth fruit, some a hundredfold, some sixtyfold, some thirtyfold</u>. Who hath ears to hear, let him hear" (Matthew 13:3-9).

2) The parable of the wheat and the tares.

Scripture

"Another parable put he forth unto them, saying, The <u>kingdom of heaven is likened</u> unto a man which sowed good seed in his field: But while

men slept, his enemy came and sowed tares among the wheat, and went his way. But when the blade was sprung up, and brought forth fruit, then appeared the tares also. So the servants of the householder came and said unto him, Sir, didst not thou sow good seed in thy field? From whence then hath it tares? He said unto them, an enemy hath done this. The servants said unto him, Wilt thou then that we go and gather them up? <u>But he said, Nay; lest while ye gather up the tares, ye root up also the wheat with them.</u> Let both grow together until the harvest: and in the time of harvest I will say to the reapers, Gather ye together first the tares, and bind them in bundles to burn them: but gather the wheat into my barn"* (Matthew 13:24-30).

3) The parable of the mustard seed.

Scripture

"Another parable put he forth unto them, saying, <u>The kingdom of heaven is like</u> to a grain of mustard seed, which a man took, and sowed in his field: Which indeed is the least of all seeds: <u>but when it is grown, it is the greatest among herbs, and becometh a tree, so that the birds of the air come and lodge in the branches thereof</u>" (Matthew 13:31, 32).

These examples given by our Savior are valuable indeed. Jesus compared his own death and resurrection in a figurative sense to the sowing of seed. The spiritual key here to be learned is that all seed brings forth a harvest. This is why you want your seed to always be sown into good ground.

Scripture

"Verily, verily, I say unto you, except a corn of wheat fall into the ground and DIE, it abideth alone: but if it die, it bringeth forth much fruit. He that loveth his life shall lose it; and he that hateth his life in this world shall keep it unto life eternal. If any man serve me, let him follow me; and where I AM, there shall also my servant be: if any man serve me, him will my Father honor" (John 12:24-26).

Jesus used this example to explain how he must die in the flesh and be resurrected by God the Father in order to redeem mankind back to himself. Jesus is the <u>HOLY SEED</u> from God. When God the Father planted his HOLY SEED in the earth in the form of his only begotten Son, it grew eternal life for all souls who would receive him as Lord and Savior. Examine the size of that harvest! What a wonderful harvest to be a part of. The Holy Bible instructs Christians how to follow Jesus in the renouncing of this wicked sinful world. This helps us separate ourselves from the world's system as we prepare our lives for the Master's use. We have work to do for God's kingdom. God is depending on us. There are lost souls in this world just waiting to be gathered into the kingdom of God. Jesus died on the cross so that all who receive him would have a right to the Tree of Life. The Tree of Life is being well guarded at this time in the Garden of Eden. No one will be permitted access to this blessed tree without the Lord's permission. The Tree of Life holds the key to eternal life with God.

Scripture

"And the LORD God said, Behold, the man is become as one of us, to know good and evil: and now, lest he put forth his hand, and take also of the TREE OF LIFE, and eat, and <u>live for ever</u>" (Genesis 3:22)*:*

"So he drove out the man; and he placed at the east of the garden of Eden Cherubims, and a flaming sword which turned every way, to keep the way of the TREE OF LIFE" (Genesis 3:24).

No sinner will have access to the Tree of Life without being blood washed by the Lamb of God, which is Christ Jesus. Therefore, get covered with the blood so that one day soon, you too may take part in the Tree of Life.

THE MANY MIRACLES OF JESUS

Jesus performed many miracles that were spoken of in the Bible. However, there were many miracles not mentioned that Jesus performed in the earth as well. Apostle John, who was known as the beloved disciple had this to say about the many miracles Jesus performed.

Scripture

> "*This is the disciple which testifieth of these things, and wrote these things: and we know that his testimony is true. And there are also <u>MANY other things which Jesus did</u>, the which, if they should be written every one, <u>I suppose that even the world itself could not contain the books that should be written</u>, Amen*" (John 21:24, 25).

We know and understand by this time, that Jesus was sent into the earth by God to walk among mankind and teach them the true will of God. This includes how to live, how to interact with others, how to love, how to forgive, how to overcome the enemy, and ultimately how to be set free from the bondage of sin. Jesus showed us all things during his visit—even how to die graciously in Christ Jesus. He was fully God and fully Man at the same time as he walked in the flesh. Anyone having a problem with this truth must take it up with the Lord on Judgment Day. I'm sure he would love to explain it all to you. Believe it or not, there are men and women in the earth who have no clue how they came to exist, yet question how Jesus could be both Man and God. Let us stop wasting time trying to analyzing everything when God forewarned us that his thoughts and ways are higher than ours. He also commanded us to trust him and lean not to our own understanding while acknowledging him in all of our ways. Therefore, let us honor the Lord as the sovereign ruler over all, trust and believe in his holy word, and we will all be alright. After Jesus experienced life and attained the age of ministry, the anointing of God came upon him while he was baptized by his first cousin, John the Baptist. John the Baptist was sent to the earth to fulfill his purpose of being a forerunner for Jesus Christ. God sent John the Baptist specifically to pave the way and announce loudly to the world that the Lord is coming. God always lets his people know what he intends to do in the earth before he does it. Remember, God originally made man to rule over everything in the earth except each other. In the Old Testament, God used his prophets to notify his people when he was about to perform changes in the earth. In the New Testament God speaks through his Son Jesus and the gospel message. Jesus performed many miracles while in the earth which all gave glory to God the Father. Many souls were converted as a result of witnessing the high number of miracles Jesus performed while in the flesh. Everyone Jesus healed had a spirit of expectation concerning their particular need. Jesus performed so many miracles that if they were all written down, there would not be enough books to contain them. When Jesus' ministry began, he fulfilled the prophecies that were written in the Old Testament book of Isaiah concerning him. The prophet Isaiah prophesied these words concerning who Jesus would become.

Scripture

"For unto us a child is born, unto us a Son is given: and the government shall be upon his shoulder: and his name shall be called WONDERFUL, COUNSELOR, the MIGHTY GOD, the EVERLASTING FATHER, the PRINCE OF PEACE" (Isaiah 9:6).

The prophet Isaiah referred to Jesus using all these excellent titles spoken of. The prophet Isaiah also prophesied that the kingdom Jesus would establish would have no end. He further explained that the sevenfold Spirit of God would be revealed in Christ. This is the seven attributes God is known for.

Scripture

"And the Spirit of the Lord shall rest upon him, the Spirit of Wisdom and Understanding, the Spirit of Counsel and Might, the Spirit of Knowledge and of the Fear of the Lord" (Isaiah 11:2).

The Spirit of the Lord was upon Jesus

Scripture

"The Spirit of the Lord is upon me, because he has anointed me to preach the gospel to the POOR; he hath sent me to HEAL the brokenhearted, to preach DELIVERANCE to the captives, and recovering of SIGHT to the blind, to set at LIBERTY them that are bruised, To preach the acceptable year of the Lord" (Luke 4:18, 19).

Jesus performed all these miracles that were witnessed by both his enemies and his followers. Anyone who had the privilege of reading and believing the Holy Scriptures had all the proof they needed when it came to who Jesus truly was. Therefore, when Jesus read in the synagogue on the Sabbath out of the book of Isaiah, the Pharisees should have been paying attention, instead of focusing on hatred. Their only problem was they fail to put two and two together. This was one of the main problems with the temple leaders known as the Pharisees. They knew how the law read; they just did not always believe it. After Jesus finished reading the Holy Scripture to those present in the synagogue, he closed the book and sat down. The Bible tells us that the eyes of all in the synagogue were fastened on him. When this occurred, Jesus said unto them, "This day is this scripture fulfilled in your ears." Jesus was clearly letting them know who he was and what he was about to do. The only problem was many refused to believe because they did not have ears to hear what thus saith the Lord.

REPENT FOR EVERLASTING LIFE

REPENT to God before Jesus returns for his church.

REPENT to God while there is still time.

REPENT to God while the blood is still running warm in your veins.

REPENT to God and run for your life to the Savior of the world.

REPENT to God and forsake everything else in life and make your soul your number one priority.

REPENT to God and become a servant for Jesus Christ and join the laborers in the Lord's vineyard.

REPENT to God and be the witness you were called to be in telling others about the good news of the gospel.

REPENT to God and accept Jesus as your Savior and receive the free gift of salvation that is freely given.

REPENT to God because the Lord chose you before the foundation of the world to be saved. We have been called of God.

REPENT to God and enter into the portal of Christ before the door is shut; just like in the days of Noah when God sealed them in the ark, and then <u>HE SHUT THE DOOR</u>.

Scripture

> "REPENT ye therefore, and be converted, that your sins may be blotted out, when the times of refreshing shall come from the presence of the Lord; And he shall send Jesus Christ, which before was preached unto you: Whom the heavens must receive until the times of restitution of all things, which God hath spoken by the mouth of all his holy prophets since the world began. For Moses truly said unto the fathers, A PROPHET shall the Lord your God raise up onto you of your brethren, like unto me; him shall ye hear in all things whatsoever he shall say unto you. <u>And it shall come to pass, that every soul, which will not hear that Prophet (Jesus), shall be destroyed from among the people</u>. Yea, and all the prophets from Samuel and those that follow after, as many as have spoken, have likewise foretold of these days. Ye are the children of the prophets, and of the covenant which God made with our fathers, saying unto Abraham, <u>And in thy seed shall all the Kindred's of the earth be blessed</u>. Unto you first God, having raised up his Son Jesus, sent him to bless you, in turning away every one of you from his iniquities" (Acts 3:19-26).

THE GIFT OF SALVATION!

Thank God for the greatest gift known to man, which is the salvation of the Lord. Our God loved us so that he came to see about us personally. He is an awesome God, full of love and compassion. His earthly children he created in his own image and likeness. He calls us little gods, and refers to us as his offspring. Jesus is the KING of kings and LORD of lords! Jesus our Lord and Savior paid the ultimate price for the sins of the entire world. Therefore, be not hard-hearted and accept the free gift Jesus died to give us all. No one in their right mind wants to be cast into the lake of fire with the enemies of God, known as Satan and his crew. The only reason mankind will end up there is because they refuse to believe. This is called blasphemy against the Holy Spirit.

Scripture

> "For God so loved the world that he gave his only begotten Son, that whosoever believeth in him should not perish, but have everlasting life.

THE LAMB'S BOOK OF LIFE:

For God sent not his Son into the world to condemn the world; but that the world through him might be <u>SAVED</u>. He that believeth on him is not condemned: but he that believeth not is condemned already, because he hath not believed in the name of the only begotten Son of God" (John 3:16-18).

THIS IS GOD'S PLAN FOR YOUR SALVATION!
THIS IS GOD'S PLAN FOR YOUR SALVATION!
THIS IS GOD'S PLAN FOR YOUR SALVATION!

THIS MESSAGE GOES OUT TO ALL FORMS OF RELIGION AROUND THE GLOBE WITHOUT MENTIONING ANY SPECIFIC GROUPS. THE QUESTION IS, HAVE YOU BEEN BORN AGAIN OF THE SPIRIT OF GOD? NO ONE WILL ENTER INTO GOD'S KINGDOM UNTIL THEY HAVE BEEN WASHED IN THE PRECIOUS BLOOD OF JESUS. EVERY SOUL MUST BE BORN AGAIN OF THE SPIRIT OF GOD. THIS IS THE FREE GIFT THAT GOD HAS EXTENDED TO ALL SOULS WHO WILL RECEIVE HIS ONLY BEGOTTEN SON. ALL WE HAVE TO DO IS BELIEVE IN OUR HEART AND CONFESS WITH OUR MOUTH THAT JESUS CHRIST IS OUR LORD AND THE RISEN SAVIOR OF THIS WORLD. THEN WE WILL INHERIT OUR NEW BIRTH UNTO ETERNAL LIFE IN CHRIST JESUS, AMEN.

Jesus shed his innocent blood on the cross at Calvary to SAVE our souls from the lake of fire. This lake of fire and brimstone was created by God for Satan, his beast, his false prophet and all of his fallen angels who were cast down from heaven with him. Mankind has the power to make his own choice where he will spend eternity. If man ends up in hell waiting to be sentenced to the lake of fire, it's his own fault. The Lord Jesus wants everyone SAVED. Jesus gave us the parable of the net in the Bible which reads like this.

Scripture

The Scripture reads, *"Again, the <u>kingdom of heaven</u> is like unto a net, that was cast into the sea, and gathered of every kind: Which when it was full, they drew to shore, and sat down, and gathered the good into vessels, but cast the bad away. <u>So shall it be at the end of the world: the angels shall</u>*

come forth, and sever the WICKED from among the JUST. And shall cast them into the furnace of fire: there shall be wailing and gnashing of teeth" (Matthew 13:47-50).

This parable teaches us that there are going to be those who accept Jesus as Lord and Savior, and then you will have others who will reject Jesus as Lord. Those who end up sentenced to the lake of fire, which is the second death, are those who rejected God's plan for salvation in his Son Jesus. This is no fault of God who has provided salvation for every soul. It will be the hardness of one's heart that will cause the will of Satan to be sought and carried out.

Scripture

The Scripture reads, *"As many as I love, I rebuke and chasten: be zealous therefore, and REPENT. Behold, I"* (**Jesus**) *stand at the door, and knock: if any man hear my voice, and open the door, I will come in to him, and will sup with him, and he with me. To him that overcometh will I grant to sit with me in my throne, even as I also overcame, and set down with my Father in his throne"* (Revelation 3:19-21).

REMEMBER THE SABBATH DAY

Remember the Sabbath day and keep it holy unto the Lord. Rest and worship is crucial for mankind. God will cause a man to be blessed more by honoring the Sabbath as opposed to laboring unending. The day Jesus rose from the dead is called the Lord's Day. This is why most Christian worshipers enter into the house of the Lord on the first day of the week to offer up their praise and worship to God. The worship of Jesus Christ as Lord takes precedent over the original exclusive Sabbath day worship in the temple. Now, Christians worship not only on Saturday, but also on Sunday, Monday, Tuesday, Wednesday, Thursday and Friday as well. Jesus said it best when he explained why the Sabbath Day was made.

Scripture

"And he said unto them, The Sabbath was made for man, and not man for the Sabbath: Therefore the Son of Man is Lord also of the Sabbath" (Mark 2:27, 28).

The Sabbath Day allowed mankind to enter into his rest which the Lord has commanded for him to do. Praise and worship is unending. This is a lifestyle that the born-again believers choose. Therefore, let us not struggle any longer over what day we should worship the Lord. Worship is a continuous lifestyle we should practice everyday. The Lord's Day is the birth of the church under the grace of God. Anyone who fails to acknowledge the Lord's Day and how he rose from the dead should re-examine themselves. Jesus laid down his life and God raised him from the dead so that all things would become new. The grace of God has now been given to this world. Sunday is the day of the resurrection of the Savior Jesus the Christ. This is a very special day to the world. This does not mean that Jesus cancelled the Sabbath by any means. We are still to labor six days and rest one. Remember, Jesus is the holy temple from above. When Jesus spoke of rebuilding the temple in three days, he was referring to himself. When Jesus Christ rose from the dead in three days, he gave the kingdom of God to man. The Pharaisees are the only ones who lacked understanding concerning this truth. They thought the Lord was referring to an actual building. Only to find out that Jesus brought his kingdom from heaven and placed it in the hands of all who would believe. This is the kingdom of God that believers now have access to. The Jews were looking for an earthly kingdom to overthrow the Roman government. Let us never forget that Jesus created all things that were made; this even includes the Sabbath day which God made for man. After being raised from the dead on the first day of the week, Jesus appeared to his disciples later that same evening.

Scripture

"Then the same day at evening, being the first day of the week, when the doors were shut where the disciples were assembled for fear of the Jews, came Jesus and stood in the midst, and saith unto them, Peace be unto you" (John 20:19).

Later, Paul the apostle preached on this very special day in the presence of the disciples which was Sunday, the first day of the week. Prior to this practice, the disciples would enter the temple on the Sabbath day where the Jews were gathered. However, the actual day that Jesus rose from the dead is nationally recognized as the Lord's Day. This event occurred after the traditional Sabbath day which would have been sometime after six oclock pm on Saturday after the sun went down. From that time until the early morning hour, Jesus rose from the dead. Mary Magdeline came and discovered that Jesus' body was gone from the tomb early that Sunday morning. For this reason, this special day is called the Lord's Day.

Scripture

"And upon the <u>first day of the week</u>, when the disciples came together to break bread, Paul preached unto them, ready to depart on the morrow; and continued his speech until **midnight**" (Acts 20:7).

In the Old Testament, they honored the Sabbath from sundown to sundown at the end of the week. The time frame involved started on Friday evening at six o'clock to Saturday evening at six o'clock, or sundown to sundown. During that time, the Jews took rest from all their labor while they read the scriptures in the holy temple. The Sabbath is still as holy now, as it was in the beginning when Jesus established it for men. The Christian born-again believers honor the day of worship and rest on the Lord's Day—the first day of the week. This special day is honored because on this day the risen Savior of the world defeated death, hell and the grave. The Holy Bible instructs us to work six days and rest one, sanctifying that day unto the Lord. Therefore, always remember to labor only six days and rest one. Jesus said it best when he told the Pharisees, "Man was not made for the Sabbath, but the Sabbath was made for man." For this cause, we should worship everyday of the week. God only requires that we rest at least one full day out of six. This is the same system God used when he created the heavens and the earth and all therein. The Lord created in six days and rested on the seventh day calling it the Sabbath. Just make sure that you come to rest and sanctify one day of the week unto God. This will give him honor and glory on the day he hallowed and blessed.

Scripture

"Remember the Sabbath day, to keep it holy. Six days shalt thou labor, and do all thy work: But the seventh day is the Sabbath of the Lord thy God: in it thou shalt not do any work, thou nor thy son, nor thy daughter, thy manservant, nor thy maidservant, nor thy cattle, nor thy stranger that is within thy gates. For in six days the Lord made heaven and earth, the sea, and all that in them is, and rested the seventh day: wherefore the Lord blessed the Sabbath day, and Hallowed it" (Exodus 20:8-11).

Consequences of Failing to Honor the Sabbath

Scripture

"And the Lord spake unto Moses, saying, Speak thou also unto the children of Israel, saying, Verily my Sabbath ye shall keep: for it is a sign between me and you throughout your generations; that ye may know that I AM the Lord that doth sanctify you. Ye shall keep the Sabbath therefore; for it is Holy unto you: every one that defileth it shall surely be put to death: for whosoever doeth any work therein, that soul shall be cut off from among his people" (Exodus 31:12-14).

When we forget about God and what he has deemed holy, it causes death. Whether this is spiritual death or mortal death in the flesh really doesn't matter. The results are the same. The Bible verses tell us that we are also cut off from among our people. This means cut off from the family of God. Since Jesus Christ provided the gift of salvation to whosoever will, this has to include the entire body of Christ. Let us not do anything that is against the holy word of God. We as born-again believers were adopted into the family of God and became heirs and seed of father Abraham. Therefore, we have to maintain our covenant with the almighty God. Our adoption came through the blood of Jesus Christ the righteous. We now have an obligation to obey the word of God whether we like it or not. We as sons of God should base all of our love and focus on what Jesus did on the cross. This will cause us to spend the rest of our days glorifying Jesus as Lord. Let us stop beating each other up for the many infirmities men struggle with in the flesh. When we do such things and still walk imperfect ourselves, we speak judgment toward others and do the same thing. This is what the Bible says about hypocritical judgmental behavior.

Scripture

"Therefore, thou art inexcusable, O man, whosoever thou art that judgest: for wherein thou judgest another, thou condemnest thyself; for thou that judgest doest the same things. But we are sure that the judgment of God is according to truth against them which commit such things. And thinkest thou this, O man, that judgest them which do such things, and doest the same, that thou shalt escape the judgment of God" (Romans 2:1-3)?

Let us be very careful when pointing the finger at our brothers and sisters just because their particular sin does not tempt us nor cause us to stumble. Remember, every soul struggles with a particular weakness. Your weakness may not be your neighbor's weakness! Your sin may not be your neighbor's sin! However, the word of God tells us to judge ourselves and we will not be judged.

Scripture

"For if we would judge ourselves, we should not be judged. But when we are judged, <u>we are chastened of the Lord, that we should not be condemned with the world</u>" (1 Corinthians 11:31, 32).

When we fail to judge ourselves, God corrects us to keep us from being condemned with the rest of the world. This is what happens when a soul has not been forgiven for his sins committed. Those who repent and ask for forgiveness through Christ Jesus, their slate is wiped clean and covered with the blood of the Lamb. That is why if the righteous fail to judge themselves, God steps in and makes the necessary correction. Unless we have attained perfection within ourselves, let us be careful how we examine others. We must focus on glorifying Jesus, the perfect Savior. Then we can get back on track and cause men and women everywhere to come to the knowledge of the gospel of Jesus Christ.

THE ARMOR OF GOD

This is the best protection the Lord has given to the righteous souls in the earth—the God-given armor of the Lord. Police officers are required to wear bullet proof vest on duty which protects their upper torso from certain caliber weapons. This protection is only limited and not full proof. Heavy caliber weapons can and will penetrate this limited body armor. Only a small area of the body is designed to be covered. However, the Lord's armor is 100 percent full proof. It protects the entire body (physical being) and spirit (spiritual being) of a man. When we put on this holy protection, it fends off the fiery darts of the enemies of darkness who operate solely in the spirit realm. This holy protection is only privileged to the sons and daughters of God through the Savior Jesus Christ. No other souls have protection against the enemies of God. These unprotected souls are vulnerble and exposed to the wiles of the devil at all times. The armor of the Lord is not material armor; it is the spiritual armor that the unbelievers cannot seem to comprehend. This is the best protection God has given to the born-again believer. They have the ability to shield themselves when they become soldiers in the army of the Lord. This totally prepares them for spiritual battle with the enemies of God. Without this precious armor, souls are completely naked and helpless against the evil demonic forces that wage war against the family of God.

Description and Purpose of this Armor

Scripture

"Finally, my brethren, be strong in the Lord, and in the power of his might. Put on the <u>whole armor of God</u> that ye may be able to stand against the wiles of the devil. For we wrestle not against flesh and blood, but against principalities, against powers, against the rulers of the darkness of this world, against spiritual wickedness in high places. Wherefore take unto you the whole armor of God, that ye may be able to withstand in the evil day, and having done all to stand" (Ephesians 6:10-13).

The Armor of God in Detail

Scripture

> "*Stand therefore, having your loins girt about with <u>truth</u>, and having on the breastplate of <u>righteousness</u>; And your feet shod with the preparation of the gospel of <u>peace</u>; Above all, taking the shield of <u>faith</u>, wherewith ye shall be able to quench all the fiery darts of the wicked. And take the helmet of <u>salvation</u>, and the <u>sword</u> of the Spirit, which is the <u>W</u>ord of God. Praying always with all prayer and supplication in the Spirit, and watching thereunto with all perseverance and supplication for all saints*" (Ephesians 6:14-18).

The Armor of God Consist of Six Pieces

1) **Truth**—this piece of mighty armor is the knowledge and truth of God's word. Without the precious knowledge of the word of God, the people will perish. We have to be convinced in our own mind concerning the word of God. Once we believe the word of God in our hearts, that's when we will worship him in spirit and in truth.
2) **The Breastplate of Righteousness**—this piece of mighty armor is the breastplate which is righteousness. We receive this armor when we choose to accept Jesus as Lord which is God's plan for our salvation. Then we become the righteousness of God. The new spirit man represents a holy character and moral conduct concerning our behavior. This produces a godly lifestyle when we are obedient to the truth of God's holy word.
3) **Preparation of the Gospel of Peace**—this piece of mighty armor means eagerness that comes from the gospel of peace. The Christian must have in his feet a sense of eagerness to contend with Satan. This piece of armor gives peace to the believer, freeing him from worrying about how powerful his adversary the devil is. Instead of focusing how powerful Satan is, our attention is drawn to how big and powerful our God is over every situation.
4) **The Shield of Faith**—this piece of mighty armor means taking God at his word by believing his promises. This kind of trust will protect one from doubting which is induced by Satan. Without faith, the

Bible teaches us that it is impossible to please God. Faith gives us hope and certainty when it comes to the issues of God.

5) **The Helmet of Salvation**—this piece of mighty armor is not for the unbeliever. This armor is for the Christian born-again believer because it deals with our salvation. This precious helmet is described as the hope of salvation and the certainty thereof. This is assurance to the chosen Christian believer that he truly belongs to God. This armor can only be obtained by faith in the gospel of Jesus Christ.

6) **The Sword of the Spirit, which is the Word of God**—this piece of mighty armor deals with the RHEMA word of God. This is the Christian's sword of protection against the enemy Satan and his devices. Knowing and believing this valuable word of God gives the Christian believer power and authority over all of the enemies of Satan. The devices of the evil one will no longer have authority to harm these believers who use the word of God to fend off wickedness. This weapon of choice, also known as the word of God is the only weapon that will work affectively against this wicked enemy called the devil.

Having put on the whole armor of God will allow the Christian born-again believers to prosper and receive the many blessings from God. Satan and his devices can no longer BLOCK the flow of blessings God has in store for his blood washed believers. They have all been properly safeguarded by the Lord's special armor. The fiery darts and the wiles (tricks) of the devil will no longer affect these well protected well covered Christian believers.

HOW TO WALK UPRIGHT BEFORE THE LORD

Did you know that it is possible for mankind to walk upright before the Lord? This is made possible when we learn to walk in the spirit and not in the flesh. Some churches may teach that no man can ever walk perfect before the Lord. Perfect in the biblical sence has often been explained by many devout scholars to mean a form of completeness. Since we all have a sinful nature and very capable of committing sin, we must fully embrace the help of the Holy Spirit. This is the only way we can be assured to avoid sin in the flesh. With the power of the Holy Ghost operating inside of us, and the word of God retraining our thought life, our life will be conformed to God's perfect will. Without these two aids that the Lord provides, no man can ever live totally free from sin. It is a fact that our spirit-man will forever war against our flesh-man all of our days while we are in the earth. However, there is a way to walk without stumbling. The Bible says it like this.

Scripture

"This I say then, Walk in the Spirit, and ye SHALL not fulfill the lust of the flesh" (Galatians 5:16).

Having the gift of the Holy Spirit and the renewing of the mind will cause us not to fulfill the LUST of the flesh. Without these gifts and principles, our lives will remain sinful. Thank God for the provision of repentance he has given to the born-again believers during this period of grace. Without the Lord's grace and mercy, we would all be lost in sin. Some churches only teach their congregations to focus solely on resisting sinful behavior. Sort of like how the Pharasiees of old did toward the Jews. Their focus was more concerned over the outward act, as opposed to the inward heart. This may sound like a form of self discipline; however, total deliverance comes with a renewed mind. The way to renew your mind is to fill your cup with the mighty word of God. Without faith in God, there is little or no word. Likewise, without the word of God, there is little or no faith. Nevertheless, focusing solely on resisting sin without the power of the Holy Ghost can be nearly impossible. When focusing solely on sinful behavior, mankind will often find himself still in bondage. We need to place our focus on the perfect Savior, who is Jesus Christ the righteous. Once we fully receive him as our Lord and Savior, then we become the righteousness of God. Not based on our works, but based on the living sacrifice Jesus made for each one of us on that rugged cross. Now all we have to do is renew the way we think. This is easier than it sounds, yet it may seem hard. First of all, we must understand that everything starts with a thought. The reason why born-again Christians struggle with sin is because they have not renewed their mind, nor have they learned how to take their thoughts captive with the word of God. When sinful thoughts come into our mind, we as Christians must take those thoughts captive immediately. Then we will learn that right thinking will cause our behavior to change itself. This puts our lives on the path to success. As long as we continue to entertain the wrong thoughts, we will remain in bondage to sin and bad behavior. There is an old saying which goes like this, "**Do what's right and it will fix what's wrong**." Focusing on the sin at hand without changing the way we think is a big waste of time. This is why we must read and study the word of God so that we can speak the word of God over every situation. The word of God is the only thing powerful enough to cancel out the devils attempt to gain control over our mind. We have to correct our way of thinking one day at a time. The word of God says it like this.

Scripture

"Finally, brethren, whatsoever things are TRUE, whatsoever things are HONEST, whatsoever things are JUST, whatsoever things are PURE, whatsoever things are LOVELY, whatsoever things are of GOOD REPORT; if there be any virtue, and if there be any praise, <u>THINK ON THESE THINGS</u>. Those things, which ye have both LEARNED and RECEIVED, and HEARD, and SEEN in me, do; and the God of peace shall be with you" (Philippians 4:8, 9).

When we think on all good things, it causes a chain reaction to occur in our life. Not only will our behavior be honorable, but we begin to reap exactly what we have sown, even when it come to our thoughts. The Bible says if we do the things which we have learned, received, heard and seen in the word of God, we will also have the PEACE of God with us always. When we do this, we will see a total change in our lives. Remember, good thoughts will always produce good behavior. The Holy Bible also teaches us to develop a relationship with the Savior Jesus the Christ as we cast all of our burdens upon him. While we are learning the will of God, Jesus is willing to take on our burdens because he knows that the more we increase in his word, the more our flesh decreases in unrighteousness. Then we can deny our flesh as we pick up our cross and follow the Lord finishing the work he has commanded of us. As we complete the work of the ministry, the Holy Ghost will continue to strengthen us for the task.

Scripture

"And he said to them all, If any man will come after me, let his deny himself, and take up his cross daily, and follow me" (Luke 9:23).

We have to understand that Jesus is the mediator between God and man. Therefore, since all men have sinned and come short of glory of God, this makes us all as filthy rags in the eyes of our Lord. This is why every soul needs to be cleansed with the blood of the Lamb. Once we come to this understanding, the Bible directs us on how to walk in the will of God without stumbling. We must remember that God has set laws and principles that we must learn to follow. When we fail to do things God's way, we fail to receive God's benefits.

Scripture

"Submit yourself therefore to God. Resist the devil, and he will flee from you. <u>Draw nigh to God</u>, and he will <u>draw nigh to you</u>. Cleanse your hands, ye sinners; and purify your hearts, ye double minded" (James 4:7, 8).

Most often, mankind will get the '<u>RESIST THE DEVIL</u>' part right. Yet they leave out the most important part of this verse of scripture. Man must first <u>SUBMIT HIMSELF</u> to the almighty God. This means to totally surrender one's self to the Lord Jesus Christ, for it is he who created all things. When we fail to submit ourselves to the Lord, we will find ourselves still entangled in a struggle with sin. Jesus has given us an open door to come to him with all of our burdens and he will give us rest.

Scripture

"Come unto me, all ye that labor and are heavy laden, and I will give you rest. Take my yoke upon you, and learn of me; for I am meek and lowly in heart: and ye shall find rest unto your souls. For my yoke is easy, and my burden is light" (Matthew 11:28-30).

The Bible teaches us that all we have to do is learn more of Jesus Christ, which is the word of God, and our transgressions will fade away. This happens when we renew and saturate our mind in the word of God. Once we get the word of God digested deep down on the inside, not only will our minds be renewed, but our actions will follow. What ever is inside of a person will always flow to the outside freely. Yes, we should resist sinful behavior; however, we will be wasting our time if we have no word of God down on the inside. We can resist like some preachers teach, but sin will keep returning without the power of God's word changing the way we think. Therefore, teach souls to meditate in the word of God night and day. This will affect the necessary change in ones life. Teach them to murmur in the word of God without ceasing. This practice will keep the will of God afresh in your mind. The next thing you know, your life will start to conform to the perfect will of God. Only God can deliver you from sin. For this reason, the Holy Spirit has been given to us as a form of strength, power and guidance. Without God's precious Holy Spirit helping us every step of the way, we are helpless in this journey called life. Therefore, cast your cares and burdens on the Master and enter into his rest.

Walking in the spirit

Let's talk about how to walk in the spirit. When we walk in the spirit, this means to walk according to the perfect will of God. Since everything in life begins with a thought, this means, our beginning must always start off right if we want out outcome to be favorable. We can walk very easily in the spirit as long as we walk according to the word of God. Anytime we think contrary to the will of God, we allow an opportunity for the wrong thought to take up root. Every action starts with a thought whether it is good or bad. Once we learn to think right, our right thoughts will then produce right behavior. Then our right behavior will produce right consequences. Always remember, the harvest is always greater that the seed planted. The same principle applies to walking in the flesh. Since we now understand that everything starts with a thought. When we think on fleshly things, this too will produce a flesh filled lifestyle. This also means we should walk in the LIGHT of love, knowing very well that Jesus is the LIGHT of the world. He has delivered every saved soul from darkness and caused them to walk in the LIGHT as men. No longer does mankind have to remain in darkness. Jesus has redeemed us from this world of sin and death. Christ has commanded us to love him with our whole being, and to love one another as we love ourselves. This is not an option folks. It's a commandment straight from God. When we walk in the spirit, this is the only way we can overcome the flesh. Without walking in the will of God, mankind will struggle and fall every time.

Scripture

"This I say then, Walk in the Spirit, and ye shall not fulfill the lust of the flesh. For the flesh lusteth against the Spirit, and the Spirit against the flesh: and these are contrary the one to the other: so that ye cannot do the things that ye would" (Galatians 5:16, 17).

The Holy Bible teaches the children of God to live and walk with the help of the Holy Ghost which God provides. We also learn that the Holy Spirit and man's flesh war against each other constantly. They are involved in a constant battle. How does one live by the spirit? First of all, by faith, Christians must believe that the Holy Spirit dwells within them. Remember, Jesus promised he would send a COMFORTER which is the Holy Spirit from God. The purpose of God's Holy Spirit or Holy Ghost is to guide us unto all truth. Christians must then submit themselves and fully surrender their own desires in exchange for the will of God. In other words, cast all of your cares on the Lord. This means we must do it God's way instead of our way. Our main concern and purpose is to live a God pleasing life. When we abide in the word of God and the LIGHT of his love, only then can we walk in the spirit without an occasion to stumble.

Scripture

"He that saith he is in the LIGHT, and hateth his brother, is in darkness even until now. He that loveth his brother abideth in the LIGHT, and there is none occasion of stumbling in him. But he that hateth his brother is in darkness, and walketh in darkness, and knoweth not whither he goeth, because that darkness hath blinded his eyes" (1 John 2:9-11).

For example, it is ungodly to sin once you come into the knowledge of Jesus Christ as Lord. However, Jesus is our Advocate and propitiation for sin in case we do. When he died on the cross at Calvary, he died for the sins of the entire world. According to the gospel of John, Jesus' last words on the cross were, "IT IS FINISHED." This means exactly what Jesus said—it is finished. The blood of Jesus covers past, present and future sins of all who believe by faith and is born again by the Spirit of God. This does not give us permission to continue in sin, God forbid that we would even think so. However, this teaches us that when we walk in the spirit and the LIGHT of Jesus Christ, sin cannot dwell in the LIGHT. Too many Christians struggle with focusing on certain sins and find themselves still bound. God's principles teach us that we need to focus our energies on spending more time in the word of God. This develops our relationship with the Savior which will cause sin to be cancelled in the life of the born-again believer. The more we love on God, the stronger our will becomes to resist sin. This is an important spiritual key to the kingdom believer. That is why great testimonies have gone forth in the name of the Lord, telling how God has taken the desire of sinful behavior away from the born-again believer. This is the supernatural power of the God we serve. All glory belongs to him, and his name is Jesus. We as believers must learn to follow the Lord's principles in order to receive his many blessings. The bodies of believers have been freed from all sin. The problem is some do not yet realize it. All we have to do is realize our freedom and be convinced as we walk in the newness of life. Just remember, the born-again spirit man cannot sin, however, the old natured man can. This is why it is necessary to walk in the spirit at all times. This avoids stumbling in the flesh.

Scripture

"Therefore if any man be in Christ, he is a new creature: old things are passed away; behold, all things are become new. And all things are of God, who hath RECONCILED us to himself by Jesus Christ, and hath given to us the ministry of reconciliation" (2 Corinthians 5:17, 18).

"For he hath made him to be sin for us, who knew NO sin; that we might be made the RIGHTEOUSNESS of God in him" (2 Corinthians 5:21).

When a man or woman accepts the Lord Jesus into their heart and confesses him with their mouth, something miraculous happens in their spirit. Their spirit is immediately SAVED by God from the hand of the enemy. This is something that the Lord does deep down on the inside. Then miraculous things start to take place on the outside. This is why we must seek more of God and not focus so much on the problems and issues at hand. The supernatural power of the living God will supply all of our needs, whatever they may be. Always give thanks unto the Lord and trust his power with all of your heart. The Lord's power is strong enough to deliver all those who will believe and not doubt.

Scripture

"Behold, I AM the Lord, the God of all flesh: is there anything too hard for me" (Jeremiah 32:27)?

THE GREAT COMMISSION

Jesus gave his remaining eleven disciples this Great Commission after he was resurrected from the dead. Jesus appeared to them in Galilee where he had appointed them to go.

Scripture

"Then the eleven disciples went into Galilee, into a mountain where Jesus had appointed them. And when they saw him, they worshiped him: <u>but some doubted</u>" (Matthew 28:16, 17).

Then Jesus gave his disciples their Great Commission.

Scripture

"And Jesus came and spake unto them, saying, All Power is given unto me in heaven and in earth. GO YE THEREFORE, AND TEACH ALL NATIONS, BAPTIZING THEM IN THE NAME OF THE FATHER, AND OF THE SON, AND OF THE HOLY GHOST: TEACHING THEM TO OBSERVE ALL THINGS WHATSOEVER I HAVE COMMANDED YOU: AND, LO, I AM WITH YOU ALWAYS, EVEN UNTO THE END OF THE WORLD, Amen" (Matthew 28:18-20).

The purpose of the local church is to make disciples of all nations, kindreds, and tongues. Those who are evangelized and converted should then be baptized, attesting to their identification with Christ and the local body of believers. The final phase of the Great Commission is to train disciples in the Lord's Christian knowledge for effective service in the ministry. The Great Commission is a command with three steps. The first step is EVANGELISM; the second step is BAPTISM; and the third step is EDUCATION in the word of God. Jesus has commissioned his disciples to saturate their local communities, and then spreading the good news of his gospel to the ends of the earth. When Jesus gave this commandment to his disciples, they probably had no clue that planes, television and internet was in their upcoming future, however, Jesus Christ knew. For it was he who gave man the vision to create all things in its proper time.

Scripture

"All things were made by him (**Jesus**)*; and without him was not any thing made that was made"* (John 1:3).

In the book of John chapter one verse 1 through 3 teaches how Jesus is the living Word of God.

"In the beginning was the Word, and the Word was with God, and the <u>Word was God"</u> (John 1:1).

"All things were made by him; and without him was not any thing made that was made" (John 1:3).

God is the one who causes man to create all things in its proper time. It is amazing how up until about the last one hundred years, man rode the backs of horses and buggy drawn carriages. Now we have cars, buses, trucks, trains, planes, and even rocket space ships that blast into outer space. We have satellites in orbit which take live pictures all over the world. Man's wisdom has increased in the last and evil days.

Scripture

"But thou, O Daniel, shut up the words, and seal the book, even to <u>the time of the end</u>: many shall run to and fro, and <u>knowledge shall be increased</u>" (Daniel 12:4).

This prophecy in the book of Daniel was concerning the end time. God is the one who provides us with all things for the good of humanity.

Scripture

"According as his divine power hath given unto us all things that pertain unto life and godliness, through the knowledge of him that hath called us to glory and virtue" (2 Peter 1:3):

Knowledge has increased in these last and evil days. We must be very careful not to attempt to steal God's glory. Let us be about our Fathers business so that one day we too can be told by the Lord, well done thou good and faithful servant.

Signs Shall Follow Them Who Believe

Scripture

Jesus said, *"He that believeth and is baptized shall be saved; but he that believeth not shall be damned. And these signs shall follow them that believe; In my name shall they cast out devils; they shall speak with new tongues; They shall take up serpents; and if they drink any deadly thing, it shall not hurt them; they shall lay hands on the sick, and they shall recover"* (Mark 16:15-18).

This explains why many fail to show evidence of these signs that Jesus said would follow the believer. The key word in this precious verse of scripture is <u>BELIEVE</u>. Jesus tells us that these signs SHALL follow THEM THAT BELIEVE! The world system we live in has attempted to brainwash our minds to doubt all things concerning anything spiritually having to do with God.

The world has trained us to believe that we have to see it, in order to believe it. This is what brings doubt in the mind concerning the word of God. When a man doubts in his mind, he is considered to be double minded. This is what the Holy Scriptures had to say.

Scripture

"But let him ask in FAITH, nothing wavering. For he that wavereth is like a wave of the sea driven with the wind and tossed. For let not that man think that he shall receive any thing of the Lord. A double-minded man is unstable in all of his ways" (James 1:6-8).

Not only does the lack of faith place us at a disadvantage with God, it further keeps us from recognizing what's real, and what's not. Remember, faith is needed for the things that cannot be seen. Only those things that can be seen require no faith. Everything we see with our natural eye is temporary. However, the things that we cannot see are eternal.

"While we look not at the things which are seen, but at the things which are not seen: for the things which are seen are TEMPORAL; but the things which are not seen are ETERNAL" (2 Corinthians 4:18).

When we doubt in our mind, this completely cancels out our faith. The word of God tells us that we can have whatsoever we say if we doubt not. Therefore, believe in your heart and doubt not, and watch the manifestation of the Lord unfold.

WE MUST FOLLOW JESUS

We must follow Jesus if we want to enter into the kingdom of God. Jesus said, "No man can come to God the Father accept by me." Everyone who belongs to Christ will listen and believe in the word of the almighty God. Those who do not belong to Christ have all refused to surrender to the word of God, it's that simple. These souls cannot hear, nor do they want to hear what God has to say.

Scripture

Jesus tells us, *"My sheep hear my voice and I know them, and they follow me. And I give unto them eternal life; and they shall never perish, neither shall any man pluck them out of my hand"* (John 10:27).

"And other sheep I have, which are not of this fold: them also I must bring, and they shall hear my voice; and there shall be <u>one fold</u>, and <u>one shepherd</u>" (John 10:16).

What other sheep is Jesus referring to that is not of this fold? Who is the Lord talking about? The other sheep he is referring to is the Gentile nations. Jesus will make atonement for all mankind, not just the children of Israel. After the Lord's death, burial and resurrection, provisions were made for all nations, kindreds, and tongues.

Scripture

"For through him, we both have access by one Spirit unto the Father. Now therefore ye are no more strangers and foreigners, but fellow citizens with the saints, and of the household of God" (Ephesians 2:18, 19).

Jesus has given salvation to all men. The Jews being God's chosen people have been given the salvation of the Lord. Even the Gentiles are no longer alienated from God, but they too have been given the salvation of the Lord. The family of God has been open to all nations of men. This is what Jesus accomplished when he laid down his precious life on that rugged cross at Calvary. All souls that accept Jesus as their Lord and Savior have been adopted into the family of God. These souls are now the righteous seed of Abraham and heirs of all the promises of God.

Power Received for the Task

Scripture

"Behold, I give unto you power to tread on serpents and scorpions, and <u>over all the power of the enemy</u>: and nothing shall by any means hurt you" (Luke 10:19).

Jesus fully equips those who are called to serve with everything needed to complete their finished work for Christ. He also makes sure we can adequately deal with the enemy of God. Our Lord truly supplies all of our needs. Jesus had announced to his disciples his coming, his rejection, and even his death to occur on Calvary. Jesus felt by that time his disciples' faith had been established enough to bear this news. Jesus spoke more openly leading up to his final hour in an attempt to prepare his disciples for what was to come. This preparation by the Lord would so disappoint the hearts of the disciples. Peter the disciple did not understand this saying because he rebuked Jesus when he spoke of his death on the cross. Peter felt he was protecting Jesus; however, he had been influenced by Satan just that quick. Peter had no idea he was under the influence of the enemy at that moment. The Lord recognized the enemy's influence and ended up rebuking Peter for his own good. If we are not careful, the enemy will try to influence our life in the same manner. We will think we are doing something good, not fully understanding the true cause of the mission we are trying to stop. This is what Jesus said to Peter after he saw Satan's influence upon him.

Scripture

"Get thee behind me, Satan: thou art an offense unto me: for thou savorest not the things that be of God, but those that be of men" (Matthew 16:23).

Jesus was letting Peter know that he should not interfere with the will and destiny of God's plan. This is an example of how easy Satan can enter one's mind when they lack knowledge. This is why God said, "My people are destroyed for lack of knowledge." The important scriptures that instruct us how to follow Christ Jesus are found in the following verses.

Scripture

"Then said Jesus unto his disciples, If any man will come after me, let him <u>deny himself</u>, and take up his cross, and follow me. For whosoever will save his life shall lose it: and whosoever will lose his life for my sake shall find it. For what is a man profited, if he shall gain the whole world, and lose his own soul? Or what shall a man give in exchange for his soul? For the Son of man shall come in the glory of his Father with his angels; and then he shall reward every man according to his works. Verily I say unto you, There be some standing here, which shall not taste of death, till they see the Son of man coming in his kingdom" (Matthew 16:24-28).

This is a very profound message from the Lord to his disciples. Jesus is telling us to deny our flesh, pick up our cross, accept his commission, and follow him daily. Being servants of the Lord, we have to perform the work he has commanded of us. Jesus told his disciples near the end of his course that some standing there would not taste of death till they saw him coming in his kingdom. Jesus died on the cross for the sins of the whole world. Those who accept Jesus as Lord will avoid the second death, which is the lake of fire. We as believers that appear to die in the flesh, actually are asleep in Christ Jesus, and await the coming of our Lord. Therefore, the saints of God do not truly die; they sleep in Jesus. They will not taste death the way the unbelieving souls will. Those who choose to reject the Lord, when they die in the flesh, they will fill the sting and face the second death. Then they will be cast into the lake of fire and brimstone forever.

Scripture

The Bible tells us, *"But I would not have you to be ignorant brethren, concerning them which are <u>ASLEEP</u>, that ye sorrow not, even as others which have no hope. For if we believe that Jesus died and rose again, even so them also which <u>sleep in Jesus</u> will God bring with him"* (1 Thessalonians 4:13, 14).

Those who die in the Lord are blessed. Death for the believer has no more sting or control over their souls. For their death is mere sleep in Jesus Christ our Lord. This also can be viewed as sleeping or in a state of rest while awaiting the return of the Lord.

Scripture

"Here is the patience of the Saints: here are they that keep the commandments of God, and the faith of Jesus. And I heard a voice from heaven saying unto me, <u>WRITE</u>, "Blessed are the dead which die in the Lord from henceforth: Yea, saith the Spirit, that they may rest from their labors; and their works do follow them" (Revelation 14:12, 13).

"O DEATH, WHERE IS THY STING? O GRAVE, WHERE IS THY VICTORY? The sting of death is sin; and the strength of sin is the law, but thanks be to God, which giveth us the victory through our Lord Jesus Christ. Therefore, my beloved brethren, be ye steadfast, unmovable, always abounding in the work of the Lord, forasmuch as ye know that your labor is not in vain in the Lord" (Matthew 15:55-58).

Every good deed done in the earth for the kingdom of God will be greatly rewarded by Jesus at the Judgment Seat of Christ. The Lord has conquered all things that the enemy introduced when sin was birthed into this world. Even the devil's fate has been sealed and his sentence already pronounced. Time in the earth just has to catch up with God's appointed time. Therefore, continue to do good work in Christ Jesus while you remain in the land of the living. Souls are leaving this earth through death in the flesh every hour of the day. However, the blessed thing about being a servant/son of the living God is that we get a chance to step over into eternity forever when God calls our name.

Therefore, the homegoing of a born-again Christian is a special event. They are on their way to be with the Lord forever. The unbelieving soul does not have it quite the same. Their future is dim. They chose to spend their eternity with the enemies of God. Whether they know it or not, their fate was sealed when they rejected the free gift of salvation which the Lord freely offered. We all have the same choice. We can either spend eternity with God in his glorious kingdom, or we will end up with the enemies of God in the lake of fire. This decision is yours to make. Please, choose correctly!

THE CHURCH

The church—that blessed body of Christ—is the centerpiece of God's kingdom. God, with all his power and might, spoke everything into existence. There was not anything made that was not made by the Lord Jesus Christ. God redeemed the church body back from the clutches of the enemy with the only sacrifice valuable enough to offer. This one valuable sacrifice was the precious blood of the Lamb. This precious blood came from God himself. Jesus being the Lamb of God was also God manifested in the flesh. Our Lord Jesus left his place in glory to visit mankind in the earth. His purpose was to come and seek and save that which was lost. His precious blood was the only commodity valuable enough to pay in exchange for the sins of this world. This whole process was part of God's plan for our salvation. Sin in the world today is a direct reflection of Adam's disobedience in the Garden of Eden. Every human born has received the sin nature of the first man Adam, with the exception of Christ. For this reason alone, man had to be delievered in the flesh by God. Thank God for Jesus establishing his church that even the gates of hell will not prevail against it. The church of Jesus Christ, which is called the body of Christ, was given birth on the day of Pentecost. This is when the Holy Spirit began to dwell on the <u>inside</u> of the born-again believers. Prior to the day of Pentecost and with the exception of just a few souls like John the Baptist, his parents Zechariah and Elizabeth, the Holy Spirit would only come <u>upon</u> those used by God. This same Holy Spirit was the Comforter that Jesus promised he would have his Father send to his church body of believers after his departure.

Scripture

"And when the Day of Pentecost was fully come, they were all with one accord in one place. And suddenly there came a sound from heaven as of a rushing mighty wind, and it filled all the house where they were sitting. And there appeared unto them CLOVEN TONGUES like as of fire, and it sat upon each of them. And they were <u>ALL FILLED</u> with the HOLY GHOST, and began to speak with other tongues, as the SPIRIT gave them utterance. And there were dwelling at Jerusalem Jews, devout men, out of every nation under heaven. Now when this was noised abroad, the multitude came together, and were confounded, because that every man heard them speak in his own language" (Acts 2:1-6).

When the Holy Ghost was given to the disciples of Jesus, others Jews and all nations in the town heard all the commotion. Then they heard their own languages in their own native tongue. When these fiery tongues rested upon the men, they each heard a personal message in their own ears. This was to inform the disciples that the SPIRITUAL BAPTISM was now to include all men. This was the birth of the body of Christ—the body that was to include all souls alike, both Jews and the various Gentile nations. Christ is returning for his one church body of believers. This church will not be shaken by the evils of this world. Therefore, we must get in, and stay in the body of Christ. Regardless of what happens to us in any way, we must stay in the church. Don't let the devil trick you from coming in or remaining therein.

If the devil attacks your body, stay in the church.
If the devil attacks your mind, stay in the church.
If you lose your job, stay in the church.
If you lose a loved one, stay in the church.
If you have trouble in your home, stay in the church.
If you have trouble in your marriage, stay in the church.
If the church members offend you, stay in the church.
If the pastor offends you, stay in the church.
If the preacher preaches a hard message, stay in the church.
If you witness fellow saints falling short of God's glory, stay in church.
If you fall short of God's glory, stay in church.

Regardless of what happens in your life, stay in the church. Stay under the ARK of God's protection. The devil is doing everything in his power to stop you from pleasing God. The devil would love to distract and deceive you causing your faith to be shaken. The Bible tells us to faint not. The devil wants us to return to his worldly influence of wicked and sinful behavior. He knows that if he can convince us to forsake God, we will lose our souls, just like he has lost his. To the church body in Christ Jesus, hold onto your faith. Stay in the body of Christ. God has given us protection and strength in the midst of other born-again believers. There is strength in numbers. Stay and fellowship among the Christians and be encouraged one to another. This will provide the strength and protection you need in your time of trouble. Continue to minister to the lost souls of this world. Remember, the Holy Spirit now dwells within us, therefore protect your temple (the body) where the Spirit of God dwells.

Scripture

"He that dwelleth in the secret place of the Most High shall abide under the shadow of the Almighty. I will say of the Lord, he is my refuge and my fortress: my God; in him will I trust (**FAITH**)*. Surely he shall deliver thee from the snare* (**DANGEROUS TRAP**) *of the fowler, and from the noisome pestilence. He shall cover thee with his feathers, and under his wings shalt thou trust: his truth shall be thy shield and buckler. Thou shalt not be afraid for the terror by night; nor for the arrow that flieth by day; Nor for the pestilence that walketh in darkness; nor for the destruction that wasteth at noonday. A thousand shall fall at thy side, and ten thousand at thy right hand; but it shall not come nigh thee"* (Psalm 91:1-7).

The Lord is letting us know that he is our protector regardless of what type of situation we may be facing. The Lord promises to shield us from all hurt, harm, and danger. He promises to destroy all of our enemies without any harm coming to us. The Lord will protect and shield those who seek refuge in the body of Christ.

CHRIST'S RETURN FOR HIS CHURCH

Jesus our Lord and Savior is going to return for his church in order to gather all the saints of God to himself. This great event will occur before the Great Tribulation Period takes place. The saints of God are referring to the souls who have received Jesus Christ as Lord and Savior while in the earth. Thank God for his plan of salvation that he has given to all who believe in the Messiah, which is Christ Jesus.

Scripture

"For the Lord himself shall descend from heaven with a shout, with the voice of the archangel, and with the trump of God: and the dead in Christ shall rise first: Then we which are alive and remain shall be caught up together with them in the clouds, <u>to meet the Lord in the air</u>: and so shall we ever be with the Lord. Wherefore comfort one another with these words" (1 Thessalonians 4:16-18).

Those of us, who are in the body of Christ, once caught up, will appear before the Judgment Seat of Christ. This judgment is for the purpose of receiving our rewards. That's right. Jesus will reward the saints of God for their diligent work that brought him glory while they were alive in the earth. This will be a glorious day when Jesus awards his faithful servants with their particular crowns of glory.

THE FIVE CROWNS OF GLORY

There are five crowns in heaven reserved for the saints of God. This event will take place at the Judgment Seat of Christ. This judgment is for the born-again believers who will be judged for their good works performed while they were alive in the flesh. Jesus will issue the appropriate crown achieved for the righteous deeds performed by his saints. All deeds that were done to the glory of God will receive recognition on this great day. All this will come to pass at the Judgment Seat of Christ, also called (THE BEMA).

Scripture

"For we must all appear before the Judgment Seat of Christ; that every one may receive the things done in his body, according to that he hath done, whether it be good or bad. Knowing therefore the terror of the Lord, we persuade men; but we are made manifest unto God; and I trust also are made manifest in your consciences" (2 Corinthians 5:10, 11).

The 'Terror of the Lord' is best understood in the general sense as 'the fear of the Lord.' This signifies a deep reverence for God, especially here particularly in view of the judgment seat which we as believers must all stand before.

Scripture

"Every man's work shall be made manifest: for the day shall declare it, because it shall be revealed by fire; and the fire shall try every man's work of what sort it is. If any man's work abide which he hath built thereupon, he shall receive a reward. If any man's work shall be burned, he shall suffer loss: but he himself shall be SAVED; yet so as by fire" (1 Corinthians 3:13-15).

This scripture explains that one does not suffer the loss of his or her salvation at the Judgment Seat of Christ. This judgment determines the loss or gain of their reward. However, their salvation will remain intact. This passage of scripture deals not with the relationship to Jesus, but the service provided for Jesus while alive in the earth. In order to be at this particular judgment, you must have already achieved a relationship with Christ. Therefore, be extremely careful that no one steals your crown. Remember, faithful perseverance through trials will guarantee a crown of life. Let us never forget that the <u>SECOND DEATH</u> is eternal destruction in the lake of fire reserved for Satan and his demonic host. This same FIRE will also include all unbelieving human beings who rejected the Son of God. Let us take a closer look at the description of the five crowns Jesus will administer to his saints.

The Five Crowns

1) INCORRUPTIBLE CROWN—Victor's Crown

Scripture

"And every man that striveth for mastery is temperate in all things, Now they do it to obtain a corruptible crown; but we an INCORRUPTIBLE" (1 Corinthians 9:25).

The many rewards that a man seeks to obtain are often received by dishonest and immoral practices. This is what the wicked world system teaches. They fully condone their behavior regardless of whatever it takes to gain the advantage over their opponent. This is not how the kingdom of God operates. The Lord gives rewards based on his perfect merit system. God sees the evil and the good of every soul at the same time. He is the only one who judges justly. The crowns that Christ will issue to them who have obtained victory over this world will be received only by the righteousness of God in Christ Jesus.

2) CROWN OF LIFE—Martyr's Crown

Scripture

"Fear none of those things which thou shall suffer: behold, the devil shall cast some of you into prison, that ye may be tried; and ye shall have tribulation ten days: be thou faithful unto death, and I will give thee a CROWN OF LIFE" (Revelation 2:10).

This Crown of Life will be waiting for the souls who loved God enough that they gave up their very life to proclaim the gospel of Jesus Christ. They call this the Martyr's Crown. These are the ones who died clinging onto their faith in God—those who suffered great persecution and tribulation for Christ's sake. This special crown is for the ones who were faithful unto death.

3) CROWN OF RIGHTEOUSNESS—For Those Who Love His Appearance

Scripture

> *"But watch thou in all things, endure afflictions, do the work of an evangelist, make full proof of thy ministry. For I am now ready to be offered, and the time of my departure is at hand. I have fought a good fight, I have finished my course, I have kept the faith: henceforth there is laid up for me a CROWN OF RIGHTEOUSNESS, which the Lord, the Righteous Judge, shall give me at that day: and not to me only, but unto all them also that love his appearing"* (2 Timothy 4:5-8).

This beautiful crown of Righteousness is reserved for all the saints of God who loved the appearing of Christ return. There are some who will be extremely happy about the coming of Jesus when he returns for his church body of believers. Then there are those who will hate his appearing. These are the hard-hearted souls who refused to let go of their evil ways so that they could continue in sin. However, those who look forward to the coming of the Lord will enjoy receiving this precious crown. The saints of God are made the RIGHTEOUSNESS of God because of what Jesus Christ did on the cross at Calvary. This free gift given to every believer qualifies them to spend eternal life with the Lord forever.

4) CROWN OF GLORY—Elder's Crown

Scripture

> *"The Elders which are among you I exhort, who am also an Elder, and a witness of the sufferings of Christ, and also a partaker of the glory that shall be revealed: Feed the flock of God which is among you, taking the oversight thereof, not by constraint, but willingly; not for filthy lucre, but of a ready mind; Neither as being lords over God's heritage, but being examples to the flock. And when the CHIEF SHEPHERD shall appear, ye shall receive a CROWN OF GLORY that fadeth not away"* (1 Peter 5:1-4).

This crown of glory is reserved for Elders, teachers and leaders who minister the good news of the gospel by feeding the Lord's precious flock of sheep. They have an awesome responsibility. These church leaders are held to a higher standard. This does not mean they should exhalt themselves as some religious organizations do. They must teach the word of God in season and out of season without intentional error. Jesus is the Chief Shepherd, and these Elders and church leaders are Christ spiritual under-shepherds. As long as they stay with the word of God, they will remain on the right track. They have been entrusted to lead and guide the flock of God into the knowledge of his holy kingdom. Christ is the author and finisher of our faith. He is the one who will give us access to his Holy City, also referred to as the New Jerusalem. Jesus Christ has a special reward that will honor our leaders at his Judgment Seat.

5) CROWN OF REJOICING

Scripture

"For what is our hope, or joy, or CROWN OF REJOICING? Are not even ye in the presence of our Lord Jesus Christ at his coming? For ye are our glory and joy" (1 Thessalonians 2:19, 20).

This crown is a crown of Rejoicing. The Bible talks about the hope and joy of rejoicing in the Lord's appearance. These are the souls who are happy to see the Lord coming back for them in the clouds. Unfortunately, there will be those who will hate his appearance. Just make sure that you are not one of them. God is our hope in glory. We are worshipers of the Lord. He is worthy to be praised above anyone and anything. Let us rejoice in the sovereignty of our Lord God. Jesus will award his crowns to all the saints who rightfully deserve them. Thank you Lord Jesus, for you are the only righteous judge.

Remember, there are two primary main judgments of God. The one you want to attend is called The Judgment Seat of Christ. The one you want to avoid is called The Great White Throne Judgment. This Great White Throne Judgment is the judgment of the dead. Trust me; you do not want to appear before that judgment.

This Great White Throne Judgment will sentence you to the lake of fire. There is no redemption or protection for those who appear before this judgment. They have chosen to reject the Lord's saving grace. Therefore, the unsaved souls will be sentenced to the same place where Satan, his beast, his false prophet and his host of fallen angels will spend their eternity. The only reason mankind will enter into this judgment is because they failed to listen and believe those who preached and proclaimed the good news of the gospel of Jesus Christ. They refused God's free gift of salvation and chose to remain in the family of the enemy. These individuals felt they were smarter than God when they had his breath in their body. This is a perfect example of what happens when we fail to surrender ourselves to the Lord. This world teaches us we can do our own thing. We must at some point discover the purpose God has for our life, or else we will also be deceived right along with the unsaved souls of this world. We must understand that the Lord called us into the sheepfold, and we answered the call. To associate with the enemy of God will likewise cause us to perish right along with him. This is the same principle that applies in the earthly realm as well. When we run with the wicked, we will likewise perish with the wicked.

DESCRIPTION OF THE KINGDOM OF HEAVEN

Have you ever wondered what the kingdom of heaven looks like? The answer to this question is found in the same place every other answer to life's many questions can be found. This place is called the Holy Bible. When we take the time to read it, we learn the truth of the whole matter. The Lord is preparing a place for the saints of God to dwell in. The old heaven and the old earth will be replaced by a new heaven and a new earth. This present universe will be cleansed from all the effects of sin. There will be no more seas; therefore, the space will be greater and capable of handling large numbers of redeemed souls from all the ages. The kingdom of God will be so beautiful that you could never even imagine all of its beauty. In your wildest dreams, you could have never imagined the glory involved in the construction of this holy city. John the apostle described it like this.

Scripture

"And there came unto me one of the seven angels which had the seven vials full of the seven last plagues, and talked with me, saying, Come hither, I will show thee <u>THE BRIDE</u>, the Lamb's wife. And he carried me away in the spirit to a grat and high mountain, and showed me that great city, the holy Jerusalem, descending out of heaven from God. Having the glory of God: and her light was like unto a stone most precious, even like a jasper stone, clear as crystal; And had a wall great and high, and had twelve (12) gates, and at the gates twelve (12) angels, and names written thereon, which are the names of the twelve (12) tribes of the children of Israel: On the east three gates; on the north three gates; on the south three gates; and on the west three gates. And the wall of the city had twelve (12) foundations, and in them the names of the twelve (12) apostles of the Lamb. And he that talked with me had a golden reed to measure the city, and the gates thereof, and the wall thereof. And the city lieth four-square, and the length is as large as the breadth: and he measures the city with the reed, twelve thousand furlongs. The length and the breadth and the height of it are equal. And he measured the wall thereof, a hundren and forty and four cubits, according to the measure of a man, that is, of the angel. And the building of the wall of it was of jasper: and the city was pure gold, like unto clear glass. And the foundations of the wall of the city were garnished with all manner of precious stones. The first foundation was jasper; the second, sapphire; the third, a chalcedony; the fourth, an emerald; the fifth, sardonyx; the sixth, sardius; the seventh, chrysolite; the eighth, beryl; the ninth, a topaz; the tenth, a chrysoprasus; the eleventh, a jacinth; the twelfth, an amethyst. And the twelve (12) gates were twelve pearls; every several gate was of one pearl: and the street of the city was pure gold, as it were transparent glass. And I saw no temple therein: for the Lord God Almighty and the Lamb are the temple of it. And the city had no need of the sun, neither of the moon, to shine in it: for the glory of God did lighten it, and the Lamb is the light thereof. And the nations of them which are saved shall walk in the light of it: and the kings of the earth do bring their glory and honor into it. And the gates of it shall NOT be shut at all by day: for there shall be no night there. And they shall bring the glory and honor of the nations into it.

And there shall in no wise enter into it anything that defileth, neither whatsoever worketh abomination, or maketh a lie: but they which are written in the Lamb's Book of Life" (Revelation 21:9-27).

This gives you a full description of the beauty of the New Jerusalem that the Lord has prepared for us. Notice that the size of the holy city is measured equal on all four sides. Therefore, the length and breadth is measured the same. This means the holy city will be just as high as it is square. The size of this beautiful place is measured 1500 miles cubed. Therefore, if placed inside the United States, this city would stretch from the Canadian border in the State of Minnesota, south to the Gulf of Mexico at the City of Houston Texas. It would also stretch from the East Coast near Washington D.C. clear across to the State of Colorado. Finally, the height of it would extend into the heavens 1500 miles straight up. The Lord God almighty has spared no expense when it involves all the wonderful things he creates for his children. He has truly prepared a beautiful place to dwell among the saints of God for all eternity. Will you be among the saints who will dwell in this sin free society with God forever and ever? That is the question!

Around God's Throne

The kingdom of heaven and the throne of God are described as a beautiful place by John the apostle. John the apostle was the youngest of all the disciples and the one whom Jesus loved. He was the same disciple chosen by the Lord Jesus to come up hither and look into the kingdom of heaven. Once shown the end time which was to come to pass, John was instructed and entrusted by God to write the book of the revelation of Jesus Christ. Then he was commanded to send these writings to the seven churches which are in Asia. However, this is a peek at the beauty surrounding the throne of God.

Scripture

"After this I looked, and, behold, a door was opened in heaven: and the first voice which I heard was as it were of a trumpet talking with me; which said, Come up hither, and I will show thee things which must be here after. And immediately I was in the spirit: and, behold, a throne was set in heaven, and one sat on the throne. And he that sat was to look upon

like a jasper and a sardine stone: and there was a rainbow round about the throne, in sight like unto an emerald. And round about the throne were four and twenty seats: and upon the seats I saw four and twenty elders sitting, clothed in white raiment; and they had on their heads crowns of gold. And out of the throne preceded LIGHTNING and THUNDERINGS and VOICES: and there were seven lamps of fire burning before the throne, which are the seven Spirits of God. And before the throne was a sea of glass like unto crystal: and in the midst of the throne, and round about the throne, were four beasts full of eyes before and behind. And the first beast was like a LION, and the second beast like a CALF, and the third beast had a face as a MAN, and the fourth beast was like a flying EAGLE. And the four beast had each of them six wings about him; and they were full of eyes within: and they rest not day and night, saying, Holy, Holy, Holy, Lord God Almighty, which was, and is, and is to come. And when those beast give GLORY and HONOR and THANKS to him that sat on the throne, and worship him that liveth forever and ever, and cast their crowns before the throne, saying, Thou art worthy, O Lord, to receive GLORY and HONOR and POWER: for thou hast created all things, and for thy pleasure they are and were created" (Revelation 4:1-11).

Those in heaven around God's throne give him glory day and night. Those who belong to God in the earth also give him praise and glory day and night in honor of his name. We have to prepare ourselves while in the earth to become worshipers of the Lord who sits on his throne. Those who truly love Jesus enjoy giving him praise and worship all the day long. This can be viewed as a dress rehearsal for the things to come in the New Jerusalem, also known as the Holy City. We will then take much pleasure in worshipping and serving the Lord throughout all eternity.

WHO IS THE HOLY SPIRIT?

The precious HOLY SPIRIT is part of the Godhead—God the Father, God the Son and God the Holy Spirit. The Holy Spirit, like the Son, is God from God. The Son, Jesus is generated or begotten, whereas the Holy Spirit proceeds from God. The TRINITARIAN relationship is a mystery to some men. However, this understanding is very clear and evident in the holy word of God. Jesus called him the COMFORTER—the one Jesus promised God the Father would send to us. This HOLY SPIRIT or HOLY GHOST is the very Holy Spirit which comes from God which the Lord allows all born-again believers to receive. This is the part of God that he shares with his beloved sons of men. The Holy Bible is not trying to say that there are three Gods which some religions use as an excuse to not follow the doctrine of Christ. There is only ONE GOD, with three distinct persons or functions. Do not be confused, this is God's business. There is only one Lord, one Faith, and one Baptism.

Scripture

The Bible reads, *"If ye love me, keep my commandments. And I will pray the Father, and he shall give you <u>another</u> COMFORTER, that <u>HE</u> may abide with you for ever, Even the Spirit of truth; whom the world cannot receive, because it seeth him not, neither knoweth him: but ye know him; for he dwelleth with you, <u>and shall be in you</u>. I (Jesus) will not leave you comfortless: <u>I WILL COME TO YOU</u>. Yet a little while, <u>and the W O R L D seeth me no more</u>; <u>But ye see me</u>: because I live, ye shall live also"* (John 14:15-19).

Jesus further tells us, *"But the <u>COMFORTER</u>, which is the <u>HOLY GHOST</u>, whom the Father will send in my name, he shall teach you all things, and bring all things to your remembrance, whatsoever I have said unto you"* (John 14:26).

Therefore, let us be comforted to know that the Holy Spirit of God will teach us all things. That's everything we need to know while we travel earth's journey. Let us have our mind focused on kingdom business. When we do this, we will have peace both in our hearts and mind. Remember, Jesus warned us not to let our hearts be troubled—neither should we allow ourselves to ever be afraid. The Holy Bible taught us that fear is first of all a spirit, and secondly, this spirit did not come from God. We know if it's not from God, it has got to be from the enemy of God known as the devil.

Scripture

Jesus said, "And when he is come, he will reprove the world of <u>Sin</u>, and of <u>Righteousness</u>, and of <u>Judgment</u>" (John 16:8).

Jesus is referring to the Comforter which is the Holy Ghost that he will send to us. Furthermore, it is explained how the Holy Spirit or Comforter will reprove or rebuke concerning three categories. These three categories are known as sin, righteousness and judgment.

1) Sin—the Holy Spirit reveals the need for redemption. The greatest sin is unbelief which causes eternal condemnation according to John 3:18. The greatest work of God is that we believe on him whom God sent to us which is Jesus the risen Savior" (John 6:29).

2) Righteousness—the Holy Spirit reveals the possibility of redemption. Jesus Christ goes to the Father after a righteous sin free LIFE, and a DEATH that will pass his righteousness onto all born-again blood washed believers. Jesus died so that we could be saved. We are the righteousness of God based on how Jesus died on the cross, taking on himself the sins of the world. Now we must accept the free gift of salvation, deny ourselves, take up our cross daily, and follow Jesus. We have an assignment to daily be about our Father's business.

Scripture

Jesus said, "And he said to them all, if any man will come after me, let him deny himself, and take up his cross <u>daily</u>, and follow me" (Luke 9:23).

3) Judgment—the Holy Spirit reveals the reality of redemption. The power of Jesus to judge Satan and to overthrow his kingdom is not future, but was accomplished at the cross during the resurrection of our Lord.

Scripture

Jesus tells us, *"Now to the judgment of this world: now shall the prince (Satan) of this world be cast out. And I, if I be lifted up from the earth, will draw all men unto me"* (John 12:31, 32).

Jesus was indeed lifted up on the cross at Calvary. Then he was also lifted up from the depths of the earth after ministering in paradise to the saints of old. Then ultimately the Lord was lifted all the way up when he ascended into the heavens witnessed by a few of his loyal disciples. This ascension took place on a mountain in Galilee. God received Jesus up into the heavens where he is now seated on the right hand of the throne of majesty. Jesus now makes daily intercession for his born-again believers as Satan constantly accuses the brethren every opportunity he gets. Finally, everytime we offer up praise and worship to the Lord, this too will lift Jesus up so that all men can still come to God.

The HOLY SPIRIT is All We Need

Do you know that the Lord thy God is ultimately all we need in the earth? This statement is not made to encourage us not to associate with one another. This statement is made to teach us that God allows his Spirit to dwell within us when we love him and accept the Lord Jesus as our risen Savior. The world has many organizations designed to connect mankind one to another. The problem is that many of these organizations are formed without God in mind. We have to be very careful what we pledge our allegiance to. The one true fellowship we really need to be concerned about is the church body of Christ. This is the family, brother, and sisterhood that we must make sure that we are part of. All other forms of brother and sisterhood in the earth cannot save your soul. This means that there are some organizations that intentionally promote unrighteous behavior. There are even some that endorse wickedness and the worship of false gods. Therefore, be careful who you associate yourself with. Birds of a feather will always flock together. We as children of God must be extremely careful of the oaths we take part in while in the earth. There are many organizations that still openly practice idolatry to this day, yet call themselves a good organization. Once we come to know Jesus in the pardoning of our sins, he sends us the Holy Spirit of God to be a present help in this day of trouble. God's Holy Spirit will teach and expose __ALL__ things for our enlightenment. This gift and privilege is only granted to the children of God, which are the redeemed of the Lord.

Scripture

> *"If ye then be risen with Christ, __seek__ those things which are __above__, where Christ sitteth on the right hand of God. Set your affection on things __above__, not on things on the earth. __For we are dead, and your life is hid with Christ in God__. When Christ, who is our life, shall appear, then shall ye also appear with him in glory. Mortify therefore your members which are upon the earth; fornication, uncleanness, inordinate affection, evil concupiscence, and covetousness, which is idolatry. For which things sake the wrath of God cometh on the children of disobedience: In the which ye also walked some time, when ye lived in them. But now ye also put off all these; anger, wrath, malice, blasphemy, filthy communication out of your mouth. Lie not one to another, seeing that ye have put off the old man with his deeds; and have put on the new man, which is renewed in knowledge after the image of him that created him. Where there is neither Greek nor Jew, circumcision nor uncircumcision, Barbarian, Scythian, bond nor free: but Christ is __all in all__."* (Colossians 3:1-11).

The Bible tells us to seek the things of God above all things. Often times there are occasions when we take our lives into our own hands. Then we start to look to other things. These other things are often allowed to become barriers to prevent us from totally surrendering to God. Remember, God requires our total allegiance which is our whole heart. When we divide ourselves, this creates confusion in our mind. We will then have trouble letting other allegiances go. Always remember this. No other organization, brother or sisterhood has a heaven or hell to place you in. Neither does any other organization have the authority to sustain you or save your very soul. Let us not forget that the wrath of God will be poured out without mixture on the sons of disobedience. These facts should always remain in the forefront of your mind when choosing to establish priorities for your life. Therefore, be real careful when you decide to attach yourself to strange fellowship organizations, especially ungodly ones. The term ungodly is referring to any organization that practices or promotes any behavior contrary to the word of God. Mankind will often seek an organization to belong to in order to satisfy that feeling of emptiness often mistaken for loneliness. The problem is, without God in your life, you will never be fulfilled. We must learn that only God can fill that void that causes a man to feel like somethings missing in his life. There's no need to continue to seek after worldly avenues anylonger. The Bible tells us that the Holy Spirit will teach us all things. Therefore, be careful pledging fellowship where Jesus Christ is not acknowledged nor praised openly. We as born-again Christians must remember that God's Spirit does indeed dwell inside all of his born-again believers. So if you claim to belong to the risen Savior named Jesus, reverence him, and never put anyone or anything above him.

Scripture

"The God of our Fathers raised up Jesus, whom ye slew and hanged on a tree. Him hath God exalted with his right hand to be a PRINCE and a SAVIOR, for to give repentance to Israel, and forgiveness of sins. And we are witnesses of these things; and so is also the <u>Holy Ghost, whom God hath given to them that obey him</u>" (Acts 5:30-32).

Remember, Jesus told us that if we love him, we will keep his commandments. Therefore, let us receive the Holy Spirit of God and finish the work Jesus commanded us to perform in the earth. Then you will have been deemed the righteous seed of the Most High.

BLASPHEMY AGAINST THE HOLY GHOST

The Unforgivable Sin

Jesus lets us know that he that is not with him, is against him. The sin of blasphemy against the Holy Ghost is unforgivable. This is the only sin where ther is no hope at all.

Scripture

"Wherefore I say unto you, all manner of sin and blasphemy shall be forgiven unto men: <u>but the blasphemy against the HOLY GHOST shall not be forgiven unto men</u>. And whosoever speaketh a

word against the Son of Man, it shall be forgiven him: but whosoever speaketh against the Holy Ghost shall not be forgiven him, neither in this world, neither in the world to come" (Matthew 12:31, 32).

Blasphemy against the Holy Ghost is when you deliberately reject the grace of God which is freely given unto salvation. This person rejects the very provision and sacrifice Jesus Christ made when he died on the cross at Calvary. This living sacrifice was made so that each and every one of us could be saved from the wrath of God to come. The Holy Spirit of the Lord performed many miracles in the earth that was evidence of his deity. To disregard these miraculous wonders performed by God is to reject the power of the true and living Savior who operated in the Holy Spirit while in the earth. Furthermore, to disregard the grace of God that provides salvation is just like telling the Lord, NO THANKS. God's Holy Spirit offers the gift of salvation to the very heart of man. To reject the Holy Spirit is to have a hardness of heart and a rebellious spirit toward anything good. Those who find themselves in this category desire to remain in darkness, rejecting the light of truth—thereby ultimately taking the will of God for granted. This act of rejection toward the sovereignty of the Creator and his holy word is BLASPHEMY against God's Holy Spirit. This is a very serious matter since the Holy Spirit is God. Anyone who rejects God's offer of salvation has in reality blasphemed the very nature of God. They cannot be saved at this point. They have taken for granted and chose not to value the precious genuine grace God has given us through his only begotten Son, Jesus Christ our Lord. When these things develop in one's mind, that very soul has made the lake of fire their eternal home. Salvation is truly impossible at this point. There is absolutely no hope for that soul. We must remember that there is only one way to God the Father. All souls must be covered with the precious blood of the Lamb, and his name is Jesus. He is the one and only God who loved us enough to lay down his very own life in place of ours. Blasphemy against the Holy Ghost is the one sin you never want to commit. Therefore, if you are currently rejecting the free gift of salvation given by God, you must turn immediately and start running toward Jesus. Your future eternal life depends on it.

DAY SEVEN

THE BOOK OF LIFE

The book of life is where you want your name to be found written and preserved by God. We are going to answer the six questions found at the beginning of this book under the day one section. The only way to be forgiven of sin and pardon from the lake of fire is to accept the only begotten Son of the living God as your Lord. Then your name will be found written in the Lamb's book of life. The Bible speaks about these books—the ones that contains our entire life and deeds whether they be good or bad; the other that contains the names of all those who have been forgiven by God. To be forgiven by God is to be washed clean in the blood of the Lamb. This is the only way to receive the salvation of the Lord. The second death is eternal punishment and torment in the lake of fire to be experienced only by Satan, his host of followers and all the lost souls of mankind. The Bible tells us that when the books were opened, the dead were judged out of those things written in these books. The dead being referred to here are the resurrected spiritually dead souls that were kept in hell awaiting the judgment of God. This also includes the spiritual dead if still alive in the earth at that time who insists on rejecting the free gift of God's salvation. These books will be opened at the Great White Throne Judgment of God. The good news is you do not have to be there!

Scripture

"And I saw the dead, small and great, stand before God; and the books were open: and another book was opened, which is THE BOOK OF LIFE: and the dead were judged out of those things which were written in the books, according to their works" (Revelation 20:12).

Now let's get back to the six questions asked at the beginning of this book concerning the Lamb's Book of Life.

THE LAMB'S BOOK OF LIFE:

SIX QUESTIONS ASKED IN DAY ONE

1) What is the Book of Life?

The book of life is a heavenly book that has written therein the names of the righteous souls who are saved and redeemed by the shed blood of Jesus Christ. The names that are found written in the Lamb's book of life will not experience the judgment of God to be poured out onto the earth, nor will they be sentenced to the lake of fire which is considered the second death. The other books spoken of will contain the deeds—both good and bad—committed in the lives of those who are judged. Nothing is hidden from the eyes of the Lord. Our sins were exposed the minute they were committed. God had a ringside seat. Every sin will be exposed against those who are judged at the Great White Throne Judgment. The many sins that mankind thought were secret will now be exposed before they are sentenced to the lake of fire. All souls that are deemed righteous will be caught up forever to be with the Lord Jesus Christ prior to this event. After the righteous souls have been judged at the Judgment Seat of Christ to determine their reward, they will forever spend eternity with God. These are the ones who will enter into the New Jerusalem, also known as The Holy City of God.

Scripture

"And all the nations of them which are SAVED shall walk in the LIGHT of it: and the kings of the earth do bring their glory and honor into it. And the gates of it shall not be shut at all by day: for there shall be no night there. And they shall bring the glory and honor of the nations into it" (Revelation 21:26).

2) Whose Book Is It?

The Holy Bible teaches us that the book of life belongs to the one worthy to open it. The Lamb of God who is Jesus Christ our Lord was the only one worthy to take the book out of the right hand of the one who sat upon the throne. The book is called **The Lamb's Book of Life**. The book of Revelation tells us that Jesus was the only one worthy to open this heavenly book.

Scripture

"And they sung a new song, saying, Thou art worthy to take the book, and to open the seals thereof: for thou wast slain, and hast redeemed us to God by the blood out of every <u>kindred</u>, and <u>tongue</u>, and <u>people</u>, and <u>nation</u>; And hast made us unto our God <u>kings</u> and <u>priest</u>: and we shall reign on the earth" (Revelation 5:9).

"And there shall in no wise enter into it any thing that defileth, neither whatsoever worketh abomination, or maketh a lie: but they which are written in the <u>LAMB'S BOOK OF LIFE</u>" (Revelation 21:27).

3) Why is there a Need for Such a Book?

The God of the universe is not only a loving God, he is a just God. Everything we do and say is being recorded by the one and only God of the universe. Therefore, on Judgment Day, the proof of mankind's wickedness will be presented as evidence. Then will God pass sentence on the wicked to spend eternity in the lake of fire and brimstone. That is why we desperately need a Savior like the one God sent us. The wages of sin is still death because God commanded it in his holy word. Jesus left his position in glory and came to the earth to die on the cross for the sins of all who will accept him as Lord. This wipes our sin-stained soul clean as the driven snow. God did this as a free gift out of his unconditional love for the sons and daughters of men. However, some have hardened their hearts against receiving this free gift from God. They have chosen to place their trust in someone or something else and have totally rejected the God of salvation. Those are the ones who are condemned because their sins are still weighing heavy upon them. They have not been washed in the blood of the Lamb. Since God is Holy, he will not look upon sin, nor allow it to be in his presence. Without the precious blood of Jesus covering us, we are as filthy rags before the eyes of God. Having your sins upon you will cause you to suffer the second death which is the lake of fire. There will be no questions asked at the Great White Throne Judgment of God. The facts will speak for themselves. There is no need for a defense attorney to plead your case, nor will you be allowed to have one. The records of their lives will tell the whole truth and nothing but. Without the saving grace and the blood of Jesus to cover their sins, the weight of their sins will totally condemn their soul forever. This is why no one can escape this judgment and sentence God will pronounce upon the unrighteous souls. Likewise, will no one escape the lake of fire whose sin has not been covered by the blood of Jesus? This eternal punishment and torment is the fate of those who rejected Jesus as Lord. This freewill choice you will make all by yourself.

4) What Happens If My Name Is Not Found In The Book Of Life?

The Bible tells us that whosoever's name was not found written in the Lamb's book of life will be cast into the lake of fire.

Scripture

> *"And whosoever was not found written in the book of life was cast into the Lake of Fire"* (Revelation 20:15).

This is one book you want to have your name written in. If your name is not written in this book, it's because of you and the hardness of your own heart. You have chosen not to accept the Savior of the world who can cover your sin-stained life. For this reason, your name had to be blotted out of the Lamb's book of life. However, if you are still alive, Jesus is still knocking at the door of your heart. It's not too late if you are able to read these words. This is an opportunity to change your mind and strongly consider spending the rest of your life serving the Lord. You must do it right now while your blood in still running warm in your veins? With this newfound knowledge, you should be running for your life to get into the church body of Jesus Christ before you die in your flesh. Don't delay, do it today!

5) How Do I Get My Name in the Lamb's Book of Life?

The Bible tells us that the book of life contains the names of the righteous souls—all souls who have been saved and redeemed of the Lord. According to the Holy Scriptures, all souls born into this world have been written down in God's precious books. Only the ones that have rejected God have been blotted out. This means that in order to be blotted out, you had to have first appeared in this precious book. We must first believe in God and the entire Holy Bible he has sent to us through his chosen people. Secondly, we must accept God's plan for our salvation and stop trying to create a false plan of our own. This plan of God involves him sending his only begotten Son into this world to be a living sacrifice for the entire world of sin. Despite our filthiness, God so loved us that he gave and sacrificed what was most precious to him. All who refuse God's plan—which is accepting his only Son as Lord—those names will not be found written in the Lamb's book of life. They have been blotted out by God. If you want your name to be preserved in the Lamb's book of life, accept Jesus as Lord and become a servant for God's kingdom. Start doing the Lord's will instead of your own will. Get on the side of the Lord while there is still time. Time in the earth verses eternity is like a drop of water compared to the size of all the Oceans put together. There is no comparison between the two time frames. Think of this way. After being in the fire ten thousand years, those who were cast into the Lake of Fire are just getting ready to be there!

6) How Do I Keep My Name Written Therein?

This is a very simple question which has a very simple answer. Once you have accepted Jesus as Lord both by belief and confession, you have now been born-again into the family of God. Now you are a child of God by faith and considered one of his covenant believers. Something miraculous starts to happen on the inside of you. Your spirit has been saved and quickened by God. Your life is being conformed to a life in Christ Jesus. The Bible tells us whosoever shall call upon the name of the Lord shall be saved. Those names that are <u>not</u> found written in the Lamb's book of life are the unsaved souls that insist on rejecting Christ as Lord. They are among the ones who have chosen not to call upon the name of the Lord. These souls have no ark of protection over their lives. Unless they turn to God and receive the salvation of the Lord, their names will be blotted out of the Lamb's book of life.

Scripture

"That if thou shalt confess with thy mouth the Lord Jesus, and shalt believe in thine heart, that God hath raised him from the dead, thou shalt

THE LAMB'S BOOK OF LIFE:

be saved. For with the heart man believeth unto righteousness; and with the mouth confession is made unto salvation" (Romans 10:9, 10).

"All that the Father giveth me shall come to me; and him that cometh to me I will in no wise cast out" (John 6:37).

"And this is the Father's will which hath sent me, that of all which he hath given me I should lose nothing, <u>but should raise it up again at the last day</u>. And this is the will of him that sent me, that every one which seeth the Son, and believeth on him, may have everlasting Life: and I will raise him up at the last day" (John 6:39, 40).

Jesus desire is to lose no one once God the Father has placed the souls in his hands. Remember, no man can come to Jesus accept God draws him first. Once the called out souls come to the Lord Jesus, his desire is to lose no one, nor cast anyone out. This does not mean that rebellious souls cannot choose to leave on their own. Every soul has a freewill spirit given by God. Let us pray that no one turns back after first putting their hands to the plow. This means tasting the word of God and then turning back to the wicked world system influenced by Satan. The Bible tells us that God will turn those souls over to a reprobate mind to do the things unseemly.

Scripture

"And even as they did not like to retain God in their knowledge, God gave them over to a REPROBATE MIND, to do those things which are not convenient; Being filled with all unrighteousness, fornication, wickedness, covetousness, maliciousness, full of envy, murder, debate, deceit, malignity; whisperers, backbiters, HATERS OF GOD, despiteful, proud, boasters, inventors of evil things, disobedient to parents, without understanding, covenantbreakers, without natural affection, implacable, unmerciful; <u>Who knowing the judgment of God</u>, that they which commit such things are worthy of DEATH, <u>not only do the same, but have pleasure in them that do them</u>" (Romans 1:28-32).

This is why we must first believe in our heart, and then confess the same with our mouth. That will determine whether or not we are true to the one who has truly redeemed us—Jesus Christ the righteous. Once a born-again believer knows the judgment of God and commits such things without repentance, God will eventually withdraw his gracious help because their minds are in unbelief and their actions are wicked continually. Then they come to a state where they begin to take pleasure in themselves and others who commit these sinful acts. God will eventually turn them over to a reprobate mind. This means to give them up and turn them completely over to their sinful acts they desire to commit in their flesh. The word of God tells us that when sin is finished it always brings on death. This means that the sinful lifestyle without repentance will eventually destroy them all.

HEAVEN OR HELL

Where Will You Spend Eternity?

John the apostle, that disciple whom Jesus loved was the only one of the twelve disciples who died of old age. Peter the apostle once asks Jesus after the resurrection what the fate of John the beloved disciple would be. This is how Jesus replied to Peter concerning the fate of John.

Scripture

"Peter seeing him saith to Jesus, Lord, and what shall this man do? Jesus saith unto him, If I will that he tarry till I come, what is that to thee? Follow thou me. Then went this saying abroad among the brethren, that that disciple should not die: yet Jesus said not unto him, He shall not die; but, If I will that he tarry till I come, what is that to thee? This is the disciple which testifieth of these things, and wrote these things: and we know that his testimony is true" (John 21:21-24).

John the apostle was chosen and entrusted by Christ to both view the end of all things, and entrusted to accurately write these prophisees to the seven churches. Jesus had John in mind when Peter concerned himself enough to question the future fate of John. This beloved disciple was chosen by Jesus Christ to receive the revelation of God's kingdom and glory. Remember, John was the only disciple that did not scatter while Jesus was being crucified on the cross. Jesus allowed John to gaze into eternity and view the ending time for the purpose of revealing it to the people of God. Jesus gave John the revelation of all things to come. Then the beloved disciple wrote it down so that it would be placed in the Holy Bible for the benefit of the church. We all have a choice where we will spend eternity. God is such a loving God that he left his home in glory, wrapped himself in flesh, entered into the earthly realm in the form of the only begotten Son, sacrificed himself to undergo the pain and agony of the flesh for his creation. Remember, man was made special from the beginning by being created in the image and likeness of God. He freely forgave our sinful nature in order to allow us an opportunity to dwell with him in his everlasting kingdom. All we have to do is BELIEVE, REPENT and ACCEPT Jesus Christ as the only way to the kingdom of God. Mankind cannot clean himself up. We need the power of the Holy Spirit, who is the Comforter that Jesus promised he would send to us after he ascended into the heavens. Please, do not reject God's message and his provision of salvation he has made for us all.

Scripture

"For God so loved the world, that he gave his only begotten Son, that whosoever believeth in him should not parish, but have everlasting life" (John 3:16).

Salvation is simple. Either you will accept Jesus Christ as Lord now, or you will confess him as Lord later on your knees in the presence of his glory. Either way, you will bow down to the KING of kings, and the LORD of lord's which is Christ Jesus. The only problem is, in the event you are one of the ones to bow down later; you will have missed your opportunity to enter into his blessed kingdom. You will be on your way to eternal DAMNATION in the lake of fire. Therefore, you will not benefit by bowing down later, even though you will still be required to. The question still remains, "Where will you spend eternity?"

THE LAKE OF FIRE

The lake of fire was developed by God for Satan and his fallen angels. The unfortunate news is that any human being who does not accept the free gift of salvation will end up there. Some have said that if God is a God of love, how then can he send anyone to hell where they will be tormented for all eternity? There is an easy answer to that question. Anyone who ends up in the lake of fire, we must realize that God did not reject them, they rejected God. They chose not to believe the word of God, nor anyone who preached and proclaimed the message. They chose not to accept Jesus as Lord. This is crucial seeing how Christ is God's only begotten Son. They chose not to believe the Holy Scriptures—both the Old and the New Testament. In essence, they just refused to believe. They have chosen their own way and their own destiny. The coming of the Messiah was prophesied in the Old Testament and manifested in the New Testament. The Holy Bible clearly gives us instruction what we must do in order to be SAVED! The word of God never said we could make up our own way back to his precious holy kingdom. We must do it God's way and his way only. If not, you have missed the mark. Let no man and his self-made religion influence you any longer. Trust in the word of God and his word alone. Stop reading books written by rebellious men attempting to create ANOTHER WAY to the kingdom of God. There is only one way. This way is clearly spelled out in the Holy Bible. Jesus said, "I AM the way, the truth, and the life, NO MAN cometh unto the Father but by me (John 14:6)!" This blessed love letter from God is not up for discussion, nor debate. We must humble ourselves and believe the Holy Bible in its entirety. Remember, God will always resist the proud! Let us not mimic others in the past that have taken bits and pieces of God's word and formed their own religions and various denominations. When there are other books used in conjunction with the Holy Bible, normally that's a dead give away to a religious cult refusing to accept the whole Word of God. Many books make reference to the Holy Bible; however, the Holy Bible refers to no other book as being superior in its content. This is because the Holy Bible is the only book written that was inspired by God himself. Let us believe and trust in the Holy Bible whether we like it or not, and we too will avoid that fiery lake of judgment to come.

Scripture

"And whosoever was not found written in the book of life was cast into the lake of fire" (Revelation 20:15).

Always remember that God did not create the lake of fire for man. Regardless of who you've talked to, never let anyone convince you that God made hell and the lake of fire for mankind. The fiery lake was created by God for the destruction and the ending judgment set forth for Satan and his fallen angels. The reason why some men and women will end up there is because they have purposely chosen to reject God and his precious free gift of salvation. In other words, they have chosen to act just like the devil. Their rebellion against God will cause them to share in the punishment established for the enemies of God. We have all heard of being guilty by association. The same rules apply to those would choose to follow and or act like the devil. When the hammer falls, anyone standing in the way is going to get smashed. Remember, hell and the lake of fire was not intended for mankind.

Scripture

Jesus said, *"Then shall he say also unto them on the left hand, Depart from me, ye cursed, into everlasting fire, <u>prepared for the devil and his angels</u>"* (Matthew 25:41).

This verse of scripture deals with the Judgment as Jesus comes into his glory and sits on his throne to separate the wicked from the righteous souls. The sheep shall be set on his right hand and the goats on his left. These wicked souls will be reminded of their evil deeds when they are judged by God. They will also have every one of their sins be exposed just prior to being cast into the lake of fire. They would have missed the opportunity to have their deeds covered with the blood of Jesus. This is why we should not allow our hearts to be hardened nor let our spirits become rebellious. However, just like the enemies of God, these wicked souls are going to allow the spirit of rebellion to overtake them as well. The Lord Jesus Christ came and sought out mankind for the purpose of SAVING THEIR SOULS from his pending judgment. When you possess a rebellious spirit and decide to reject God, this is not the Lord's fault. As a matter of fact, God just happens to have a place for the rebellious wicked spirits to dwell. When you make the choice not to spend eternity with God, there is a place waiting to receive you. It starts in hell and ends in the lake of fire. Therefore, if any man or woman ends up in hell and then sentenced to the lake of fire just remember, it's their own fault.

These souls have rejected the free gift of salvation given by the one and only God who loves them unconditionally. We are saved by the grace of God and not by works lest any man should boast. Salvation is not earned; it is a free gift from the Lord.

THE END OF SATAN—THE BEAST AND THE FALSE PROPHET

Scripture

"And the devil that deceived them was cast into the lake of fire and brimstone, where the beast and the false prophet are, and shall be tormented day and night for ever and ever" (Revelations 20:10).

If we allow ourselves to get caught up in this world's system and fail to search out the Creator of the universe, we cause ourselves to be condemned. The very God of all creation has every breath we take in his precious hand. We should never take this fact for granted ever again once we come into the knowledge of God.

Scripture

"And the God in <u>whose hand thy breath is</u>, and whose are all thy ways, hast thou not glorified" (Daniel 5:23b).

This verse was explaining the time Daniel interpreted the writing on the wall for King Belshazzar who failed to humble his heart before God. The prophet Daniel was letting the king know that God controls our very breath, which should not be taken for granted. Therefore, remember, you have a choice whose side you will end up on. God offers forgiveness to anyone who is willing to accept him. For this reason, never let it be said that God sends any man or woman whom he created in his own image and likeness to a place of torment. Mankind sends his own soul to the lake of fire all by himself. This is why we must all REPENT and ask the Lord for forgiveness for our sins committed against him. We must all be covered with the blood of Jesus, who is the Lamb of God that taketh away the sins of the world. This is not normal blood that was shed on that rugged cross on Calvary. This precious blood that Jesus shed for the sins of the world came from God the Father. Therefore, it was both precious and priceless. The Bible teaches us when Jesus returns, it's going to be just like in the days of Noah. Noah closed the door to the ark, and God sealed them in; that's when the people outside the door all perished. Jesus is going to shut the eternal door to everlasting life in the New Jerusalem, in that great and terrible day of the Lord. The best gift of all is eternal life with God to anyone who will accept the Lord's plan of salvation.

THE NEW HEAVEN AND THE NEW EARTH

The Holy City / The New Jerusalem

John the apostle saw this Holy City coming down from God out of heaven prepared as a bride adorned for her husband. That's right; God is bringing his Holy Temple called the Holy City down from heaven to mankind.

Scripture

> *"And I saw a new heaven and a new earth: for the first heaven and the first earth were passed away; and there was no more sea. And I John saw the holy city, New Jerusalem, coming down from God out of heaven, prepared as a bride adorned for her husband. And I heard a great voice out of heaven saying, Behold, the tabernacle of God is with men, and he will dwell with them, and they shall be his people, and God himself shall be with them, and be their God. And God shall wipe away all tears from their eyes; and there shall be no more DEATH, neither SORROW, nor CRYING, neither shall there be any more PAIN: for the former things are passed away. And he that sat upon the throne said, Behold, I make all things new. And he said unto me, Write: for these words are true and faithful. And he said unto me, It is done. I AM Alpha and Omega, the beginning and the end. I will give unto him that is athirst of the fountain of the water of life freely"* (Revelation 21:1-6).

This beautiful kingdom is what God has designed and prepared for his children. Those who love Jesus will look forward to his return. Then, once the Lord receives the body of Christ, these blessed souls will never be separated from the Lord ever again. Jesus is not only the Savior of the world; he is the Lamb of God. John the apostle witnessed and wrote about the new kingdom of God. He told us how God will bring the New Jerusalem down to the earth out of heaven. This is a marvelous gift from God he will present to his chosen people. We serve an awesome God who cares deeply for all of his creation. However, this earth as we know it will one day soon be burned up and totally consumed or refashioned with fervent heat. All the sinfulness will be burned away. There will not be a trace of it left.

Scripture

"But the day of the Lord will come as a thief in the night; in the which <u>the heavens shall pass away with a great noise, and the elements shall melt with fervent heat, the earth also and the works that are therein shall be burned up</u>. Looking for and hasting unto the coming of the day of God, wherein <u>the heavens being on fire</u> shall be dissolved, and the elements shall melt with fervent heat? Nevertheless we, according to his promise, look for New Heavens and a New Earth, wherein dwelleth righteousness" (2 Peter 3:10-13).

Remember, we are running in a Christian race for our lives to reach the kingdom of God. Jesus has already paid the price in full for our salvation. If we slow down, we may faint. If we faint, we will become easy prey and get caught by the enemy's devices. Therefore, let us stay strong in the faith. We must never look back as we continue to press toward the mark of the high calling of God.

Scripture

Paul the apostle said, *"Brethren, I count not myself to have apprehended: but this one thing I do, forgetting those things which are behind, and reaching forth unto those things which are before, I press toward the mark for the prize of the high calling of God in Christ Jesus"* (Philippians 3:14).

Let us keep our sights set on Jesus our Lord. For he has already blazed the trail through the course we must follow which illuminates the way to eternal life in the kingdom of God. This course or trail Jesus made is very narrow and not wide. Therefore, there are not many ways to this holy kingdom. There is only one!

Scripture

> *"Looking unto Jesus the Author and Finisher of our faith; who for the joy that was set before him endured the cross, despising the shame, and is set down at the right hand of the throne of God"* (Hebrews 12:2).

Let not your heart be troubled. Refrain from allowing hardness to set in. Remember, Jesus is knocking at the door of your heart. Jesus said whosoever opens the door; he will come in and sup with them. Don't let the devil deceive you with the distractions of this world. He knows as long as he can keep you distracted and spiritually asleep, you will be condemned right along with him. Satan knows as long as your spiritual eyes are closed, you will never notice that slow roller coaster ride to hell that you are on. Many of us found ourselves on that same slow roller coaster ride at one time in our lives. Thank God we had the spiritual awakening to realize it and get off before it reached its end. This is eternal life in the kingdom of God being offered to all who will come to the Lord Jesus Christ RIGHT NOW!

Scripture

> *"Behold, I stand at the door, and knock: if any man hear my voice, and open the door, I will come in to him, and will sup with him, and he with me. To him that over cometh will I grant to sit with me in my throne, even as I also overcame, and am set down with my Father in his throne"* (Revelation 3:20, 21).

> *"I am Alpha and Omega, the beginning and the end, the first and the last. Blessed are they that do his commandments, that they may have right to the <u>TREE OF LIFE</u>, and may enter in through the gates into the City"* (Revelation 22:13, 14).

Now you have a final decision to make with all this new found knowledge you possess. Will you choose to be a child of God, or will you choose to remain a child of Satan? Unless you accept Jesus as Lord, you will remain a child of Satan! The choice is up to you. You do not have to be separated from God forever. No one has to spend eternity in the lake of fire with Satan and his followers unless this is your personal choice!

THE LAMB'S BOOK OF LIFE

Will your name be found written therein?

See you in the Kingdom of God

GLOSSARY

These are just a few names mentioned in the Bible and there significant meaning which describes each individual or place. Names were very important in the days of old. They should likewise remain just as equally important today.

AARON—a teacher, lofty, mountain of strength.

ABEDNEGO—servant of light; shining.

ABEL—vanity, breath; vapor.

ABRAHAM—father of a great multitude.

ABSALOM—father of peace.

ADAM—earthy; red.

ADONAL—he is my Lord; he runs everything, my owner.

AHAB— uncle, or father's brother.

AHASUERUS—prince; head; chief.

AHIMELECH—my brother is a king; my king's brother.

AMEN—"truly," or "so be it."

AMOS—loading; weighty.

ANANIAS—or Ananiah, a cloud of the Lord.

ANDREW—a strong man.

ANGEL—messengers of God, spiritual beings.

ANTICHRIST—an adversary to Christ.

APOLLONIA—perdition, destruction.

APOLLOS—one who destroys, destroyer.

APOLLYON—a destroyer.

ARAB—multiplying; sowing sedition; a widow; a locust.

ASHER—happiness.

ASA—physician; cure.

BAAL—master; lord.

BAALIM—idols; masters; false gods.

BABEL—confusion; mixture.

BABYLON—same as Babel.

BARABBAS—son of shame, confusion.

BARNABAS—son of the prophet, or of consolation.

BARTHOLOMEW—a son that suspends the waters.

BATHSHEBA—the seventh daughter; the daughter of satiety.

BELIAL—wicked, worthless.

BELSHAZZAR—master of the treasure.

BELTESHAZZAR—who lays up treasure in secret.

BEN—a son.

BENAIAH—son of the Lord.

BENJAMIN—son of the right hand.

BERNICE—one that brings victory.

BETH-EL—the house of God.

BETH-LEHEM—house of bread.

BIBLE—the WORD, the book, the voice of God to man, both the Old and New Testament.

BOAZ—or booz, in strength.

CAIN—possession, or possessed.

CAIPHAS—he that seeks with diligence; one that vomiteth.

CALEB—a dog; a crow; a basket.

CANAAN—merchant; trader; or that humbles and subdues.

CANDACE—who possesses contrition.

CEPHAS—a rock or stone.

CHRIST—anointed.

CUSH—Cushan, Cushi, Ethiopians; blackness.

CYRUS—as miserable; as heir.

DAN—judgment; he that judges.

DANIEL—judgment of God; God my judge.

DARIUS—he that informs himself.

DATHAN—laws or rites.

DAVID—well-beloved, dear.

DEBORAH—word; thing; a bee.

DEVIL—accuser.

DELILAH—poor; small; head of hair.

DIANA—luminous, perfect.

DIDYMUS—a twin; double.

DORCAS—a female roe-deer.

ED—witness.

EDEN—pleasure; delight.

EGYPT—that troubles or oppresses; anguish.

ELEAZAR—help of God, court of God.

ELI—the offering or lifting up.

ELIJAH—God the Lord, the strong Lord.

ELIMELECH—my God is king.

ELISABETH—Elizabeth, the oath, or fullness, of God.

ELISHA—salvation of God.

ELOHIM—The Creator, the one who speaks things into existence.

ELRAUH—he is the God who seeth thee, when no one else can.

EL-SHADDAD—God All Mighty.

EMMANUEL—God with us.

ENOCH—dedicated; discipline.

ENOS—mortal man; sick; despaired of; forgetful.

EPHRAIM—fruitful; increasing.

ESAU—he that acts or finishes.

ESTHER—secret, hidden.

ETHAN—strong; the gift of the island.

ETHIOPIA—blackness; heat.

EUNICE—good victory.

EVE—living; enlivening.

EZEKIEL—the strength of God.

EZRA—help; court.

FELIX—happy, prosperous.

GABRIEL—God is my strength.

GIDEON—he that bruises or breaks; a destroyer.

GOLIATH—passage; revolution; heap.

HABAKKUK—he that embraces; a wrestler.

HAGAR—a stranger; one who fears.

HAGGAI—feast; solemnity.

HAM—hot; heat; brown.

HEBER—one that passes; anger.

HEBREWS—descendants of Heber.

HEROD—son of a hero.

HEZEKIAH—strength of the Lord.

HOSEA—Hoshea, savior; safety.

IMMANUEL—God with us.

ISAAC—laughter.

ISAIAH—the salvation of the Lord.

ISHMAEL—God that hears.

ISRAEL—who prevails with God.

JABEZ—sorrow; trouble.

THE LAMB'S BOOK OF LIFE:

JACOB—that supplants, undermines; the heel.

JAMES—same as Jacob.

JAPHETH—(unknown)

JASHER—righteous; upright.

JASON—he that cures.

JEDIDIAH—beloved of the Lord.

JEHOSHAPHAT—the Lord is judge.

JEHOVAH—self subsisting, the God who keeps his covenant with his people.

JEHOVAH-JIREH—the Lord will provide.

JEHOVAH-M'KADDESH—God who sanctifies.

JEHOVAH-NISSI—the Lord my banner, the God who gives victory.

JEHOVAH-ROPHE—he is the God who gives you health, and heals you.

JEHOVAH-SABIYOSE—Lord of hosts, he protects you.

JEHOVAH-SHALOM—God of peace.

JEHOVAH-SHAMMAH—the Lord is there.

JEHOVAH-TSIDKENU—the Lord our righteousness.

JEREMIAH—exaltation of the Lord.

JEROBOAM—he that opposes the people.

JESSE—gift; oblation; one who knows.

JETHRO—his excellence; his posterity.

JEW—same as Judah.

JEZEBEL—chaste.

JESUS—savior; deliverer.

JOB—he that weeps or cries.

JOEL—he that wills or commands.

JOHN—the grace or mercy of the Lord.

JONAH—a dove; he that oppresses; destroyer.

JONATHAN—given of God.

JOSE—raised; who pardons.

JOSEPH—increase; addition.

JOSHUA—a savior; a deliverer.

JOSIAH—the Lord burns; the fire of the Lord.

JUDAH—the praise of the Lord; confession.

JUDAS—praise of the Lord.

LAZARUS ---assistance of God.

LEAH—weary; tired.

LEVI—associated with him.

LOIS—better.

LOT—Lotan, wrapped up; hidden; covered; myrrh; rosin.

LUCIFER—bringing light.

LUKE—luminous; white.

MALACHI—my messenger; my angel.

MANASSEH—forgetfulness; he that is forgotten.

MANOAH—rest; a present.

MARCUS—polite; shining.

MARK—same as Marcus; polite and shining.

MARTHA—who becomes better; provoking.

MARY—same as Miriam.

MATTATHIAS—the gift of the Lord.

MATTHEW—gift of Jehovah.

MELCHIZEDEK—king of justice.

MESHACH—that draws with force.

MESSIAH—anointed.

METHUSALEH—he has sent his death.

MICAH—poor; humble.

MICHAL—who is perfect?

MILLO—fullness.

MIRIAM—rebellion.

MORDECAI—contrition; bitter; bruising.

MORIAH—bitterness of the Lord.

MOSES—taken out; drawn forth.

MYRA—I flow; pour out; weep.

NAHUM—comforter; penitent.

NAPHTALI—that struggles or fights.

NATHAN—given; giving; rewarded.

NAZARITE—one chosen or set apart.

NEBO—that speaks or prophesies.

NEBUCHADNEZZAR—tears and groans of judgment.

NICODEMUS—victory of the people.

NIGER—black.

NIMROD—rebellion (but probably an unknown Assyrian word)

NOAH—repose; consolation.

OBADIAH—servant of the Lord.

OBED—a servant; workman.

OMAR—he that speaks; bitter.

PAUL—small; little.

PETER—a rock or stone.

PHILEMON—who kisses.

PHILIP—warlike; a lover of horses.

PILATE—armed with a dart.

PONTIUS—marine; belonging to the sea.

POTIPHAR—bull of Africa; a fat bull.

RABBI ---Rabboni, my master.

RACA—worthless; good for nothing.

RAHAB—proud; quarrelsome (applied to Egypt).

REBEKAH—fat; fattened; quarrel appeased.

REUBEN—who sees the son; the vision of the son.

RHODA—a rose.

ROMAN—strong; powerful.

RUFUS—red.

RUTH—drunk; satisfied.

SAMSON—his sun; his service; there the second time.

SAMUEL—heart of God; asked of God.

SAPPHIRA—that relates or tells.

SARAH—lady; princess; princess of the multitudes.

SATAN—contrary; adversary; enemy; accuser.

SAUL—demanded; lent; ditch; death.

SETH—put; who puts; fixed.

SHADRACH—tender, nipple.

SHEBA—captivity; old man; repose; oath.

SHEM—name; renowned.

SILAS—three, or the third.

SIMEON—that hears or obeys; that is heard.

SIMON—that hears; that obeys.

SOLOMON—peaceable; perfect; one who recompenses.

STEPHANAS—crown; crowned.

STEPHEN—same as Stephanas.

THE LAMB'S BOOK OF LIFE:

TABITHA—clear-sighted; a roe-deer.

TABOR—choice; purity; brusing.

THADDEUS—that praised or confesses.

THOMAS—a twin.

TITUS—pleasing.

TYRE—Tyrus; strength; rock; sharp.

URIAH—Urijah, the Lord is my light or fire.

ZEBEDEE—abundant; portion.

ZECHARIAH—same as Zachariah; memory of the Lord.

ZEDEKIAH—the Lord is my justice; the justice of the Lord.

ZEPHANIAH—the Lord is my secret.

ZERUBBABEL—a stranger at Babylon; dispersion of confusion.

ZION—monument; raised up; sepulcher.

ZIPPORAH—beauty; trumpet; mourning.

ZOAR—little; small.

COMING SOON List of Books

*Absent in the Body, Present with the Lord
   What happens when we die?
*The Wiles of the Devil
   The true enemy behind the scenes
*The Divine Healer
   Overcoming sickness as a born again believer
*How to Receive God's Increase
*What Makes Jesus God
*The True Descendants of Adam
*The Value of Salvation
   God's shedding blood
*The Other Side of the Cross
   Choose Christ, or remain on the other side
*Raising your Children According to the Word of God
*The Ten Commandments
   Past or Present

Better to be on the devils hit list because you serve the LORD, than to be on Satan's slow rollercoaster ride to Hell and not know it!

Minister Carl Brice

And it shall come to pass, that whosoever shall call on the name of the LORD shall be saved (Acts 2:21).

And he said unto them, I beheld Satan as lightening fall from heaven. Behold, I give unto you power to tread on serpents and scorpions, and over all the power of the enemy: and nothing shall by any means hurt you. Notwithstanding in this rejoice not, that the spirits are subject unto you: but rather rejoice, because your names are written in heaven (Luke 10:18-20).

Jesus Christ our Lord

Printed in Great Britain
by Amazon